Dynamical Cognitive Science

Dynamical Cognitive Science   Lawrence M. Ward

A Bradford Book
The MIT Press
Cambridge, Massachusetts
London, England

This book was set in Times New Roman in 3B2 by Asco Typesetters, Hong Kong, and was printed and bound in the United States of America.

Library of Congress Cataloging-in-Publication Data

Ward, Lawrence M.
  Dynamical cognitive science / Lawrence M. Ward.
    p. cm.
  "A Bradford book".
  Includes bibliographical references and index.
  ISBN 0-262-23217-0 (hc. : alk. paper)
  1. Cognitive science. 2. Change (Psychology). 3. Time—Psychological aspects.
I. Title.
BF311 .W2695   2001
153—dc21   2001044336

Contents

Preface

Life is change.
How it differs from the rocks.
—Jefferson Airplane, *Crown of Creation*

The times they are a-changin'.
—Bob Dylan

Changing time, timely change, change creating time, time measuring change—the themes of this book are change and time in various permutations and combinations. The book also deals with nonlinearity, chaos, randomness, and stochastic models, the use of computers to study complicated systems of differential equations, systems theory, complementarity, the importance of formal models, methods from physics and mathematics for the analysis of cognitive systems, and interdisciplinarity, among other topics. Dynamical cognitive science is a potpourri of the old and the new, the borrowed and the "true" (in the carpenter's sense, meaning "linear").

Many have proclaimed it was about time we began to focus on dynamics in cognitive science—or in psychology as a whole. Gregson (1983) was perhaps the most forceful of the moderns, but you will find many others referenced within, notably, van Gelder and Port (1995), Port and van Gelder (1995), Kelso (1995), van Gelder (1998), and Beer (2000). Their articles and books discuss the advantages and disadvantages of the dynamical approach to cognition and provide many examples of its usefulness in cognitive science. The present book is both more and less than these others. It is more because it discusses different topics in different ways, for example, noise and relaxation oscillators. It is less because it often touches on material covered in depth elsewhere and does not address at all approaches championed by other dynamical authors, for example, the dynamical psychophysics of Gregson (1988, 1992) and the dynamical hypothesis of van Gelder (1998). *Dynamical Cognitive Science* is intended to be a deep introduction to the field. Its purpose is to whet appetites, not to give a complete meal: although it treats usually neglected topics such as noise in depth, where it considers deep topics such as time and differential equation models of cognition, it does so in interesting, rather than exhaustive ways.

The book's thirty-five chapters are relatively short. Some introduce important topics presented elsewhere in detail, others together present an important topic in depth (e.g., chaps. 14–19 on noise). Each chapter is self-contained, making a few major points or introducing a few important topics amply yet succinctly, so that it can be read at a short sitting. Although I hope something in the book will appeal to a wide range of readers, from cognitive psychologists and neuroscientists to computer scientists, engineers, physicists, mathematicians, and philosophers, I do not expect that every reader will find every chapter of interest. Thus mathematicians will probably want to skip over sections where familiar equations are explained, just as physicists will the introductory discussions of the master equation, quantum theory, and oscillators. On the other hand, psychologists will probably find most of the chapters of interest, and much of the material new. Although some chapters are difficult, there is really no serious mathematics in the book, only relatively simple equations that will become familiar as readers progress. I hope to show how the relevant mathematical forms (mostly difference or differential equations) can be approached in a more-or-less empirical way, especially by computer exploration, so that their meaning and usefulness to cognitive science is revealed.

This book is much less than I had hoped it would be, or than it could have been had I spent ten more years working on it. The cascade of new dynamical work being undertaken by psychologists and other cognitive scientists promises to undercut the timeliness of one theme of this book, that dynamics should form a core approach to cognitive science. On the other hand, coming after decades of neglect, the new work makes a wide-ranging, comprehensible, yet deep introduction to the promise of the dynamical approach even more timely.

I was helped by many people, not least by those whose work I have cited and adapted, and by countless other colleagues from whom I have learned over the past thirty years. I owe special thanks to Christian Richard, who read much of the text and provided astute comments; my graduate students Shuji Mori, Odie Geiger, Robert West, John

McDonald, David Prime, and Matt Tata, who kept me thinking and put up with my obsessions; my other students and research assistants, especially Amanda Jane, Sharna Hurwitz, and Sarah Knowlden, who managed the references and the permissions, and Sim Desai and Dan Rootman, who helped get the stochastic resonance studies going; my colleagues and friends Cindy Greenwood, Birger Bergerson, Steve Marion, and other members of the Crisis Points Group at the University of British Columbia (UBC), from whom I learned an enormous amount, especially about stochastic dynamics; my colleague and friend Frank Moss, who first inspired and then conspired in the study of stochastic resonance; my graduate school mentor and friend Gregory R. Lockhead; my wife, Brigitte Renahte Voegtle, who has endured the curse of the absent-minded professor for over ten years; and finally my mother, Sarah Mabel Johnston Ward Walls, who has always supported and encouraged me. Preparation of the book was funded by an ongoing operating grant from the Natural Sciences and Engineering Research Council (NSERC) of Canada, which has funded my research for over twenty-six years, and by a major thematic grant from the Peter Wall Institute for Advanced Studies at UBC to the Crisis Points Group, of which I am a member.

Chapter 1
Magic, Ritual, and Dynamics

In the magic of incantation, a formula of exorcism or of cursing possesses the virtue of subjugating to the will of him who pronounces it (in the right "ritual" conditions as to words, intonation, rhythm) beings and things in the world above and in the world here below.

—Maurice Bouisson, *Magic*

1.1 Magic and Ritual

Why begin a book on dynamical cognitive science with a discussion of magic and ritual? Surely not to make an analogy between mystery and science. Surely not to suggest that magic and ritual are fertile fields to plow with mathematical models. And surely not to contend that our current understanding of these topics should form prototypes for the modeling process. Why, then? Because they dramatically illustrate the fundamental insight that, along with the rest of the universe, human behavior *unfolds in time*. This include both covert behaviors involved in sensation, perception, and cognition and the overt, observable motor behaviors from which we cognitive scientists must infer those covert behaviors.

What, then, can we glean from magic and ritual to inspire us to study dynamical cognitive science? Magic and ritual are deeply embedded in the human condition. For much of history, magic and ritual ruled human behavior, and for many so-called primitive peoples, they still do. Magic, and ritual based on it, explained the mysteries of the world, informed religions, and helped humans cope with a powerful and uncaring natural world. Of the three forms of magic, sympathetic (like attracts like), incantational (see chapter epigraph), and talismanic (certain objects have magical power), incantational has been considered the most powerful: the words and numbers used in incantations are held to have real power to affect the actions of people. "Man observes that nature is sometimes

שברירי

בריר י

ריר י

יר י

ר י

י

Figure 1.1
Magical formula to exorcise Shabriri.

hostile and sometimes favourable to him and in this fact he sees a manifestation of the anger of the spirits—or of their good disposition. One
must, then, treat the spirits as one would treat men whom one *cannot
dispense with*" (Bouisson 1960, 95; emphasis mine). Because speech and
music were known to influence the actions of other people, sometimes
almost miraculously, many people felt there was a strong basis for believing that they would influence the "spirits," the forces that generated the
natural phenomena that ruled their lives.

An example of an incantation is the formula (fig. 1.1) from the
Babylonian Talmud used to exorcise the demon Shabriri, who was said to
cause blindness. The magical formula, repeated before drinking at night,
consists of the demon's name (written here in Hebrew letters on the top
line of the figure), pronounced six times, with ever fewer of its syllables
(Shabriri, Briri, Riri, Iri, Ri, I). The demon is supposed to waste away as
the syllables of his name are removed and thus not be able to do his evil
work of blinding unsuspecting drinkers from the water jar.

As illustrated by the Shabriri formula, incantational magic involves
formulas of rhythms, intonations, and words performed *in the correct
order*. Of course order is important even in ordinary speech. Indeed, it is
a truism that word order can determine meaning, for example, "shark-
eating man" versus "man-eating shark." And intonation can also affect
meaning. For example, rising pitch toward the end of an English sen-

tence indicates a question; falling pitch indicates a statement of fact. Listen to yourself pronounce the following sentences: first, "The eggs are done?" and then, "The eggs are done." In poetry, the effect of word order, rhythm, and intonation is even more striking. Read the following poem, by Robert Bringhurst (1995, 100) out loud:

II Parable of the Harps

In the drum of the heart
Are the hoofbeats of horses—the horse
Of the muscles, the horse of the bones.

In the flutes of the bones are the voices
Of fishes—the fish of the belly,
The fish of the fingers and limbs.

In the streams of the limbs
We are swimming with fishes
And fording with lathering horses.

Love, in this bed full of horses
And fishes, I bring to the resonant gourds
Of your breasts the harps of my hands.

You can almost feel the horses thundering in your heart, or feel yourself in the river, swimming fluidly with the fishes. But try reading aloud the following permutation of the poem:

the swimming In bones. Are the
Love, of the horses—the horse the
muscles, the horse Of the breasts

heart In the bones I bring of the fish
Of fishes—the lathering of belly,
fording The resonant gourds. flutes of the

harps In the drum of fishes limbs
We are And fishes, are the streams
with limbs And fish with horses.

in this of the bed of fingers
to the horses and of the voices
Of your hoofbeats the full of my hands.

Not only has the meaning of the poem been destroyed, but also the meaning of its rhythm and intonation. Indeed, it is no longer a poem, only a word salad. A good poem can bring tears to the eyes. Word salad just confuses, and can even signal mental illness. For example, people with untreated schizophrenia often utter strings of words that resemble the "tossed" version of Bringhurst's poem.

1.2 Dynamics

The unfolding of behavior in time, especially that of human speech, has been a dominant theme in our understanding and subjugation of nature, as reflected by the dominant role played by dynamics in science, especially in physics, from Aristotle to Galileo to Kepler to Newton to Einstein and into the modern era. Quantum electrodynamics (QED), the foundation stone of modern physics, is essentially dynamical; indeed, according to Feynman (1985), it consists of only "three little *actions*" (emphasis mine): electrons and photons move in space-time and electrons scatter photons.

Given the historical importance of magic, music, and rhythm, the preeminent role of dynamics in physics, and the emphasis on change over time in the other sciences (e.g., reactions in chemistry and evolution and development in biology), it is somewhat surprising that the dominant approaches to cognitive science, and to psychology as a whole, are statical rather than dynamical. That is, empirical laws and theoretical statements, when expressed formally, are written as

$$B = f(x_1, x_2, x_3, \ldots, x_n), \tag{1.1}$$

where time is not a relevant variable, rather than as

$$B = f(x_1, x_2, x_3, \ldots, x_n, t), \tag{1.2}$$

where time enters as an important variable.

A good example of a statical law in psychology is the well-known psychophysical power law, sometimes called "Stevens's law," expressed in the following equation:

$$R = cS^m, \tag{1.3}$$

which describes reasonably well how responses (R) in a psychophysical scaling experiment vary with the intensity of the stimulus (S). For example, we might ask a subject to give a number (a "magnitude estimation") that indicates how loud a sound seems each time it occurs. When we play several sounds, each of a different intensity, several times each, and plot our subjects' average responses on a graph (see fig. 1.2), the results closely fit the curve of equation 1.3, which we can then use to calculate a value of R close to the one our subjects would give for any sound, even those to which they did not give a number. Because different people give similar numbers to the same sounds (Stevens 1975), this procedure is used routinely to predict people's responses to sounds when designing music halls, airports, and hearing aids.

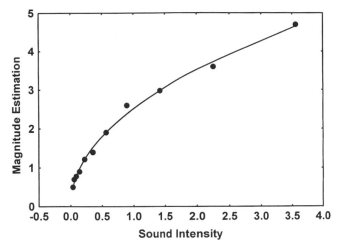

Figure 1.2
Stevens's law (curve) summarizes psychophysical scaling data (dots).

As useful as Stevens's law is, it does not describe everything of interest about subjects' responses in a psychophysical scaling experiment. Subjects do not always give the same numbers when presented with the "same" physical stimulus (the error bars were omitted in fig. 1.2). Of course, as the quotation marks around "same" indicate, all stimuli differ, no matter how hard we try to get them to be the same. Air currents, voltage fluctuations in a sound generator, increasing fatigue of loudspeaker cones, rising or falling temperature and air pressure, and so forth together produce trial-to-trial fluctuations in sound pressure at the eardrum even for the same nominal sound stimulus. And subjects change, too. Blood pressure rises and falls, attention wavers, digestion proceeds, viruses and bacteria multiply and die, and so forth. It would be a miracle if subjects and stimuli were exactly the same on any two occasions. In fact, subjects often give dramatically different responses to the "same" stimulus at different times, and often give the same response to dramatically different stimuli presented on different occasions. A psychophysical scaling experiment is necessarily extended in time, and the behavior involved in making psychophysical judgments fluctuates over time, even when the experimenter strives to make the situation identical from moment to moment.

How should we deal with these fluctuations? In psychophysics, one tradition, attributed to S. S. Stevens (1975), has been to ignore them. The justification is that we are not usually interested in the fluctuations in subjects' blood pressure, digestion, sleepiness, and so forth over the course of a psychophysical scaling experiment. Nor are we interested in the unavoidable differences in the stimulus magnitude from trial to trial. These effects reflect our incomplete control over the experimental situation and are nuisances. We therefore agree simply to call these fluctuations "error variance," to be "averaged away" (as in fig. 1.2). A different tradition, beginning with Fechner (1860) and continuing through Thurstone (1927) and Green and Swets (1966), is to use the *amount* (but not the *timing*) of the fluctuations to measure sensation and sensory discrimination. Thus Fechner built his famous law of sensation on what we now call "Weber's law," that the difference threshold (the smallest intensity difference that can be reliably detected) is proportional to the stimulus intensity at which it is measured, $\Delta I = kI$, where ΔI is the difference threshold and I the stimulus intensity. This proportionality arises because response variability generally increases with stimulus intensity. In signal detection theory (and related approaches), an important measure of stimulus discriminability, d', is defined as the difference between the means of two assumed probability distributions of sensory effects of stimuli divided by their common standard deviation, the latter representing the amount of fluctuation in those sensory effects. Just how those fluctuations are distributed over time is irrelevant (but see Link 1994). Thus, whether a nuisance or a fundamental concept, psychophysical variability is usually treated as "error" rather than as temporally distributed information about cognitive processes. Both traditions ignore time, even though fluctuations over time can provide fundamental information about the processes generating the behavior in question. This point applies not only to psychophysics, but also to most of the work being done in cognitive science today.

It is undeniable that in some cases the temporal distribution of response variability adds nothing to our understanding of the phenomenon we are studying. On the other hand, however uninteresting the temporal distribution of these fluctuations might seem to be, it takes on new meaning when juxtaposed with several significant observations from physics and biology and from physical methods applied to human behaviors. First, such temporally distributed fluctuations are ubiquitous; indeed, in quantum mechanics and statistical physics, they are fundamental (see chap. 13). Second, these random processes can actually "drive" physical and biological phenomena by falling into one or the other of several "basins of attraction," depending on random fluctuations early in the process. They can determine, for example, which of two equally rich food sources will be exploited by an ant colony (e.g., Beckers et al. 1990). Random choices made by the first ants to reach a choice point bias the probabilities of choices made by ants reaching the choice point at a later time (via the pheromones they deposit), leading to a strong "preference" for one food source over the other. Importantly, random choice fluctuations of the same size occurring at a later time in the process, once a preference has developed, have no effect on which source is preferred. In this and in many other cases, the *timing* of the fluctuations is all important. Third, the random fluctuations can convey valuable information when observed in human behavior. For example, fluctuations that occur with a certain type of periodicity, called "$1/f$" or "pink" noise (see chap. 15), are diagnostic of stochastic processes that interact at several scales of time; $1/f$ noise characterizes the residual response variability in standard experimental tasks of cognitive science (see chap. 16). Finally, even deterministic processes can create fluctuations that appear random (Chan and Tong 2001). For example, the logistic difference equation

$$Y_i = a Y_{i-1}(1 - Y_{i-1}), \tag{1.4}$$

although simple and completely deterministic, demonstrates extremely complicated, effectively random behavior for values of $a > 3.58$. Only dynamical analysis of time series of behaviors can reveal the differences between such deterministic processes and processes characterized by white noise.

In making these same points, other authors (e.g., Gregson 1983, 1988; Port and van Gelder 1995; Kelso 1995) have also argued that dynamics should be central to cognitive science and to psychology as a whole. Nevertheless, even though more and more cognitive scientists are using dynamical metaphors, and even though some are using dynamical system theory to analyze behavioral experiments, the practice of dynamics is still not widespread. This is so partly because dynamics is complicated and difficult, requiring considerable sophistication in mathematics and other disciplines with a large technical content, and partly because some practitioners of the dynamical approach (e.g., Gregson 1983, 1988) have set it against the more traditional approaches, arguing for a Kuhnian paradigm shift in psychology. Unfortunately for the latter, not all statical theories of psychology can be subsumed as special cases under dynamical theories (see chaps. 8 and 9). Finally, psychology's reluctance to embrace dynamics lies partly in our having few well-worked-out examples of the benefits that accrue when the dynamical approach is taken (see, for example, Kelso 1995). In a discipline such as economics, where prediction of the next values of a time series (e.g., stock market prices) has obvious benefits, dynamics is understandably central. In psychology, however, the benefits of dynamical analysis are not so clear.

Sometimes a dynamical analysis simply generalizes a statical theory to other situations and data, particularly where values fluctuate in time, as in the psychophysical case (see chap. 11). Sometimes, however, the dynamical analysis provides a fundamentally different theoretical approach to an old problem, with novel predictions following from the dynamical theory. Beer (2000) describes one such dramatic case in the "A-not-B" error in infant reaching: infants 7 to 12 months old continue to reach for an object in the one of two opaque containers they have been trained to reach for, even after they have seen the object being hidden in the other one. Whereas Piaget argued that the error is the result of applying an immature concept of object permanence to the task, a dynamical analysis suggests that it is caused by an immature goal-directed reaching system (Thelen et al. in press). The dynamical model also accounts for the dramatic context effects that have been observed in this task. Moreover, it makes the novel prediction that, under the right conditions, the error should be observed in older children as well because it arises from general properties of the perceptual-cognitive-motor system controlling goal-directed reaching. Thus, if confirmed, the dynamical theory would dramatically change our understanding of infants' performance in goal-directed reaching, and perhaps even our assessment of concepts such as object permanence in child development.

In light of the possible benefits, this book aims to overcome the considerable obstacles to the centrality of dynamical analysis in cognitive science. It aims to describe some tools of dynamical analysis simply and clearly, so that even mathematically unsophisticated researchers can see how they are used. It aims to show how dynamical and statical approaches are complementary and mutually informative. And finally, it aims to provide examples of the increases in understanding that accrue when cognitive science is informed by both dynamical and statical analyses.

Chapter 2

Sequence

The various sections of the Torah were not given in their correct order. For if they had ... anyone who read them would be able to wake the dead and perform miracles. For this reason the correct order of the Torah [is] known only to the Holy One....

—Rabbi Eleazar ben Pedath, quoted in Gershom Gerhard Scholem, *On the Kabbalah and Its Symbolism*

The mind which any human science can describe can never be an adequate representation of the mind which can make that science. And the process of correcting that inadequacy must follow the serial steps of an infinite regress.

—J. W. Dunne, *The Serial Universe*

Just about all of the interesting hypotheses we have about how social systems function imply at their base an imagined scenario of interaction, a scenario invariably sequential in character.

—John M. Gottman and A. K. Roy, *Sequential Analysis*

2.1 The Serial Universe

It is often best to begin at the beginning. In the case of sequence, the beginning has to do with the nature of the universe itself. In his charming little book, from which the second epigraph above is taken, Dunne (1934, 28) argued that the universe "*as it appears to human science* must needs be an infinite regress" (emphasis his). In this context, a "regress" is a question that can be answered only by asking another, similar question, which of course leads to asking still another, similar question, and so forth, to infinity. For example, a child learning arithmetic might attempt to answer the question "What is the largest integer?" The child first considers whether there is a larger number than "1" and discovers that "2" is larger than "1," which leads to another question, whether there is a number larger than "2," and so forth. Because, "1" can always be added to any

Figure 2.1
Dunne's serial painter (1934).

integer, this series of questions can go on forever. Although Dunn felt we cannot know whether the universe is actually an infinite regress, he tried to convince his readers that, as revealed by science, it must be so. Without going into the details of Dunne's arguments, let us briefly consider his theory of "serialism," which contains a compelling case for treating the objects of science, including cognitive science, as observations in *time*.

Figure 2.1, from Dunne (1934), illustrates the dilemma in which we find ourselves. We are like the artist trying to portray himself and all of his knowledge of the scene before him in a single painting. He is frustrated in this by the fact that he himself is always outside the frame of the picture he paints. Thus he must paint a series of pictures, each perhaps more complete than the last, but all subject to the limitation that the information displayed must be less than the information involved in creating the display. Gödel (1931) dealt with a similar problem, how to prove all of the true statements within a consistent formal system, and Penrose (1994) argued that the resulting nonalgorithmic nature of human understanding of the world is the hallmark of human consciousness.

Dunne's theory of serialism (1934) contends that, as self-conscious beings, we are able to differentiate ourselves from "the world" (including other humans). Like the artist pictured above, however, we are unable to treat this predicament systematically except as an infinite regress. And because time is regressive in just this sense, each instant outside of and containing all of the prior instants, viewing all experience in terms of time provides the required descriptive framework. This framework introduces the notion of *change* and allows us to consider causing changes both in ourselves and in the world. Change, in turn, creates the possibility of experimental science: it allows us to interfere with what we observe and to record the results of that interference. This interpretation of experiments is an axiom of quantum physics. Thus, at the most fundamental level of science, we are forced to be regressive, to describe events in time, and to consider sequence.

2.2   The Problem of Serial Order in Behavior

Karl Lashley is probably best known today as the psychologist who searched for, but failed to find, the engram (the specific, localized neural substrate upon which memories were laid down) in a series of brilliant experiments with rats (e.g., Lashley 1950). However, he was also one of the earliest psychologists to point out (Lashley 1951) that every type of behavior, from moving to speaking to designing a building or writing a book, temporally integrates sequences of actions in complex ways—ways that cannot be explained by how the behaving organism responds to sequences of external stimuli. He asserted that especially complex action sequences are absent in animals that lack a cerebral cortex, such as insects. He considered complex, temporally integrated actions to be especially characteristic of human behavior. He rejected the "associative chain theory," in which execution of each element in a chain of reflexes provides the stimulus for the next, as an explanation for temporal integration because it is unable to account for myriad empirical facts. One striking example is in typing on a keyboard, in which the various motor acts can follow each other in any progression, such as the various ones that make up the very sentences I am typing here. The letter "e" does not invariably follow the letter "r," the letter "a," or any other letter, although in English, the letter "z" seldom (and then only in typos) follows the letter "c." (in Polish, on the other hand, ...). Similarly, the phonemes that make up a spoken word can follow each other—and coarticulate—in nearly any sequence at all. Moreover, sequences never before uttered by a person (take the novel pseudoword "baffit") can be uttered perfectly the first time, without any learning whatsoever. In speaking, typing, running in unfamiliar terrain, sight-reading music, and so forth, the novel action sequence consists of low-level units organized into a hierarchical structure that seems to be governed from above.

Lashley (1951) rejected "commonsense" answers about how temporal order is imposed on the elementary units of an action sequence, arguing for a new approach, one in which the brain is a dynamic, constantly active system. An input to such a system, rather than exciting a single, isolated, reflexive pathway, causes widespread changes in the entire brain system, much as gusts of wind, tossed stones, a swimmer's strokes, and so forth cause ripples on the surface of a lake. And just as the surface of the water is always active and its activity always the product of the many competing and cooperating influences, in Lashley's view, action is temporally integrated under the influence of reverberatory circuits in the brain created by the interaction of inputs with ongoing and preceding activity. More specifically, Lashley contended that all stimuli perceived and all actions generated by an organism are distinguished in terms of a system of spatial coordinates; that, once representations ("traces") of stimuli or movements have been discriminated in this system, they are "scanned" by a separate system of the brain that translates the spatial into a temporal order. Similarly, a series of stimuli received in a particular temporal order are represented internally as different loci in the spatial system, and then read out in the appropriate (or a changed) temporal order by the scanning system. Finally, a prescribed series of actions, naturally represented in different spatial loci within the motor system, is activated by the scanning system and thus produced externally in the appropriate temporal sequence. Lamenting that Lashley had not described his scanning mechanism in sufficient detail, Bryden (1967) proposed another, slightly more detailed mechanism, in which stored "ordering systems" specify inhibitory and excitatory interactions between memory traces of stimuli and action units in their control of output pathways. The overlearned order of reading words from left to right in English, for example, imposes a difficult-to-change ordering on human subjects' reporting of visual and auditory stimuli. Bryden also used his theory to explain both the order in which items to be remembered are rehearsed, and data in several other paradigms.

It is remarkable how modern Lashley's words sound when read today, even though his program is only beginning to be followed. An excellent example of recent work in the spirit of Lashley's dynamical approach is

Clancey's detailed and fascinating computational analysis (1999) of what he calls "conceptual coordination." Whereas, in "situated cognition" (Clancey 1997), concepts could be coupled (simultaneously activated) and inferred (sequentially activated) under the control of a (physical, social, mental) situation, in conceptual coordination, associations between concepts in memory operate as either simultaneous or successive neural activations in the brain. Clancey (1999) also argued that many of the organizers of cognitive behavior thought to be innate, such as grammar, might be learned and might constitute a kind of virtual machine running in the brain's basic neural architecture (cf. chap. 35). In Clancey's system (1999, xvi), "ordered behavior in time might be constructed and composed dynamically from simple processes of sequential and synchronous activation of categories." This view contrasts mightily with the usual analyses of memory and conceptualization, which emphasize static, connected structures such as semantic networks, and provides a dramatic example of the conceptual benefits that accrue from a dynamical analysis of cognition.

2.3   Markovian Analysis of Behavior

One of the most direct ways to analyze sequences of behavior, at least when the behavior can be categorized into several simple categories, is to consider the sequence as a series of transitions between *states* of a behaving system, where each transition occurs with a particular probability. When, in a sequence of probabilistic state transitions, the next state depends only on the current state, we have what is called a "Markov chain," and the process from which the chain arises is called a "Markov process" (see also chap. 12). A Markov process is described fundamentally by its *initial state vector*, which gives the probabilities for each of the states of the system at the start of a chain, and its *transition matrix*, which summarizes the probabilities of transitions between each of the states. An example of a simple transition matrix for a three-state Markov process is given in figure 2.2.

Notice that, because the probabilities in the matrix are *conditional* on the state at time t, for example, $P(0 \text{ at } t+1 \text{ given } 1 \text{ at } t) = P(0 \mid 1) = 0.1$, the rows in figure 2.2 sum to 1.0. Notice, also, that a transition from states 0 and 1 to any of the three states is possible; for example, the probability of a $0 \rightarrow 1$ transition is 0.6. However, if the chain arrives at state 2 the only transition possible is to state 0. A series of states, or a Markov chain, generated by this transition matrix would look something like this:

State at time t + 1

	0	1	2
0	0.2	0.6	0.2
State at time t 1	0.1	0.8	0.1
2	1.0	0.0	0.0

Figure 2.2
Typical Markov transition matrix.

0 1 1 1 1 1 1 2 0 0 1 0 1 1 1 1 1 0 1 1 1 1 0 0 2 0 1 2 0 1 1 1 1 1 1 1 ... Notice that this chain fragment is dominated by state 1, the most likely transition out of both state 0 and state 1; once in state 1, the process either stays there (with probability 0.8), goes back to state 0, or goes to state 2, from which it always goes back to state 0 again. State 1 is close to being an *absorbing state* (which it would actually be if the probability of a 1 → 1 transition were 1.0). Occasionally the lower probability transitions 0 → 0 or 0 → 2 occur, both of which result in 0 again and another chance to enter state 1 with high probability. Interpreting the states as categories of behavior, say reading the *TV Guide*, watching a TV show, and getting a snack for states 0, 1, and 2, respectively, we could use the transition matrix in figure 2.2 as a model for the sequential behavior of a person who likes to watch TV. Notice that figure 2.2 does not exactly describe any one chain, only the overall "look" of all chains generated by sampling the probability distributions ("realizations") described by the transition matrix.

The fundamental mathematics of this approach was developed extensively by mathematicians and physicists, and the approach has been applied in areas of psychology concerned with change ever since Miller 1952 introduced the idea to us. The mathematics is closely related to the analysis of contingency tables with chi-square statistics, and also to Shannon and Weaver's information theory (1949). Indeed, a type of chi-square test can be used to establish the necessity of a Markov analysis based on observation of a particular sequence of behaviors. Other statistics can also be calculated that allow comparison of transition matrices across individuals or groups. In the 1950s, Markov modeling was applied especially successfully to animal learning (e.g., Bush and Mosteller 1955) and, in the 1960s, to human concept learning (Trabasso and Bower 1968). In the latter application, the states involved were explicitly cognitive states that represented the subject's internal hypothesis as to the concept the experimenter was using the generate the series of exemplars and non-exemplars to which the subject had to respond. Because Trabasso and

	Frequency t + 1				Probability t + 1	
	0	1	Sums		0	1
0	25	6	31	0	0.81	0.19
1	6	162	168	1	0.04	0.96
			199			

Figure 2.3
Frequency and probability matrices for the talking sequence.

Bower's analysis (1968) is somewhat complicated, however, I will illustrate the Markov approach with an example from the extensive work on sequential analysis of social interactions described in Gottman and Roy 1990, which also described in detail how to use the technique for analysis of a wide range of behaviors, including language behavior (cf. sect. 2.2). Because the techniques are easy to use, the statistics familiar, and the mathematics related to very deep results in physics (see chap. 13), sequential analysis via Markov models remains one of the most attractive tools for dynamical cognitive science.

As an example of the first steps in a Markov analysis of a sequence of behaviors, consider the following sequence of states described by Gottman and Roy (1990) from a study of conversational interaction by Jaffe and Feldstein (1970). Here the states refer to whether a particular one of the conversationalists is talking (state 1) or remaining silent (state 0—the other person is talking) and describe one minute of conversation:

1111111110001111111111111111111111111111111111111111111111

1111111111111111111110000000000000000001111111111111111111

111111111111111001111111111111111111001111111111111111111

11111111111010000000011111111

The frequency and probability transition matrices for this sequence are shown in figure 2.3. The frequency matrix was created by counting the numbers of transitions of each type in the sequence above; the probability matrix (whose entries actually only estimate the "true" probabilities), by dividing each entry in the frequency matrix by its row sum (e.g., $25/31 = 0.81$). The value of χ^2 for this frequency matrix is 118.99, which is much larger than the 99.9th percentile of the χ^2 distribution with 1 degree of freedom (10.82), indicating that the observed frequencies of transitions are very unlikely ($p \ll 0.001$) to have been generated by sequentially independent samples from the overall, unconditional probability distributions of the two states. In other words, there is tendency for the speaker, once having started talking (in state 1) to persist in talking, and a similar, although not quite as strong, tendency to persist in silence once having fallen silent. Another way to see this is to calculate the unconditional probabilities of silence and talking by dividing the total numbers of occurrences of the two states (31 and 168 for silence and talking) by the total number of elements in the chain (199), yielding $P(\text{silent}) = 0.16$ and $P(\text{talking}) = 0.84$. These probabilities can be compared with the conditional probabilities from the transition matrix, $P(0\,|\,0) = 0.81$ and $P(1\,|\,1) = 0.96$. Clearly, because these conditional probabilities are larger than the corresponding unconditional probabilities, there is a tendency to remain in the same state over time, even when the transition that brought one to that state is unlikely, for example, $P(0\,|\,1) = 0.04$. The Markov transition matrix captures this tendency simply and elegantly, and predicts similar, although not identical, sequences in other settings. Similar analyses (e.g., Gottman and Roy 1990) have been effectively applied to marital and other social interactions, resulting in useful predictions and insight about underlying processes.

Chapter 3

Rhythms of Behavior

It can now be said with assurance that individuals are dominated in their behavior by complex hierarchies of interlocking rhythms. Furthermore, these same interlocking rhythms are comparable to fundamental themes in a symphonic score, a keystone in the interpersonal processes between mates, co-workers, and organizations of all types on the interpersonal level as well as across cultural boundaries. I am convinced that it will ultimately be proved that almost every facet of human behavior is involved in the rhythmic process.

—Edward Twitchell Hall, *The Dance of Life*

3.1 The Dance of Life

Hall (1983) was one of the first to observe that humans in all cultures are engaged in a rhythmical "dance" when they interact with each other. Studying films of people interacting in a wide range of situations, from laboratory to field, and both within and across cultures, he documented both the actual rhythms and the intriguing variety of these rhythms, especially across cultures. Moreover, he also described the dramatic ways in which rhythms can affect performance, relationships, enjoyment of life, and the outcomes of interactions between cultures. Rhythm is one of the most elementary and at the same time one of the most profound categories of sequential behavior. Rhythmical time series are simple and yet they exhibit a compelling structure.

Interestingly, the rhythms of interpersonal behavior are not easy to see or to describe in English. When Hall asked some of his Chicago-born American students to view his films of people interacting and to report what they saw, it usually took them many hours of viewing before they began to notice and interpret the nonverbal gestures and other movements of the people in the film. On the other hand, when he asked Spanish-American students to view the same films, they were able to see the rhythmical dance right away. What was the difference? According to Hall, the Spanish-American students came from a culture in which rhythm and repetition are foundations of interaction, whereas the other students were from a verbal culture that trained people to seek variety and avoid repetition. Moreover, the Latin culture (and others, such as African) emphasize the connectedness of people and their embeddedness in a cultural context, whereas the dominant North American culture emphasizes the uniqueness of individuals and their isolation from others. This leads also to different views of time in those cultures: the Latin and African cultures have a polychronic, or "many clocks" view of time, whereas the North American culture has a monochronic view of time, with just one clock, the physical one on the wall or on the wrist that says when events such as classes, meetings, or vacations are to begin and end. For Hall, the rhythms of life generate a great variety of types of time, illustrated in his mandala of time in figure 3.1. Although we will not explore most of these types of time, their characterization is consistent with the view of time as *constructed* and *evolving* put forth in chapter 4. It is instructive to com-

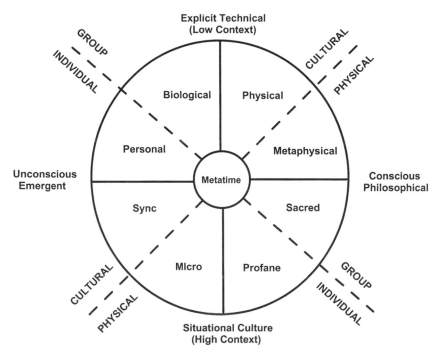

Figure 3.1
Mandala of time. (After Hall 1983.)

pare this polychronic view of time with the nested hierachy of times proposed by Fraser (1982), and discussed in chapter 4.

3.2 Music and Rhythm

One topic that creates both a desire to attend to rhythm and a vocabulary with which to describe it is music. Even here, however, we find that Western music and music in the rest of the world treat rhythm quite differently. In his beautiful book, Robert Jourdain (1997) explores the many facets of music and its construction and appreciation by the human brain. He considers two very different notions of rhythm that dovetail nicely with Hall's conceptions. *Meter* consists of metronomic patterns of accentuated beats, whereas *phrasing* consists of more organic, irregular but structured temporal organizations of musical "shapes." Or, as Jourdain (p. 130) puts it: "Meter is brick, phrasing is poured concrete." The regular beat of rock music, indeed of most Western music, is meter at its strongest. Try tapping your fingers on a surface at a steady rate. Soon you will find yourself accentuating some taps and not others: *one*-two, *one*-two, and so forth. Even perfect, metronomic pulses are organized into groups of beats (e.g., Povel 1981). The *one*-two-three, *one*-two-three meter of a Viennese waltz is what lays the foundation of the dance of the same name, a three-step that, at least for beginners, proceeds with one foot movement per beat. In parallel with the monochronic Western dance of life, most Western music is informed by a single meter, a monorhythm. In contrast, meter in "world music" is often polyrhythmic, consisting of several interacting meters. African drumming is perhaps the quintessential example of polyrhythm, often incorporating four or more different meters into a single fabric that seems to ebb and flow like a tide. Such rhythmic elaboration is attractive when only a few, rather cumbersome instruments, like drums, are available.

As an example of the powerful influence of phrasing on our appreciation of music, Jourdain analyses "The Pink Panther" by Henry Mancini. Figure 3.2 shows the score for the first few bars of this unforgettable piece of music. The rather simple meter is shown at the bottom of the figure; the groups of notes comprising musical phrases and subphrases are indicated at the top. Note that the phrases are easier to understand when listening to or humming the music than when visually inspecting the score. You might wish to try humming the tune from memory while perusing figure 3.2. It is clear that the phrasing builds a complex hierarchical structure. This structure strongly organizes our perceptions of the music and, in this

Figure 3.2
Meter and phrasing in "The Pink Panther." (From Jourdain 1997, p. 123. © 1997
by Robert Jourdain. Reprinted by permission of HarperCollins Publishers, Inc.)

instance, creates even more complexity by sometimes accentuating and
sometimes undercutting the meter. All of this creates a driving piece of
music that we cannot help moving to, although these movements do not
include any kind of simple underlying oscillations, such as those made
when we tap out the beat of a piece of rock music.

Meter is clocklike; it is involved in measuring temporal intervals. It
creates temporal order with an underlying *pulse*, which entrains the other
meters, even complex ones like syncopation and polyrhythms. In contrast,
the perceptual present, memory, and anticipation work together to generate phrasing, or the large-scale temporal structure of music. In dance,
we move to the rhythm of a piece, trying to feel or to convey the music's
rhythmical structure, both meter and phrasing. Jourdain argues, however,
that rhythm does not arise from movement. Rather, it is generated by the
brain in an effort to organize perception and cognition along the temporal
dimension. Rhythm, especially phrasing, is largely learned and may depend on oscillators in the brain that are engaged in structuring experience in "phrases" (see chap. 31). Some phrasings are clearly related to the
organic way we act in the world, and to the temporal contingencies of the
evolutionary niche we occupy. Others are constructed in creative acts of
elaboration of our musical vocabulary.

3.3   Rhythms in the Brain

In another beautiful book Scott Kelso (1995, xvii), describes how the
brain, conceptualized as a "pattern-forming, self-organized, dynamical system poised on the brink of instability," creates rhythms. He begins with
an account of a clever finger-twiddling experiment, which he explains

using the Haken, Kelso, and Bunz (HKB; 1985) model of coordination. An example of *synergetics*, the interdisciplinary theory of pattern formation created by Haken (1983), the HKB model is the basis for Kelso's description of how the brain organizes itself to create the rhythmical flow of behavior, including perception and learning.

Although Kelso used a back-and-forth motion, let us try a tapping version of Kelso's task, one that connects more closely with musical rhythm. Place your hands on a surface in front of you, thumbs touching, index fingers in the air pointing away from you, and the other three fingers of each hand curled underneath, out of the way. Now try tapping one finger on the surface while lifting the other one in the opposite direction, away from the surface, then lifting the tapping finger and tapping with the other one, repeating this alternate tapping motion at the same, relatively slow rate for a while (imagine you are playing a bongo drum for a very slow Latin ballad). This tapping is called "antiphase movement" because the homologous muscle groups in your two hands are doing different, opposing, things at the same time. Now try "in-phase" movements, where your fingers are moving in the same direction (up or down) and tapping at the same moment. Here homologous muscles that move your index fingers are doing the same thing at the same moments. Now go back to antiphase tapping at a slow rate and begin to speed up your tapping rate (following a metronome's clicks is a good way to force the higher tapping rate). As the tapping rate increases, you will find it increasingly difficult to continue tapping in antiphase, finally succumbing and switching to in-phase tapping. Now try beginning with in-phase tapping. You will find that you are comfortable tapping in phase at any rate, including the very slow ones at which antiphase tapping also seems comfortable. We could say that in-phase tapping is "stable" over the entire range of tapping rates, whereas antiphase tapping is only stable at slower rates, becoming "unstable" at higher rates. The instability causes the switch to in-phase tapping. The HKB model, briefly described below, explains this dramatic difference in the stability of the two tapping patterns (for the full account, see Kelso 1995).

We can describe the results of Kelso's experiment (1995) in terms of a single variable, the *relative phase*, ϕ, between the movements of the two fingers, measured by subtracting where one finger is in its up-down cycle (its *phase*) from where the other one is at the same moment in time, relative to a canonical position (say touching the surface). If we consider an entire up-down cycle to be a circle, with the canonical position at 0, each cycle has magnitude 2π (the number of radians in a circle;

$\pi = 3.141593\ldots$); thus relative phase can be anything between 0 and 2π. For example, if one finger is down (phase $= 0$, touching the table) when the other is up (phase $= \pi$, halfway around the circle), then the relative phase is $\pi - 0 = \pi$ (or vice versa, $0 - \pi = -\pi$). The finger-tapping experiment result is that a relative phase of 0 (or, equivalently, 2π, in phase), with the fingers always at the same phase of their movements, is stable at all rates, whereas a relative phase of π (or $-\pi$, antiphase), with each finger moving in the opposite direction from the other, is only stable at slow rates, switching to $\phi = 0$ at some critical speed of cycling (degrees per second). Notice that relative phase is unchanged if we reverse which finger is in which position. For example, $\phi = \pi$, whether the left finger is down and the right one up or vice versa. Relative phase is also unchanged if we shift time by one entire period, adding or subtracting 2π. For example, 0 and 2π are identical, as are relative phases of π and 3π (or $-\pi$ and π). We can express these spatial and temporal symmetries in terms of a mathematical function, $V(\phi)$, that stands for the behavior of the two fingers: $V(\phi) = V(-\phi)$ and $V(\phi + 2\pi) = V(\phi)$, respectively. What is the simplest function V that could display these two symmetries and also describe the results of the experiment? As Kelso (1995) explains, temporal symmetry implies that V is periodic and thus can be expressed as a Fourier series, a sum of sine and cosine functions (see, for example, Ramirez 1985 and chap. 14 for more). Spatial symmetry means that V has only cosine functions because $\cos(x) = \cos(-x)$. Because we want the simplest model that just does the job, we need only the first two terms in the series:

$$V(\phi) = -a \cos \phi - b \cos 2\phi, \tag{3.1}$$

the equation for the HKB model of coordination. Figure 3.3 shows graphs of equation 3.1 for various values of b/a, which is interpreted as related to rate of tapping, f, by $b/a = k/f$, where k is a constant. Large values of b/a correspond to slow tapping, and the smaller the value of b/a, the faster the tapping. Finally, for any value of a, if $b = 0$, $b/a = 0$, and tapping is the fastest it can be (f approaches infinity). When this happens, $V(\phi) = -a \cos \phi$, as shown in the bottom right-hand graph.

We can interpret the graphs in figure 3.3 as a two-dimensional landscape on which a ball (representing a particular value of the phase relation ϕ) is rolling around, subject to a downward force (e.g., gravity). When the ball is in a valley, it cannot get out unless energy is exerted to raise it above one of the adjacent hills (a "potential barrier"), which represents a stable state of the system (black ball). If there is no adjacent hill, the ball could easily roll downhill into a valley, and it is in an un-

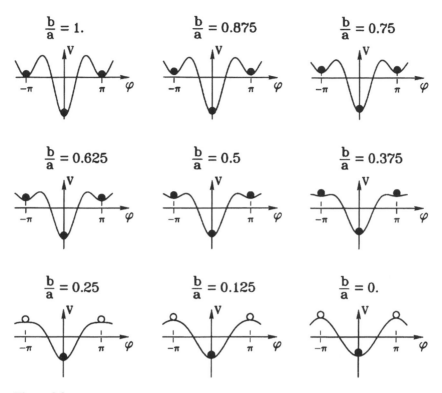

Figure 3.3
The Haken, Kelso, and Bunz (HKB; 1985) model of coordination. (From Kelso 1995. Reprinted by permission of The MIT Press.)

stable state (white ball). Notice that there is always a center valley with a black ball in it, regardless of the value of b/a. Thus, if tapping in phase (ball in center valley, $\phi = 0$), a person can easily keep on doing this, no matter whether the tapping rate becomes higher (b/a gets smaller) or lower (b/a gets larger). However, if a person begins tapping in antiphase ($\phi = \pi$ or $\phi = -\pi$) at a high rate (bottom row of graphs), the state is unstable, and the slightest fluctuation will send the ball rolling downhill toward the nearest (and only) stable state, $\phi = 0$. If a person begins tapping at a slow rate, say at $b/a = 1$, and gradually speeds up, the terrain gradually changes with the tapping rate until, once again, the system becomes unstable and eventually falls into the stable state, $\phi = 0$. This happens at some critical value of b/a, in this case near $b/a = 0.25$. The parameters b and a, and the critical value of b/a, could be different for each person, but when the correct values are fitted to the data, the model describes each person's phase-switching behavior quite nicely. Moreover, because the fingers are controlled by the brain, the HKB model can be interpreted as a description of the self-organized, coordinative behavior of those parts of the brain involved in generating rhythmical movements, just the kind of thing demanded by both music theory and by the dance of life. The HKB model is an excellent example of the application of dynamical systems theory to explain the temporal integration of behavior. The central role played by fluctuations in the dynamics of behavior, specifically, in precipitating movement between states and, more generally, in synergetics, is a major theme of the chapters to come.

Chapter 4

Time

Time flies, time dies.
—Jonathan Larson, "One Song, Glory," from *Rent, The Musical*

What really matters anyway is not how we *define* time, but how we measure it.
—Richard Phillips Feynman, Robert B. Leighton, and Matthew L. Sands, *The Feynman Lectures on Physics*

Ordering behaviors in a sequence is not enough. For many reasons that will become apparent if they are not already, we need to locate behaviors in *time*. But what *is* time? Despite its central role in their subject, most authors writing about dynamics do not discuss the nature of time, perhaps because they realize just how difficult it is to discuss properly. Failure to deal with the nature of something as fundamental to dynamics as time, however, can lead to inadequacies in the resulting theory. Changes of a system over time are observed, categorized, and analyzed, but the role of time in these changes is relegated to a symbol (usually, t) in a differential equation. (On the deep problems time poses, see Russell 1945 and Van Bendegem 1992 for reviews of work before and after 1945, respectively; see also Coren, Ward, and Enns 1999 for a conventional discussion of the role of time in perception and cognition.) Here, in touching on some of the very deep problems that remain, I adumbrate a coherent view that will serve our present purposes.

4.1 Space-Time

The time employed assumptively in most discussions of dynamical systems, including the few that exist on the dynamics of behavior or of cognition, is the *absolute* space-time of Newtonian, or classical, physics. In this system, dimensions, in which moving particles exist, are infinite in

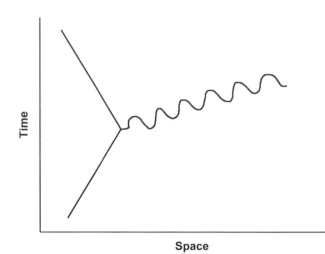

Figure 4.1
A Feynman diagram of an electron (straight lines) moving in time and space and emitting a photon (wavy line) at a certain time and place.

extent and axiomatically or definitively given. For example, figure 4.1 shows a "Feynman diagram," which Richard Feynman (1985) invented to keep track of the possible paths of photons and electrons in doing calculations in quantum electrodynamics. Similar diagrams are used in discussions of cosmology to illustrate the evolution of the universe and in many other areas of physics. In such diagrams, space and time are represented as two dimensions: space is relegated to one dimension, and time to the other. In psychological diagrams, the space dimension might be changed to a psychological variable, such as anxiety or the probability of a correct response to a short-term memory probe, but the time variable is unchanged. This absolute time is treated as a variable in an equation and is measured by physical clocks. It appears either as an explicit variable, for example, in $d = rt$, where d is distance, r is rate of movement, and t is time; or as an implicit variable, for example, in $F = ma$, where F is force, m is mass, and a is acceleration, the rate of change of the rate of change of position, $d(dx/dt)/dt$. The calculus is not crucial to understand acceleration at this point; I will indicate and explain it when it is.

Where did the idea of absolute time come from? According to Feynman, Leighton, and Sands (1963), there was no precise way to measure time when philosophers (e.g., Plato and Aristotle) first began to discuss it. Galileo first measured time intervals in his inclined plane experiments by counting his heartbeats (pulse). Later, to gain more precision, he created better clocks based on pendulums. The drive to create better clocks has continued until the present day, when physical time is measured by the vibrations of the cesium-60 atom and other exotic oscillators. Having a good measuring system for time also allows us to measure other important variables. For example, distance can also be measured in terms of absolute time as long as speed is constant. One useful application of this idea is in radar: radio waves are bounced off objects, whose distance, d, is calculated from $d = ct/2$, where c is the speed of light and t is the time from emission of the radio wave by the emitter until its detection by the receiving attenna.

In contrast to the absolute space and time of physics, the space and time of Leibniz (1714/1956) were defined by relations among an infinite number of particles (he called them "monads") that had no extension in either space or time. Although various aspects of Leibniz's philosophy are problematic from the point of view of dynamics, especially the assumption that monads cannot interact, the idea of *relational* space and time itself is not. Consider a set of identical elements, or particles, in the abstract. To speak of one, rather than another, there must be some property by which the one can be discriminated from the other. The most elementary such property is *location* in space. If the two differ in location, then I can point to one or the other and say, "That is the one I mean." In physics, elementary particles are of this nature: two photons or two electrons of the otherwise same quantum properties are interchangeable except for a difference in spatial location. When I can discriminate two otherwise identical elements in this way, I can say that space is "generated" by the relationship between the two. The unit of space is the "difference" between the elements that allows the discrimination. Time then arises from treating the two (or more) spatial locations in some *order*. *Interval* (or *duration*) is generated by movement (change) from the first to the second, whereas *period* is generated by movement from the first to the second and back again. In the simplest case, interval is generated by two successive pointing events (cf. Wittgenstein 1961). Elements that can be distinguished spatially but not temporally are *concurrent*, or simultaneous. In some general systems theories, space and time are "constructed" through the interactions of the system with its environment which causes the differentiation of initially identical elements, first in space and then in time (Alvarez de Lorenzana 2000).

Whether we consider time to be relational or absolute, a fundamental relationship between space and time is that time can be represented by distribution in space plus order (or sequence). By this, I mean that if we have a set of events represented at different spatial locations, and impose an order on that set, then moving between the locations in that order generates a temporal sequence of the events. If speed of movement is constant and fast enough, then covering the space between event representations can reconstruct the time distribution of those events. Lashley (1951; see also chap. 2) argued that the events of animals' (including humans') experience are stored in the brain as a spatial distribution but are reproduced when required in a sequence from the spatial representation, thus creating the temporal distribution of the events, their serial order. A similar mechanism is thought to produce new sequences of behaviors (and thoughts) in a particular serial order that itself often has significant meaning (as in speech). This (re)production of the temporal from the spatial may very well be a clue as to a useful way to think about the unfolding of behavior in time.

4.2   The Arrow of Time

Time is more than order and interval, however. As James (1890) and many others have pointed out, and everyone knows intuitively, there is a *sense* to time as experienced by humans (and perhaps other animals), a *direction* in which the order proceeds preferentially. We look out from the "saddle point" of the present, as James called it, remembering the past and predicting the future. We experience a sense of time passing, or flowing as a river flows. Our very consciousness has been metaphorized as a "stream" flowing, and we all know that streams do not flow uphill. Where does the directionality of time come from?

The easy answer given by physics is the second law of thermodynamics: entropy always increases in an isolated system. Entropy, originally concerned with the flow of heat between objects, is now interpreted as a measure of disorder, so that the second law now reads that isolated systems evolve toward a more disordered (more probable) state. For example, if we put a cold ice cube in a warm glass of cola, the ice cube will melt as the heat flows from the cola and the glass to the ice, and the result will be a glass of cooler and somewhat diluted cola (but no ice). All of the fluid in the glass (and the glass itself, neglecting the surrounding air) will come to have the same temperature and the entropy of the system will be larger than at the moment when the ice cube entered the glass. In this explanation, the arrow of time represents the system's evolution from less probable (more organized) states to more probable (less organized) states. The passage of time is simply a statistical phenomenon. In a beautiful lecture on this question, however, Thomas Gold (1965) demonstrated that even these statistical tendencies do not suffice. By simply reversing all processes in the universe, we can build a coherent picture in which time goes in the opposite direction; we are left with order without direction. Like Kant, Gold concluded that it is we who give time a direction through our experience of its flow. He argued that this experience arises because memory is more accurate than prediction (simulation): we look out from the "now" in two directions that are asymmetrical, labeling the more accurate one to be what already happened, the less accurate to be what is yet to happen. This emphasis on memory, particularly "episodic" memory (Tulving 1983) is entirely consistent with James's ideas. What we remember feels more solid than what we think will happen in the future (but see Roediger 1996). The latter is usually generated by mental simulations (Kahneman and Tversky 1982), though occasionally we experience powerful and accurate "intuitions" about the future.

Gold's explanation for time's arrow is consistent with another modern view of time as itself evolving along with the universe. Fraser (1982) argued that pure, symmetrical succession is the time of the physical world, whereas asymmetrical time (past, present, future) is the time of the biological and the psychological worlds. Just as the universe has evolved from the big bang singularity, so time has evolved from the *atemporal* (chaos of photons traveling at the speed of light), to the *prototemporal* (probabilistic specification of temporal positions; no meaning of "moment"; world of subatomic and atomic particles), to the *eotemporal* (simultaneities of chance; pure succession; ideal clock; directionless, symmetrical time; physicist's and dynamicist's *t*), to the *biotemporal* (simultaneities of need; physiological present; evolutionary or developmental past; predictive future; living organisms), and finally to the *nootemporal* (simultaneities of intent; mental present coexisting with physiological present; remembered past; imagined future). Of course all of these times exist now, in a nested hierarchical complex that is still evolving as humans (and perhaps other creatures) create ever more complex informational and interactional environments (cf. Hall 1983 and chap. 3). This notion is similar to one in which each dynamical system has its own characteristic cycle time for information exchange between elements (Alvarez de Lorenzana and Ward 1987), except that, for Fraser (1982), the very nature of time, not just its unit, is different at the different levels of the hierarchy. Fraser's view reminds us that eotemporal interval should not be taken to be the only property of time relevant to dynamical cognitive science. The directionality of biotemporal and nootemporal time can even help us unravel the temporal complexities of cognitive behavior (see fig. 4.2 and chap. 5), and the existence of different time scales informs the frequency structure of temporally distributed fluctuations (chaps. 14–19).

4.3 Measuring Time

In spite of (or perhaps in reaction to) Feynman's statement in the second epigraph above, I have defined time in some detail, although, at least until dynamical cognitive science is more advanced, we must be content with a series of observations made at a series of moments of eotemporal clock time, on which we must impose somewhat artificially the directionality of nootemporal or biotemporal time. The clocks we use today are very accurate compared to the first clocks used by Galileo. Nonetheless, those first clocks were based on a fundamental principle that is important today. Galileo noticed that the period of a particular pendulum was always the same, even though the distance it traveled might change as the initial energy imparted to it was dissipated by friction (at least as measured by his pulse). A clock is merely a process that has a regular period, usually of movement between two states. Agreement among clocks is the standard by which we decide which are the best clocks. In cognitive science, we often use computer clocks based on oscillations in a crystal. Such oscillations are highly regular and can be very fast, making it possible to measure the timing of events to microseconds or even more precisely, though the significant differences cognitive scientists are interested in are usually on the order of 10 milliseconds (e.g., of reaction time). My rule of thumb is that measurement should be at least an order of magnitude more precise than the differences I want to detect, so that time measurement error does not make it harder to detect the meaningful difference, which usually means measuring time to the nearest millisecond. This should be sufficiently precise for most cognitive and behavioral time series, and is probably more precise than necessary for conscious cognitive behavior, which proceeds at about four operations per second (see chap. 16).

Even if we measure time with a very precise clock, we often cannot observe behavior as precisely. A behavioral time series is composed of a series of observations that persists for a total time period, T, in which the observations are separated by an interval, Δt, both measured in, say, seconds of clock time. For example, consider recording, once per second, at which part of a complex painting I am looking. The period, T, puts a lower limit on the temporal regularities we can observe: if any occur more

Figure 4.2
For eotemporal time either direction of events makes sense, whereas for bio-
temporal and nootemporal time only the top-to-bottom direction makes sense.
(After Fraser 1982.)

slowly than a frequency of $2/T$ we will not see them because a cycle begun during the observation period will not be completed while we are still collecting observations. For example, if we collected our looking observations for $T = 100$ seconds, we would not notice a regular waxing and waning of my attention that caused me to gradually speed up my scanning behavior to a maximum, slow it down to a minimum, and so forth, repeating the cycle every 10 minutes (600 seconds). Such behavior would have a temporal frequency of $1/600 = 0.0017$ Hz. We would notice some change of scan rate over our observation period, but it would not be sufficient to tell us whether the change was regular or just a drift or trend for that one observation period (causing our time series to be nonstationary; see chaps. 11 and 12). Similarly, the *sampling rate*, the number of observations (samples) per second, or $1/\Delta t$, imposes an upper limit on what we can observe in the time series: we cannot see regularities whose frequency is greater than $1/2\Delta t$, or what is called the "Nyquist frequency." If all relevant regularities occur below the Nyquist frequency, then we can be confident of having seen them all if only we sample for a long enough duration. If however, there are any regularities above that frequency, they will contaminate our time series in a process called "aliasing," which arises from discretely sampling a continuous function at a rate that is too slow to capture all of its regular fluctuations. Although the effects of aliasing can be dealt with or avoided (see Press et al. 1992), anyone dealing with time series should be aware of them and of the limitations of discrete sampling of a continuous process.

Moreover, we should be mindful that quantum theory may sometimes apply even to cognitive behavior (see, for example, Hecht, Schlaer, and Pirenne 1942 on the absolute threshold of only six photons for vision). The quantum theory uncertainty principle for time, $\Delta t = h/\Delta E$, where E stands for energy and h is Planck's constant (6.6254×10^{-27} erg sec), means we cannot simultaneously measure both time and energy for a physical system to any desired degree of accuracy. If we want more precision in knowing *when* something happened, we are forced to give up precision in measuring *what* it was that happened (energy change). Of course this minimum error is actually very small and would hinder neither classical physics nor ordinary cognitive science, where time is usually measured to the nearest millisecond. Nevertheless, it serves to remind us that, in measuring one aspect of a system, we may disturb that system, making measurement of another aspect less precise. If we think of time as generated by changes in large-scale systems the uncertainty principle might apply even to humans.

Finally, there is the issue of continuity. Whereas, in physics and most dynamics, time is a continuous dimension, represented by the real numbers, discrete time might better characterize the unfolding of cognitive behavior in time, which could create discrete time instants, abrupt transitions between instants and places, like a Markov chain or a finite state machine transition between states with no intermediate positions. Although such an idea might seem inconsistent with the laws of physics, at least those of classical physics, it need not be. As Kilmister (1992, 58) puts it: "All change, whether it be generation of a new element or incorporation of new information, takes place in discrete steps and the sequence of steps is the process." At least some physics can be reformulated in terms of the calculus of discrete differences, in which the time derivative is the difference between the values taken by a variable at two neighboring time instants, and differentiation causes time shifts—a novel aspect that does not follow from differentiation of a continuous variable (see, for example, Kauffman and Noyes 1996). Finally, some of the most difficult conundrums of modern physics, such as quantum gravity, can perhaps be understood in terms of a quantized or discretized time and space (t'Hooft 1989). How this view bears on dynamical cognitive science will be discussed in chapter 5.

Chapter 5

Cognitive Processes and Time

Time travels in divers paces with divers persons.
—Shakespeare, *As You Like It*

We might ... say this of time: It ambles with action, trots with thought, gallops with sensation....
—Herbert F. Crovitz, *Galton's Walk*

"How about me?" he yelled, "Am I to be just like a clockwork orange?"
—Anthony Burgess, *A Clockwork Orange*

5.1 Temporal Unfolding of Cognitive Behavior

In chapter 4, I set forth a constructive view of time, in which a cognitive process unfolds by progressing through a series of *states*, constructing time as it goes. In other words, the system *changes*. Rather than thinking of these changes as occurring in time, we can think of them as creating time itself. We do this by using the states as markers of time; we measure time by counting the number of state changes between recurrences of the same state. As Crovitz (1970) emphasized, following Galton, thoughts recur. Thought is cyclic. One way to construe this statement is by representing a cognitive system as a finite state machine. Tipler (1994) argued that humans can be modeled as finite state machines because they are quantum systems, and all such systems can be modeled as finite state machines. A *finite state machine* is simply a finite set of states and a transition matrix that records the probabilities of transitions between each state and each of the others. The Markov chains discussed in chapter 2 are examples of finite state machines. Clocks can be represented as finite state machines, usually with two states and with the probabilities of a transition from one state to the other near 1.0. A more complicated

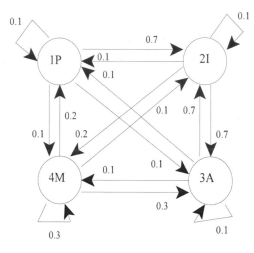

Figure 5.1
A simple finite state machine.

example is shown in figure 5.1, where the machine has four states (note that the transition probabilities are shown near the arrowheads), and the cyclic behavior is not at all clear. In particular, there is no absorbing state into which the system will collapse, and no guarantee that a certain state, once reached, will recur when the same preceding cycle of states recurs. And yet the system does cycle. There are only $4^4 = 256$ possible four-state cycles (including cycles like $3 \rightarrow 3 \rightarrow 3 \rightarrow 3$), for example, and each must recur many times in a long sequence generated by the machine. The cyclicity is simply more exotic, the rhythm hard to discern from such a representation. Let us pretend that the system as diagrammed represents one spouse's cognitive and emotional state vis-a-vis the other as follows: 1P = passion; 2I = indifference; 3A = annoyance; 4M = mild affection. What does the diagram capture about the cyclic nature of this particular long-term relationship at a particular moment in time? It seems that, for the spouse under consideration, passion is a short-lived emotional state (probability of staying in that state is only 0.1, versus 0.9 for changing to another state), whereas indifference (2I) is the most common state (sum of transition probabilities to that state is the greatest at 1.6). The short cycle of indifference (2I) to annoyance (3A) and back again is quite common: the probabilities $P(2I \rightarrow 3A)$ and $P(3A \rightarrow 2I)$ are both high. Of course, the probabilities can themselves evolve. For example, Sternberg (1986) argued that passion is a common state at the beginning of a romantic relationship (all probabilities leading to passion are high, including the

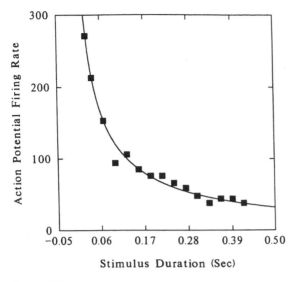

Figure 5.2
Adaptation of the visual receptor complex. (From Ward 1991.)

probability to stay there, implying that probabilities leading away from passion are low), but the likelihood of passion wanes as the relationship progresses, eventually reaching a somewhat low state in most relationships (perhaps similar to the probabilities in figure 5.1).

The ever-precessing sequence of cognitive and emotional states is only one example of the many aspects of cognitive behavior that demand description in terms of temporal unfolding. Although none is fully developed into a dynamical systems theory, let us briefly consider a few other compelling examples, beginning with information input. Everyone knows that sensory systems adapt, that the response of, say, the visual system to a patch of light striking the retina is greatest at first and then rapidly wanes until steady state is reached. If we think about this process as one of acquiring information, as Kenneth Norwich (1993) has, then adaptation represents a series of states of increasing knowledge about what is out there. Although we typically represent adaptation as continuous with time (see fig. 5.2), according to Norwich's theory it is actually discrete, depending on a series of samplings of the stimulus energy by the receptor. The state of the receptor–ganglion cell complex before the light has struck the retina is one of ignorance about the light's intensity. After the light strikes, the receptor begins both to acquire information about its intensity and to lose information as it "forgets" the content of earlier samples. Eventually, a state is reached in which the forgetting exactly equals the acquiring: equilibrium. Any change in the light input disturbs this equilibrium, and causes the receptor to change its response. First the firing rate jumps to a new level above the previous equilibrium rate as the receptor–ganglion cell complex enters the state of ignorance of the current light intensity, and then it falls, through a series of intermediate states representing information acquisition, to a new equilibrium state that represents the balance of information acquisition and loss for the new light intensity.

Adaptation is just one of the many processes involved in the microgenesis of a visual percept (see, for example, Kalmus and Bachmann 1980), which also includes the time course of feature extraction, object formation, categorization, identification, comparison with other perceptual objects, application of semantic rules, evocation of associations, and so forth. These processes have been studied repeatedly and thoroughly in every perceptual system, but seldom with the aim of completely describing the temporal unfolding of the percept. One particular time-critical aspect of visual perception is the sequence of eye movements made when scanning a scene. Figure 5.3 shows how these movements occur even when scanning a scene at rest; they are much more critical when scanning a scene in motion, as when driving a vehicle or viewing a film. Enormous efforts have been expended in understanding eye movements, although usually within certain contexts, such as reading (e.g., Just and Carpenter 1976, 1987), driving, flying, or searching a scene, with an emphasis on the information extracted rather than on the complex interplay of that information with the process of scanning itself. If the eye movement system were to be represented as a finite state machine, with each state defined by the part of a given scene focused on, then it is clear that different scan patterns could be described by different state transition matrices, and that such matrices would both depend on the preconditions of a particular situation and dynamically (and complexly) on the information being extracted. Eye movements in a situation in which the scene itself is also changing, perhaps as a result of movement of the body in response to the information extracted from the previous scene, would be described by a sequence of transition matrices generated by the interaction of the extracted information and the goals of the person.

Many more examples of temporal unfolding in cognition could be adduced. Learning is obviously a time-critical process, including both timing aspects (see sec. 5.2) and unfolding as the knowledge or skill state of the organism changes. Memory, the record of that learning, is also

Figure 5.3
Eye movements (*bottom*) while scanning a picture (*top*). (After Yarbus 1967.)

dynamical (see sec. 5.3). But beyond these obvious examples are others. Indeed thinking itself cycles, creates time, and unfolds in the time it creates. The exercise of logic is sequence critical, and thus time critical. A mathematical or logical proof only works if the steps are presented and cognized in the correct sequence. Although a proof can be modeled by a degenerate finite state machine, what is more interesting is a human's understanding of a proof, which can be modeled by a much more complicated finite state machine, with many intermediary states and probably changing matrices of transition probabilities (memory). Problem solving also has its own rhythm, which can be arrived at by asking people to verbalize their thinking during problem solving (e.g., Ericsson and Simon 1993), or by having them make judgments about how close they might be to a solution. Metcalfe 1986 and Metcalfe and Wiebe 1987 on subjective "feeling of knowing" are two such studies. In Metcalfe 1986, subjects solving insight problems were actually less likely to give the correct solution when they felt "hot" (i.e., the solution was imminent) than when they felt only "lukewarm" (not very close to a solution but on the right track). Metcalfe and Wiebe 1987 showed that this pattern holds only for insight problems; for algebra problems, subjects' feeling that they were very close to a solution did indeed correctly predict their subsequently obtaining that solution. In both studies, time series of judgments of feelings of "warmth" were collected as subjects solved problems. Although the focus of the studies was on the inherently temporal aspect of predicting performance (both by the subjects themselves and by normative ratings), the analysis was not extended to modeling the full time series. It would be informative to make a finite state machine model of those time series, in which the probability of switching from the various states of warmth into other such states and into the absorbing "problem solved" state could be estimated from the transitions occurring in the various empirical time series. Such a model, by displaying the overall dynamical properties of the process of solving insight problems, could perhaps suggest additional hypotheses about the mechanisms involved.

5.2   Timing of Cognitive Behavior

Many cognitive science phenomena seem to involve a different aspect of time, what we might call "timing," where the occurrence of stimuli or states at particular times and places seems to matter the most. For example, in visual masking (e.g., Kahneman 1968; Enns and Dilollo 2000), given appropriate spatial relations, it is exactly *when* the masking stimulus occurs with respect to the onset and/or offset of the target stimulus that determines the masking effect. If the two overlap in time, then brightness masking occurs. If the target precedes the mask by about 60–100 msec, then maximal backward masking occurs; if vice versa, then forward masking. And if target and mask are more than 200 msec apart in time, then usually no masking occurs at all. The very names of the phenomena are informed by the temporal relationship between the stimuli. Similar examples occur in the orienting of attention (e.g., Wright and Ward 1998), inhibition of return (e.g., Klein 2000), priming (e.g., Houghton and Tipper 1994), alerting (e.g., Sokolov 1975), and warning (e.g., Woodworth 1938), among many other processes.

But timing actually involves synchronizing two or more processes unfolding in time. In masking, for example, the microgenesis of the percept of the target stimulus interacts with that of the masking stimulus at a critical moment in that of the target. If the target percept is already fully formed, it is perceived. When masking occurs, the percept of the mask has undermined the processes leading to the perception of the target. The situation is similar in the other timing examples: timing is always about the relationship between two or more unfoldings in time.

5.3 Memory

Memory would seem to be the cognitive process that most directly addresses time. Memory differentiates the past from the present, and the differences between the "feeling" of a memory and the feeling of an anticipation might help to differentiate both from the future (see chap. 4). In discussing memory, we suppose that the cognitive system is always changing and that current inputs have lasting effects that may wax (learning, consolidating) or wane (relaxing, forgetting) over time. What is the nature of this inherently temporal process?

One axiom of the modern understanding of memory is that it is *constructive*, and therefore inherently dynamical. Memories are not simply records sitting on a library shelf, waiting for a librarian to take them off and bring them out into the bright light of working memory. When we remember an episode from our past, we actively build the "memory" from traces of perceptual and cognitive activations of the brain that were triggered by the episode we are remembering (literally "re-bringing to mind"). These old traces are recycled in the current context, with current activations contributing strongly to the remembered experience. Although it is useful to classify memory into various types, including sensory, procedural, episodic, gist, implicit, explicit, working, and repisodic, each type abides by the same underlying principle: changes in the brain at one time affect the activity of the brain at a later time (see Squire 1987). Indeed, this principle can be extended to all forms of "memory," including computer memory, genetic memory, and even more abstract systemic memory, implying that there might be a universal model for memory that would illuminate the human case (Clancey 1999; Minelli 1971), possibly in the form of a finite state machine, where memory processes would be modeled by changing of state transition probabilities.

In the absence of such a universal model, we must work at modeling the memory states of the human or other animal brain. Because the activation sequence of the entire brain is too complex to model as a finite state machine at the neural level or lower, we will have to be content with models at a fairly high level for the present. A few such models are already available to serve as a foundation, for example, network models of associative memory (e.g., Anderson 1976; Rinkus 1996). Many models of working memory have been proposed, although not at the same level of detail. A particularly intriguing one conceptualizes working memory as a push-down stack, much as some memory registers are organized in computer operating systems. Similar models could be created for processes of cognitive development, both for the learning of thinking skills (including memory skills) and for the learning of facts. In these models, finite memory states should not be confused with the "stages" of the various stage theories of cognitive development, such as Piaget's (1954). One particularly interesting cognitive ability to model would be memory for sequence. As I discuss in chapters 28–30, our perception of sequence is biased, and at least part of this bias depends on our memory for the order in which recent events have happened. There is a considerable, though sporadic, literature on sequential aspects of memory. One interesting set of recent studies (Houston 1999; Wegner, Quillian, and Houston 1996) differentiated the effect of instructions to suppress memory for a film, on memory of the sequence of events from that on memory for the events themselves. Another recent study (Woltz et al. 1996) showed that general sequence memory was more useful than specific sequence memory in skill acquisition. A third (Clancey 1999) describes in detail an inherently dynamical theory of memory based on the distinction between simultaneous and sequential activations of concepts in the brain (see chap. 3).

In general, memory (along with most other cognitive phenomena) exists at many timescales, from very short (1 msec or less; physical and chemical processes in the brain), to fairly short (25 msec; memory scanning), to medium (250 msec; conscious operations), to fairly long (seconds, minutes; short-term or working memory), to very long (hours, days, years; episodic memory) to longer still, (centuries; scientific research, organizational memory), to evolutionary (millennia; evolution of cognitive processes). In particular, more precise modeling of explicit, autobiographical memory systems, including their evolution, could contribute greatly to the solution of the problem of consciousness (see Donald 1995). Although some of these topics are taken up in later chapters, many others must await the future efforts of dynamical modelers.

Chapter 6
Systems and General
Systems Theory

What is a system? As any poet knows, *a system is a way of looking at the world.*
—Gerald M. Weinberg, *An Introduction to General Systems Thinking*

There exist ... systems [whose] quantization in space encompasses their structure; their quantization in time represents their orbits.
—Arthur S. Iberall, *Toward a General Science of Viable Systems*

Some while after the Beginning, there was Newtonian science. And Ludwig von Bertalanffy said, "Let the whole system be greater than the sum of its parts." Norbert Wiener added, "Let negative and positive feedback flow throughout the system." Ross Ashby whispered, "Let the system have the requisite amount of variety to manage its environment." And general systems theory was born. This book could be viewed as an attempt to embed cognitive science firmly in a general, dynamical, systems framework. Many of the concepts used thus far, and of those used later on, can be traced to fundamental general systems theory (for a fine introduction, with articles by many of the most important practitioners, see Klir 1972a). General systems theory embodies many of the formal theories whose use I advocate in analyzing cognitive behavior, including the theory of finite state and stochastic machines, Turing machines, and the like. Ironically, however, systems theory remains a somewhat obscure discipline, usually taught in engineering schools and occasionally also in business schools. Some of its concepts have been co-opted by the more modern and fashionable "complexity theory" (e.g., Waldrop 1992). As we will see, systems concepts are crucial to the development of dynamical cognitive science. I can only introduce a few of the major ideas here and in the following chapters, leaving readers who wish to apply these ideas in their respective contexts to pursue them in greater detail elsewhere.

6.1   Systems

What *is* a system and why is it relevant to dynamical cognitive science? As Weinberg (1975, 52) says in his excellent introduction to general systems theory, and in the first epigraph above, *"a system is a way of looking at the world."* A point of view is necessary because even that tiny part of the world, the human brain, is complex, containing around 100 billion neurons and probably more than 10 trillion synapses. Indeed, even when we try to limit our attention to a single cognitive system, we run into complexity that demands a point of view. One way of coming to grips with this problem is to contemplate the "Bremermann limit" (Bremermann 1962). At approximately 10^{93} bits (a bit is a Binary digIT, 0 or 1, equivalent to a Boolean logic truth value, a unit of Shannon information; see Shannon and Weaver 1949), the *Bremermann limit* represents the processing capacity of a digital computer the size of the Earth (6×10^{27} grams) over the time the Earth has existed (10^{10} years at about 3.14×10^7 sec/ year $= 3.14 \times 10^{17}$ sec), assuming a maximum processing rate of 2×10^{47} bits/sec/gram. Many reasonable computation problems are beyond the Bremermann limit. For example, even a simple problem in Boolean algebra (the logic implemented by general-purpose computers and universal Turing machines) can quickly exceed it. Klir (1972b) gives an example of implementing on a computer a function that maps a set of n logic (0 or 1) input variables to a set of n logic output variables using what are called "universal elements" or computing modules. He shows that the number of bits involved in determining how to implement this function for various numbers of input variables, n, is $N = n \cdot 2^{2^{n+1}}$. For $n = 1$, $N = 16$, but for $n = 8$, $N = 10^{155}$ and for $n = 10$, $N = 10^{617}$—the latter is more than 500 orders of magnitude greater than the Bremermann limit. (Special theoretical methods are used to solve these and related problems in computer design.) Because similar computational problems arise in science, it is clear we must simplify. And whenever we simplify, we implement a point of view. Building a model or a scientific theory (see chap. 7) is a way of simplifying, of making the otherwise overwhelming complexity manageable.

Thus a system is a theoretical construct that simplifies nature. Nonetheless, the system must be complex enough to manage relevant aspects of its environment. For example, in a human memory system, there must be enough complexity (or what Ashby called "variety") to deal with remembering the things a human has to remember (grocery lists, words of a language, faces of relatives and friends, rules of games). Ashby (1958) called this principle the "law of requisite variety." It was extended by many, including Beer (1979), who pointed out that there are various ways a system could amplify its own variety to cope with the much larger amount of relevant variety from the environment. Finally, Alvarez de Lorenzana and Ward (1987) argued that systems should be placed into an evolutionary context, in which those with ever-increasing variety emerge from an environment also increasing in complexity. They identified two principles by which a system evolves: *combinatorial expansion*, a linear process whereby the system develops the unrealized potential in its fundamental properties; and *generative condensation*, a nonlinear process whereby complexes of the elements of the old system recombine to create fundamental elements of a new system with new possibilities. Both processes operate through system-environment interaction. They argued that, through successive stages of combinatorial expansion and generative condensation, the universe has evolved from the first, simple physical systems (such as the hydrogen atom), through ever-increasing complexity of physical, chemical, biochemical, biological, and finally social and intellectual systems into the world we experience today. Each of these system levels can be described by its own fundamental properties, including units of time and space unique to the interactions taking place between the system elements at that level (see chap. 4). In this way, a cognitive system is no different from others, and should be characterized by the relevant fundamental systemic properties, such as time and space units, information input capacity, and potential for combinatorial expansion.

One principle that makes some systems easier to deal with is the "square root of n law": variances of statistics obtained by sampling from probability distributions decrease as the sample size increases (see Schrödinger 1944/1967). For example, the standard deviation of the distribution of means of random samples taken from any probability distribution (the standard error of the mean) is equal to the population standard deviation divided by $\sqrt{n}$. For very large systems, then, we can find statistical regularities. On the other hand, for very small systems, such as simple machines, we can successfully analyze behavior in terms of the interactions of their individual components. For systems of medium size, however, neither approach works well; in such systems, we observe fluctuations of many sizes, irregularities and lack of predictability, and great theoretical difficulty. Unfortunately, systems of medium size, such as cognitive systems and even brains (for some purposes at least), are the rule. With medium-size systems, we seldom benefit from the square root of n law: the simplification we must undertake will cause us to omit many important

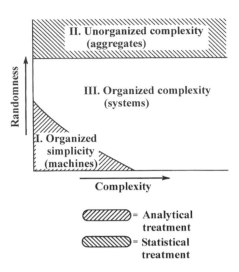

Figure 6.1
Where general systems thinking fits in. (From Weinberg 1975, p. 18. © 2001, 1975
by Gerald M. Weinberg. All rights reserved. Reprinted by permission of Dorset
House Publishing.)

elements, relations, or both. Thus we can expect deviations from theoretical predictions to occur with regularity, whereas regularity in system
behavior will seldom be seen. Figure 6.1 illustrates what we must deal
with in most medium-size systems, and especially in cognitive systems—
organized complexity, the most difficult type of system to understand, but
also potentially the most rewarding.

6.2   General Systems Theory

It is not enough to acknowledge that we are dealing with systems of
medium size and then go on to do our usual science. As we simplify and
search for statistical and other regularities, we must be constantly aware
that we *have* simplified, and that there are other points of view not represented by the one we are taking. Other researchers will take some of
those points of view, and what might emerge eventually is a kind of *order
of the second degree*: laws about the laws of what we are studying. Those
who have applied general systems theory across the various fields of
science and engineering have come up with quite a few laws about laws.
Some are useful and others appear whimsical, but all contain a grain of
truth about how to deal with organized complexity, the realm in which we

Table 6.1
General Systems Laws (Laws about Laws)

Name	Content
Composition law (Weinberg)	The whole is more than the sum of its parts.
Decomposition law (Weinberg)	The part is more than a fraction of the whole.
Principle of indifference (Weinberg)	Laws should not depend on a particular choice of symbols.
Principle of difference (Weinberg)	Laws should not depend on a particular choice of symbols, but they usually do.
Principle of invariance (Weinberg)	Change can be understood only by observing what remains invariant, and permanence only by what is transformed.
Fundamental theorem (Gall)	New systems mean new problems.
Law of large systems (Gall)	Large systems usually operate in failure mode.
Law of function (Gall)	Systems tend to oppose their own proper function.
Law of growth (Gall)	Systems grow.

Sources: Weinberg 1975 and Gall 1975.

nearly always find ourselves in cognitive science. Table 6.1 lists a few such general system laws, just to reveal their flavor.

Probably the most famous of the general systems laws listed in table 6.1 is the "composition law": the whole is more than the sum of its parts. This law refers to what has been called "emergence," the idea that a simple combination of the properties of the separate elements of a system does not describe the properties of the system itself. One famous example is that of the water molecule, H_2O. Water molecules freeze at $0\,°C$, whereas both oxygen and hydrogen, its constituents, are gases at that temperature. Water does not become a gas until $100\,°C$. We now understand why water has these properties (and others that do not match those of hydrogen and oxygen): they arise because of the unique geometry of electrical charge created by the hydrogen and oxygen atoms when joined into a water molecule. This geometry is now understood in terms of quantum electrodynamics, but it is not a simple linear combination of properties of hydrogen and oxygen atoms. It is the relationship between its constituent atoms that create water's properties; its atoms must be joined in just the right way. Thus water's properties are said to be "emergent" because they cannot be obtained directly from the properties of its constituents. Cognitive systems often seem to exhibit "emergence"; indeed, time and again, the most elusive cognitive phenomenon of all, human consciousness, has been said to be "emergent" relative to the human brain.

A final important distinction in this brief introduction to general systems theory is that between open and closed systems. The ideal system of thermodynamics and science in general is *closed*, meaning that *all* influences on system behavior are known and either under control or fully described. In a closed system, entropy (or disorder) always increases with time. In contrast, all *real* systems are *open*, meaning that they are in contact with a larger environment that produces uncontrolled and possibly undescribed inputs. The Earth, which receives some of the extravagant outpouring of energy from the Sun, is just such an open system, as are the many constituent systems on its surface. Some systems, such as those in physics experiments using particle accelerators, can be sufficiently isolated from the larger environment that fairly simple descriptions of their behavior will be accurate. Open system are the rule, however, and their behavior reflects this openness. The most interesting open systems are those far from equilibrium, in which some of the energy input is used to maintain self-organized patterns: thermal convection cells, for example, or exotic chemical reactions such as the Belusov-Zhabotinski reaction, or possibly even human consciousness (see Prigogine and Stengers 1984; Kelso 1995).

6.3 Dynamical Systems Theory

Dynamical systems theory attempts to describe the temporal unfolding of a system. It is concerned with two fundamental concepts, those of *change* and *time*, both of which I have discussed in earlier chapters. There are two standard ways to mathematically describe a dynamical system (von Bertelanffy 1972): an *external description*, which consists of a set of transfer functions, usually expressed as systems of linear equations relating inputs to outputs; and an *internal description*, which consists of a set of n simultaneous partial differential "equations of motion,"

$$\frac{dY_i}{dt} = f_i(Y_1, Y_2, \ldots Y_n), \tag{6.1}$$

where Y_i represents the system state variables and $i = 1, 2, \ldots n$. (If your mathematical training did not include calculus, be assured there will be gentler and more helpful introductions to such equations in chapter 8.) The important thing to note here is the "*dt*" in the denominator of the first term, which means that the equations are expressing the *rate of change* of the system state variables, $Y_1, Y_2, \ldots Y_n$, with respect to time, t. Although this is standard physical (eotemporal) time, depending on the state variables and the time measurement, these "equations of motion" can become very exotic indeed. However difficult they may be to work with, we need to face them, for they formally describe important system properties, such as wholeness and sum, growth, competition, and equilibrium (von Bertelanffy 1968). In doing so, they describe the "motion" of the system in *state space*, an *n*-dimensional space in which the current state of the system is represented as a vector (one value for each state variable) and in which the changes of values of these state variables (i.e., the changes in the system's state) are represented as *trajectories*, or paths. Trajectories can be divided into categories, such as *asymptotically stable* (all trajectories sufficiently close to a particular one approach it asymptotically with time), *neutrally stable* (all trajectories sufficiently close to a particular one stay in its vicinity), and *unstable* (all trajectories sufficiently close to a particular one diverge from it with time). When the equations of motion defined by equation 6.1 are linear, many things can be said about the system described by them. Systems described by nonlinear differential equations, though they often exhibit dramatic instabilities and are harder to understand, are nevertheless the most interesting systems, and the ones on which we will concentrate in this book. After a brief diversion to establish some important concepts about theories, models, and scientific understanding in chapter 7, we will return to the development of a dynamical system theory approach to cognitive science in chapter 8.

Chapter 7

Science and Theory

Even the artists appreciate sunsets, and the ocean waves, and the march of the stars across the heavens.... As we look into these things we get an aesthetic pleasure from them directly on observation. There is also a rhythm and a pattern between the phenomena of nature which is not apparent to the eye, but only to the eye of analysis; and it is these rhythms and patterns which we call Physical Laws.
—Richard Phillips Feynman, *QED*

Why should I presume to tell you, my scientist readers, what *I* think science is? There are two reasons. First, I simply cannot resist the natural temptation to inject a few memes (Dawkins 1976) on this topic into your brains. Second, you need to understand what I am trying to do, even if you do not agree with me. Knowing the framework within which *I* do science, you can compare it with your own and judge accordingly. I should tell you that I have been heavily influenced by physics, especially by quantum mechanics, through a few of its practitioners most willing to put themselves on public display, such as Richard Feynman (1965, 1985) and Erwin Schrödinger (1944/1967).

7.1 The Mandala of Science

Michael Ovenden was a very good astrophysicist, colleague, and friend of mine, who died too young at 62. We often argued about what science is and how it should be used, before, during, and after the meetings of the General and Applied Systems Workshop at the University of British Columbia, which we both regularly attended and to which we both regularly contributed. In Michael's highly rigorous view, only physics (perhaps including astrophysics) had achieved the status of a true science. Figure 7.1 shows my version of the basic elements of his view. (In Michael's version, there was only one arrow, labeled "intuition," between "theory"

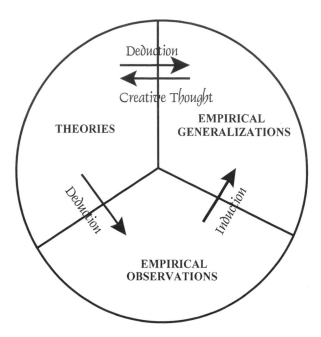

Figure 7.1
Ovenden-Ward mandala of science.

and "empirical generalizations," and it went in the direction of the arrow
I have labeled "creative thought.") Michael held a dualist stance on the
relation between mind and matter, believing that the inspiration to create
a useful scientific theory came from a mysterious place to which we had
no access, not even in principle. Thus he rejected the idea that psychology
would or could ever become a science.

Although Michael never convinced me to eschew psychology, he did
influence the way I think about science, along the lines displayed in figure
7.1, whose mandala divides science into *products* (theories, empirical
generalizations, and empirical observations) and *processes* (deduction,
induction, and creative thought). Cognitive scientists study the processes
of science; we and other scientists can of course use them without
understanding their mechanisms. These ideals of deduction and induction
(arguing from the general to the specific and vice versa) are described
precisely and applied rigorously by mathematicians and logicians in the
context of proving theorems in formal systems. As practiced by scientists,
however, they can range from loose arguments and wild speculations to

precise mathematical or other formal derivations. Creative thought is still somewhat of a mystery, although we have studied it for many years. Some (e.g., De Bono 1970) think it requires some nonlinearity and others (e.g., Crovitz 1970) argue for a random element. The ability to make analogies and sophisticated guesses, to see patterns and relations, to hold many facts and concepts simultaneously before the mind's eye, and unusual perseverance—all seem to contribute to successful creative thought.

The mandala emphasizes that science is a system, a whole that is different from the sum of its parts. Indeed, the necessity of all parts and the sufficiency of none are why Ovenden thought that only physics was a true science. He argued that biology, chemistry (though he wavered here), psychology, and other "sciences" were not true sciences chiefly because they lacked deep formal theories whose precisely verifiable quantitative predictions had been extensively tested. Physics does possess such theories, for example, quantum electrodynamics (see Feynman 1985), quantum mechanics as a whole (see Baggott 1992), and general relativity (Einstein 1961; Thorne 1994). In biology, Darwin's theory of evolution by natural selection, now quite modified and sophisticated, finds itself in nearly every modern biologist's toolbox, yet profound theoretical problems remain (see, for example, Kauffman 1993). The remarkable "central dogma" of molecular biology, that DNA and its associated molecules both carry and implement the genetic code that informs the variety of life on this planet, is fairly well accepted, yet there is still no comprehensive theory about how the information encoded in DNA interacts with its environment to form and regulate a life-form (see Nass 1970). Cognitive science abounds with theories of perception, memory, reasoning, language production, and understanding, many of which are comprehensive and quantitative, such as the entropy theory of perception (Norwich 1993) and the wave theory of psychophysics (Link 1992), or comprehensive and formal in a different way, such as Newell's SOAR approach (1990) to cognition. Yet none has attained anything near the scientific rigor of quantum mechanics or general relativity.

If we are to more closely approach the impressive accomplishments of physics, we must incorporate a dynamical component into cognitive theory, and into psychological theory as a whole. And because of the complex systemic nature of cognitive and psychological phenomena, the dynamical component will have to be in the form of dynamical systems theory. This book aims to convince at least some of its readers on both these points.

7.2   Formal Theories

Although theories come in many types, I favor formal theories, a bias shared by at least some others in cognitive science. A formal theory is distinguished by its reliance on a few, precisely stated, fundamental principles from which rigorous application of logical manipulations can then produce a large variety of useful implications. Maxwell's theory of electromagnetism is an elegant and important, though difficult to understand, example of a formal theory in physics. Basically, what Maxwell did was to transform Faraday's ideas about electrical and magnetic lines of force into a precise mathematical theory (see Born 1962; Wise 1979). The theory's fundamental axioms are written in the form of four partial differential equations:

$$\nabla \cdot \mathbf{E} = \rho/\varepsilon \tag{7.1}$$

$$\nabla \cdot \mathbf{B} = 0 \tag{7.2}$$

$$\nabla \times \mathbf{E} = -\frac{\partial \mathbf{B}}{\partial t} \tag{7.3}$$

$$\nabla \times \mathbf{B} = \mu\sigma\mathbf{E} + \mu\varepsilon\frac{\partial \mathbf{E}}{\partial t} \tag{7.4}$$

In these equations, $\mathbf{E}$ stands for the electrical field intensity, $\mathbf{B}$ for the magnetic field intensity, ρ for electrical charge density, ε for the dielectric constant, μ for the atomic weight (relative to that of hydrogen) of the electrical conductor (e.g., a copper wire), and σ for the conductivity of the electrical conductor (values for copper, silver, gold, and platinum are high). Finally, $\partial/\partial t$, the partial differential operator, means to take the partial derivative of the relevant multivariable function in the numerator (in this case, $\mathbf{E}$ or $\mathbf{B}$) with respect to the variable in the denominator (in this case, t, or eotemporal time); here, we are interested in the rate of change of $\mathbf{E}$ or $\mathbf{B}$ with respect to time. $\mathbf{E}$ and $\mathbf{B}$ are vector-valued functions of space, that is, each "value" of the function is a vector in geometric space (specified by coordinates x, y, z). Vectors have both a direction in space (the orientation of the vector with respect to the axes of the space) and a length, or magnitude (how far from the origin—0,0,0—the end of the vector is). The symbol ∇ related to $\mathbf{E}$ and $\mathbf{B}$ by the raised dot in the first two equations stands for the differential operator "divergence" or simply "div," the scalar product of the operator (a partial differential expression in the spatial coordinate vectors) with the relevant vector-valued function, in this case, $\mathbf{E}$ or $\mathbf{B}$. Scalar products of vectors produce a scalar, or nonvector, number, at each point in space. The symbol ∇ related to **E** and **B** by the "$\times$" in the other two equations stands for the differential operator mathematicians call "curl," the vector product between the operator and the relevant vector-valued function, which produces another vector at each point in space (instead of a scalar, as with "div").

It is not necessary to understand these equations completely to grasp their beauty and fundamental importance. Equations 7.1 and 7.2 describe how electricity and magnetism behave separately. In words, equation 7.1 means that whenever an electrical charge (ρ/ε) occurs, an electrical field (**E**) appears that exactly balances the charge everywhere in space. Equation 7.2 means that a magnetic field (**B**) is not accompanied by any free magnetic "charges"; such charges do not exist. Equations 7.3 and 7.4, which contain the curl operator, describe how electricity and magnetism interact. Equation 7.3 states that every magnetic "current" created by the displacement or disparity of magnetic force lines in space induces an electric field in a perpendicular direction (minus sign on the right). Similarly, equation 7.4 states that every electrical current, including one made up entirely of the displacement or disparity of electrical charge density in a vacuum, induces a magnetic field. When the values of the constants representative of the vacuum are entered into equations 7.3 and 7.4, the equations describe the mutually generating propagation of the electrical and magnetic fields that make up a "light wave" or photon. Notice especially that the theory consists of a set of partial differential equations in time and space variables. The equations describe the distribution of electrical and magnetic force over space and how these distributions change in time. This (relatively) simple theory thus describes *all* electrical, magnetic, and electromagnetic phenomena, including those of light itself, with incredible precision. One of the crowning achievements of Einstein's special theory of relativity was that Maxwell's equations could be derived in it. If they had not been, Einstein's theory would have been incorrect.

In physics, the formal, mathematical statement *is* the theory, and any accompanying verbal or pictorial explication is secondary, which makes physics difficult even for the initiated because mathematics requires careful and often deep thought—and virtually impossible for the uninitiated because the combination of jargon and difficult mathematics is impenetrable. This situation is unfortunate, but in my opinion the advantages of formal theory outweigh its disadvantages. These advantages are spelled out quite nicely by Feynman (1965), and include both the enormous simplifying and precision-inducing character of mathematical expression, and the bringing to bear of the entire reasoning framework of mathematics on the problem at hand. As Feynman wrote, "it is impossible to explain honestly the beauties of the laws of nature in a way that people can feel, without their having some deep understanding of mathematics. I am sorry, but this seems to be the case" (pp. 39–40).

But cognitive science is not physics, and I know many will object that, in our context, formal theory is too restrictive and the simplifications required too radical, that informal theories are richer, admit a wider variety of interpretations capturing a wider range of phenomena, and so forth. Many of these objections are well taken. As Platt (1964, 352) put it: "The logical net is coarse but strong, the mathematical net is fine but weak." By the "logical net" he meant an informal but correct understanding of a phenomenon, expressed in words or perhaps in flow or structural diagrams, with perhaps an equation or three thrown in. Such an understanding is necessary before proceeding to a formal statement: although it is "coarse" and cannot make detailed quantitative predictions, it is nevertheless "strong," in that it does indeed capture the essence of the understanding. In this sense, other scientists, especially Faraday, had understood the relation between electricity and magnetism somewhat before Maxwell wrote his equations, and had even expressed some of their understanding formally, as equations summarizing empirical generalizations (e.g., Ohm's law, $E = IR$). Thus, too, the mathematical theory produced by Maxwell when he wrote his four simple equations was "fine" because it made precise quantitative predictions about a vast range of electromagnetic phenomena, including those of light waves, but it was "weak," in that if any of those predictions proved wrong, to even the slightest extent, the theory was disconfirmed. Many people will nevertheless feel that Faraday's pictures of interacting electrical and magnetic fields, though they do not do the work that Maxwell's equations do, give them a better grasp of electromagnetism than do Maxwell's equations.

It is possible to be formal without being mathematical. Gregg and Simon (1967) argued that some sort of symbolic information-processing language might be more appropriate than mathematics for cognitive science. They showed how Trabasso and Bower (1970) in formulating their Markov chain theory of concept learning, often had to resort to informal theory because mathematical theory failed to apply to some important, empirical phenomenon; how, when they recast the informal theory into a formal symbolic language, much like a computer programming language, it captured the concept learning phenomena quite well while avoiding the inconsistency and imprecision usually associated with informal theory; and how they could mathematize the formal information-processing theory whenever necessary to generate and test quantitative predictions. Such an approach is certainly still a viable one to pursue in cognitive science; an excellent example is Newell's SOAR theory (1990).

Although quantitative precision has always been and still is the goal of the physical sciences, when we move into the realm of nonlinear dynamics and cognitive science, such precision may not be generally attainable. Systems described by nonlinear differential equations often have an extreme sensitivity to initial conditions: even a small amount of error in the specification of the initial or current conditions of such a system will cause the predicted trajectory of the system to diverge radically from the actual trajectory. Although the system might end up in the predicted region of the system state space, its precise state at any given time will not be predictable with the precision required by most physical theories. This situation is called "chaos" (see chap. 23). Discussing the consequences of this lack of predictability for sciences that deal with nonlinear dynamics, Kellert (1993) argued that we might need to adopt a new approach to these sciences, in which the prediction of patterns of change would replace the prediction of precise values of system state variables. In such an approach, formal theories would be just as desirable because the need for consistency and precision of ideas would be just as great, but the goals of these theories would be accurate predictions of patterns of change, rather than of change magnitudes. Because system dynamics are often best studied as geometrical figures, the emphasis may well become more geometric. Nevertheless, the goal of precise and deep understanding remains intact.

7.3 Principle of Complementarity

According to Weinberg's principle of complementarity (1975, 120): "Any two points of view are complementary." No one point of view provides the entire understanding. Sometimes different points of view are contradictory—that is just the nature of the world. Paradoxes will arise and may be resolved, but there will always be multiple points of view. Two good examples are the wave/particle duality of light (photons; see chap. 13) and the Heisenberg uncertainty principle (measurements of one aspect of a system interfere with knowledge of other aspects). In the context of dynamical systems theory, Weinberg's principle reminds us that, having had to simplify, to adopt a point of view, and to accept some uncertainty about a system's behavior, we can take other points of view that, provided they are of equal rigor and depth, will undoubtedly contribute different elements to our understanding of the system we are studying. This is not a license to abandon scientific rigor and speculate wildly, but simply a reminder that sometimes, as in the wave/particle duality of light, complementary points of view can all be useful, even though each is incomplete. I expect this will often be the case in dynamical cognitive science.

Chapter 8

Dynamical versus Statical Models

[Re] Zeno's argument of the arrow[:] The natural view ... is that there are *things* which *change* [but] philosophers have developed two paradoxes.... How ridiculous to say there is no arrow! say the "static" party. How ridiculous to say there is no flight! say the "dynamic" party. The unfortunate man who stands in the middle and maintains that there is both the arrow and its flight is assumed by the disputants to deny both; he is therefore pierced, like Saint Sebastian, by the arrow from one side and by its flight from the other.

—Bertrand Russell, *A History of Western Civilization*

Nothing is permanent except change.

—Heraclitus

8.1 Theories, Models, and Data

Theories are grand things, even informal theories. Ideally, they are general and yet parsimonious, broadly applicable and yet succinct. A theory is a system within which to think about many specific phenomena. Again, we can take our pick from several prominent examples in physics, such as general relativity or quantum mechanics. Within these theories, models of more specific situations can be created, for example, a model of how light interacts with a sheet of glass in quantum mechanics (actually, quantum electrodynamics; see Feynman 1985). Psychology does have a few such theories, a prominent example being signal detection theory. Itself an application of statistical decision theory to detection of signals by radio receivers, this engineering theory was applied to human performance and has since become very widely used as an approach to measuring performance independent of motivational biases (e.g., Green and Swets 1966; Macmillan and Creelman 1991). Many models have been created using the theoretical constructs of signal detection theory. A prominent example is the excellent model of auditory intensity perception developed by

Braida and Durlach (1988). In both physics and psychology, specific models are consistent with a particular, more general theory and use its terminology, but are actually *applications* of the theory in a restricted domain.

Of course, models also can be created in the absence of theory. In this case, although it holds true that the elements and relations in the model system (often a mathematical system) represent the elements and relations of the actual system being modeled (often an empirical system), no generally accepted theoretical principles, or only broad, informal theoretical frameworks, are invoked to connect the model with a wider domain of phenomena. This is common practice in psychology, especially in domains like perception and cognition, where much progress was made from the 1960s through the 1980s with information-processing models of restricted domains such as attention, speech, judgment, and decision making. For this reason, I will be referring mostly to models, although my (perhaps distant) goal remains the development of a general theoretical system within which cognitive phenomena can be modeled. Some candidate systems have been proposed, for example, Newell's SOAR system (1990), Anderson, Matessa, and Lebiere's ACT-R system (1997), Norwich's entropy theory of perception (1993), and Link's wave theory of psychophysics (1992).

A final point that needs to be reiterated here is that theories and models, however formal, serve as a guide to the collection, analysis, and interpretation of empirical data. There are no such things as data divorced from a theoretical framework, just as there is no such thing as an object divorced from its inertial framework (Newton). Even an informal, "commonsense" framework gives meaning to data collected within it, which is only to emphasize the importance of being explicit about our theories and models. Although the mere selection of phenomena to observe reveals what the accompanying theory is about, it is not always enough to reveal the assumed relationships between those phenomena and an informal, implicit theory or model. Thus, to take full advantage of Weinberg's principle of complementarity (chap. 7), let us always state our guiding theories explicitly and precisely.

8.2 Statical Models

Most theories and models in psychology are statical models. As mentioned in chapter 1, a statical model assumes, at least implicitly, that the relevant state of the modeled system remains constant, and specifies the relations between the various state variables of that system. If the model is formal, there is an *equation of state* that relates the measured values of the variables for some particular state. For example, either Fechner's or Stevens's psychophysical law is an equation of state. Let us revisit Stevens's law (eq. 1.3):

$$R = cS^m,$$

which states that, whenever the psychophysical system (experimenter, stimulus, subject, response; see Ward 1992) has a particular value of the experimenter's stimulus, S, the value of the subject's response, R, will be cS^m (with some error, of course). Although equation 1.3 is the simplest kind of equation of state, relating just two variables of a system, much can be done with it (see, for example, Geschieder 1997; Marks 1974). Music halls are designed according to its predictions of responses to the intensity of the music at various places in the halls, lawsuits are launched against polluters regarding the smelliness or loudness of their byproducts, and theories of sensory system function are tested noninvasively by measuring the parameters, especially m, of this equation under various conditions. What is perhaps most important, equation 1.3 summarizes fundamental relationships between important concepts; indeed, in some cases, it defines the concepts themselves. Stevens (1975) interpreted the exponent m to be the operating characteristic of the sensory transducer: different values of m measured for different sensory modalities (e.g., brightness in vision and loudness in hearing) reflected the different energy transduction principles of the various sensory modalities.

Possibly more familiar to most readers will be the many statical models of the human memory system that have appeared over the past 150 years. Enduring theoretical distinctions are those between *short-term* (or primary) and *long-term* (or secondary) memory systems and between *episodic* and *semantic* memory systems; a more recent popular model distinguishes between *implicit* and *explicit* memory systems. These informal models each define two conceptually separate memory systems that vary on several key properties. For example, the explicit memory system is said to control memory performance that is "initiated and guided by a conscious plan or by an intention to recollect specific prior episodes" (Graf 1994, 682), whereas the implicit memory system is involved when some prior episode influences present behavior in the absence of any such conscious plan or intention to recollect that episode. This leads to several empirical practices, such as asking subjects explicitly to remember in tests of explicit recall but giving them various priming tasks, such as stem completion, to test implicit memory. As proposed by Mandler (1980), implicit and explicit memory are said to be related to the underlying psychological processes of integration and elaboration. In this view (see also Graf 1994), implicit memory is the result of integration processes that make connections between the various features of perceptual objects during their perceptual processing, whereas explicit memory results from the elaborative processing that relates different perceptual objects in terms of their meaning. Note that although memory is inherently a temporal phenomenon (see chap. 5), such models emphasize the relationships between variables outside of time. For example, much is made in the memory literature of the observation that amnesiac patients often show substantially more implicit memory, sometimes near "normal," for past episodes than they do explicit memory (indeed, amnesia is *defined* by a lack of explicit memory). In other words, the (informal) state equation is as follows: amnesiac state implies low (relative to normal) explicit memory but high implicit memory, whereas nonamnesiac state implies high explicit memory and high implicit memory.

8.3   Dynamical Models

A dynamical model is concerned with a succession of states, that is with change, and thus with time because that is the dimension associated with change. Every dynamical model has time as a variable, although it is often represented implicitly. The prototypical dynamical model is a differential equation, such as the following simple linear one:

$$\frac{dx}{dt} = at, \tag{8.1}$$

where dx/dt, the derivative of x with respect to t, represents the rate of change of the variable x with respect to time, t. The dx and the dt, called "differentials" (after which differential equations are named), refer to infinitesimal changes of x in infinitesimal intervals of time. The equation describes the limit of change in the value of the state variable x as the change in t (time interval) becomes very small. Equation 8.1 states that the rate of change increases linearly with t, beginning at the value 0, when $t = 0$, that is, $a \cdot 0 = 0$. With time measured in seconds, if $a = 0.001$, then 1,000 seconds after $t = 0$, the variable x is changing at a rate of 1 unit per second, whereas at $t = 10,000$, it is changing at a rate of 10 units per second. Thus the rate of change increases with time. What does this mean about the behavior of the state variable x? We might suspect that, because

the rate of change just keeps on increasing, meaning that x keeps changing faster and faster forever, x itself would grow forever (or until something broke down). To find out for certain, we solve equation 8.1, which
involves multiplying both sides of the equation by dt and integrating each
side with respect to the variable in the differential on that side (integration
in calculus is the inverse of differentiation). Here the solution is an *explicit*
function of time because t appears on the right-hand side of the differential equation. When we solve equation 8.1 in this way, we obtain as one of
the solutions

$$x = a\frac{t^2}{2}.$$ (8.2)

(For the purists, I assumed that the difference of the two constants of
integration equals zero.) Now, beginning with $x = 0$ at $t = 0$, it should
be clear that x will grow forever on an ever-steepening curve, just as we
suspected. This may be a useful model of the national debt, or love in a
lover's dream, but it is not going to be too useful in dynamical cognitive
science. Most useful models in dynamics have more interesting, and more
limited, behavior. In particular, feedback often limits the growth of a
state variable, as we will see shortly.

Let us first consider another differential equation, however:

$$\frac{dx}{dt} = ax.$$ (8.3)

Because t does not appear on the right-hand side of the equation, the
solution of this differential equation is an *implicit* function of time. To
solve it, we need to rewrite the equation as $dx/ax = dt$ and then integrate
as before. The result is (again assuming that the difference of the constants of integration is zero)

$$x = e^{at},$$ (8.4)

as is well known in the literature of differential equations. In this exponential growth equation, if $a > 0$, then there is again growth without
limit, whereas if $a < 0$, there is a decline toward an asymptote of zero. If
$a = 0$, then $x = 1$ for all time, that is, the system does not change with
time. There are many other, more useful, differential equations, to be
sure, and most are functions of more than one variable, although they are
usually not easy to solve, especially when they are nonlinear. (For those
interested in actually doing this kind of modeling, Morrison 1991 provides summaries of many of the important techniques.) It is often possi-

ble, however, to find an approximation to differential equations in the form of difference equations, and work with these on a computer, as we will see shortly.

Without feedback, a dynamical model is boring, whereas, with it, the model becomes both useful and fascinating. Let us add some feedback $(-bx^2)$ to equation 8.3:

$$\frac{dx}{dt} = ax - bx^2 \tag{8.5}$$

Notice that $-bx^2$ is a negative term and will decrease the rate of change of x more and more as x gets larger and larger, offsetting the tendency of the rate of change to increase linearly with x according to the first term. Solving Equation 8.5 results in another implicit function of time,

$$x = \frac{c}{1 + (c/x_0 - 1)\ \exp[-a(t - t_0)]}, \tag{8.6}$$

where $c = a/b$. Figure 8.1 shows a graph of this *logistic equation*. When $0 < x_0 < a/b$, $a > 0$ and $b > 0$, then x approaches $x_0 + a/b$ as $t > t_0$ increases. Starting at t_0, growth is exponential for a while but then, as the feedback begins to make itself felt, slows down, leading to an asymptote of the variable at $x_0 + a/b$. Equation 8.6 is more useful than equation 8.4, having served for example, to model the consumption of a nonrenewable resource, such as petroleum (see Meadows et al. 1972). Indeed, its appli-

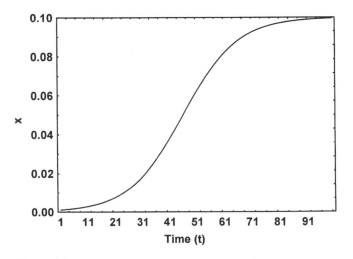

Figure 8.1
Graph of the logistic equation (eq. 8.6) for $a = 0.1$, $b = 1$.

cation in this area predicted that domestic oil production in the United States would decline as the available oil was discovered, produced, and consumed, until there was little left. Similar models might be usefully applied in cognitive science to the consumption of limited cognitive resources, such as memory, attention, or processing effort. In this case, however, the temporal unfolding might be over seconds, minutes, or hours, rather than over years.

There are two other important ways of setting up dynamical models. One is to use a difference equation, such as the logistic difference equation

$$x_{n+1} = ax_n - ax_n^2, \tag{8.7}$$

whose resemblance to equation 8.5 is apparent (though it behaves altogether differently). A difference equation assumes that time changes in equal and discrete jumps, so that the index n is taken to be integers representing equally spaced moments of time. Difference equations are closely related to differential equations, and often differential equation models can be turned into a difference equation models and studied by computer simulation, an approach much in vogue today. The relation to differential equations can be made clearer by subtracting x_n from both sides of equation 8.7 and then writing the left side, $x_{n+1} - x_n$, as Δx. Dividing both sides by $\Delta t = 1$ (by assumption), which leaves the right side unchanged, and suppressing the subscript n on the right, we obtain

$$\frac{\Delta x}{\Delta t} = x(a - 1) - ax^2, \tag{8.8}$$

which looks very much like differential equation 8.4, with the finite differences Δx and Δt replacing the differentials dx and dt. I will discuss the striking behavior of the logistic difference equation 8.7 in chapter 24 and show how it can be used as a model for memory in chapter 26. (For a very good practical introduction to the details of working with difference equations, see Goldberg 1986, which also includes examples of models in psychology and other fields.)

The other approach to setting up a dynamical model is simply to add a time index to a statical model. For example, equation 1.3 can be turned into a dynamical model simply by adding a time index to the variables, in this case a discrete trials index, i:

$$R_i = cS_i^m, \tag{8.9}$$

which describes the response on the ith trial as a function of the stimulus intensity on that trial. Now the model states that all of the trial-to-trial variation in psychophysical judgment responses can be accounted for by the variation in nominal stimulus intensity (controlled by the experimenter) from trial to trial. Because this is not the case in any published scaling experiments, an error term must be added to equation 8.9 to account for the residual variance. Now the question becomes, is the error simply random, or is it correlated with some other variables, in particular with previous values of R_i or S_i, say R_{i-1} or S_{i-1}? The model of equation 8.9 can usefully include more terms and even if it does the residual variance might still retain some structure. Chapter 11 summarizes the dynamical analysis of psychophysical judgment using equation 8.9 as a starting point. DeCarlo and Cross 1990 presents the detailed development of one of the resulting models of psychophysical judgment and also describes this method of developing a dynamical model in a way applicable to other modeling problems.

8.4   Why We Need Both Statical and Dynamical Models

Statical models seem to be more popular, and are arguably more useful, in biology, psychology, sociology, and so forth, than they are in physics and economics, at least partly because in the former fields the fundamental concepts depend more on the classification of phenomena. In other words, specifying the fundamental phenomena requires recognizing that a particular event falls into a particular category (Rapoport 1972). For example, in psychophysics, the decision to study sensory magnitude as a function of the stimulus intensity requires that "sensory magnitude" be given meaning. Fechner (e.g., 1860) spent a great deal of time and effort doing just this; psychophysicists have continued his effort for over 140 years, making invaluable use of the statical models of Fechner's and Stevens's laws as they have (cf. Ward 1990). Similarly, the study of human memory has involved repeated efforts to develop concepts that capture the important memory phenomena in ways that allow us to discover reliable empirical regularities. The distinctions mentioned earlier, and the models they have spawned, have led to impressive advances in our understanding of how behavior depends on previous experience. Thus, without useful statical models in these fields, it is doubtful that scientists could agree on the relevant phenomena of study. Although a dynamical model can always be built as long as a time series of events can be obtained for study, the meaning of the events used to inform the dynamical model needs to be anchored in some larger conceptual framework. A highly confirmed statical model can be a useful anchor. Moreover, when studying a field in which there are many useful statical models, the body of knowledge they summarize both informs any future efforts at model building and concept discovery, and provides a fertile ground for testing the generality and accuracy of dynamical models. Statical models produced by collapsing dynamical models over time must agree with other, highly confirmed statical models or the original dynamical models are suspect. For example, any dynamical model of psychophysical judgment must in some way or other collapse to a statical psychophysical law (e.g., eq. 1.3; see Gregson 1988). Thus, consistent with Weinberg's principle of complementarity, dynamical models complement existing and future statical models—they do not replace them.

Chapter 9

Dynamical and Structural Models

One of the more remarkable aspects of the connectivity of the cerebral cortex is the fact that when a given area A sends an output to area B, area B sends a return output back to area A.... This is such a ubiquitous arrangement that there are only a few exceptions to it.

—Semir Zeki, *A Vision of the Brain*

These topological features are at times the most essential ones in the descriptions of many systems.

—Anatol Rapoport, "The Uses of Mathematical Isomorphism in General Systems Theory"

9.1 Structural Models

I argued in chapter 8 that statical models are useful to dynamical modeling because they provide a framework within which dynamical models can be constructed and tested. Of course they are also useful in their own right because they define, categorize, and often make sense of the elementary phenomena with which a science is concerned. In both of these roles, statical models often take the form of what I call "structural models." That is, they achieve their goal by specifying a set of elements and describing the interrelations between these elements, emphasizing which elements are connected to which other elements (and can thus affect them causally). This emphasis on *connectedness of elements* is central to the role of structural models in dynamical cognitive science because it provides significant constraints on the form of any dynamical model describing the time evolution of the structurally modeled system.

A compelling example of the importance of such constraints comes from a comparison of various structural models of the brain. Descartes modeled the brain as a pump that distributed the humors, via the nerves, to the muscles and so caused behavior, much as a water pump distributes water through tubes to drive fountains. Clearly, any dynamical model of the brain based on Descartes's theory would involve hydraulic theory, and its basic elements would be pump chambers, tubes, and fluids. In contrast, the telephone switchboard model of the brain, in vogue after the electrochemical nature of nerve conduction was discovered and telephones invented, would require wires and switches and would involve the flow of electrons through those wires. Finally, the more modern models of the brain, based on computer metaphors, require elements such as flip-flops organized in registers, again with wires communicating between them. In these models, however, the flowing substance is digitally encoded information (in the form of electrical pulses). Although dynamical models derived within these three frameworks would undoubtedly share some aspects, they would differ from one another more often than not. For example, if a tube filled with fluid is cut, the fluid can drain out of any connected part of the system, causing total breakdown (as when an artery is cut and all of the blood drains from a body). In contrast, if a wire is cut, electrons can no longer flow from one terminus of the wire to the other, but electron flow is still possible in the other wires of the circuit (however altered it might be according to the laws of electrical circuits). Finally, if an information channel is cut, clearly information can no longer pass through that particular channel, but, rerouted, it might very well get to its destination by another pathway, and the system's functioning might be affected hardly at all.

9.2   Graph Theory

An excellent formal system within which to model system structure, graph theory involves a *graph*, defined as a set of points (*vertices* or *nodes*) in space and a set of interconnecting lines (*edges*) between them; for each pair of vertices, there either is or is not a connecting line. If the edges have an arrowlike direction associated with them, then the graph is said to be "directed"; each vertex has an *in-degree*, the number of edges directed toward that vertex, and an *out-degree*, the number of edges directed away from that vertex. Figure 9.1 shows an example of a directed graph, with the edge direction specified by the arrowhead on each edge.

   Finite state machines (see fig. 5.1), electrical circuits, and perhaps even brain circuits are all directed graphs, whose important function is to specify what is connected to what. A *path* between two vertices is a list of the vertices that have to be traversed to get from one to the other; DAC is a path between vertices D and C in figure 9.1. A path is *simple* if, as in

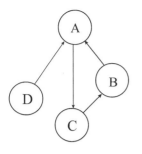

Figure 9.1
Directed graph.

DAC, no vertex in the list is repeated. A path such as *ACBA*, because its beginning and ending vertex are the same, is called a "circuit" or "cycle," (a circuit is simple except for the first and last vertices). A graph with no cycles is called a "tree." Favorite data structures in computer science, trees have also been used for structural models in psychology (e.g., Sattath and Tversky 1977). A graph is *connected* if there is a path from every vertex to every other vertex in the graph. The graph in figure 9.1 is not connected: there is no path connecting *C* to *D*, among other pairs of vertices. If a graph with *N* vertices has fewer than *N* − 1 edges, it cannot be connected; if it has more than *N* − 1 edges, it must have a cycle and thus cannot be a tree. Although a tree has exactly *N* − 1 edges, not all graphs with exactly *N* − 1 edges are trees. If there are *weights* on the edges, as in figure 5.1, where they represent state transition probabilities, the graph is a weighted graph. Finite state machines are thus directed, weighted graphs.

Because graph theory is an enormous topic in mathematics, I can only, as before, touch on a few less enormous topics relevant to it (for a basic text, see Berge 1985). The computer science literature contains a huge range of graph theory applications, including many relating to cognitive science, for example, expert systems (see Cowell et al. 1999) and directed weighted graphs used as models of stochastic systems (for an excellent detailed account, see Lauritzen 1996). Many theorems have been proven about various types of graphs, especially about the simplest ones. Many of these concern methods to ascertain whether and how many paths or cycles exist in a certain type of graph, or what might be the most efficient way to get from one vertex to another. The celebrated traveling salesman problem, in which all of the vertices in a graph must be traversed at least once, by the shortest possible route, is an example of a particularly fruitful graph theory problem. These static graphs might be used directly as the basis for a dynamical model concerning the temporal unfolding of the system state defined by the vertices. Such a model has been suggested for the cognitive neuroscience of attention, in which different, connected brain areas "light up" (show activity above the background level) successively as a cognitive task is performed (e.g., Posner and Raichle 1994). Of course graphs can change. The main category of dynamical graph studied is the *random* graph, where links "grow" among the initially defined set of vertices, and where a probability distribution over the vertices associated with the growth of the links between them provides constraints on the emerging structure. For a given set of probability distributions, there are many possible, different realizations of the random graph so defined. The relevant theorems of such a graph define the probability distributions for whether the graph is connected, how many indegrees its vertices have, how many paths there are from one vertex to another, and so forth. One common application of such graphs is that of predicting the extent and lifetime of disease epidemics. Cognitive science applications might include understanding the spread of information in a brain or in a culture.

Although much of the sophisticated mathematical analysis of directed graphs can be done only on graphs that have no cycles, such as trees, real systems always have cycles, as do most abstractions of real systems, so that the directed graphs representing them should also have cycles. This situation presents a dilemma for mathematical analysis. One solution, suggested to me by Priscilla Greenwood (personal communication), involves a particular way of introducing dynamics to the graphical structure. It can be illustrated by a planar graph, such as in figure 9.1, which has a cycle. The idea is to add a unidirectional time dimension perpendicular to the spatial dimensions (think of it as rising vertically from the page for figure 9.1), and then to replicate copies of the graph along the time dimension. Each copy of the graph represents one instant in time during which only one edge is "active" (represented by, say, a solid line), whereas the remaining edges are passive (represented by, say, dotted lines). This scheme transforms cycles in space into helices (or spirals) in space-time. For example, beginning at vertex A at time t_1 the cycle $ACBA$ in figure 9.1 becomes the helix $(A, t_1)\ (C, t_2)\ (B, t_3)\ (A, t_4)$. Because of the difference in time coordinates between (A, t_1) and (A, t_4), the helix never gets back to the origin, there are no cycles, and mathematical analysis can proceed on the augmented graph. This is just one illustration of how the introduction of a time dimension can make a model more useful and the modeler's task easier in some ways (see also Weinberg 1975; chap. 6). Of course the analysis of helices is routine in molecular biology and, interestingly, also in music theory, where musical pitch takes the form of a helix.

Directed graphs are already used by many cognitive scientists as models of system structure. The example of such a model shown in figure 9.2 is a *flow diagram*, albeit a very complicated one. Of course such models are not analyzed to determine whether they are connected (they usually are not), or how many "shortest" paths there are between particular nodes, or really for any of the myriad other mathematical properties of directed graphs. In these flow diagrams, it is the graph's local properties, such as the content of the nodes and the presence or absence of particular edges, that dominate its analysis. The model is really a "sufficiency" demonstration, showing how the properties of a particular empirical phenomenon, such as the experience of a visual image in the case of figure 9.2, could arise within the structure of the functional nodes depicted. Such a flow diagram also could be dynamicized by adding a time dimension and allowing only one active edge per frame. I can imagine a quite complicated time evolution in such a complicated graph, one that might even resemble some of the information processing done in support of everyday human behavior (given that this system is supposed to represent the human mind). Moreover, because the graph in figure 9.2 certainly has cycles, such treatment would allow some of the more global, graph-theoretic properties of the model to be explored, perhaps with interesting implications for understanding the behavior the graph represents. Finally, it is likely that explanation of human behavior would require that several edges be simultaneously active. As long as the active edges do not form any cycles within a single frame, the mathematical analysis should not be compromised. The result would be a dynamical model with several helices developing, and possibly intertwining, over the same time period. A model like this, with one helix emphasized and the others relatively suppressed, has been suggested, in principle, as a description of human consciousness (Dennett 1991).

It is also possible to see the brain itself as a directed, weighted graph, as mentioned earlier and as hinted at in the first epigraph at the beginning of this chapter. Indeed, topological maps of brain connections are commonplace in neuroscience. A famous example is the map of the myriad interconnections (edges) between anatomically distinct parts (vertices) of the macaque monkey visual system. Figure 9.3 shows a modern version by van Essen and Deyoe (1995). Although portrayed as an undirected

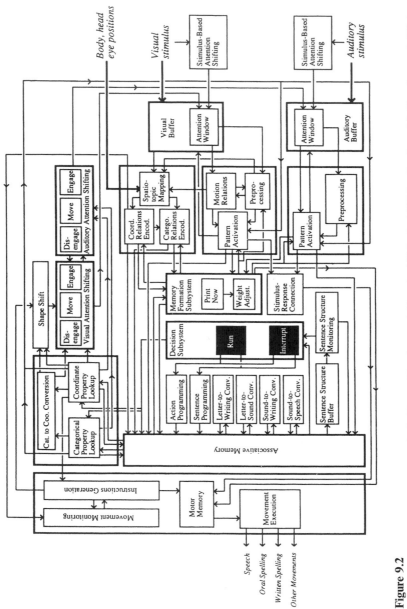

Figure 9.2
Directed graph of the human mind. (From Kosslyn and Koenig 1992. © 1992 by Stephen M. Kosslyn and Olivier Koenig. Reprinted with permission of The Free Press, a Division of Simon & Schuster, Inc.)

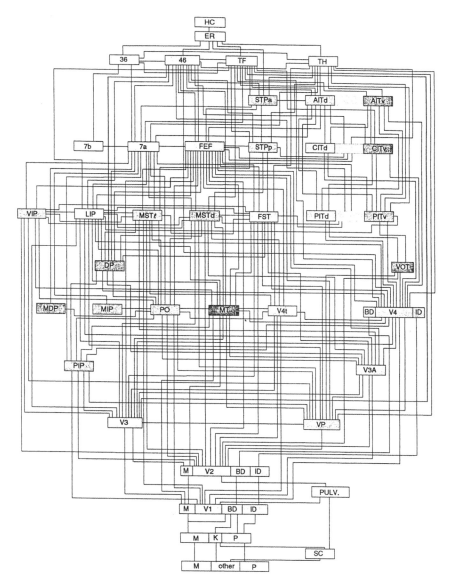

Figure 9.3
Graph of the monkey visual system. (From van Essen and Deyoe 1995. Reprinted by permission of The MIT Press.)

graph, most if not all of the edges actually are two-way, or rather two different edges, one in each direction (Zeki 1993). Although the accurate depiction of the complete form of such a model is a distant goal of the field of neuroscience, useful submodels might already be possible in the spirit of figure 9.3 and of the work of Posner and Raichle (1994). Such structural models would depict several anatomically connected, functionally related brain areas, and would specify the order of functional activity in performance of a particular behavior by depicting the series of active edges (and nodes) along the time axis. Several such models could be juxtaposed, with appropriate connections, to expand the model's applicability, and the possibility of several edges being simultaneously active could be introduced. Again, the temporal unfolding of such a model would be complicated, and would be a starting point for the development of a dynamical model of brain activity that would admit of mathematical analysis to discover the global properties of the structure and their implications for brain function.

A final relevant topic in graph theory is that of the scale of the graph. Whereas a simple system can be represented by a simple planar graph such as in figure 9.1, or by a more complicated, time-evolving graph such as those just discussed, both types consisting of just a single scale level, many complex systems, with multilevel groupings of vertices, whose edges connect the nodes within a group and the various groups of nodes, must be represented by multiscale graphs such as the graph in figure 9.2. These multiscale graphs, though much more difficult to analyze mathematically, are also more likely to be realistic models of actual cognitive systems. (Several examples, especially those producing "colored" noise, will be discussed in later chapters.)

9.3 Interplay between Dynamical and Structural Models

As just discussed, the dynamics of a system are both informed and constrained by the structure within which they operate. Dynamics also can create structure, however, such as a heat cell when a fluid is heated from below, which then sustains itself. Here the original structure of the fluid, which consisted of loosely interconnected molecules moving randomly with respect to one another, changes when heat is added in a particular way to a much more tightly bound set of molecular motions in particular, spatially distributed directions. In the case of a complex system such as the brain, there are important distinctions to be made between statical structure (e.g., sensory pathways), dynamical structure (e.g., synaptic

plasticity that creates changing connections between neurons), dynamically created structure (e.g., momentarily active cell assemblies, conceptually in the same category as a heat cell), and pure dynamics (e.g., a
stochastic process or a finite state machine). We can always find revealing
structure, even in pure dynamics (e.g., a stationary law in a stochastic
process; see chap. 12). Thus we must face the prospect that a dynamical model alone, even if deliberately created without a structural basis,
still introduces structural aspects to its analysis. We must be prepared to
recognize and deal with this structure, for it often forms an important
product of the dynamical analysis. Indeed, some authors consider the
geometric flavor of nonlinear dynamical analysis to be its most important,
and in many cases its only, usable product (e.g., Kellert 1993). Finally,
there is the prospect of building dynamical models that implement realistic structural assumptions even as they explore the consequences of
changes in structure, whether of the brain or of more abstract cognitive
systems. Neural network models are one promising example of this possibility, although, to portray ongoing dynamics, they would have to be
developed somewhat differently from how they are today. Such models
are directed, weighted graphs at one level, although their processing
power vastly exceeds such a simple structure. Chapter 34 reveals the tip of
the neural network iceberg in the context of dynamical models.

Chapter 10

Deterministic versus Stochastic Dynamical Models

A linear universe is a physical impossibility....

Even numerical methods do not cope with all the difficulties of nonlinear equations.... Statistical modeling must be applied at some level or stage of development.

—Foster Morrison, *The Art of Modeling Dynamic Systems*

10.1 Deterministic Models

All of the models discussed thus far have been *deterministic*, which simply means that they contain no random elements. And what is *random*? I explore this very difficult and important question in several contexts (especially in chaps. 11 and 22). The answer is elusive; indeed, as Mark Kac (1983, 406) has stated: "From the purely operational point of view the concept of randomness is so elusive as to cease to be viable." He meant that it is impossible to tell whether a particular sequence, say of heads and tails produced by coin tosses, was produced by actual coin tosses or by an arithmetical procedure designed to mimic the outcomes of coin tosses. In this sense, a deterministic, completely predictable, arithmetical process behaves in the same way as something presumed to be random and unpredictable (unless the coin is severely biased). To take this even further, it is possible to create a computer algorithm (a deterministic one that produces the same sequence every time it is run) that will mimic any "random" process whatever (see also Kac 1984). Thus, when I say the model "contains no random elements," I mean to say that it is a simple one-to-one function, that the values of the state variables completely determine a system's state, and that there is no variability of behavior of the system for a given set of state variable values. For example, in the statical model of equation 1.3, $R = cS^m$, each value of S gives rise to one and only one value of R, always the same one regardless of other conditions. Similarly, even the dynamical version of that model (equation 8.9), $R_i = cS_i^m$, has the same property. On each occasion, i, there is one value of S and one value of R. Whenever the S is the same as some other S, the R is also the same. There is no error variability; the value of S *completely determines* the value of R.

Of course these are ideal, theoretical models, although the model is supposed to express some underlying "truth" that obtains in the real world. However, tests of such theoretical statements always involve the "real" real world and all of its myriad complexity. We can never isolate our system from all other influences. Thus, when we set up an experiment in psychophysical scaling, say, and present a particular S to our subjects on several different occasions, we find that the same subject often responds with different Rs on those different occasions. There is variability in R even though the value of S was nominally (not actually—that is also impossible to control exactly) the same. Moreover, different subjects also respond to the same S with different Rs even if only presented once. In what sense, then, could we say such a deterministic model "holds"? We assert that the model holds "on average," that it holds for the central tendency of the different values of R observed for each value of S. We accept the difficulty of isolating our experimental system from all other influences and simply relegate the effects of those influences, giving rise to the variability in R, to a "noise" term. Effectively, we divide our models into two classes: theoretical and empirical. The theoretical model is what we want to assert, whereas the empirical model is realistically what we have available. All empirical models contain a noise term, reflecting the uncontrolled influences in our experiment or observation. Theoretical models often do not contain a noise term because we are uninterested in "other influences" we cannot control. Even when the theoretical models do contain a noise term, however, it is almost never a term that attributes any *structure* to the noise, particularly temporal structure. It is almost always only the *amount* of noise that we model, not its *temporal distribution* (again, there are significant exceptions).

Thus far we have considered only the simplest deterministic models. Because they change either not at all or only very slowly relative to the timescales of interest, all statical models are called "type 0" by Morrison (1991). The simple dynamical models he calls "type I": here, because of the precision with which they can be specified, theoretical models are clearly distinguished from their empirical counterparts. When we move into the realm of differential and difference equations things become a bit less clear, although there is still a class of models among these that yields precise solutions. These are called "class I, type I" systems by Morrison (1991). They include differential equations that can be solved precisely, without error, such as equation 8.1 (with solution eq. 8.2). We run into trouble almost immediately, however, when we encounter differential equations whose solutions involve unavoidable error, "class II, type I" systems such as equation 8.3 (solution eq. 8.4). The solution is an exponential equation; because the number e is irrational (its exact value can never be known, only approximated with increasing accuracy), there will always be some rounding or truncation error involved in its evaluation. Although this will often be trivial, sometimes it will not (see Morrison 1991, 178).

The problem of error becomes more severe for what Morrison (1991) calls "type II" systems, used when data are very precise or abundant, so that the data depart from any type I model. Here a special technique creates a series of models and uses power series expansions to account for the departure of the real system from the ideal model, with each created model providing somewhat better approximation to the data until the accuracy is sufficient for the purpose at hand. Although as Morrison states and demonstrates, these highly intricate and difficult methods are of dubious value today because of the availability of numerical simulations on computers, nonetheless, they illustrate that, even for a relatively simple deterministic system, small perturbations (such as those caused by the planets of our solar system acting gravitationally on each other) can be important and can complicate the modeling effort.

"Chaotic" or "type III" systems pose an additional problem: they are differential or difference equations whose behavior is so complex it actually seems random in many ways (see chaps. 23 and 24). Such equations do not have to be complicated to behave in a complicated way. The logistic difference equation, (e.g., eq. 8.7) discussed repeatedly in this book and in every book dealing with chaos theory, is a perfect example. Exceedingly simple in its geometric form (its nondynamical map is a parabola), it behaves wildly and cannot be predicted in principle. On the other hand, many systems of nonlinear differential equations also behave wildly and have geometric forms that are more complicated and difficult to grasp. As we will see in chapter 24, it is difficult to distinguish chaos from randomness, although many people like the idea of the underlying determinism in chaotic models (notice there is no "random variable" in equation 8.7). Although computer simulation techniques have been a great help, we are still often faced with "Bonini's paradox," where the behavior of a computer simulation model is as difficult to understand as that of the empirical system that inspired it. Various techniques exist to analyze these models, including statistical ones. Their importance here is that they emphasize that even deterministic models can behave in ways that are difficult to distinguish from randomness. Indeed, as soon as we move away from the simple, statical, idealized model represented by Stevens's law (and many other psychological theories), we encounter randomness. Although this randomness shares many characteristics with the more usual random error that permeates our data and that sometimes is the basis for powerful models, it also contains different, exotic elements that arise from temporal unfolding.

10.2 Stochastic Models

A stochastic model is one in which randomness plays some role, often a profound role inherent to the phenomenon modeled. A simple dynamical empirical model of psychophysical judgment, such as

$$\log R_i = \hat{m} \log S_i + \log \hat{c} + \varepsilon_i, \tag{10.1}$$

is stochastic. In this model the ε_i term is the *random variable*, which represents a series of samples from some probability distribution, usually the normal distribution with mean zero and some nonzero standard deviation. In the empirical model, the random variable is the "noise" term—it is simply there to represent the variability that cannot be captured by the model. When we move into the theoretical domain, however, because the "noise" is not taken to be important theoretically and constitutes a considerable nuisance during theoretical calculations or derivations, the random variable is commonly dropped. One of the major themes of this book is that this practice has concealed some extremely interesting phenomena from us. That neglected noise often has temporal structure, and when it does, it deserves to be modeled. In particular, the temporal relationships buried in the noise can reveal important aspects of the process under study (see chaps. 14 through 19).

There are several domains in psychology where formal modeling has been quite well developed and successfully applied to empirical data, among them learning, measurement, perception, attention, and psychophysics. The field of mathematical psychology has become quite sophisticated, with a wide variety of modeling approaches, although it continues to have less impact on mainstream psychology than it deserve to. Importantly, stochastic *theoretical* models have played a large role in mathematical psychology; indeed, entire books have been written on the subject, including Green and Swets 1966, a classic on signal detection theory (the sina qua non of stochastic statical models); the excellent Townsend and Ashby 1983; and Luce 1986 which concentrates on response times, as reaction times are often called. These books, and many others, describe myriad stochastic theoretical models, including some dynamical ones. For example, Luce 1986 describes a model by Pacut (1978), where information about a sensory signal, whose appearance is to be reacted to as quickly as possible (simple reaction time), accumulates until it exceeds some response criterion, at which time a response is made. Only one of the many models proposed to describe simple reaction time, the Pacut model assumes that the accumulation of information about the signal is perturbed by "additive random noise." (Luce, 1986, 154). In this model, $A(t)$ represents the total information accumulated by time t; and a response is made when $A(t) > C(t)$, where $C(t)$, the criterion, is a normally distributed random variable. $A(t)$ is influenced linearly by $S(t)$, the signal amplitude, which is taken to be 0 for $t < 0$ and 1 for $t \geq 0$, and additively by $w(t)$, the noise, again normally distributed with mean zero and variance proportional to elapsed time from signal onset. The model can be written as a differential equation:

$$\frac{dA(t)}{dt} = -\beta[A(t) - \alpha S(t)] + \frac{dw(t)}{dt}, \tag{10.2}$$

which states that the momentary change in accumulated information about the signal is proportional both to the signal amplitude and to the current amount of information, plus some noise. But for the noise, equation 10.2 would be a simple linear differential equation; the deterministic part would be a "type I" model. The addition of the noise complicates matters however. The solution to equation 10.2, for $A(0) = A_0$, where A_0 is also a normally distributed random variable, is

$$A(t) = \alpha + e^{-\beta t}\left[A_0 - \alpha/t + \int_0^t e^{\beta x}\, dw(x)\right], \tag{10.3}$$

which states that at any time, t, the accumulated information is a random variable composed from a constant, α, representing the coupling to the signal, plus a complicated, random term representing both the (random) starting amount of information, A_0, and the weighted integral of the noise over the time since signal onset. This random walk from a random starting place proved to be too complicated to apply directly (Luce 1986), although a special case does fit some reaction time data fairly well, and a discrete version would not be difficult to simulate. Notice that this model describes what happens over time on a single trial of a reaction time experiment. Such models are typically evaluated by deriving their predictions about the variation of expected values of reaction times with causal factors, such as signal amplitude, and about the (usually somewhat asymmetrical) form of reaction time distributions, in both cases collapsing across all of the trials on which reaction time is measured under a given set of conditions. Only a single scale of time, that of a single reaction time trial amounting to perhaps several hundred milliseconds, is modeled. Even though there is no attempt to model either longer timescales (e.g., an entire experiment) or shorter ones (e.g., neuronal conduction times) nonetheless, the model is already "too complicated."

Another approach to stochastic modeling in psychology is to represent response variability directly, usually by making the dependent variable of the model the probability of a response. All signal detection theory models are of this character, as are most of the very general psychophysical models described by Falmagne (1985). In one such statical model of psychophysical judgment,

$$p(\text{yes}) = [1 + e^{-(I-\mu)/\theta}]^{-1}, \tag{10.4}$$

the probability of saying, "Yes, I see it," to the presentation of a faint flash of light is modeled as a logistic function of the light intensity, I, with μ representing the absolute threshold for light under the given conditions, and θ representing the steepness of the change from never seeing the light to always seeing the light (the "fuzziness" of the threshold). This function has a similar graph to that of figure 8.1, except that here the abscissa is stimulus intensity rather than time. In such a model, the decision process is considered to be hidden, so that only probabilistic predictions can be made from the model; the outcome of any single trial in an experiment is unpredictable. This situation is reminiscent of quantum theory (see chap. 13), in which randomness is considered to be necessary, and not simply the result of ignorance. Of course, such a model could be made dynamical by introducing time, and made even noisier by adding a noise term. Alternatively, a dynamical model could be constructed from the start, in which the temporal unfolding of the decision process would give rise to the variability in the psychophysical decisions made in such a way that the model of equation 10.4 would describe the expectation of the dynamical model's outputs as a function of light intensity.

Thus, for many different reasons and in many different ways, cognitive science must utilize, and has utilized, stochastic models. Many sophisticated stochastic models have already been proposed, although most are either statical, or dynamical over only a limited range. Nonetheless, the techniques used in these models have proved to be highly effective, and will continue to be so when applied in a wider dynamical context. Still more sophisticated techniques are available in mathematics and in physics, as the material discussed in chapters 12 and 13 reveals; such techniques will come into wider use as dynamical cognitive science matures.

10.3   Do We Need Both?

Deterministic models capture the basic, nonstochastic processes of a system, addressing central tendencies in an elegant (though not always simple) way, whereas stochastic models address variability directly, albeit sometimes only by averaging over it or putting it into a catchall random variable (noise) term. Importantly, the two types of models can lead to different outcomes even when applied to the same data. This is perhaps most clearly demonstrated in the context of psychophysical scaling, where S. S. Stevens (1975) pointed to the conflict between the *poikilitic* (based on variability) function called "Fechner's law," $R = a \ln(S/S_0)$, and Steven's own psychophysical power law, $R = cS^m$, based on central tendencies of direct scaling judgments. Because these two functions can be fitted to different statistics of the same judgments, they actually reveal two different aspects of those judgments, another example of the ubiquity of Weinberg's principle of complementarity (chap. 7). The same possibilities exist in dynamical models. In the dynamical context, stochastic models account for or describe the structure of fluctuations over time, whereas deterministic models describe trends. Useful models sometimes have both deterministic and stochastic parts (see chaps. 11, 12, 30). And, as pointed out above and in other places (e.g., Morrison 1991), the distinction between variability and trend blurs when the deterministic model is nonlinear, as in chaos (see chap. 24).

Chapter 11

Linear Time Series Analysis

ARIMA models are not arbitrarily fit to data, but rather are built empirically.
—Richard McCleary and Richard A. Hay, Jr., *Applied Time Series Analysis for the Social Sciences*

The vast literature on linear time series analysis can only be woefully adumbrated in fewer than ten pages. Indeed, it is only because the literature *is* so vast and the number of helpful works so numerous that I can get away with this. The most useful of the helpful works, in my opinion, is McCleary and Hay 1980, quoted above, on which the first two sections of this chapter are mostly based. Another good book is Gregson 1983, which argues forcefully for a change in emphasis in psychology from statical to dynamical modeling, although those without excellent mathematical background will find it hard going. A third, for those preferring to have it from the horse's mouth, is an original and influential synthesis, Box and Jenkins 1976.

11.1 Time Series and Noise

If you have been reading straight through, you will by now have a fairly clear idea of what a time series is. But a little redundancy on important matters never hurts, and time series is the most important idea in the book. As defined by McCleary and Hay (1980, 30): "A time series is a set of ordered observations: $Y_1, Y_2, Y_3, \ldots, Y_{t-1}, Y_t, Y_{t+1}, \ldots$" The key idea is that the observations are *ordered in time*, and this temporal order is denoted by the ubiquitous subscript. Any observed time series is considered to be a single realization of an underlying stochastic process (chapters 9, 12, and 13 discuss stochastic processes more generally). By modeling the process that generated the temporal order, linear time series analysis contrasts mightily with the most common practice of cognitive science research, which is to collapse observations across time, disregarding the order in which they were made.

The basic stochastic process of linear time series analysis, and the only one we will consider here, is the "white noise" process (see also chap. 14). If we had a time series made up only of successive samples from a white noise process, a simple model of it would look like this:

$$Y_t = b_0 + a_t, \tag{11.1}$$

where b_0 is a constant representing the level of the process, and a_t is a sample from a Gaussian (or normal) distribution with mean zero and constant variance σ_a^2. Because all such noise samples are assumed to be independent, a_t represents independent identically distributed, or *i.i.d.*, noise. Also, the samples are assumed to be taken at equally spaced time points, although the actual time intervals could be anything from nanoseconds to many years, even unit intervals of "system time." This is the null hypothesis of time series analysis. If a time series consists of, for example, a set of reaction times that can be modeled in this way, then the mean reaction time, which will equal b_0, will be a good representation of the situation and the temporal order of observations will be irrelevant: there is no temporal structure. All of the fluctuations we observe in such a reaction time series would be "caused" by the addition of independent samples of white noise, which have no temporal structure. Of course, as you will see in this and later chapters such is seldom the case. Either the noise is colored (see chap. 15), or there is some other, possibly nonlinear temporal structure in the series. Nonetheless, knowing for certain there is no temporal structure in the noise is better than making an unsupported assumption that there is none.

11.2   ARIMA (p, d, q)

The three processes—autoregression (AR), integration (I), and moving average (MA)—that combine to form the "autoregressive integrated moving average" of ARIMA are the ones used to model the generation of most linear time series. Each process is represented by a specific kind of linear model discussed below. A convenient convention to describe what kind of model best fits a particular time series is to write "ARIMA (p, d, q)," where p, d, and q stand for the order of AR, I, and MA types of model, respectively. Whereas AR and MA models are rarely combined (see McCleary and Hay 1980 for a detailed discussion of the reason, and sec. 11.3 for an example of a combination), both types are commonly combined with I models. After briefly describing the first-order processes (higher orders are easily generalized) of each type of model, I will summarize the procedure used to identify which type applies to a given time series, using the autocorrelation and partial autocorrelation functions.

The simplest departure from the null hypothesis model of equation 11.1 occurs when the underlying process adds, or *integrates*, successive samples of noise (called "shocks" in the parlance of linear time series analysis). The Brownian motion discussed in chapter 14 is a good example of such a *random walk*, in which a tiny particle starts out at some position in space-time and each subsequent position is obtained by moving a random amount along each spatial axis. Thus the position of the particle at any time is represented by the algebraic sum of its separate movements along each spatial axis at all previous times. Such a process is modeled by

$$Y_t = Y_{t-1} + a_t, \tag{11.2}$$

where each new value of the variable Y_t is composed of the previous value plus a sample of white noise. One interesting aspect of the behavior of this model is that its time series show substantial *drift*, that is, what appear to be steady movements in one direction or another for long periods of time. Stock market prices are good examples of drifts. These drifts might be mistaken for *trends*, that is, situations in which real change is taking place in an underlying process over time. An example of a trend would be motor learning, for example, learning to ride a bicycle, in which the level of skill really is increasing over time, although large random fluctuations also occur. Equation 11.2 can be modified to include an additive constant to account for such a trend, and a *t*-test can be done to determine whether it is necessary. If either a drift or a trend occurs in a time series, then it is *not stationary* and must be *differenced* to remove the trend or drift before any other model is fitted. To difference a series, each observation is simply subtracted from the one immediately following, to create an ordered series of differences: $d_1, d_2, \ldots, d_{t-1}, d_t, d_{t+1}, \ldots$ This new time series can then be examined for further drifts or trends, possibly requiring more differencing, or checked for applicability of AR or MA models. The number of times differencing is done becomes the value of the d parameter in the ARIMA description. For example, a series rendered stationary by a single differencing operation, and having no significant AR or MA parameters, would be ARIMA (0, 1, 0). It is common for behavioral times series to require differencing at least once because processes such as learning and fatigue, which would cause trends, are difficult to avoid in cognitive science experiments, and processes that depend on each previous position in some state space and cause drifts, such as evidence accumulation, are also ubiquitous in such experiments.

Although random shocks persist in a time series, the influence of each one may decrease as time passes. This is probably the simplest case in which a stochastic process has a temporal structure worth modeling. In AR models, the decreasing influence of random shocks is modeled by including a multiplicative parameter on previous observations. In the simplest case, this looks like

$$Y_t = \phi_1 Y_{t-1} + a_t, \tag{11.3}$$

where $-1 < \phi_1 < 0$ or $0 < \phi_1 < 1$. Because ϕ_1 is a fraction, each shock has an exponentially decreasing effect (ϕ_1^n for a shock n time intervals back in the series) on the current value of the series. This behavior is called "autoregression," hence the name of the model. A time series requiring a model like that of equation 11.3, would be an ARIMA $(1, 0, 0)$ model; a series that had to be differenced once before fitting such a model would be an ARIMA $(1, 1, 0)$ model. An ARIMA $(2, 0, 0)$ would require inclusion of two previous observations, their respective multiplicative parameters, and so on for higher orders.

Shocks persist indefinitely in both I and AR models, albeit their influence decreases exponentially in AR models. In MA models, a given shock persists only for a finite, usually short, number of observations. The simplest MA model is

$$Y_t = a_t - \theta_1 Y_{t-1}, \tag{11.4}$$

where, again, $-1 < \theta_1 < 0$ or $0 < \theta_1 < 1$, and each shock persists for only one observation in the past. If shocks persist for two observations, we will need two parameters, one for each of the two previous observations, and so on for higher orders. The first-order MA model is represented as ARIMA $(0, 0, 1)$ and for a once-differenced series ARIMA $(0, 1, 1)$. We seldom see an ARIMA $(1, 1, 1)$ model because AR and MA processes show parameter redundancy, that is, they are mirror images of each other mathematically (see McCleary and Hay 1980).

Although we now know *what* linear, noise-driven models can be fitted to time series data, we do not know *how* to accomplish the fitting—the task of model *identification*, which relies on two statistics calculated on the time series at hand, the *autocorrelation function* (ACF) and the *partial autocorrelation function* (PACF). To statisticians, a correlation is a normalized covariance, namely, a covariance divided by a variance-like term, actually, the product of two standard deviations. The covariance (cov) of a set of paired numbers, say (x_i, y_i) representing two time series, is the average summed product of deviations of the separate members of each pair from their respective means, m_x and m_y:

$$\text{cov}_{xy} = \frac{\sum_i (x_i - m_x)(y_i - m_y)}{N - 1},$$

where $i = 1$ to N. The variance (var) is the covariance of a variable with itself, for example,

$$\text{var}_x = \frac{\sum_i (x_i - m_x)(x_i - m_x)}{N - 1},$$

where $i = 1$ to N, and the standard deviation is the square root of the variance, $\text{sd}_x = \sqrt{\text{var}_x}$. Thus $\text{correlation}_{xy} = \text{cov}_{xy}/(\text{sd}_x \cdot \text{sd}_y)$. Notice that the product of standard deviations in the denominator is like a variance. Physicists usually refer to the summed product of the numbers in each pair $(\sum_i x_i \cdot y_i)$, possibly normalized by dividing by the number of pairs, as the correlation, because that is the core of the concept. Everything else is normalization required to make comparisons across contexts. Here I use the statisticians' definition, what the physicists call the "dimensionless covariance" because dividing by the product of standard deviations cancels out the physical (or other measurement-related) dimensions of the quantities involved.

An autocorrelation, as you might have suspected (or already known) is a correlation of a time series with itself at a certain *lag*, which refers to the difference in subscript values between each observation in the series and the observation at an earlier or later time step. For example, if we have a series 3, 5, 7, 5, 8, 2, 4 ... then the autocorrelation for lag 1 is between the values 3, 5, 7, 5, 8, 2, 4 ... and 5, 7, 5, 8, 2, 4 ..., or alternatively the pairs of values (3, 5), (5, 7), (7, 5), (5, 8), (8, 2), (2, 4), (4, ...) ... The ACF consists of the set of autocorrelations at all possible lags, 0 through $N - 2$ (because it is symmetrical, we usually consider only one direction). The autocorrelation at lag 0 is always 1 because it is the variance of the entire series divided by the same variance, and is undefined for lags greater than $N - 2$ because at least two pairs are required for the variance to exist. Autocorrelations are estimated very well at small lags but are increasingly poorly estimated at higher lags as the number of pairs available becomes smaller. For short time series, none of the autocorrelations is estimated very well. The PACF is the set of partial autocorrelations at all lags, where the partial autocorrelation at a specific lag is the autocorrelation at that lag, with the autocorrelations at smaller lags "partialed out" (see again McCleary and Hay 1980).

Conveniently, the various ARIMA models produce time series with unique ACFs and PACFs, so that model identification can be accomplished by inspecting these functions for the time series of interest (see McCleary and Hay 1980 for the derivations). Of course, white noise alone produces a null ACF and PACF because, by definition, it is composed of independent samples from a Gaussian, or normal, distribution, whereas the ARIMA (0, d, 0) integrated process produces an ACF with significant correlations at several lags, with the ACF gradually decreasing as lag increases. Differencing such a process d times creates a null ACF and PACF. AR processes produce ACFs that decrease exponentially with lag and PACFs that have a significant correlation at only the number of lags that represent the order of the process. MA processes create the opposite kind of picture, with ACFs that have significant correlations only at the number of lags that represent the order of the MA process, and exponentially decreasing PACFs. Figure 11.1 shows examples of ACFs and PACFs for ARIMA (1, 0, 0) and ARIMA (0, 0, 1) processes, where either $0 < \phi_1 < 1$ or $0 < \theta_1 < 1$. The pictures for $-1 < \phi_1 < 0$ or $-1 < \theta_1 < 0$ are similar. The AR process with negative ϕ_1 has an ACF with correlations of exponentially decreasing absolute value but alternating signs at successive lags and the significant PACF correlations are all negative. In the MA process with negative θ_1, the ACF and PACF are both positive at all lags instead of negative as they are in figure 11.1. After using the ACF and PACF of a time series, in combination with these prototypical patterns, to accomplish model identification, the parameters of the model can be *estimated*, the residuals (remaining variability after the model is fitted) *diagnosed* (they should be white noise), and the model put into *use* (see again McCleary and Hay 1980). In sections 11.3 and 11.4, I illustrate how the linear time series approach can be applied to time series relevant to dynamical cognitive science.

11.3   ARIMA Model of Time Estimation

In the four experiments reported in Ward 1996, six human subjects produced 1,000-point time series consisting of the intervals between 1,001 successive presses of a computer keyboard spacebar. Endogenous time series were produced by having subjects attempt to press the spacebar at 1 sec, 3 sec, and "natural" or "random" intervals, without any timekeeping aids. In my ARIMA analysis of these time series, none of the time series was stationary (a chronic problem with psychological time series); all were therefore differenced once to render them so. In three of the experi-

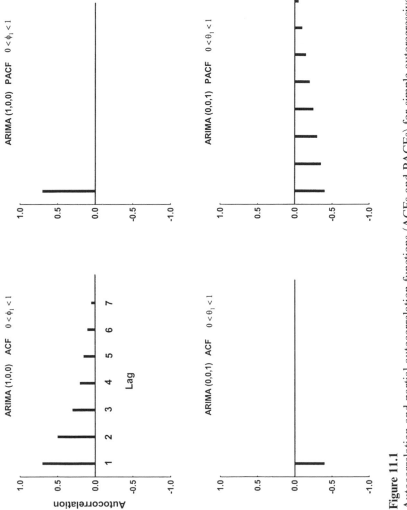

Figure 11.1
Autocorrelation and partial autocorrelation functions (ACFs and PACFs) for simple autoregressive integrated moving average (ARIMA) models. (After McCleary and Hay 1980.)

ments, the ACFs and PACFs generally resembled the MA pattern shown in figure 11.1, so the best model was ARIMA (0, 1, 1) (including $d = 1$ for the differencing) in which random shocks persisted for only one observation, with average $\theta_1 = 0.789$ for 1 sec, 0.600 for 3 sec, and 0.605 for natural intervals. In one case, an additional MA parameter, and in another case a negative AR parameter, was required. All of the fits were very good, indicating that the MA model was appropriate for these data, and the ACFs and PACFs of the residuals of the fits for all series were uniformly null, indicating that the fitted models were statistically adequate. Thus, when humans are attempting to reproduce a series of remembered eotemporal intervals, a random fluctuation introduced to one interval influences only the next one, as we might expect from the fact that the end of one interval marks the beginning of the next one.

The random instructions, on the other hand, produced some contrasting behavior: three subjects had null ACFs (after differencing). Which means they actually were able to produce a series of intervals uncorrelated except for a trend or drift—an ARIMA (0, 1, 0) model. It seems likely that there was indeed drift, again because the end of one interval marked the beginning of the next, thus we would expect drift from the sum of uncorrelated intervals. This performance was remarkable, given the difficulty most people have in producing a random sequence (see chap. 29). Perhaps the temporal interval context made it difficult for these subjects to employ their usual "randomness" heuristics, and thus to produce their usual, correlated, series. The other three subjects in this experiment required ARIMA (0, 1, 2) models to describe their data, meaning that the "random" instruction induced them to create a correlation of their present interval with the intervals both one and two back in the sequence, a result to be expected from most people attempting to behave randomly. The ARIMA analysis clearly differentiated between the random and the other instructions, although, for three of the subjects, it simply increased the persistence of the previous shocks. Importantly, even after all of this (interesting) linear temporal structure was removed from these time series, they still displayed evidence of nonlinear structure, perhaps chaos (see Ward 1996 and chap. 26).

11.4   Mixed Regression-ARIMA Model of Psychophysical Judgment

For a second, more complicated, example of the application of ARIMA analysis, consider the following time series made up of magnitude estimation stimuli, S_n (here pure tones varying in intensity), and responses, ME_n (here numbers produced by human subjects that are supposed to be proportional to the perceived loudnesses of the tones): $S_1 ME_1 S_2 ME_2 S_3 ME_3 S_4 ME_4 \ldots S_n ME_n \ldots$ In a series of papers, I and several other researchers applied multiple linear regression to create empirical models of such time series. In this technique, the logarithm of each response is considered to be a joint function of the logs of current and previous stimuli and responses up to some lag. The logarithms of stimuli and responses are used to allow linear regression to be applied; the theoretical model on which the analysis is based resembles Stevens's psychophysical power law (e.g., eq. 1.3), with added terms for previous stimuli and responses. A good empirical model for most magnitude estimations can be expressed as follows: (Jesteadt et al 1977; Ward 1979):

$$\log ME_n = \beta_0 + \beta_1 \log S_n + \beta_2 \log ME_{n-1} - \beta_3 \log S_{n-1} + \varepsilon, \qquad (11.5)$$

where ε stands for residual error.

DeCarlo and Cross (1990) analyzed the same time series differently, combining the regression technique with an ARIMA analysis. They argued that the dependency of the current response on the previous response should be seen in the context of "correlated error," which is exactly the ARIMA assumption. Thus they first regressed $\log S_n$ and $\log S_{n-1}$ on the current response, equation 11.5, with the "$\beta_2 \log ME_{n-1}$" term removed. The result of removing this term was to make the coefficient of $\log S_{n-1}$ positive rather than negative as in equation 11.5, producing a very different regression equation. When DeCarlo and Cross then applied an ARIMA analysis to the residuals of the new regression equation, they found that an ARIMA (1, 0, 0) process fit these residuals very well, implying that $\beta_2 \log ME_{n-1}$ in equation 11.5 could be replaced by $\phi_1 e_{n-1}$:

$$\log ME_n = \beta_0 + \beta_1 \log S_n + \beta_2 \log S_{n-1} + \phi_1 e_{n-1} + \varepsilon, \qquad (11.6)$$

where ϕ_1 is the AR parameter. Notice that β_2 is the coefficient of $\log S_{n-1}$ in equation 11.6, and that it is now positive. Although both equations 11.5 and 11.6 fit the data well, they have very different theoretical implications, which have still not been reconciled.

DeCarlo and Cross argued that equation 11.6 is a better empirical model for such time series than is equation 11.5 because $\log S_{n-1}$ and $\log ME_{n-1}$ are highly correlated in the time series. (Indeed, in psychophysical scaling, most of the variance in the responses is produced by variations in the stimuli, meaning that the two variances are highly correlated.) Such correlations between regression variables cause serious problems for regressions, a problem that I and others dealt with by fixing the order of entry of variables into the regression to be the assumed causal order. Although effective, this approach is empirically inferior to dealing with only uncorrelated regression variables. DeCarlo and Cross's approach (1990) has this advantage, and also an effective way, ARIMA, to deal with the structure in the residual variance. The question is whether to allow the theoretical stance to be dictated by the empirical model that is easiest to use. Because both theoretical approaches have been confirmed by separate experiments and seem useful, the issue continues to be undecided. This controversy demonstrates that although ARIMA (and linear regression) can be extremely useful techniques, they are only tools, and limited ones at that, as we will see in chapters to come.

Chapter 12

Probability Theory and Stochastic Processes

Although gamblers have undoubtedly learned a great deal from probability theory, they clearly never learn—or in any event never accept—the main lesson probability theory can teach about gambling ... "If you keep on gambling, you will lose."

—Warren Weaver, *Lady Luck*

A *model* is a simplified description of how something is supposed to work. We hope. A *stochastic* model says this something is working with the help of some random, or stochastic, component. It is a kind of cop-out. Really we don't know how this something works, exactly ... so we make a stochastic model.

—Priscilla E. Greenwood, lecture notes for mathematics 608

12.1 Dynamical Cognitive Science and Mathematics

As you might have gathered by now, I feel that mathematics should play a central role in dynamical cognitive science. Mathematics is the "Queen of the Sciences," the preferred language of the most successful ones, such as physics, and the bane of the less successful aspirants. Or, to quote Feynman (1965, 40): "Mathematics is *not* just another language. Mathematics is a language plus reasoning [—it] is a tool for reasoning" (emphasis his). As in all science, algebra is ubiquitous in dynamical science; the role of calculus, especially that of differential and difference equations, has been extensively developed, as is only natural: the differential calculus is about change, and so is the science of dynamics. On the other hand, the role of probability theory in dynamical science has been relatively neglected, probably because noise often has been considered a nuisance rather than an important process worthy of study (see chap. 14). This chapter is therefore devoted to revealing a few important aspects of a branch of probability theory that may have a profound bearing on dynamical cognitive science: nonlinear stochastic processes. The emphasis here is on the unfolding of these processes in time, and on what kinds of statements we can make about the general behavior patterns followed by such processes. In passing, some of the equations used in earlier chapters will be considered from a slightly more mathematical point of view. Chapter 13 will describe the success physics has had applying a similar approach; chapters 12–14 will describe what can be gained from adopting a stochastic modeling approach to dynamical cognitive science.

12.2   Stochastic Processes: A Random Walk to Ruin

To begin gently, I am going to describe a classical, simple stochastic process, one we have already met in a different guise in earlier chapters. It is formulated in a gambling context for interest, but has been applied in physics (Brownian motion) and other areas and lays the groundwork for later discussion (see Feller 1968). Consider a fair gambling game in which a gambler with a stake, s, competes against a gambling house with stake S, both in dollars. The gambler bets \$1 on each play, wins that bet with probability p and loses it with probability q, where $p = q = 0.5$ (note $p + q = 1$). Think of a fair coin being tossed and the gambler wins if heads appears and loses if tails appears. The gambler plays until his or her stake is lost—or the bank is broken. What is the probability that the gambler will be ruined? What is the probability distribution of the duration of the game (i.e., what are the various probabilities that the game will continue for various numbers of plays until one of the end states is reached)? What is the expected time until the game ends (i.e., until one or the other player is ruined)? This game is an example of a restricted random walk problem. In the random walk conceptualization of the problem, a particle moving about on a line in discrete jumps takes the place of the gambler. The particle starts at position s and jumps about the line until it reaches either of two other positions, the origin (0) or another position $s + S$, called "absorbing barriers" (if there are no absorbing barriers, the walk is unrestricted). For the random walk, p and q are the probabilities of moving to the right (toward $s + S$, or winning) or to the left (toward 0, or losing). When $p = q$, the walk is symmetric. When $p > q$, the particle tends to drift toward the right; when $p < q$, the particle tends to drift toward the left.

Now we will see why this section has the strange subtitle it does. Returning to the gambling game, let us analyze the fair version ($p = q = 0.5$; see Weaver 1963 for a simpler and clearer but longer analysis). Imagine you are the gambler and you are at Monte Carlo, an establishment that has a very large stake, S. Because you begin with your stake, s, the possible outcomes after one play, each with probability 0.5, are that (1) you have $s + 1$ and Monte Carlo has $S - 1$ or (2) you have $s - 1$ and Monte Carlo has $S + 1$. With each successive play, your fortune grows or diminishes by random increments and decrements of \$1, until sooner or later one of the end states is reached. To calculate the probability of your ruin in this game, P_R, we set up a difference equation:

$$P_R(s) = 0.5 \cdot [P_R(s + 1) + P_R(s - 1)], \tag{12.1}$$

which follows from the two equiprobable outcomes of each play: that you will either win a dollar or lose a dollar. We also know some boundary conditions: that $P_R(0) = 1$, that is, ruin is certain if you have lost all of your money, and $P_R(s + S) = 0$, that is, ruin cannot happen if you have won all of the money. We can guess that P_R is linearly related to s (if we are wrong, the solution will not work): $P_R(s) = a \cdot s + b$. Inserting the values of $P_R(s)$ found at the boundary conditions into this linear equation, we have $1 = a \cdot 0 + b$ when you have lost all of your money, and $0 = a \cdot (s + S) + b$ when you have won all of Monte Carlo's money. From the first of these two equations, we see that $b = 1$; inserting this into the second gives $a = -1/(s + S)$. Plugging these values for a and b into the original linear equation, we obtain the solution

$$P_R(s) = \frac{S}{s + S}, \tag{12.2}$$

which yields some shocking predictions. For example, if you begin gambling with \$1,000, and the house has \$100,000,000 (a not unrealistic assumption for Monte Carlo), your probability of ruin is $P_R(\$1,000) = \$100,000,000 \div \$100,001,000 = 0.9999900001$. Thus it is virtually certain that you will lose all of your money, *even though the game is "fair."* If, however, the game is slightly favorable to the house, $p < q$ (as is almost always the case), you will lose with even greater certainty because the random walk will "drift" toward ruin, as if the thin line you are walking on is tilted toward the left.

If you are interested in gambling, or even in probability theory, you will probably want to know more about how long such "fair" games can be expected to last. The (finite) expected duration of the random walk to ruin given a player's initial stake s, $D(s)$, satisfies a difference equation similar to equation 12.1 when $p = q$:

$$D(s) = 0.5 \cdot [D(s + 1) + D(s - 1)] + 1, \tag{12.3}$$

with boundary conditions $D(0) = 0$ and $D(s + S) = 0$. The solution to equation 12.3 is $D(s) = s \cdot S$. Thus, in a friendly game where each player begins with $100 and they play until one or the other wins all of the money ($200), the expected duration of the game is $100 \times 100 = 10,000$ plays. If each play took 30 seconds (to flip the coin and exchange money), the game would last $30 \times 10,000 = 300,000$ seconds or 83.33 hours. Almost four days of gambling entertainment for a mere $100, which I will wager is much longer than you would have predicted in the absence of such an analysis. For our wealthier player at one play per second at Monte Carlo, the game would last on average $1,000 \times 100,000,000 = 100,000,000,000$ seconds or about 3,171 years. Of course this picture is changed if p and q are not equal. The difference equation and its solution are more complicated because they must contain p and q. The game is shorter when $p < q$ than when $p = q$, and longer when $p > q$. Finally, the probability that a game will last any particular number of plays can be derived using a similar difference equation approach (see Feller 1968).

The random walk toward ruin I have just described can be expressed as a linear stochastic process in terms of the position of the particle (you) on the line at some (discrete) time (equivalent to the current amount of money in your pocket at Monte Carlo) as a function of where it was at the previous moment:

$$X_{n+1} = X_n + \varepsilon_{n+1}, \tag{12.4}$$

where $\varepsilon_{n+1} = 1$ with probability p, and $\varepsilon_{n+1} = -1$ with probability q. (This form emphasizes that the process is unfolding in time.) The process described by equation 12.4 is actually an example of the autoregressive (AR) process, which has the more general form:

$$X_{n+1} = \theta \cdot X_n + \varepsilon_{n+1}, \tag{12.5}$$

where θ is a real number, and ε_{n+1} is a random variable that can have any probability distribution whatever. Notice that this is similar to the model described by equation 11.3, an ARIMA $(1, 0, 0)$ or AR(1) model, except that there $-1 < \theta < 0$ or $0 < \theta < 1$. This is actually an infinite family of models or linear stochastic processes, each different value of θ yielding a different model or process. Stochastic processes can be written even more generally as

$$X_{n+1} = f(X_n, \varepsilon_{n+1}), \tag{12.6}$$

where n is a discrete index (time or space; may be continuous), the values of ε_{n+1} are random, and the function f, called the "parameter" of the model, has some relevant properties, such as continuity, boundedness, and linearity. If the function f is nonlinear, then we have a *nonlinear stochastic process*, as in the following equation:

$$X_{n+1} = \theta \cdot X_n^\beta + \varepsilon_{n+1}, \tag{12.7}$$

where β is also a real number. Because equation 12.7 is a nonlinear function, its parameter, (θ, β), is similar to those of the logistic and other chaotic equations. In general, linear stochastic models are easier to analyze and are better behaved than nonlinear stochastic models, as are their deterministic counterparts. Nonlinear models can exhibit very bizarre, but interesting, behavior as the possibly already exotic behavior of the nonlinear deterministic part (called the deterministic "skeleton") is kicked around by the stochastic part (see sec. 24.3).

Mathematicians like to describe stochastic processes in terms of the probability distributions that characterize them; these descriptions are called the "laws" of the processes (see Grimmett and Stirzacker 1992 for more on the mathematics of stochastic processes). In other words, they describe a stochastic process by specifying the probabilities with which the various possible states of the system, X_n, can occur. These probabilities are affected both by the deterministic part and by the stochastic part of such a process. If their probability distributions do not change depending on where in the state space the processes are operating, then they are said to be "stationary," and the laws "stationary laws." For the random-walk-to-ruin process, unfortunately, a stationary law does not exist, which means that the probabilities of the different possible states are continually evolving as the process continues. However, for the more general AR process of equation 12.5 with the ε_{n+1} samples from a Gaussian distribution with mean zero and standard deviation σ, and $-1 < \theta < 0$ or $0 < \theta < 1$, a stationary law does exist. Let us assume $\theta = 0.5$. In this case, if we consider just the deterministic part of equation 12.5, $X_{n+1} = \theta X_n$, as n grows very large the process converges to 0 (e.g., if $X_0 = 1$, we have the sequence 1, 0.5, 0.25, 0.125, 0.0625, ...). Whereas the stochastic part of equation 12.5 would keep the process jumping around, the deterministic part would cause it to drift always toward zero, so that the jumping around would be overlaid on this drift toward zero. The stationary law is just the distribution of the noise in this case (and whenever $-1 < \theta < 0$ or $0 < \theta < 1$), a Gaussian distribution as specified.

12.3   Critical Points in Stochastic Models

If the AR process of equation 12.5 has a stationary law whenever $-1 < \theta < 0$ or $0 < \theta < 1$, what happens when θ is outside these boundaries? Let us again consider only the deterministic part of the process, this time with $\theta > 1$, say $\theta = 2$. For $X_0 = 1$, for example, we obtain the sequence $1, 2, 4, 8, 16, \ldots$, and for $X_0 = -1$, we get $-1, -2, -4, -8, -16, \ldots$, clearly heading for $+\infty$ and $-\infty$, respectively. When $\theta < -1$, the sequences grow toward *both* $+\infty$ and $-\infty$ in sign-alternating jumps that grow larger and larger. For example, when $\theta = -2$ and $X_0 = 1$, we have $1, -2, 4, -8, 16, -32, 64 \ldots$ In any case, even though the stochastic part causes the process to jump around, unrelenting movement toward infinity takes the process away from any particular neighborhood, so that it never settles down into a stationary law.

What if $\theta = 1$ or $\theta = -1$? Mathematicians call these cases "critical points," at which stationarity is not even defined (so that the process could be considered not to have a stationary law at these points) because no probability measure is possible. In this case, no probability measure is possible because the variance of the process is not a constant, but rather increases as n increases (as it also does in the cases $\theta > 1$ or $\theta < -1$). To see this, consider that

$$\text{var } X_n = \text{var } \sum_i \varepsilon_i = n \text{ var } \varepsilon_i \to \infty \quad \text{as } n \to \infty,$$

which makes the points $\theta = \pm 1$ interesting, but why are they "critical"? They are critical because they divide the behavior of the AR process into two cases: behavior that possesses a stationary law ($-1 < \theta < 0$ or $0 < \theta < 1$) and behavior that does not ($\theta > 1$ or $\theta < -1$). (Notice that if $\theta = 0$, then this is just a simple white noise process, whose stationary law is that of the noise.) In general, the character of any stochastic process (eq. 12.6) depends on its parameter (the function f in our terminology), usually in a continuous manner. If there is a break, or discontinuity, in this dependency, the value of the parameter at that point is the critical point or *critical value* ("critical point" refers more to the position of the process in the abstract parameter space at which the change in behavior occurs). Clearly, such critical points are important in the description of any stochastic or deterministic process, even a linear one. They are even more important in nonlinear processes because they tend to herald very exotic behavior. For example, in the deterministic logistic equation (eq. 1.4), the parameter value $a = 3.58$ is a critical value. For $a < 3.58$, the equation behaves relatively tamely, jumping in a predictable sequence from one periodic point to another (although the number of periodic points depends on the value of a and can become quite large). However, for $a > 3.58$, chaos ensues, literally. For some values of $a > 3.58$, there is an infinity of periodic points and the behavior of the equation is chaotic (see chap. 24). Notice that, in the case of the logistic equation, the critical point is not defined in terms of a stationary law, but rather in terms of a different aspect of the system behavior, the number of periodic points and the presence of chaos.

Finally, let us consider the nonlinear stochastic process of equation 12.7. Does this process have any critical points? Here we must think in terms of a two-dimensional parameter space. Notice that the two parts of the parameter can work in opposition or can reinforce each other. Thus, in some parts of the parameter space, whenever $\theta > 1$ or $\theta < -1$ *and* $\beta > 1$ or $\beta < -1$, we have a situation similar to that of equation 12.5: θX_n^{β} will tend toward some infinity and there will be no stationary law. When both $-1 < \theta < 1$ and $-1 < \beta < 1$ are true, on the other hand, there will be a stationary law, because θX_n^{β} will tend toward either zero or some other fixed point or points under these conditions. If $\theta > 1$ or $\theta < -1$ and $-1 < \beta < 1$, or vice versa, things get interesting. Whether there is a stationary law will depend on the actual values of θ and β, on which one wins the competition. In general, the values of θ will have to be more extreme than those of β because multiplication is less powerful than exponentiation. Clearly, however, the critical points of this model, though complicated and not easy to figure out, remain important to characterizing the model's behavior.

12.4   Ergodicity and the Markov Property

Two other mathematical concepts that bear on stochastic processes should be introduced here. The first, ergodicity, has to do with stationary

	Stake of player 1 on play n+1										
	0	1	2	3	4	5	6	7	8	9	10
0	1	0	0	0	0	0	0	0	0	0	0
1	.5	0	.5	0	0	0	0	0	0	0	0
2	0	.5	0	.5	0	0	0	0	0	0	0
3	0	0	.5	0	.5	0	0	0	0	0	0
4	0	0	0	.5	0	.5	0	0	0	0	0
5	0	0	0	0	.5	0	.5	0	0	0	0
6	0	0	0	0	0	.5	0	.5	0	0	0
7	0	0	0	0	0	0	.5	0	.5	0	0
8	0	0	0	0	0	0	0	.5	0	.5	0
9	0	0	0	0	0	0	0	0	.5	0	.5
10	0	0	0	0	0	0	0	0	0	0	1

(Row labels at left: Stake of player 1 on play n = 0, 1, 2, 3, 4, 5, 6, 7, 8, 9, 10)

Figure 12.1
Transition matrix for fair coin toss game with equal stakes of $5.

laws; the second, the Markov property (first encountered in chap. 2), with sequential behavior. Mathematicians call a stochastic process "ergodic" if it converges to a unique stationary law, no matter where in the state space it begins, that is, no matter what the initial probability distribution over the various states of the system is. The AR(1) process discussed in section 12.3 is ergodic because no matter what the initial position of the particle, the drift of the deterministic part toward zero would assure that eventually the stationary distribution would be reached. Of course, the farther from zero the initial position was, the longer on average it would take to reach the final, stationary distribution.

Mathematicians call a stochastic process a "Markov process" (after the mathematician Andrey Andreyevich Markov) if the next state of the system depends only on the present state, and not at all on any other states, previous or future (see Feller 1968). The random walk to ruin is a Markov process (or Markov *chain* in this case) in which each next state depends only on the present state (although the number of these might be very large). Consider the gambling situation in which two gamblers each have only $5 (let us say you are tossing a fair coin with a friend). Here there are only eleven possible states, and the probability of moving between them can be neatly summarized in a transition matrix (figure 12.1) in which "0" and "10" are absorbing states (the transition matrix for player 2 is the same as figure 12.1, with "player 2" substituted for "player 1").

Chapter 13

Stochastic Models in Physics

Limited information about the dynamics of a system and uncontrollable influences on the system often mean that it can only be considered as a statistical system.

—Josef Honerkamp, *Statistical Physics*

13.1   The Master Equation

Physicists approach the modeling of intrinsically stochastic processes somewhat differently from the way mathematicians do, as described in chapter 12 (see Plischke and Bergersen 1994; van Kampen 1985). Their approach, which is both very general and compatible with that of mathematicians, can also be of considerable use in dynamical cognitive science. Physicists usually begin with a description of a physical situation (naturally). The required description is a *mesoscopic* one, somewhere between the *microscopic*, in which noise consists of the fluctuations in position and momentum of each of a very large number of elementary particles, and the *macroscopic*, the level of classical Newtonian physics, in which noise is unimportant because there are so many particles that their individual fluctuations can be ignored. In a mesoscopic description, noise is important but it is treated globally, by describing its probability distribution. Usually, we think of physical systems as composed of particles in motion, such as electrons flowing in a wire. At the mesoscopic level, the states of this system could be the different numbers of electrons flowing in the conduction band at a given time, which means that the electrons are "free": they are not occupying any orbits around nuclei of atoms, thus can move along the wire. We are not interested in exactly which electrons are flowing, however, but only how many are flowing and how many are bound in orbits around nuclei. The number of electrons flowing is related to classical variables such as current, I, but the classical treatment considers only its mean, or characteristic value, as in Ohm's law: $E = IR$, where E stands for electromotive force (voltage) and R for resistance.

In the mesoscopic description, we assume that the system changes between states by *stochastic transitions*, that is, we assume that transitions between states occur probabilistically and on a short timescale relative to the timescale under study. In our electron example, there would be a certain probability that a transition between x and $x + 1$ electrons in the conduction band would occur at any moment. Whether it actually occurred at a given moment would be the result of some stochastic process, probably inherently unavailable to our observation. Let q be the state of such a dynamical system. Figure 13.1A shows part of the temporal unfolding, or time evolution, of such a system. Let $W(q_{new} \mid q_{old})$ be the rate of transitions between states q_{old} and q_{new}. The type of model we are interested in is the one specified by the entire set of rates W for all possible states q_{old} and q_{new}. Our model description of the system is in terms of the probability of state q occurring at time t: $P(q, t)$. Because we are interested in how $P(q, t)$ changes over time (the dynamical aspect), we write a *master equation* (e.g., Nordsieck, Lamb, and Uhlenbeck 1940) that describes these changes in the most general way possible:

$$\frac{\partial P(q, t)}{\partial t} = \int [W(q \mid q')P(q', t) - W(q' \mid q)P(q, t)] \, dq', \qquad (13.1)$$

where q and q' are any two states, and the indefinite integration is over the entire set of possible states. Basically, what equation 13.1 says is that the rate of change of the probability that the system is in state q at any time t, $P(q, t)$, is equal to the weighted "sum" over all possible system states of the difference between the likelihoods that (1) being in some other state with probability $P(q', t)$, the system will at that time make a transition into state q; and (2) already being in state q with probability $P(q, t)$, it will make a transition out to some other state. The weighting is by the transition rates that characterize each state. This partial differential equation describes the time evolution of the *probability distribution* of system states, *not* that of the state of the system itself. This distinction is critical to understanding how to use this approach. What is of interest here is whether and, if so, when there is an equilibrium in the probability distribution, that is, whether a particular, stable, probability distribution comes to describe the state transitions of the system. This is analogous to the property of stationarity in the mathematical theory of stochastic processes (chap. 12). Notice that the master equation also describes a Markov process because it is assumed that the system state at the next moment of time depends only on the state at the current moment of time (chap. 12). Figure 13.1B displays an example of the time evolution of a probability distribution toward equilibrium.

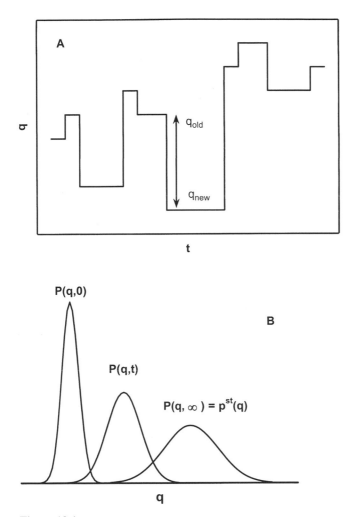

Figure 13.1
(*A*) Time evolution of a simple physical system; (*B*) time evolution of a probability distribution toward equilibrium.

Physicists consider the master equation to be "solved" if they can find the probability distribution $P(q, t)$ that satisfies equation 13.1 for arbitrary values of the probabilities at time $t = 0$. For example, $P(q, t) = (1/\sqrt{2\pi}) \exp(-q^2/2)$ indicates that the final, stationary probability distribution is Gaussian, or normal. Although it is not always easy to solve the master equation, general methods have been worked out and many special cases have been studied (e.g., van Kampen 1976, 1985). The general method consists of substituting equations for the W rates into equation 13.1 and applying various boundary conditions and other facts. In the more complicated cases, computer simulations are required to explore the evolution of the probability distribution, especially for some of the stochastic processes of interest to cognitive scientists, such as multiplicative noise, self-similar processes, and fractal processes. Finally, if we consider only the general location of the probability distribution and ignore its spread (see fig. 13.1B), the mesoscopic description is consistent with the macroscopic description in the form of classical-type laws (although these may be nonlinear).

13.2 Quantum Physics

The approach to statistical physics briefly outlined in section 13.1 is concerned with the evolution of the probability distribution describing the mesoscopic statistical fluctuations in a dynamical system. Quantum physics is concerned with the evolution of a related but quite different aspect of a particular dynamical system: the *probability amplitude* for a *quantum system* to assume a particular state. Quantum theory addresses a microscopic scale of energy, space, and time, and on that scale energy (at least) comes in little chunks (called *quanta*) when we measure it. To describe the evolution of a quantum system over time, however, we need to use a different concept, that of the *wave function*, represented by a lowercase psi with a subscript, ψ_n. The first postulate of quantum theory is that the state of a quantum system is described completely by the wave function, where the subscript n stands for quantum numbers, one for each coordinate of the space in which the wave function is defined (see Baggot 1992). The wave functions represent probability amplitudes for the quantum system to assume various possible states, such as for an electron to occupy particular regions of space or to move at particular speeds. The probability (or probability density for continuous, infinite systems) is given by the square of the wave function, or, because the probability amplitude is a complex number (e.g., $a + ib$, where $i = \sqrt{-1}$), by $|\psi^2| =$

$\psi^*\psi$, where ψ^* is the complex conjugate of ψ (e.g., $a - ib$). Although the theory can be quite complicated, for present purposes we do not need to go into these complications. In this section, we will simply consider an alternative way of thinking about how a system unfolds in time that has proven to be very useful in physics. In fact, it is the foundation of quantum electrodynamics (see Feynman 1985), one of the two most successful theories in physics, the other being Einstein's general theory of relativity.

Another important postulate of quantum theory is that observable quantities (the quantities we measure in experiments) are represented by mathematical *operators*. Although it is easiest to think of the operators of normal arithmetic, such as addition or multiplication, the operators in quantum theory can be much more complex. Indeed, the quantum theory idea is that *measurement* consists of applying an operator to the wave function, where the operator is essentially a description of the experimental system in all of its aspects, including especially the way in which measurements are made. One of the most famous equations of physics, the Schrödinger wave equation,

$$\hat{H}\psi = E\psi, \tag{13.2}$$

when written this way, uses what is called the "Hamiltonian operator," $\hat{H}$. Equation 13.2 mathematically describes the measurement of a system's energy, using two separate operators: the kinetic energy operator and the potential energy operator. Whereas the kinetic energy operator involves differentiation, the potential energy operator usually involves only multiplication. In equation 13.2 (technically, an *eigenvalue equation*; see Baggot 1992), the Hamiltonian operator operates on a wave function to yield that same function times the system's total energy, E.

The version of the Schrödinger equation in equation 13.2 is time independent: it does not describe the time evolution of a quantum system, but rather the system at some fixed time, even though it contains a differential operator for the kinetic energy (energy of motion). To introduce time into the Schrödinger equation, we need to change our notation slightly. Physicists use a notation invented by Dirac (1958), representing the state of a quantum system by putting special brackets around the wave function symbol: $|\psi_n\rangle$, and by calling it "state vector." Expressing this state vector as a combination of more primitive vectors that define a special kind of phase space called "Hilbert space," lets us use some powerful mathematical ideas. Thus expressed, state vectors are represented by boldface capital psi without a subscript: $|\Psi\rangle$. We can now write the time-dependent form of the Schrödinger equation:

$$ih\frac{\partial}{\partial t}|\Psi\rangle = \hat{H}|\Psi\rangle,\tag{13.3}$$

where $i = \sqrt{-1}$ and $\hbar = h/2\pi$, h being Planck's constant. This equation states that the rate of change of the system's state vector over time depends on the Hamiltonian operator's action on that state vector. Integrating equation 13.3 (see Baggot 1992) yields

$$|\Psi\rangle = \hat{U}|\Psi_0\rangle,\tag{13.4}$$

where

$$\hat{U} = e^{-i\hat{H}t/h},\tag{13.5}$$

$|\Psi_0\rangle$ is the state of the system at some initial time $t = 0$, and $|\Psi\rangle$ is its state at some later time. The complicated exponential term represented by equation 13.5 is called the "time evolution operator." With it, equation 13.4 describes the time evolution of a quantum system (how it unfolds in time) as continuous and deterministic in the probability amplitudes of all the different possible states of the system in a linear superposition (see again Baggott 1992).

But then where do the probabilities come from? Most physicists think about them in this way: the "act" of experimental observation "collapses" or "reduces" the wave function, producing a single "real" quantum state from the set of evolving, superposed (and possibly partly imaginary) "possible" states with a probability equal to the square of the amplitude for the system to assume that state. That is, although we can only observe states of a quantum system with various probabilities, the system evolves between our observations deterministically, not probabilistically. The process by which observation creates real quantum states by reducing the wave function is a fundamental mystery, often called the "quantum measurement problem." In one popular interpretation of the theory, the wave function only represents our knowledge of reality, and has no reality in itself. In another, the observation actually creates the reality. Whichever interpretation we accept (and there are still others; see Baggott 1992 or Penrose 1990), we are clearly dealing with a way of understanding a dynamical system very different from the way in which dynamical stochastic systems are understood. Some suggestions about dynamical cognitive systems are reminiscent of this approach, for example, as Neuringer and Voss (1993) see it, chaos theory both explains the unpredictability of human behavior and provides it with a deterministic foundation (see chap. 30). Thus the formulations of quantum physics could prove to be more generally useful, especially in dynamical cognitive science.

13.3   Complementarity Redux

Let us return to the time-independent version of the Schrödinger equation (eq. 13.2). The E in that equation is called the "eigenvalue," and the wave function an "eigenfunction," of the Hamiltonian energy operator. The requirement that the eigenvalue be real, that is, observable, whereas the eigenfunction and the operator can be complex (and have imaginary components), puts a considerable constraint on the mathematical form of the operator. Only a certain kind of operator, one with real eigenvalues for the indicated wave function, can be considered. Even with this restriction, however, when we want to measure the value (actually its *expectation value*, a kind of mean, called an "observable") yielded by applying an operator in the course of an experiment, there is no inherent limit to the precision with which that value can be measured. For example, we could, in principle, measure the energy of a particle emitted by a radioactively decaying atom as precisely as we wished. Suppose, however, we wish to measure a second property of our decaying atom, say the time at which that particle was emitted. To do so, the mathematics requires that the two operators to be applied (one for the energy and one for the time) *commute*. That is, it must not matter in which order the two operators are applied to the wave function that describes the decaying atom—either way, the resultant eigenvalues, the observables, must be the same. This is actually true neither for energy and time operators nor for position and momentum operators, which do not commute. Indeed, it does not seem to be true for any pair of operators applied to the same quantum system, which means that, in general, we can measure only one property of a quantum system (determine the expectation value of its operator) to arbitrarily high precision. The value yielded by application of any other operator will be increasingly uncertain as we more precisely determine the value yielded by the first. Such pairs of observables are said to be "complementary."

A more direct way to think about complementary observables is in terms of what the operators represent, an observer's real impact upon a quantum system. For example, to observe the position and momentum of an electron, we might throw photons at it. When the electron scatters a photon so that it enters our eye or some other photon-detecting device, we can determine its position (at the moment it scattered the photon). The higher the energy of the photon we throw at the electron, the more precisely we can determine where the electron was. On the other hand, the higher the photon energy, the bigger the "jolt" it gives the electron, changing its momentum in an unpredictable way. If we use lower-energy photons, we will be more certain about the momentum of the electron because the random jolts will be smaller, but less certain about its position. Heisenberg (1927) expressed this as an "uncertainty principle," based on the idea that measurement of the two quantities requires two different kinds of measurement device and that the use of the one interferes with the use of the other. Mathematically, this is expressed as two operators that do not commute.

Neils Bohr had a very different interpretation of Heisenberg's uncertainty principle, which he made into a philosophical principle (see Baggott 1992 for an excellent discussion). Bohr felt that the uncertainty principle, and complementary observables in general, represent a limit on *what we can know*. For Bohr, it was the very concepts of the complementary observables that were interfering with one another; they represented two complementary, not conflicting, ways of viewing the quantum system and the world.

In Ward 1990 and 1992, I explored the notion of complementarity more fully for psychophysics; Baird (1997) has taken it even further, proposing complementary psychophysical theories. In chapters 6–10, we applied Weinberg's principle of complementarity to yield complementary approaches to understanding cognitive systems, a theme we will pursue in later chapters.

Chapter 14

Noise

The earliest noise phenomena discovered were thermal noise [by Einstein in 1906] and shot noise [by Schottky in 1918]. In our opinion, these two noise processes are still the prototypes of all observed characteristic noise phenomena in and out of thermal equilibrium.

—Karoline M. van Vliet, "Classification of Noise Phenomena"

14.1 What Is Noise?

Experimental data in cognitive science are noisier than those in physics, but not as noisy as those in social or clinical psychology. By this I mean that much of the variance in the dependent variables remains unexplained by the independent (or manipulated) variables. For example, consider an experiment (described in greater detail in chap. 16) where subjects responded to the onset of a target stimulus with a key press. About 60% of the variance in the reaction times of individual subjects was accounted for by the fact that there were either one, two, or four response alternatives in different conditions. This can be expressed as a linear regression equation:

$$RT = \hat{m} \cdot NR + \hat{b} + \varepsilon, \tag{14.1}$$

where RT is median reaction time, NR is the number of response alternatives available, $\hat{m}$ and $\hat{b}$ are constants to be fitted, and ε is "error" or "noise." This noise represents the 40% of variance in individual reaction times that remained "unexplained." Such noise is responsible for the "error bars" around the points in a typical plot of mean data, where the bars represent the sample standard deviation or standard error, usually assumed to be estimates of parameters of an "error distribution" sampled from on each trial. As chapters 11–13 describe, these samples of noise are assumed to cause fluctuations in behavior over time. How could noise do this? And what is noise anyway? Why can it not be gotten rid of? Does it have any structure at all, particularly temporal structure? In what follows in this and the next few chapters, I address these and other questions in an attempt to make the study of noise a respectable pursuit in dynamical cognitive science.

The error, or noise, in an experiment such as the one I just described is generally considered to have two sources. The first and assumed source of most noise in cognitive science and any other behavioral science is ignorance of the details of the uncontrolled variation of independent variables that are causally related to the dependent variables. When there is some knowledge of uncontrolled variation of independent variables, the noise caused by them in the dependent variables can be "partialed out" statistically, thus providing an "explanation" for some more of the response variance. Even if we knew everything about all of the relevant variables in an experiment, however, there would still be an irreducible minimum of "essential noise," whose source—the second source—is the unknowable. The universe is a quantum system, as are all objects and events therein. Quantum systems *necessarily* evolve outside of our awareness, that is, we *cannot* know the details of their evolution (see, for example, Baggott 1992). A statistical prediction of the state of a quantum system is the best that can be done (at least in the orthodox interpretation of quantum mechanics; see chap. 13). Moreover, measurement entails uncertainty, and the Heisenberg uncertainty principle (see again Baggott 1992) describes the way in which even measurement at the quantum level involves uncertainty. In this case, and in many at the classical level as well, measured variables trade off: more certainty in the value of one entails less certainty (more error or noise) in the value of another. Ultimately, all noise is quantum noise because the precision in the measurement of any set of variables is limited by quantum noise. Measurements usually also contain much ignorance noise because all of the relevant variables are seldom controlled, even in precise physical measurement. Moreover, much of what is called "excess noise" in physics, that is, noise in excess of thermal or shot noise, is "colored noise" (see chap. 15), which is both exotic and generic in dynamical systems. Thus a discussion of physical noise and its sources and types will reveal valuable information about how to cope with and understand the behavioral and physiological noise that characterizes the results of experiments in cognitive science.

One very useful distinction is that between external and internal noise (e.g., van Kampen 1987). External noise is caused by a force outside of a system acting on that system. A good example is the turbulence of the earth's atmosphere acting on the light rays from distant stars, causing them to twinkle. This kind of noise has two properties: (1) it does not affect the actual behavior of the system of interest (the amount of light generated by a distant star is not affected by the atmosphere's turbulence); and (2) it is connected to that system by some coupling mechanism and, in principle, can be switched off (or by passed, as when the Hubble telescope in earth orbit views the star from outside the earth's atmosphere). In contrast to external noise, internal noise is an integral part of the system of interest, and participates completely in its temporal unfolding. "It originates from the fact that matter consists of particles, or, as in photons, from the fact that energy is quantized." (van Kampen 1987, 4) A good physical example is the current noise described in chapter 19: the electrical current in a wire with a constant voltage source (say a battery) fluctuates randomly. According to van Kampen (1987), such internal noise often arises from the cooperative effect of many system elements (e.g., electrons in current noise) rather than from fluctuations in the behavior of individual elements.

One useful way to describe all external noise, and also internal noise in a system whose temporal unfolding is described by a linear equation, is with what is called a "Langevin equation," after one of the early physicists who studied Brownian motion, the random motion of particles in a fluid caused by thermal noise (such as dust motes dancing in the air of a sunlit room—a type of internal noise). An example of such an equation is the one Langevin applied to Brownian motion:

$$\frac{dv}{dt} = -\beta v + \lambda(t), \tag{14.2}$$

where dv/dt is the momentary rate of change in the velocity, v, of a particle embedded in a fluid, β is the coefficient of friction of the fluid, and $\lambda(t)$ is the force exerted by the other molecules in the fluid on a given particle. Langevin's insight was to describe $\lambda(t)$ stochastically, that is, to describe the influences of the other particles on the motion of a given particle as a probability distribution, in this case described by only its mean (assumed to be zero) and its variance, which depends in turn on a few other parameters. The resulting equation successfully describes the fluctuations of Brownian motion in any fluid as long as the friction coefficient is known. Thus a typical Langevin equation contains a deterministic term, which describes the temporal unfolding of the system, and a stochastic term, which describes the stochastic (or noisy) influences of outside forces on that unfolding. In the case of our dust mote, the (linear) deterministic term describes the effect of friction (external noise) on the particle's motion, whereas the stochastic term describes the effect of other particles in the system (internal noise). Friction slows the particle, whereas other particles in the system cause no net change in the particle's motion, although, from moment to moment, they can either speed or slow the particle, sometimes by a large amount. Notice the resemblance between equations 14.1 and 14.2. Linear regression equations are a type of Langevin equation written in the form of a difference equation (although eq. 14.1 is not a dynamical equation because time does not enter into that equation).

Unfortunately, a Langevin approach does not suffice for all types of internal noise. If the temporal unfolding, or time evolution, of a system is described by a nonlinear equation, then an attempt to model the internal noise using a Langevin approach leads to contradictions (van Kampen 1987). In this case, we have to use what is called a "mesoscopic" description of the system. "It differs from the microscopic level in that it is coarse-grained.... It differs from the macroscopic level ... in that the state of the system is not specified by certain values of these variables, but by a probability distribution of them. The evolution is expressed by the time dependence of this distribution function" (van Kampen 1987, 7). This approach, using the master equation, has already been described in some detail in chapter 13. Here it suffices to point out that most of the interesting systems we will study in this book are nonlinear ones with internal noise, so that, in principle, the master equation approach applies to them, and especially to systems generating "colored noise" (see chap. 15).

Another useful typology of noise was suggested by van Vliet (1981), who argued that internal noise could be classified according to four principal distinctions: (1) thermal versus nonthermal; (2) microscopic versus mesoscopic; (3) lumped (discrete) versus distributed (continuous); and (4) classical versus quantum (all noise is ultimately quantum noise, but sometimes a classical description suffices). According to van Kampen (1987), these four distinctions correspond roughly to which microscopic constant of nature determines the noise amplitude. Regarding the first distinction, the strength of thermal noise always involves Boltzman's constant, k, multiplied by the temperature, T. For example, the variance of the stochastic variable $\lambda(t)$ in equation 14.2 is proportional to kT. The Brownian motion described by equation 14.2 is a prototypical example of thermal noise.

van Vliet (1981) also suggested a superdistinction between characteristic and noncharacteristic noise. Characteristic noise is reducible to elementary events with time constants and can be described by a Langevin, master, or other elementary equation. Noncharacteristic noise is not so reducible: there are no "elementary" events involved, and the fluctuations arise as a cooperative phenomenon. An example of noncharacteristic noise, according to van Vliet, is a particular variety of "colored noise" called "$1/f$ noise" (discussed in considerable detail in chaps. 16–19). The important point to keep in mind about noncharacteristic noise is that it cannot be described by conventional means. And the important overall concept to remember is that noise, though it might seem undesirable, is ultimately a fundamental aspect of the very phenomena we are studying; as such, it must be described with the same care as any other fundamental aspect.

14.2   Probabilistic Description of Noise

Because careful descriptions of noise often involve probability distributions and their properties, I will here briefly review two of the most commonly used probability distributions, plotted in figures 14.1A and 14.1B. (If you find this material overly difficult, you might consult the first few chapters of a good textbook on probability theory, such as Feller 1968, for a gentler introduction to these concepts.) Whereas sample spaces with a finite number of outcomes assign probabilities directly to each outcome, continuous probability distributions are characterized by probability density functions that assign a probability density, rather than a probability, to each of an infinite number of possible outcomes, or sample points. Probabilities in such infinite sample spaces are integrals of the probability density function over some (still infinite) set of sample points. The integral of the density over all sample points must equal one. The distribution function is the integral of the density function regarded as a function of its upper limit of integration, and assigns a probability to each of a series of sets of sample points. Often the expected value and the variance of a probability distribution suffice to characterize it, but sometimes other moments must be used. When noise is characterized as a series of independent samples from a set of identical probability distributions, we say that it is "independent, identically distributed" (i.i.d.) noise.

The simplest probability distribution is the *uniform distribution*, which has the same probability density,

$$p(x) = 1/(b-a), \tag{14.3}$$

for every possible sample point, x, where a and b are the lower and upper bounds of the real interval over which the probability density function is

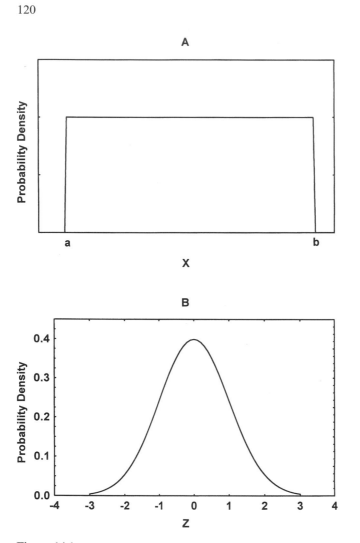

Figure 14.1
(*A*) The uniform probability distribution; (*B*) the standard Gaussian probability distribution.

defined. Equation 14.3, the uniform probability density function, is plotted in figure 14.1A. The most common uniform distribution is the one defined over the unit interval [0,1], so that $p(x) = 1$ in the interval [0,1] and 0 elsewhere, and

$$\int_0^1 p(x)\, dx = \int_0^1 1\, dx = 1.$$

The expected value of this distribution is 0.5 and the variance is 1/12. One very useful property of the uniform distribution is that if the interval $[b - a]$ is partitioned into n identical subintervals, the probability of a random sample from the distribution falling into a given subinterval is the same for each subinterval and equal to $1/n$. The distribution function of the uniform distribution is a straight line whose slope is $1/(b - a)$ and whose y-intercept is a. Thus the distribution function of the unit uniform distribution is a straight line whose slope is 1 and whose y-intercept is 0.

Probably the most commonly used probability distribution is the *Gaussian distribution* (named after Carl Friedrich Gauss, the great mathematician who invented it) or "normal" distribution. The famous "bell curve" of the Gaussian describes so many aspects of the natural world it is small wonder that it also describes noise in so many dynamical systems. Its density function is

$$p(x) = \frac{1}{\sigma\sqrt{2\pi}} \cdot e^{-(x-\mu)^2/(2\sigma^2)}, \tag{14.4}$$

where the parameters μ and σ are the expected value and standard deviation, respectively. Its distribution function unfortunately cannot be evaluated analytically and must be approximated numerically. Tables of the distribution function of the standard normal distribution, which has $\mu = 0$ and $\sigma = 1$, are ubiquitous, and approximation schemes abound. The standard normal probability density function is plotted in figure 14.1B. Notice that, since $\mu = 0$ and $\sigma = 1$, the standard normal probability density function can be written

$$p(z) = \frac{1}{\sqrt{2\pi}} \cdot e^{-z^2/2}, \tag{14.5}$$

where $z = (x - \mu)/\sigma$. Thus the abscissa of the graph in figure 14.1B is in units of z. The Gaussian distribution has many wonderful properties, perhaps the most profound of which is that it is the limiting form of many other distributions. For example, the Poisson distribution, which characterizes radioactive decay, emission of photons by a light filament, and many other random processes, becomes Gaussian in the limit as its rate parameter approaches infinity. Moreover, the distribution of sums or means of samples from any distribution, including the uniform distribution, becomes more like the Gaussian distribution as the number of samples increases. This creates both a popular and easy way to simulate the Gaussian distribution, namely, by summing samples from a uniform distribution, and a popular rationale for assuming Gaussian fluctuations in many situations. Any normal distribution can be transformed into the standard normal by applying the z-transform described in the context of equation 14.5, for example, when researchers simulate sampling from the standard normal distribution by summing samples from a uniform $[0,1]$ distribution. If, say, they take a sum of twelve samples from the uniform distribution, that is, $y = x_1 + x_2 + \cdots + x_{12}$, where the x_i are the samples from the uniform, then $\mu = 0.5(12) = 6$ and $\sigma = \sqrt{(12/12)} = 1$, so that $z = (y - \mu)/\sigma = (y - 6)/1 = y - 6$. The value of z represents a single sample from an approximately standard normal distribution.

14.3 Spectral Properties of Noise

Random noise can also be described by its power spectrum, although this was originally thought to be a meaningless exercise because random noise was supposed to have no periodic structure (see, for example, Bell 1960). A power spectrum is based on the Fourier transform, which expresses the relationship between time domain and frequency domain descriptions of any physical process. The Fourier transform of a function of time, $h(t)$, is written

$$H(f) = \int_{-\infty}^{+\infty} h(t) \cdot e^{2\pi i f t} \, dt, \tag{14.6}$$

where $H(f)$ is a function of frequency, f, measured in Hertz (Hz). The square of the Fourier transform, $H(f)^2$, is called the "power spectral density," and expresses the amount of temporal fluctuation that can be described by a combination of sine and cosine waves at a particular frequency f. The power spectrum of a function of time is a plot of the squared Fourier transform versus frequency, usually in log-log coordinates for convenience (i.e., $\log H(f)^2$ versus $\log f$). The power spectrum of real, discretely sampled time series is usually estimated by a method called the "fast Fourier transform" (FFT), which gives the power spectral density in each of several small bands of frequencies into which

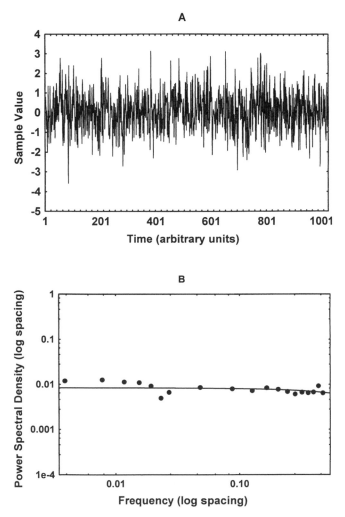

A

B

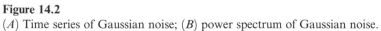

Figure 14.2
(*A*) Time series of Gaussian noise; (*B*) power spectrum of Gaussian noise.

the relevant frequency range is divided, usually referred to by indicating the center frequency of the band (see, for example, Press et al. 1992).

For example, consider a series of 1,024 samples from a Gaussian probability distribution. Although this is a relatively short time series, it is in the range of time series lengths to be expected in cognitive science experiments, and it is sufficient to illustrate the expected power spectrum of Gaussian noise for such time series. I generated such a time series (using a computer of course) and did an FFT to obtain the power spectrum (averaging the higher frequency bands into larger bins containing several adjacent bands as suggested by Mandelbrot 1998). The time series is displayed in figure 14.2A and its power spectrum in figure 14.2B. The power spectrum is relatively flat (slope $= -0.004$) over the range of frequencies involved, which means that all the frequencies contributed roughly equally to the fluctuations of the time series. The ideal power spectrum for such "white" noise has slope equal to zero. Of course, because any real system can have only a finite amount of power (the area under the power spectrum curve), this and any other spectrum must eventually have both a high- and a low-frequency cutoff, where the spectral power density becomes zero. Descriptions of noise in terms of its power spectrum have become commonplace, and we will be using such descriptions routinely in the next several chapters, as we continue our search for temporal structure in noise.

Chapter 15

Colored Noise

When the ticks in my Geiger counter exhibit $1/f$ noise I must conclude that the nuclei influence each other's decays, or that they remember the supernova explosion in which they were born, or that I have made a mistake.

—N. G. van Kampen, "Some Theoretical Aspects of Noise"

If you have not found the $1/f$ spectrum, it is because you have not waited long enough.

—Stefan Machlup, "Earthquakes, Thunderstorms, and Other $1/f$ Noises"

15.1 The Ubiquity of Colored Noise

What do a Bach concerto, alpha waves, heartbeats, earthquakes, thunderstorms, electrical current, reaction times in cognitive science experiments, mistakes, and chaos all have in common? The answer is that time series of fluctuations characteristic of these phenomena all exhibit a $1/f$ power spectrum. Here I explore the meaning of this answer; in later chapters I discuss possible reasons why it is true. My opening question, far from being merely rhetorical, is both substantial and profound and leads to a second such question. Why is it that phenomena so diverse all share the same power spectrum of fluctuations, yet other, seemingly similar phenomena, such as Brownian motion and white noise (see chap. 14), do not?

As noted in chapter 14, *white noise* is a time series of fluctuations having roughly equal spectral density at all frequencies in a given range. A good example of white noise is a time series of samples from a Gaussian, or normal, distribution. Figure 14.2 showed that the power spectrum of such a time series is roughly flat (zero slope in log-log coordinates). What this means is that there are no correlations whatsoever between samples taken at one point in the time series and those taken at any other; the samples are independent and identically distributed (i.i.d.). Although a single strong periodicity in the time series will of course be displayed as a single peak in the power spectrum at the frequency of the periodicity, the correlations in the time series of fluctuations from a Bach concerto, alpha waves, heartbeats, and so forth occur at several timescales, from very long range to very short range, with no one preferred timescale. Using a computer and equations 16.2–16.5 I created a time series of such fluctuations, which is displayed in figure 15.1A, where you can see the long-term correlations in the time series as gentle undulations, overlaid by higher-frequency fluctuations. The power spectrum of this time series, from a fast Fourier transform (FFT) and in a log-log plot, is shown in figure 15.1B. The slope of the best-fitting straight line through this power spectrum, treated in log-log coordinates, is not zero, but roughly equal to -1. Noise with this spectral "shape" is called "pink noise" because it is dominated by relatively low frequencies, but has some higher frequencies in it—just as light that appears pink to human eyes is dominated by low-frequency (long-wavelength) photons, but has some higher-frequency (short-wavelength) photons in it. As the supposed signature of a very interesting type of dynamical system called a "complex system" (Waldrop 1992), pink noise has proved notoriously difficult to explain (see chaps. 18 and 19). I will have more to say about complex systems, but for now it suffices to point out that, wherever pink noise appears, it is reasonable to look for other exotic phenomena, even in some cases the one called "chaos" (see chap. 23).

Another type of "colored noise" (noise whose power spectrum is not flat), and one that is easier to understand, is "brown noise." Probably the most famous example of brown noise is Brownian motion, which can be represented by a running sum of a time series of samples from a probability distribution with mean zero. The sum represents the current position of a particle buffeted by other particles in a fluid (see chap. 14); it is a kind of random walk. By sampling from a Gaussian distribution and adding the successive samples to create a running sum, I created some hypothetical Brownian motion. The time series of positions (momentary values of the running sum) is shown in figure 15.2A, and its power spectrum, again from an FFT and in a log-log plot, in figure 15.2B. It is clear that low-frequency fluctuations are even more dominant in brown noise, to the point where the series stays in the same neighborhood for relatively long periods of time. The power spectrum reflects this dominance by low

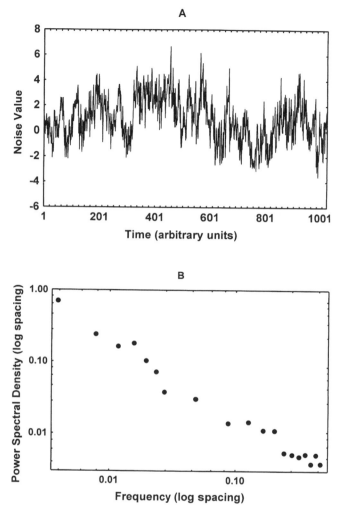

Figure 15.1
(*A*) Time series of pink noise; (*B*) power spectrum of pink noise.

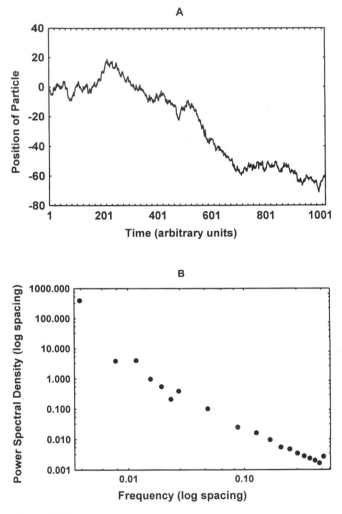

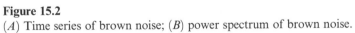

Figure 15.2
(*A*) Time series of brown noise; (*B*) power spectrum of brown noise.

frequencies, since the slope is about -2 in the log-log plot (this result can be derived theoretically; see, for example, van Vliet 1981).

Some noise is even darker than brown noise; the slopes of the log-log plots of the power spectra of such "black noise" are more negative than -2 (Schroeder 1991). One dramatic and important example is the flooding of the Nile river, whose fluctuations have a power spectrum with a slope of -2.8. Such a spectrum means that the minimum yearly level of the Nile (recorded from 622 to 1469 C.E. by the Egyptians) changes only very slowly over periods of many years, leading to both droughts and wet centuries and profoundly affecting human welfare in the region.

These represent only a few of the many examples of colored noise in nature. More will be discussed later in this chapter and in chapters 15 and 16. For now, remember that far from being an exotic rarity in our world, colored noise is so common, and occurs in such an interesting array of dynamical systems, including cognitive systems, that its presence demands exploration and explanation.

15.2   The Vicissitudes of the Exponent α

One convenient and economical way to describe the power spectra of colored noises is with an equation such as the following:

$$S(f) = kf^{-\alpha}, \tag{15.1}$$

where $S(f)$ is the power spectral density (say, from an FFT), f is temporal frequency (in Hertz), k is a constant determined by specifics of the system such as the mean and variance of the noise, and α is the crucial parameter that determines the "color" of the noise. When we take the logarithm of both sides of equation 15.1, as we did when plotting the power spectra in figures 14.2B, 15.1B and 15.2B, we obtain

$$\log S(f) = \log k - \alpha \log f, \tag{15.2}$$

a linear equation in the variables $\log S(f)$ and $\log f$, with slope $-\alpha$. Thus, for pink noise $-\alpha = -1$ (fig. 15.1B), for brown noise $-\alpha = -2$ (fig. 15.2B), and for black noise $-\alpha < -2$. White noise has $-\alpha = 0$, implying that $\log S(f) = \log k = $ constant (fig. 14.2B). Because the minus sign is somewhat awkward to carry around, in what follows I am going to drop it in front of α in most cases, but you should remember that it is supposed to be there. Moreover, as is customary in the field, I will from now on write "$1/f$ noise" when $\alpha = 1$, omitting the exponent.

It would be an ideal world if only a few, integer values of α occurred, like the values taken by the quantum numbers associated with atoms. And such precise and sparse values do occur in some physical theories. For example, as mentioned above, it can be shown theoretically that the power spectrum of Brownian motion has α = 2 (and thus −α = −2). But the real world, unfortunately, is not that neat. Many different values of α appear in different systems, and it is not yet clear which factors are responsible for these variations. Some theories in physics seem to explain some of this variation. For example, Bell's explanation (1960) for pink noise that occurs in electrical current in a wire also explains why the exponent of frequency varies somewhat with the type of material of which the wire is made (but see van Kampen 1987 and chap. 19). There are, however, no accepted theories of pink noise in living systems or in cognitive systems; even physicists consider pink noise to be a mystery: a steady stream of papers in physics journals contain models their authors claim reveal why pink noise is so ubiquitous (e.g., Kaulakys 1999).

One reason for nonideal exponents appearing in equation 15.1 (or for nonideal slopes in eq. 15.2) is that we cannot observe time series for an infinite time. This is especially important for higher values of α, such as those greater than two (or −α < −2), which describe black noise. Black noise could characterize seemingly catastrophic phenomena other than Nile flooding, such as fluctuations in global temperature or in the numbers of living members of endangered species of animals (Schroeder 1991). The power spectra of such phenomena might be only asymptotically black, approaching, say, an exponent of α = 3 according to the following equation (Schroeder 1991):

$$S(f) = \frac{T^4 f}{1 + (T^4 f^4)}, \tag{15.3}$$

where T is the time period over which the phenomenon is observed. As T gets very large, the 1 in the denominator of equation 15.3 becomes irrelevant and the equation approaches $S(f) = 1/f^3 = f^{-3}$. However, when T is small, the equation fluctuates wildly for different values of T, with the extreme fluctuations depending on just how long T is. If we wait long enough, anything is possible (as in the second epigraph above). If the observation period is long enough, we can be fooled by one of these extremes (e.g., several unusually hot summers) into thinking that the entire process has changed (permanent global warming) when it may be, in fact, only an unusually "black" part of the black noise time series. It is thus very difficult to discriminate permanent shifts in a time series (non-stationarity) from expected extreme fluctuations in black noise in which the underlying generating process has not changed at all.

A measure of fluctuations that is especially useful for black noises, where the distance between different states appears to grow larger with time, is called the "rescaled range" and is symbolized by R/S (Schroeder 1991). The range, R, is the maximum value minus the minimum value of the variable in a stationary time series over the time interval observed, whereas the scaling factor, S, is the sample standard deviation of the set of values in the time series over that same interval. The range is a "first power" measure of the dispersion of values in the time series, whereas the standard deviation is based on a "second power" measure of the dispersion—it is the square root of the sample variance, where

$$\text{Var} = \sum_{i}^{n-1}(x_i - \bar{x})^2/(n-1).$$

For colored noise, the rescaled range is proportional to the time interval, Δt, raised to a power, H:

$$\frac{R}{S} = \Delta t^H. \tag{15.4}$$

The exponent H, called the "Hurst exponent" after its inventor H. E. Hurst, can be easily measured for a particular time series as the slope of a plot of $\log R/S$ versus $\log \Delta t$, in the same way as is done for the power spectrum. Importantly, for any time series,

$$\alpha = 2H + 1, \tag{15.5}$$

so that the exponent of the power spectrum can be obtained from the Hurst exponent or vice versa. Thus Nile flooding, with $\alpha = 2.8$, has a Hurst exponent of 0.9, brown noise has $H = 0.5$, pink noise has $H = 0$, and white noise has $H = -0.5$. The Hurst exponent is a simple measure of persistence, or memory, namely, how long we can expect a given fluctuation in a time series to be reflected in future values of the series. The more positive the Hurst exponent, the longer the persistence (memory). Another way to talk about this is in terms of relaxation time, which is the time it takes for a system to "relax" from the effect of a given fluctuation into its equilibrium, or steady, state (which it may never do because there will be future fluctuations to relax from). Relaxation times will appear prominently in many discussions in the chapters to come.

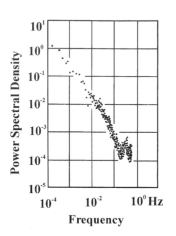

Figure 15.3
Biological pink noise from the human heart. (From Musha 1981.)

15.3 Colored Noise in Living Systems

To many people, the most intriguing aspect of colored noise, especially pink, or $1/f$, noise, is its appearance in both nonliving and living systems. Ever since Schrödinger (1944/1967) wrote about the paradoxes entailed by consideration of living things as physical systems, a bridge between nonliving and living systems has been sought. Pink noise may be a clue to nature of the long-sought bridge (or it may be a red herring that will lead us astray). If the underlying dynamic processes giving rise to pink noise in nonliving systems can be understood, perhaps this understanding can be extended to living systems. The same reasoning can be extended, in turn, to cognitive dynamical systems, ultimately to consciousness and the mind. Perhaps pink noise can reveal something fundamental about mental processes. This idea is considered seriously in chapters 16 and 17.

Two good examples of pink noise in living systems come from studies of muscles. Musha (1981) reported a study of fluctuations of the time intervals between successive R peaks (reflecting muscle contractions) of the electrocardiogram of the human heart. The power spectrum of an example time series plotted in log-log coordinates is shown in figure 15.3. As the figure makes clear, the power spectrum is just about $1/f$ (i.e., the log-log slope ≈ -1) over several decades of frequency. Figure 15.3 is a good example of power spectra from "real" time series. Notice it has a small peak at about 0.3 Hz, the frequency at which the subject was breathing, and clearly it influenced the heart's contractions. Musha

(1981) also reported an early study of the postural sway of the body on a platform, the slope of the power spectrum, plotted log-log, was −1 for frequencies lower than 1 Hz, and slightly greater than that for higher frequencies. Musha suggested that the power spectrum is related to the mechanism of posture control, and more recent studies have confirmed this (Lauk, et al. 1998). Biological pink noise also occurs both in the brain (chap. 17) and in the behavior of the whole human—to which we turn next.

Chapter 16

$1/f$ Noise in Human Cognition

The [$1/f$ music] was judged ... to be much more pleasing than ... (either white noise or $1/f^2$ music).... Indeed, the sophistication of this "$1/f$ music" ... extends far beyond what one might expect from such a simple algorithm, suggesting that a "$1/f$" noise (perhaps that in nerve membranes?) may have an essential role in the creative process.

—Richard F. Voss and John Clarke, "'$1/f$ Noise' in Music and Speech"

16.1 Music and Time Perception

The search for the relevance of $1/f$ noise to human cognition began with Voss and Clark 1975, quoted above. Although the paper was ignored for twenty years, it finally came to the attention of psychologists and has stimulated a recent burst of work in several laboratories. What Voss and Clarke did was to create several time series by digitizing the analog fluctuations of sound intensity and fundamental frequency (well below the "audio" frequencies of the sound waves themselves) in recorded music and voices played over the radio. Then they performed fast Fourier transforms (FFTs) on the time series to obtain the power spectra of the fluctuations (see chaps. 14 and 15). Their most famous result is shown in figure 16.1, the power spectrum for Bach's Brandenburg Concerto no. 1. Although two small peaks are apparent at about 2.5 Hz and 5.6 Hz, caused by the rhythmic structure of the piece, the spectrum below 1 Hz ("0" on the $\log_{10}(f)$ axis) is approximately $1/f$. Similar results were obtained for average time series of sound intensity fluctuations for Scott Joplin piano rags, classical music, rock music, and a news and talk station. The results for fluctuations of fundamental frequency were somewhat different, with only classical music exhibiting a broad-range $1/f$ power spectrum. The news and talk spectrum was the most deviant, with peaks representing the average length of an individual speech sound (0.1 sec)

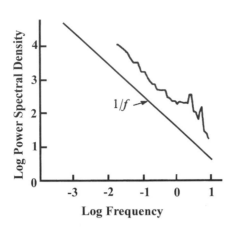

Figure 16.1
Power spectrum of amplitude changes in Bach's Brandenburg Concerto no. 1.
(From Voss and Clarke 1975. Reprinted with permission from *Nature*. © 1975,
Macmillan Magazines, Limited.)

and the average time for which a particular person talked (100 sec). The
meaning of speech is only weakly correlated with the structure of fundamental sound frequency changes, whereas that of music is usually carried
directly by such changes, which comprise the melody (but see Boon and
Decroly 1995). On the other hand, important meaning is carried by sound
intensity fluctuations in both music and speech. And that meaning seems
to be most esthetically pleasing when the intensity fluctuations are
roughly $1/f$.

Independently of Voss and Clarke, Musha (1981) summarized several
studies establishing a role for $1/f$ noise in biological systems, particularly
in human perception. His own experiments established that the power
spectra of some cartoons (based on spatial frequency fluctuations) are
approximately $1/f$, whereas those of some "realistic" paintings and
photographs are $1/f^2$, and some impressionistic paintings have spectra
somewhere between the two. Takakura et al. (1979) found that the pain-
relieving effectiveness of transcutaneous electrical stimulation was doubled
(from 35% to 70%) by synchronizing the electrical pulses with $1/f$ noise.
Thus $1/f$ fluctuations are associated both with pleasure and with the
absence of pain.

In the first of the more recent studies of $1/f$ noise in human behavior,
Gilden, Thornton, and Mallon 1995, human subjects were asked to estimate various time intervals repeatedly (only one at a time) for many
linked intervals; time series were constructed of the errors of the estimates

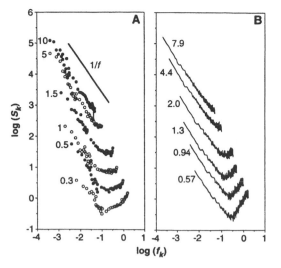

Figure 16.2
(*A*) Power spectra of fluctuations in time estimations; (*B*) power spectra from a model. (From Gilden, Thornton, and Mallon 1995. Reprinted with permission from *Science*. © 1995, American Association for the Advancement of Science.)

(target time interval minus estimate for each estimate). When Gilden, Thornton, and Mallon performed FFTs on these time series, they found the average power spectra shown in figure 16.2A. The numbers labeling the various spectra are the durations that were being repeatedly estimated (10 sec, 5 sec, ..., 0.3 sec). Clearly, the spectra are close to $1/f$ below about 0.2 Hz. Also, notice that the longer the time interval estimated, the lower the frequencies of the spectra, reflecting the duration of the time period over which the experiment continued (see also sec. 15.2). After reading Gilden, Thornton, and Mallon 1995, I reanalyzed some of my own time estimation data in the same way (Ward 1996 and chap. 11). I found similar power spectra near $1/f$ for time intervals of 1 sec and 3 sec, as well as for "random" and self-selected "preferred" intervals, even though my data were generated in a different way. This finding is robust.

Time estimation is traditionally modeled in psychology by assuming that the intervals bounded by subjects' key presses are produced by the interaction of two processes, an internal clock to time the interval and a motor program to generate the key presses at appropriate moments, both of them also sources of white noise. Gilden, Thornton, and Mallon 1995 changed the traditional model only slightly, by assuming that the internal clock was a source of $1/f$ noise, whereas the motor program remained a source of white noise. Figure 16.2B shows the power spectra of simulated time interval generation according to this modified model. The numeric labels on the different spectra are the ratios of the amount of $1/f$ noise to the amount of white noise in the respective time series, assuming that the longer the time interval to be estimated, the relatively more $1/f$ noise contributed by the internal clock. Clearly, the modified model accounts well for the empirical spectra, including the increasing amount of power and the flattening of the spectra at high frequencies as the time intervals decrease, both of which reflect the increasing prominence of the white motor program noise at shorter intervals.

16.2   Reaction Time

A few months after Gilden, Thornton, and Mallon 1995 appeared, and after informal input by Daniel Gilden about similar experiments he was performing, Keith Clayton presented another significant study (Clayton and Frey 1997) of $1/f$ noise in human behavior at the August 1995 meeting of the Society for Chaos Theory in Psychology and the Life Sciences. This study was the first reported measurement of power spectra of time series of reaction times, perhaps the most ubiquitous dependent variable used in cognitive science. Despite more than a century of use, however, seldom before had the temporal structure of the *variability* of reaction times been analyzed. Clayton and Frey (1997) created three conditions of a simple classification task, varying in memory load. In the simplest, subjects pressed one key if a visual stimulus was an "X"; another key if it was an "O." In the other tasks, subjects had to press one key if the current stimulus was the same as the one on the previous trial, and another if not; similarly, in the most difficult task, one key if the current stimulus was the same as the stimulus two trials before, and another if not. Clayton and Frey found that the power spectra of the time series of reaction times in the three tasks were different. The slope of the power spectrum at the lower frequencies for the simplest task was about -0.46; for the one-trial-back, same-different task, it was -0.35; and for the two-trial-back task, it was -0.26. Thus the slopes varied with memory load, being steepest (most like $1/f$ noise) for the simplest task and approaching white noise for the most demanding. Interestingly, Clayton and Frey also reported power spectrum analyses of time series formed from iteration of the logistic difference equation (eq. 1.4; see chaps. 1 and 24). They discovered that when the single parameter of the equation equals 3.97, forming a time series that is at the "edge of chaos" (see chap.

24), its power spectrum has a slope of about -0.33 at the lower frequencies. Thus pink noise might even appear in the equations of chaos theory.

Gilden (1997) reported similar experiments using several of the most common reaction time tasks, including mental rotation, lexical decision, serial search, and parallel search. Gilden fitted a version of the same model he and colleagues had used for the time estimation data described earlier to the residual variability (left after subtracting out the mean reaction times) in the time series for each task:

$$\text{Error} = (1/f^{\alpha})_n + \beta \cdot N(0, 1), \tag{16.1}$$

which says that the error on the nth trial is composed of two components: the nth term of a $1/f^{\alpha}$ noise with mean 0 and variance 1; and a sample from the standard normal distribution, namely, $N(0, 1)$—white noise. The constant β determines the relative contributions of the $1/f^{\alpha}$ and white noises. Gilden found that this model explained over 90% of the residual variance in each of the tasks. The $1/f^{\alpha}$ noise accounted for from about 0.2 to about 0.4 of the residual variance, the rest being white noise. Moreover, the values of α ranged from 0.7 to 0.9, indicating that the power spectra of the time series of deviations of the reaction times from the mean were near $1/f$ at frequencies below about 0.1 Hz. Thus near-$1/f$ noise characterizes many of the commonest behavioral tasks used in cognitive science laboratories.

Impressed by the work of Gilden indicating the ubiquity of the $1/f$ power spectrum in human behavioral data, and that of Clayton and Frey revealing the possibility that the exponent could be affected by experimental manipulations, I and a colleague (Ward and Richard 2001) decided to investigate specific components of the processes giving rise to the $1/f$-like noise. We had read the description of Schroeder (1991) of a simple set of three "relaxation"equations that, when summed, would yield a close approximation to $1/f$ noise. We were aware also of at least three timescales of brain and cognitive processes that might be contributing to such noise; they are summarized in table 16.1. Considering each timescale, τ, to be that of a relaxation or memory process, over which activity at a particular moment in time would decay exponentially in its influence on future activity, each of the timescales introduces a correlation scale according to $\rho = e^{(-1/\tau)}$, where ρ represents the correlation scale; it ranges between nearly 1 (for τ approaching infinity) and nearly 0 (for τ approaching 0). A correlation scale value of near 1 means that a given fluctuation would influence future fluctuations for a relatively long time, whereas a correlation scale near 0 means that a fluctuation would influ-

Table 16.1
Timescales in the Cognitive and Brain Systems

Process (eqs. 16.2 to 16.4)	Timescale τ (msec)	Cycle Frequency (Hz)	Brain System	Cognitive System	Behavioral Task
X	1 to 2.5	1,000 to 400	1 to 10 neurons	Preconscious	Peripheral sensory processing
Y	10 to 25	100 to 40	10s to 100s of neurons: within area circuit	Unconscious	Sternberg (1966) STM scanning task
Z	100 to 250	10 to 4	1,000s to millions of neurons: between-area loops	Conscious	Crovitz (1970) strobe matching task

ence future fluctuations for only a very short time. Schroeder (1991) showed that the sum of three such processes, with timescales spread over at least two decades, is sufficient to approximate $1/f$ noise. We modified Schroeder's equations to yield the following set:

$$X_n = \rho_x X_{n-1} + (1 - \rho_x^2)^{1/2} S_x E_{x,n} \sigma \tag{16.2}$$

$$Y_n = \rho_y Y_{n-1} + (1 - \rho_y^2)^{1/2} S_y E_{y,n} \sigma \tag{16.3}$$

$$Z_n = \rho_z Z_{n-1} + (1 - \rho_z^2)^{1/2} S_z E_{z,n} \sigma \tag{16.4}$$

$$W_n = (X_n + Y_n + Z_n) + \beta \cdot G_n \tag{16.5}$$

In equations 16.2–16.4, X_n, Y_n, and Z_n represent noise generated at three timescales; ρ_x, ρ_y, and ρ_z represent correlations at those scales. They function like the parameters of autoregressive (AR) processes, introducing some proportion of a previous fluctuation into each new fluctuation, with that contribution decreasing exponentially over the course of the time series (see chap. 11). The S terms, which are our most important addition to the system, are constants that allow us to manipulate at each level separately the amount of uncorrelated white noise, E, relative to that of correlated noise (first term). The σ term in each equation was added to account for the overall differences in the variance of the time series in different cognitive tasks; it does not affect the slope of the power spectrum, but only its overall position on the spectral power (vertical) axis. Finally, in equation 16.5, the X_n, Y_n, and Z_n terms are then combined with more white noise (βG_n) to produce each successive time series noise value. Note that equation 16.5 is an expanded version of Gilden's model, equation 16.1, in which the term ($X_n + Y_n + Z_n$) represents the $1/f^\alpha$ process. This modified version, however, provides information about the dynamics previously hidden in the "$1/f$ black box." Also, as I already mentioned, each of equations 16.2–16.4 is basically a first-order autoregressive (ARIMA(1,0,0)) process with parameter ρ_x, ρ_y, or ρ_z, all between 0 and 1, with the term to the right of the plus sign constituting the added white noise (see eq. 11.3). Adding together several ARIMA(1,0,0) processes with a wide range of parameter values turns out to be a very general way to create time series with $1/f$-like power spectra and might be a clue as to the necessary and sufficient conditions for such time series to arise (Greenwood and Ward 2001; chap. 19).

Although Clayton and Frey (1997) had found that increased memory load decreased the power spectrum exponent α, their task was not the same for all conditions, thus it is uncertain exactly what was affecting the exponent. To find out which scale level was causing the change in exponent, we (Ward and Richard 2001) created a similar decision task in which only the decision load, represented as the number of stimulus and response alternatives, varied between conditions. In our task, subjects either pressed a single key as soon as any one of two short lines appeared in the display (one-choice), pressed one key for a shorter line and a different one for a longer line (two-choice), or pressed the correct one of four different keys corresponding to one of four lines of different lengths that could appear (four-choice). In one of several control experiments, subjects had to press a different, arbitrary, key of the four available on each trial of the task as soon as any line whatsoever appeared, as in the one-choice task except for the rotation among different response keys. We did this to remove the possibility that any exponent changes might arise solely from the differences between the tasks in the number of motor acts required. Our data were very similar to those of Clayton and Frey (1997), although the power spectrum slopes varied more across conditions, with the one-choice task yielding almost $1/f$ spectra for several subjects. Figure 16.3A shows the average spectra for each of the conditions across eleven subjects (each subject ran all conditions in partially counterbalanced orders). The slopes for these average spectra were -0.61, -0.36, and -0.24 respectively for the one-, two-, and four-choice conditions, and the linear fits (in log-log coordinates) are very good ($r^2 = 0.99$, 0.97, and 0.96, respectively,

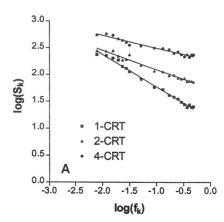

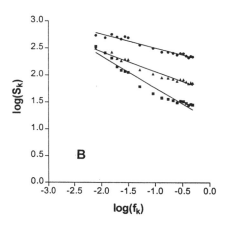

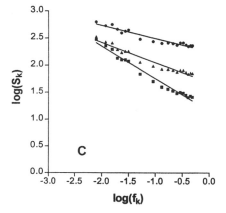

Figure 16.3
Power spectra of reaction time fluctuations for 1-choice (1-CRT), 2-choice
(2-CRT), and 4-choice (4-CRT) conditions from (*A*) subject data, (*B*) simulations
of equations 16.2–16.5 with only S_y varying, and (*C*) simulations of equations
16.2–16.5 with only β varying. (From Ward and Richard 2001.)

for the three conditions). The traditional cognitive psychology model that best fits our decision task is a Sternberg memory-scanning model, in which some set of remembered representations (1, 2, or 4 of them) must be scanned exhaustively for a match before a response can be made.

As table 16.1 indicates, this implies that the middle timescale, at about 10–25 msec per operation, would be most affected by our experimental manipulation because that is the timescale at which the psychological operations involved in Sternberg scanning are said to take place. We did computer simulations of equations 16.2–16.5, varying the contribution of the uncorrelated noise at the middle time scale only (S_y in equation 16.3), to produce the simulated spectra shown in Figure 16.3B. For these simulations we used $\tau_x = 1$, $\tau_y = 10$, and $\tau_z = 100$ so that $\rho_x = 0.368$, $\rho_y = 0.905$, and $\rho_z = 0.990$. The simulations shown in figure 16.3B came from runs in which $S_y = 1.9$ for one-choice, 0.9 for two-choice, and 0.1 for four-choice, with slopes nearly identical to those of the subject data (-0.59, -0.37, and -0.25, respectively) and nearly identical linear fits ($r^2 = 0.95$, 0.97, and 0.95, respectively). The interpretation of this result is that the more decision alternatives there are, the more dominant is the correlation at the middle timescale, causing the spectrum to flatten progressively. This interpretation seems reasonable because the correlation at the middle timescale is introduced by the Sternberg memory-scanning process operating at that scale. Varying S_x or S_z also causes changes in the spectra, but the resulting spectra are not nearly linear in log-log coordinates and the slope changes we found are difficult to simulate.

Another possible way to simulate the spectra shown by the subjects is to manipulate only β in equation 16.5, much as Gilden (1997) did. In this case, the contrast is between an unaffected $1/f$ process and added white noise, with the white noise process dominating more, the larger β is. Simulated spectra from this manipulation are shown in figure 16.3C. In these spectra, $\beta = 1.4$ for one-choice reaction times, $\beta = 2.4$ for two-choice reaction times, and $\beta = 3.5$ for four-choice reaction times, meaning that white noise is more dominant relative to $1/f$ noise, the greater the decision load. Again, the slopes (-0.60, -0.37, and -0.24) are nearly identical to those in the subjects' data, as are the linear fits ($r^2 = 0.98$, 0.95, and 0.93, respectively). Because in Gilden's model the white noise is supposed to arise from the manual response process, this approach implies that manual response noise plays a greater role the more responses are available, a reasonable statement. Because these spectra also do a fairly good job of mimicking the data, there is some ambiguity remaining as to the best way to model these data. Because, however, our control one-choice experiment with four arbitrary responses gave roughly the same results as the one-choice experiment with only one response (average power spectrum slope $= -0.55$), however, we do not think this latter explanation is the best one. Whichever interpretation is eventually accepted, it is clear that there is interesting temporal structure in the "noise" that plagues experiments in cognition, and there are indications of how that structure can be revealed. Perhaps future studies, following up on ours, Clayton and Frey's, and Gilden's, will be able to propose and test detailed models in which the modeled cognitive processes naturally give rise to such temporally structured noise.

Chapter 17

$1/f$ Noise in the Brain

[The brain is an] enchanted loom, where millions of flashing shuttles weave a dissolving pattern, always a meaningful pattern though never an abiding one....
—Charles Scott Sherrington, *Man and His Nature*

The study of systems with strong interactions of many degrees of freedom is one of the most important subjects in physics.
—E. Novikov et al., "Scale-Similar Activity in the Brain"

17.1   Neural Activity

Whether a loom or a lake (see chapter 2) is the basis of the metaphorical dynamical brain, our understanding of the dynamics usually begins with its basic functional units, the neurons. As noted in table 16.1, there are many levels of organization of neurons in the brain, from the ion channels in their walls and the second messenger systems in their somata, to the (numerically) huge interconnected networks that insinuate their fingers into every area of the entire brain. Although it is surely these many temporal and spatial scales that together make of the brain a special kind of self-organizing system, analysis of brain activity usually begins with the neural action potential level. This is because one of the main ways neurons communicate among themselves and convey information from one place in the brain to another is by sending trains of action potentials along their axons to synapses with dendrites of still other neurons. Each action potential causes the release of transmitter substance across the synapse, stimulating the receiving neuron into firing action potentials of its own. Because the action potentials are virtually all identical, the information they convey must be encoded in their time relations. The neuron's instantaneous rate of firing (i.e., of generating action potentials) is the dimension usually considered to encode the information, but more recently the time interval between successive pulses has also been suggested as an encoding dimension (e.g., Singer 1999). Also, synchrony between the firing rates of several neurons in a network is supposed to be important, possibly as a solution to the "binding problem" of cognitive neuroscience (Engel et al. 1999; see chap. 35). Of course because it will be affected by the ever present noise, the transmission of information by neurons cannot be completely precise. The noise will manifest itself in changes in the rate with which action potentials are generated by the neuron, and possibly in changes in the speed with which each one propagates down the axon. The noise arises from sources such as fluctuations in the ionic concentrations inside and outside the axon and other "channel noise" (White, Rubenstein and Kay 2000), fluctuations in the temperature of the surrounding fluids, and the decaying effects of previous action potentials received by the neuron. Some channel noise has been shown to be $1/f$, probably arising from the vibration of hydrocarbon chains in the lipids in the nerve cell membrane affecting conductance of potassium ions through the membrane (Lundström and McQueen 1974). The effect of previous action potentials is perhaps the most interesting in the present context, however, because it resembles a memory or relaxation process source for $1/f$ noise. After each action potential is generated, the neuron experiences an absolute refractory period of about 1 msec, during which no new action potentials can be generated, and an exponentially decreasing relative refractory period of an additional several msec, during which the probability of generating a new action potential gradually increases. Thus the generation of a particular action potential affects the probability of generating another one for quite some time afterwards; the neuron "remembers" its previous activity and that memory is combined with current inputs to yield current activity.

Musha (1981) did some provocative experiments on the effects of previous action potentials on the time encoding of information by the giant axons of the squid, the easiest of all axons to work with, extensively studied since they were discovered by J. Z. Young. First, by exciting successive action potentials with an electrical pulse, Musha showed that the refractory period also decreases the speed of transmission of the action potential in the axon, dropping from near 25 m/sec for the first excitation to near 10 m/sec for later ones. Clearly, this would affect the encoding of information, whether the instantaneous rate of firing or the inter–action potential interval were the encoding dimension. After stimulating the axon with sequences of random electrical pulses (white noise), Musha recorded time series of the fluctuations in the time density (the inverse of transmis-

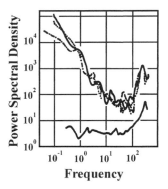
Frequency

Figure 17.1
Power spectra of speed of action potentials in squid giant axons. (From Musha 1981.)

sion speed) of action potentials traveling down the axon. The power spectra for several such time series of density fluctuations are shown in figure 17.1, along with the power spectrum of the electrical pulses that stimulated the action potentials (at the bottom of the graph). Below about 10 Hz, the action potential power spectra are approximately $1/f$, whereas the spectrum of the stimulating pulses in that frequency region is white (flat). Thus the neurons, the basic building blocks of the brain, themselves display $1/f$ noise in the foundational mechanism of information transmission, the conduction of action potentials along the axon. Interestingly, Musha and Higuchi (Musha, 1981) had demonstrated the resemblance of the fluctuations of action potential speed to fluctuations of the speed of automobiles in traffic. The $1/f$ fluctuations in the traffic model are attributed to the "bunching" of the cars as they are forced to slow down by their proximity to other cars, a property of a more general statistical queueing theory approach to $1/f$ noise first described by Bell (1960) and summarized in chapter 19.

17.2 Magnetoencephalogram Recordings

From the perspective of physics, the brain is a system with strong interactions of many degrees of freedom. It consists of perhaps 100 billion neurons, each with up to 10,000 connections to other neurons. These connections form hierarchical (and nonhierarchical) groups, from small groups of tens of neurons to large groups consisting of entire sensory, cognitive, or motor processing areas, such as the visual cortex, with many

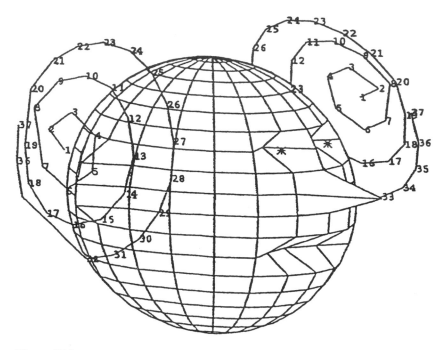

Figure 17.2
Positions of magnetoencephalogram (MEG) channels. (From Novikov et al. 1997.
© 1997 by The American Physical Society.)

millions of neurons. In physics, such systems are usually described by a
"similarity regime" (see sec. 18.3), in which similar behavior is observed
at several scales. Under certain conditions, a $1/f$ power spectrum of temporal fluctuations can arise from such a similarity regime. Novikov
et al. (1997) recorded the magnetoencephalogram to establish the existence of such a regime in the human brain. To do this, they had to use a
superconducting quantum interference device (SQUID), which allowed
them to record the magnetic field at the surface of the brain generated by
the flow of electrical current in and around neurons. They placed sensors
in an array around the heads of their two human subjects and had them
lie down in a relaxed way. The placement of the sensors is shown in figure
17.2. Then they recorded the magnetic field strength at each sensor location at 231.5 Hz (one record every $1/231.5 = 0.0043$ sec) for 30 min to
form time series for analysis.

Figure 17.3 shows a representative power spectrum from one of the
sensors for each of the two subjects (left, female; right, male). These

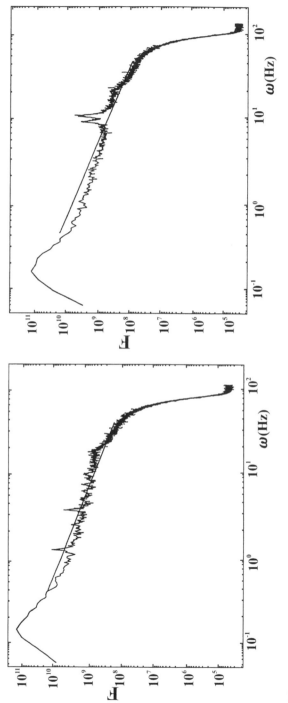

Figure 17.3
Power spectra of magnetoencephalogram (MEG) time series. (From Novikov et al. 1997. © 1997 by The American Physical Society.)

spectra show peaks at a few specific frequencies (about 1.5 and 4 Hz for the female; about 10 Hz for the male) reflecting endogenous brain rhythms such as the alpha wave (see sec. 17.3). More interesting are the average slopes of these power spectra, represented by the straight lines in the graphs. These lines have slopes of -1.03 and -1.19, respectively over the range 0.4 to 40 Hz, very near the -1 expected for $1/f$ fluctuations. Power spectra for other sensors were very similar. Moreover, taking the difference between pairs of sensors usually eliminated the peaks and yielded even more stable $1/f$ spectra. The average spectrum slopes for the two subjects over all pairs of sensors were -0.98 and -1.28, for the female and the male, respectively. Further analyses of the data established that the scale similarity implied by the $1/f$ spectra was relatively "local," meaning that it extended over only limited brain areas, probably related to the shared function of those areas. Thus the spontaneous activity of functionally related chunks of the human brain exhibits $1/f$ noise. This finding supports the assumptions made in chapter 16 regarding the origin of the $1/f$ spectra in human cognition.

17.3 Electroencephalogram and Event-Related Potential Recordings

A less exotic and less expensive way of noninvasively studying brain activity is to record the electrical field at the scalp generated by the electrical current flowing around and through the neurons when they generate action potentials (see Picton, Lins, and Scherg 1995). This recording is called the "electroencephalogram" (EEG), and its study has yielded much information about brain activity in humans. Among other things, common EEG brainwaves, such as the alpha wave can be used to classify mental illnesses (e.g., John 1977) and the stages of sleep (e.g., Dement 1974). When the EEG is used to record brain potential fluctuations over shorter intervals in response to particular sensory stimuli, the recording is called an "event-related potential" (ERP). Cognitive neuroscientists use ERPs extensively to characterize the brain activity related to stages of information processing in humans (see chap. 33). However, as might be expected, ERPs are small signals (often < 2 microvolts, or μv) buried in noise (often > 60μv). Thus the typical ERP study averages ERPs from many trials, taken in a sequence, and thus achieves a relatively clear and noise-free picture of the brain activity that occurred on each of the 50–100 or more trials on which a given stimulus was presented. Although it seems difficult if not impossible to imagine obtaining a time series of single ERPs that could be investigated with the fast Fourier transform (FFT), I and a col-

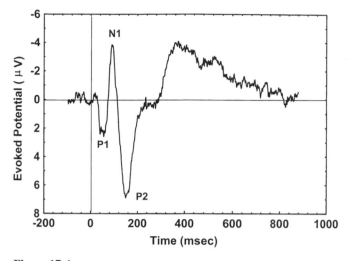

Figure 17.4
Typical event-related potential (ERP) at Cz location to a sound stimulus. (From McDonald and Ward 1998.)

league (McDonald and Ward 1998) did just that; schemes are being pro-posed (e.g., Jaśkowski and Verleger 1999) to remove at least some of the background noise from recorded individual ERPs in a more general way.

In our study, MacDonald and I used an ERP that was larger than most and very robust, one evoked by the presentation of a 50 msec, 1,000 Hz pure tone at 80 dB to a human subject seated in a very quiet (35 dB background noise) sound-attenuating room. In this context, the tone sounds fairly loud, and the ERP it evokes is quite large. Figure 17.4 shows one typical *average* ERP to this tone, averaged over 1,000 presenta-tions. Several things should be noted about such ERPs before we con-sider their temporal distribution. First, the graph displays the electrical voltage recorded at electrode site Cz, in the center of the top of the head, the best site at which to record the activity in the auditory cortices. At Cz, the electrode records electrical fields from both auditory cortices, located in the left and right temporal lobes of the brain, just above the ears, as well as from other brain areas. The electrical voltage at Cz was measured in reference to another electrode site, in this case a site just over the mas-toid bone at the base of the skull behind the ear. In figure 17.4, the elec-trical voltage is displayed as it varied over time from about 100 msec before the tone was presented to about 800 msec after the presentation began. Second, the prominent neural activity components labeled P1, N1,

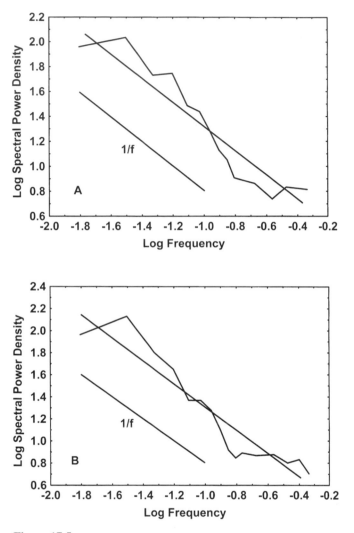

Figure 17.5
Power spectra of event-related potential (ERP) time series: (*A*) 5 msec before end of prestimulus baseline; (*B*) N1 peak amplitude. (From McDonald and Ward 1998.)

and P2 in figure 17.4 correspond to neural activity in the auditory cortices and elsewhere in the brain at different intervals after the tone was presented, Third, these components are quite large, for example, the N1 component deviates about 5 μv from baseline (the period to the left of the vertical axis at 0 msec), making them good candidates for a time series FFT analysis. Finally, the EEG during the baseline period is quite flat, indicating that the auditory cortex showed no systematic activity just before the onset of the tone.

McDonald and I recorded time series of 1000 ERPs from tones presented every 2 sec under two conditions, in one of which the subject ignored the tones and in the other of which he counted them. This made only a small difference to both the average ERPs (figure 17.4) and the FFT analyses, and so I will present only the count condition results. We decided to look at the time series formed from two points on the ERPs, one 5 msec before stimulus onset and the other 96 msec after it, at the average location of the N1 peak. We did FFTs on the time series formed from the 1,000 successive ERPs taken 2 sec apart at each of these points. Figure 17.5 shows the resulting power spectra, one from the N1 peak and one from the prestimulus period. Both are approximately $1/f$ and are typical of all of our results. Not only is the evoked activity of the brain $1/f$, but also the noise in which the evoked activity is embedded—and which possibly characterizes the process generating that evoked activity— is also $1/f$. It is clear that the human brain is characterized by $1/f$ noise in many activity regimes, from ion flow in neurons to activity evoked by external stimuli. The challenge now is to discover the functional implications of this fact.

Chapter 18

Models of $1/f$ Noise

The author has for some time believed that the inverse-frequency spectrum must be due to some form of *co-operative* phenomenon ... that it is a property of the behaviour of the whole complex of electrons in the conduction band, and not a property of the mechanisms associated with the individual electrons.

—D. A. Bell, *Electrical Noise*

18.1 The Simplest Case

The simplest, most direct way to produce a power spectrum defined by the equation

$$S(f) = 1/f^{\alpha} \tag{18.1}$$

is to add together a set of periodic (sine and cosine) functions with the frequency amplitude weighted according to equation 1.1 and random relative phase. Alternatively, we can produce the required power spectrum indirectly, by filtering a broadband noise through a low-pass filter with a shoulder that falls off as $1/f^{\alpha}$ (see Corsini and Saletti 1987). However, because they merely reproduce the definition, equation 18.1, these approaches seem like cheating. What is needed is a description of how colored noise, and in particular $1/f$ noise ($\alpha = 1$ in eq. 18.1), arises naturally and inevitably from the cooperative activity of the elements of dynamic systems (possibly at the "edge of chaos"; see Kauffman 1993). Outlined below are a few of the most compelling accounts of how $1/f$ noise can arise in dynamic systems. (One not covered in this chapter, but discussed in chapter 16, is the presence of correlations in a time series at several timescales covering at least two log units; others not covered here or in chapter 19 can be found mostly in the physics literature; just search for "$1/f$.")

18.2   Multiplicative Noise

Remember from chapter 14 that, when noise is added to a dynamical
equation (the Langevin approach) as in equation 14.2, the noise simply
blurs the dynamics. Caused by some force acting on the dynamical system
from the outside, such noise is called "external noise" (van Kampen
1987). Although in principle it can be switched off, in practice this is
seldom possible. In contrast, multiplicative noise is *internal* noise, arising
from the dynamical system itself. Being a part of the system's dynamics,
internal noise cannot even in principle be switched off; it is a collective
or systemic phenomenon arising because matter consists of particles or
because energy is quantized. The simplest way to model internal noise
is with a system in which such noise constitutes the *only* dynamics. An
example of this approach was created by Thurner, Feurstein, and Teich
(1997). They used a system composed of a set of variables $w_i(t)$, $i = 1$ to
N, where the value of each variable at time $t + 1$ equals its value at time t
multiplied by a noise term λ_i:

$$w_i(t + 1) = \lambda_i w_i(t), \tag{18.2}$$

and where λ_i is a sample from a probability distribution. The values of
λ_i are independent and identically distributed (i.i.d.; see chap. 14). The
system of N variables is "coupled," in other words, a correlation between
their values is introduced, by requiring that

$$\sum_{i=1}^{N} w_i(t) = N. \tag{18.3}$$

Thus, on each iteration of the model, after equation 18.2 has been applied
to fresh samples of noise, the new values of $w_i(t)$ are multiplied by

$$N / \sum_i w_i(t),$$

implementing equation 18.3. Notice that this also makes the average
value of the variables equal to 1 because, after the transformation,

$$\sum_i w_i(t)/N = N/N = 1.$$

The model also requires that

$$w_i(t) > w_0 \geq 0, \tag{18.4}$$

so that the noise tends to make all of the variable values larger, a tendency that is held in check by the application of equation 18.3 on each

iteration. Notice that, in this model, all changes in variable values are induced by the multiplicative noise. That is, without the influence of the multiplicative noise, there would be no dynamics at all.

Thurner, Feurstein, and Teich (1997) simulated the temporal unfolding of this multiplicative noise system on a computer, drawing the λ_i from a uniform distribution and recording the successive values taken by each of the N variables $w_i(t)$ at each time point t. They then calculated the fast Fourier transform (FFT) of the time series for a representative individual variable (i.e., an arbitrary value of i) and used it to obtain a typical power spectrum for the system. This spectrum approached $1/f$ as the lower bound w_0 approached zero, and was approximately flat (white noise) for $w_0 > 0.8$ and $N > 50$. In addition, the occurrence frequencies of values taken by the variables $w_i(t)$ over a large number of time steps were a power function of the values themselves, with the exponent depending on w_0, the other side of the self-organized criticality explanation of the $1/f$ power spectrum (see sec. 18.3).

A similar but more complicated approach is to combine additive and multiplicative noise according to the following general differential equation:

$$\frac{dx}{dt} = \lambda(t) \cdot x(t) + \eta(t), \tag{18.5}$$

where $x(t)$ is the system variable, $\lambda(t)$ is the multiplicative noise, and $\eta(t)$ is an additive noise (see Nakao 1998). The meaning of the different terms of equation 18.5 varies with the situation. For example, in an economic model, $x(t)$ could represent the wealth of a country; $\lambda(t)$, the (noisy) rate of change of wealth from internal production dynamics; and $\eta(t)$, noise from outside sources such as the world economy, wars in other countries, and so forth. Nakao (1998) and others have demonstrated that this model, which can be applied to many situations, both physical and nonphysical, does reproduce the prototypical power law of amplitudes and the associated $1/f$ power spectrum of systems characterized by self-organized criticality (see sec. 18.3).

18.3   Self-Organized Criticality

What do sandpiles, the game of life, earthquakes, turbulence in liquids, and stock prices have in common? According to Per Bak (1990), they are all examples of *self-organized criticality*, whereby a dissipative dynamical system with many degrees of freedom operates far away from equilibrium

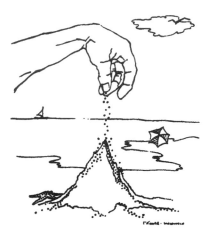

Figure 18.1
Self-organized sand pile. (From Bak 1990. © 1990. Reprinted with permission from Elsevier Science.)

near a point of instability, called "criticality"; because it does so by itself, without any fine-tuning by an external driving influence, the system is said to be "self-organized." At the point of instability, small fluctuations can give rise to events of any size, and the likelihood, or probability density, of any particular size of event, $D(s)$, is a power function of the event size, s:

$$D(s) = ks^{-\tau}. \tag{18.6}$$

In other words, the larger the event (the more elements it involves), the less likely it is to occur, although if we wait long enough, eventually an event of any size (up to the system size) will occur. For Bak (1990), the prototype of a self-organized critical system is a model of a sandpile created by dropping sand grains one at a time onto a particular location (fig. 18.1). As the pile grows, avalanches of various sizes occur until eventually the sides of the pile settle into a particular "critical" angle, at which the pile "is barely stable with respect to small perturbations" (Bak, Tang, and Wiesenfeld 1987, 382). As the sand grains continue to be dropped on the pile, avalanches of all sizes (up to the size of the pile) occur with a probability distribution like that described by equation 18.6. The sandpile looks the same no matter at what scale it is viewed, from the scale of the individual grain of sand to the scale of the movement of many grains in large avalanches. Such systems are called "self-similar."

How, then, do self-organized critical dynamical systems give rise to $1/f$ noise? According to Bak, Tang, and Wiesenfeld (1987), they do so inevitably in the following sense. First, the lifetime of an event in the system, t, is related to the size of the event, s, by the equation $t^{1+\gamma} \approx s$, or, solving for t, $t \approx \exp[\log s/(1 + \gamma)]$, where γ is the rate at which the event propagates across the system elements. For example, in the sandpile, t would be the lifetime of an avalanche; the larger the avalanche, the longer the lifetime because the larger avalanches take longer to occur, involving as they do energy transfers between many elements over large distances. Given this relation, the distribution of lifetimes can be calculated from the distribution of event sizes:

$$D(t) = (s/t) \cdot D(s(t)) \cdot \left(\frac{ds}{dt}\right) \approx t^{-(\gamma+1)\tau+2\gamma} \equiv t^{-\beta} \qquad (18.7)$$

The power spectrum of the probability density function of lifetimes (eq. 18.7) is given by

$$S(f) = \int [(t \cdot D(t))/(1 + (f \cdot t)^2)] \, dt \approx f^{-2+\beta}, \qquad (18.8)$$

which states that the power spectrum is a power function of frequency, f, with exponent equal to $-2 + \beta$ (you can ignore the integral expression in the middle if you find it puzzling). Thus a power law for the size distribution of events in a system exhibiting self-organized criticality (eq. 18.6) implies a power spectrum for the temporal fluctuations that is $1/f$-like. In fact, we can calculate the exponent of the power spectrum from the exponent of the size distribution, τ, and the rate of event propogation, γ, by plugging the expression for β from equation 18.7 into the expression for the exponent in equation 18.8. Using α for the exponent of the power spectrum function of f, as usual (eq. 18.1), we have $\alpha = -2 + [(\gamma + 1)\tau + 2\gamma]$. In a computer simulation example given by Bak, Tang, and Wiesenfeld (1987), τ was measured to be 0.98, and γ was about -0.188, which means that β was about 0.42 and the slope of the power spectrum $(-2 + \beta = -2 + 0.42)$ was -1.58. In other words, $S(f) \approx 1/f^{1.58}$. (Actually, Bak, Tang, and Wiesenfeld measured β directly and thus did not have to worry about γ; I inferred it from their numbers.) In another case, they obtained $\beta = 0.90$ and $S(f) \approx 1/f^{1.1}$. More recently, Maslov, Tang, and Zhang (1999) reported $1/f$ power spectra for the dynamics of model sandpiles confined to narrow stripes (almost one-dimensional). For these models, however, the $1/f$ power spectrum was not related to power

law distributions of avalanche sizes: the constraints on the sandpiles
resulted in the almost continual avalanches making only small changes to
the configuration of sand grains. The memory of the system for previous
configurations was nonetheless quite long and led to the observed $1/f$
power spectrum.

18.4   Center-Surround Neural Network

This model, based on the center-surround organization of neural networks in sensory systems and elsewhere in the brain, is perhaps the one
most directly relevant to dynamical cognitive science. Usher, Stemmler,
and Olami (1995) simulated a type of neural network that exhibits $1/f$
fluctuations in the temporal dynamics of individual units, although its
overall behavior is a type of self-organized criticality. They created a
100×100 lattice of model neurons, with each functioning like an integrate-and-fire neuron (see chap. 22), that is, each neuron summed exponentially decaying (20 msec time constant) voltage inputs and "fired" a
pulse if the total voltage reached a threshold. After firing, the neuron
voltage was reset by subtracting the threshold. Each model neuron
received excitatory inputs (pulses) from N other neurons in a disklike
region around it, and inhibitory inputs from a ring of N neurons outside
the disk. In other words, each neuron modeled the center-surround organization found in many regions of the brain, especially in sensory cortex
(see, for example, Zeki 1993). In addition, each cell received external
noise in the form of Poisson-distributed excitatory pulses of magnitude
$1/N$ arriving at a rate λ_P. The relative weights of the excitatory and
inhibitory inputs were $W_E = \alpha/N$ and $W_I = \beta W_E$.

Of course the behavior of this network varies with the values of the
parameters α, β, and λ_P. When β, the relative weighting of inhibitory
inputs to each neuron, is a substantial fraction of α, the relative weighting
of excitatory inputs, for example $\alpha = 1.3$ and $\beta = 0.67$, clusters of high
firing activity develop and move around the lattice. Figure 18.2 shows the
path of one such cluster over successive 50 msec intervals (1 msec is the
simulated cycle time of the network, activity is summed over 50 msec
intervals to yield the clusters). Interestingly, the behavior of these clusters
varies as a function of the external noise input λ_P. When λ_P is relatively
small, the clusters move randomly, but as λ_P is increased, the movements
take on a pattern, becoming unidirectional at high values of λ_P, which
results in diagonal stripes in the long-term average activity picture. At

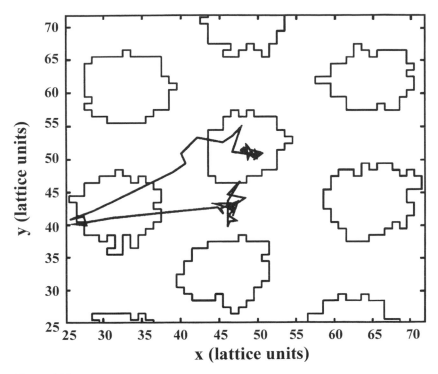

Figure 18.2
High-activity clusters move on the center-surround lattice. (From Usher, Stemmler, and Olami 1995. © 1995 by The American Physical Society.)

intermediate values of λ_P, the movement ceases and the clusters show a rigid spatial structure.

Where, then, is the $1/f$ noise in all of this? It turns out that the behavior of single units in the lattice exhibits the required fluctuations, but only for certain parameter values. First, the values of α and β must be appropriate for producing the slowly moving clusters shown in figure 18.2. Then the value of λ_P must be such that the clusters are in the transition region between "fluid" (random movement) and "crystalline" (no-movement) regimes. Under these conditions time series of the individual units' firing rates show near-$1/f$ fluctuations. Now, apparently, under these same conditions changes in the value of β also change the responsiveness of the model neurons to "stimuli," in this case small changes in the external input rate λ_P. Figure 18.3 shows the mean spike rate per millisecond for a region of the lattice of model neurons where the external

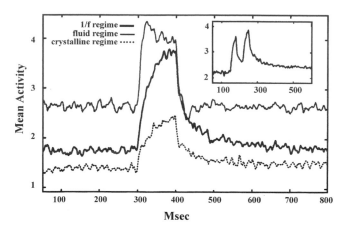

Figure 18.3
Responses of model neurons in various parameter regimes to stimuli; note priming
effect in inset. (From Usher, Stemmler, and Olami 1995. © 1995 by The American
Physical Society.)

input rate to the excitatory center neurons of the region was raised by
12% for a brief interval. Such a stimulus, is equivalent to a brief change in
the mean amount of energy impinging on a sensory receptor, for example,
a flash of light to the retina of the eye. For lower values of β, which result
in relatively less inhibition from the surrounding inhibitory neurons, the
system is more fluid (and the power spectrum more like white noise), and
the model neurons exposed to the stimulus give a very strong but quickly
decaying response, which indicates no "memory" (top trace of fig. 18.3).
For higher values of β, which result in relatively more inhibition from the
surrounding neurons, the system is more rigid or crystalline (and the
power spectrum more like black noise), the stimulated neurons respond
only weakly to the stimulus, and the weak response decays only slowly
to baseline, indicating perhaps too much "memory" even for a weak
response (bottom trace). For the value of β that yields $1/f$ fluctuations,
however, the response from the stimulated neurons is both vigorous and
has just the right amount of memory, like Baby Bear's porridge, decaying
to a level close to baseline over an interval of about 100 msec (middle
trace). Priming is said to have occurred when presentation of a stimulus
facilitates the response to a subsequent stimulus presentation (e.g., Posner
1978), as demonstrated by the response to two successive stimuli illustrated in the inset of figure 18.3, where the response to the second stim-

ulus, which occurs while the response to the first is still decaying and is relatively far from baseline, is even more vigorous than the first response. Priming is a ubiquitous psychological phenomenon observed in many paradigms, from memory to attention to perception and even possibly subliminal perception (e.g., Marcel 1983). That this neural network exhibits priming *only* in the $1/f$ parameter regime implies that there might be something special about that regime in neural computation and in the functioning of real brains.

Chapter 19

Statistical Theory of $1/f$ Noise

The simplicity of the $1/f$ spectrum encourages speculation ... that some general statistical considerations may account for it.... It appears that the prevalence of $1/f$ noise is nearly equivalent to the assertion that distribution functions for logarithms of rates tend not only to be broad but to have wings that fall off much less sharply than Gaussians.

—M. B. Weissman, "Survey of Recent $1/f$ Theories"

Differentiating a logarithmic cumulative distribution results in a $1/f$ spectral density....

—Stefan Machlup, "Earthquakes, Thunderstorms, and Other $1/f$ Noises"

One cannot understand a $1/f$ noise without searching beyond its spectrum and the search for a single explanation becomes hopeless.

—Benoit Mandelbrot, *Multifractals and $1/f$ Noises*

19.1 What Must Be Explained

The characterization of $1/f$ noise depends on the concept of a power spectrum, which is the square of a Fourier transform of a time series, a correlation function, or a probability distribution arising from some kind of a random process. The temporal structure of the stochastic process is revealed through the distribution of frequencies of deterministic periodic functions of time. Although this idea is accepted today, it was not always. In his excellent discussion of electrical noise, Bell (1960) mentioned that at one time it was seriously questioned whether a time-varying random process could properly be said to possess a power spectrum, or even a Fourier transform. Because a mathematical technique can be applied wherever the conditions for its application exist, a Fourier transform of any function can be obtained. The result may not have any meaning, however, and this is what was questioned. It is now clear that not only does the Fourier transform of a temporal random process exist, it also has a meaning that is similar to, although somewhat more abstract than, that of a Fourier transform of any other time-varying function, with obvious implications for the existence of the power spectra of random processes. In fact, the concept of the Fourier transform applies strictly only to mathematical functions and all such are abstractions. Any application to real measurements is only approximate, almost always through the fast Fourier transform (FFT), although if the measurements are exquisitely fine and frequent, the approximation can be very close. Thus a random process does have a meaningful power spectrum, even if it is only flat, as in white noise.

Another problem with the characterization of $1/f$ noise is that the $1/f$ power spectrum can be strictly true only over a very limited range of frequencies; there must be both high- and low-frequency bend points. The high-frequency bend point exists because Planck's constant determines a scale, the quantum scale, for both length and time (the Planck length and the Planck time). Above this point, the power spectrum of a $1/f$ noise becomes $1/f^2$ (e.g., Machlup 1981). The low-frequency bend point exists because of the Nyquist limit: the measurement time must be at least the inverse of the frequency (e.g., to measure noise at 0.1 Hz, measurement time must be at least 10 sec). But in practical situations, the limits are even narrower than this. Measurement times are usually severely limited, and only the most esoteric (and expensive) experiments reach even halfway to Planck limits. Thus we are usually looking at power spectra that are $1/f$-like over only a few decades (powers of 10) of frequency, sometimes only over one decade. Moreover, the spectra involved are usually obtained via the FFT, as mentioned earlier, the square of which measures the power spectral density in a small set of rather large (e.g., 1/32 octave), discrete frequency bands. Thus, although pure theory often stumbles over technical issues, the need for explanation is actually for a much less demanding set of facts. What must be accounted for is (1) that the power spectrum of a time series is $1/f$-like over one or more decades of frequency, and (2) that such power spectra are so ubiquitous—they appear far more often in time series than would be expected on the basis of "ordinary physics" or even of "ordinary cognitive science."

19.2 Queuing in a Wire

Scientists have been searching for a more general explanation of $1/f$-like noise for many years, and it was early recognized that some general statistical considerations might be deeply implicated (see Weissman epigraph above). Bell (1960) was one of those who searched, and he proposed an ingenious theory, based on statistical queuing theory, of how $1/f$ noise arises in current fluctuations in an electrical circuit. In Bell's theory, as is common in physics and electronics, electrical current is conceptualized in terms of the flow of *carriers* (either electrons, which have negative charge, or "holes," which have positive charge) through a wire. Let us think in terms of electrons in a copper wire. The electrons can exist in an electron shell around an atom in a bound state—or in an excited, unbound state, where they are free to move through the wire with other excited electrons in what is called the "conduction band." The electron is excited from the bound state by the absorption of a quantum of energy (a photon). After it spends some time in the conduction band, participating in the current flow, it can fall back into the bound state by emitting a photon and joining the other electrons bound to a particular electron shell around a specific atom or molecule. This process repeats itself at random times throughout the duration of the current flow. In other words, the electrons oscillate randomly between bound and excited states. It is some aspect of this process that generates "current noise," which has a $1/f$ spectrum over many decades of frequency.

Bell (1960) conceptualized the problem of explaining current noise in a different way from the usual. Instead of asking how long, on average, a carrier stays in the conduction band, he asked, "If a carrier has once been excited into the conduction band, how long is it likely to remain there before it (rather than its neighbors which may have arrived in the conduction band earlier or later) chances to fall back to a bound level." (Bell 1960, 231) From this point of view, the problem appears to be one of congestion: for a given electron to fall back into a bound state, there must be a "vacancy" in the vicinity. The vacancy the electron left when it moved into the conduction band may not be available, either because it moved away or because some other electron now occupies its former home. Moreover, wherever it is, there is likely to be a lineup (or queue) for the available vacancies in the bound state (available electron shells with fewer than a full complement of electrons) because, by chance, electrons may have bunched up at a particular place in the wire (even though other vacancies may have no lineup and may stay vacant for a long time). Thus, even though the average time an electron spends in the conduction band may be only a few microseconds, the fluctuations of the number of electrons in the conduction band, which are the source of current noise, can exhibit periodicities over tens of thousands of seconds. Figure 19.1

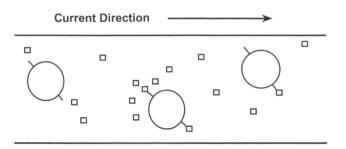

Figure 19.1
Cartoon of carriers (squares) queuing in a wire.

shows a cartoon of this situation: the circles represent copper atoms with (for illustrative purposes only) two electron sites (short lines on the circle) per atom. If an electron site is occupied by an electron (small square), then that site is not available for any other electrons to occupy. The atom in the center of the diagram is shown with several electrons clustering around it. None of these electrons can occupy either site in the atom until one of the electrons in one of the sites leaves the site vacant by joining the conduction band. Thus there is a queue of electrons in the conduction band waiting for a vacant site in that area of the wire, even though there are vacant sites in another atom some distance away (at the left of the wire).

The statistical description of this queuing situation, called "queuing theory," has been known for some time (see Feller 1968, 1971). Bell (1960) was able to (loosely) map the situation of electrons flowing in an electrical current through a wire onto a particular variation of queuing theory. In particular, he was able to discover an expression for the probability distribution of the time an electron spent waiting in a queue. Each probability density in the density function was a summation of a set of exponential distributions that had a time constant τ_i. Bell argued that the various exponential distributions in the sum should be equally weighted because each had an equal probability of occurring. It was known that a time series generated by summing samples from such an equally weighted set of exponential distributions with widely varying time constants leads to a power spectrum that is proportional to $1/f$, whereas the power spectrum of a time series formed from samples from a single exponential distribution is proportional to $1/f^2$. Bell therefore concluded that the $1/f$ power spectrum of current noise arises from the statistical properties of the electrons' queuing behavior while in the conduction band. He also showed that various departures of power spectra from $1/f$, in particular, the dependence of the slope of the power spectrum on the particular conductor or semiconductor (the material from which transistors are made), can be explained by variations in how the summation arises or in the limits over which it occurs.

Bell's approach (1960) was one of the first to offer a general explanation for why so many real dynamical systems exhibit $1/f$-like power spectra. It is sufficient that some process of the system generate an equally weighted set of exponential distributions with a wide range of time constants that all sum to produce at least a part of the time-varying behavior of the system. As an interesting corollary, this process is most likely to be a cooperative phenomenon, one that results from the interactions of all of the system's elements (e.g., the queuing of carriers in a wire), rather than from the actions of individual elements. Indeed, it may be useful to think of it as a queuing process in a very general sense, although there are other stochastic processes that could result in the required statistical description of temporal behavior. For example, a collection of neurons could generate $1/f$-like fluctuations because of the action of reverberatory circuits at several timescales, as described in section 16.2: the necessary exponential distributions with different time constants would be generated as circuits of different sizes "relaxed" or "forgot" their response to a particular input. The larger the number of neurons involved (or entrained) in the circuit, the more slowly it would relax to the unperturbed state (the larger would be the time constant for that distribution). In such a case, queuing theory would not describe the route to the required set of exponential distributions, and the relaxation approach would lead to a better mechanistic understanding.

19.3   ARIMA(1, 0, 0)

Another interesting aspect of the example explored in chapter 16 is that the set of exponential distributions need not be complete for an approximation of a $1/f$ spectrum to exist. In that example, only three relaxation processes are involved and the approximation is quite close. Moreover, because the three are ARIMA(1, 0, 0), or AR(1), processes (as hereafter abbreviated; see chap. 11), that is, linear autoregressive processes, the dynamical processes need not be nonlinear. The most important requirements of the set of distributions involved are (1) that there be several of them; (2) that their time constants be spread over at least two decades;

and (3) that they be more or less equally weighted. These three requirements correspond to those stated in chapter 16: several widely spread timescales and no one preferred timescale. Thus what I am asserting here is that *any* process giving rise to these properties will exhibit $1/f$-like fluctuations. Dynamical systems made up of many complexly interacting elements will often exhibit this kind of fluctuation because of the cooperative or emergent behavior of the elements in producing the dynamical behavior of the system (see chap. 6). The challenge is to show, in any particular instance, just how the necessary exponential distributions and time constants arise.

Several authors have argued that particular combinations of linear processes can be responsible for $1/f$-like behavior. Milotti (1995) developed a modern version of Bell's model (1960) of current noise that depends only on linear processes and some very general mathematical properties of them. Hausdorff and Peng (1996) showed that the simple linear superposition (summation) of random processes acting on several timescales, in a process they called "multiscaled randomness," could lead to $1/f$-like behavior similar to that found in many biological systems. Granger (1980; Granger and Ding 1996), an economist, was perhaps the first to suggest aggregating AR(1) processes to produce time series exhibiting $1/f$-like behavior. His work has been developed further by mathematicians (e.g., Leipus and Viano 2000). Finally, Kaulakys and Meškauskas (1998) and Kaulakys (1999), apparently unaware of the earlier work, proposed using events whose recurrence times obey an AR(1) process to produce $1/f$ noise.

In Greenwood and Ward 2001, we attempted to generalize this AR(1) approach. As noted in equation 11.2, an AR(1) process is written

$Y_t = \phi_1 Y_{t-1} + a_t,$

where here $0 < \phi_1 < 1$ and a_t is a sample from a white noise process. If $\phi_1 = 0$, then the process just produces a time series of samples of white noise, which has a flat power spectrum, whereas if $\phi_1 = 1$ the process is an integrative process, for example, a random walk, and produces a time series with a power spectrum proportional to $1/f^2$. Consider that the flat power spectrum of a time series of white noise samples is equivalent to a spectrum proportional to $1/f^0$. Thus, as others have also noticed, the $1/f$ power spectrum is in some sense *between* the power spectra produced by these two limiting AR(1) processes. We speculated that perhaps the power spectra of AR(1) processes with parameter values between those producing the limiting power spectra would be close to $1/f$, or at least $1/f$-like.

Although the power spectra of time series generated from individual AR(1) processes with $0 < \phi_1 < 1$ are not completely linear in a log-log plot, they do have linear sections at the higher frequencies, and the slopes of these sections are between 0 and -2, approaching these numbers as limits as the parameter value of the AR(1) process approaches 0 or 1, respectively. Importantly, when several such AR(1) processes, with parameters sufficiently far apart, are added together to form a single time series, the entire power spectrum becomes roughly linear in a log-log plot, reflecting the $1/f$-like behavior of the time series. Figures 19.2A and 19.2B reiterate the point that only three such processes are sufficient (notice that, again, we have averaged groups of points at higher frequencies in these spectra, as recommended by Mandelbrot 1998). Indeed, the more such processes are added together, the flatter the power spectrum becomes. Figure 19.2A was created from FFTs of 100 separate realizations of time series 1,024 observations long, each made up of the sum of three AR(1) processes—with white noise sampled from $N(0, 1)$ and with parameters (ϕ_1) of 0.1, 0.5, and 0.9. Figure 19.2B shows an analytical calculation of the same power spectrum, obtained by adding together the calculated power spectra of the three separate AR(1) processes:

$$S_{total}(f) = S_{0.1}(f) + S_{0.5}(f) + S_{0.9}(f), \tag{19.1}$$

where the power spectrum for each separate process with parameter ϕ_i was calculated from

$$S_i(f) = \frac{1}{2\pi(1 + \phi_i^2 - 2\phi_i \cos f)}, \tag{19.2}$$

taken from Brockwell and Davis 1996. Clearly, the summated AR(1) process gives a good approximation to a $1/f$ power spectrum (slopes of both straight lines are -1.03), in this case, across about two decades of frequency. Thus the simple aggregation of linear random processes at several scales can give rise to a time series with a $1/f$ power spectrum (cf. Hausdorff and Peng 1996).

19.4 Multifractals and Wild Self-Affinity

In his several works on multifractals, Benoit Mandelbrot (e.g., 1998) has made arguments similar to those above. Pointing out the several mechanisms by which $1/f$-like power spectra can arise, he evocatively described the exotic and subtle manifestations of such mechanisms, in particular, ways in which the time series arising from different mechanisms differ,

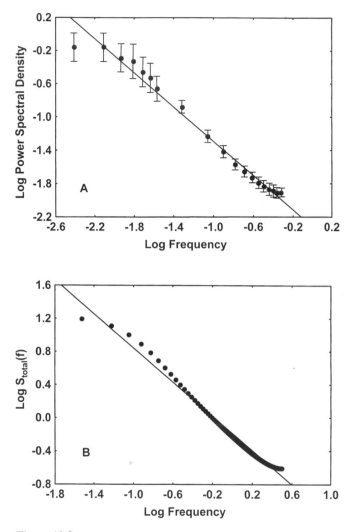

Figure 19.2
(*A*) Approximate $1/f$ power spectrum (mean ± 1 sd) from a Monte Carlo simulation of the sum of three first-order autoregressive [AR(1)] processes; (*B*) approximate $1/f$ power spectrum calculated for the sum of three AR(1) processes. (From
Greenwood and Ward 2001.)

despite their similar power spectra. However, I disagree with his conclusion that there is no real commonality between these mechanisms except that revealed by their power spectra. The statistical considerations described above provide a unifying theme that goes beyond the mere specification of a $1/f$ power spectrum. In particular, the statement that cooperative systemic behavior leads to $1/f$-like fluctuations seems to me to be a powerful explanatory device. A marriage of general systems theory with "complexity theory" (which relies on discovering $1/f$ power spectra but seldom goes further) promises new directions for both.

Mandelbrot's main point (1998) is that the $1/f$ power spectrum is only one of a set of symptoms for what he holds to be a more fundamental concept, *self-affinity*, which requires that the graph of the function specifying a process be invariant under a set of linear transformations (i.e., stretching or shrinking along each axis). Mandelbrot argues that, for the power spectrum of a noise to be proportional to $f^{-\alpha}$, it is sufficient that the noise be self-affine (and also not too weird). Because he has experienced no case of $1/f$ noise that is not self-affine, he uses "$1/f$ noise" and "self-affinity" interchangeably, although he believes that the two terms do not have the same explanatory status: "The analytic term $1/f$ *noise* is misleadingly specific, while the geometric term *self-affinity* is realistically general" (81). If self-affinity and $f^{-\alpha}$ power spectra imply each other (see Greenwood and Ward 2001), then either can be seen as fundamental. However, as is his wont, Mandelbrot opts for the geometric description as more revealing and more fundamental. This point of view resembles that of the promoters of chaos theory (see chaps. 23–27). It reveals a tension between the classical way of doing science, which depends heavily on analytic descriptions of phenomena and theories, and the many competing new paradigms, such as chaos theory, complexity theory, and Mandelbrot's self-affinity theory, which often depend on geometric arguments and descriptions. Such descriptions can be less satisfying than classical ones, although sometimes they are all that is possible (see Kellert 1993). At any rate, Mandelbrot (1998) provides many tools for the further specification of wildly self-affine processes in terms of the mechanisms from which they arise. Such specification is surely of value any time the mechanism of a $1/f$-like noise is to be explained.

Chapter 20

Stochastic Resonance

Noise in dynamical systems is usually considered a nuisance. But in certain non-linear systems, including electronic circuits and biological sensory apparatus, the presence of noise can in fact enhance the detection of weak signals. This phenomenon, called stochastic resonance, may find useful application(s)....

—Kurt Wiesenfeld and Frank Moss, "Stochastic Resonance and the Benefits of Noise"

20.1   What is Stochastic Resonance?

Stochastic resonance (SR) is a nonlinear cooperative effect in which large-scale stochastic (random) fluctuations (e.g., noise) are entrained by an independent, often periodic, weak fluctuation, or signal, with the result that the weak signal fluctuations are amplified, with sometimes spectacular results. In other words, the noise displays the same periodic behavior as the signal, even though the signal is very weak, and even though the noise has no periodic behavior of its own. Chapters 21 and 22 discuss many situations of interest to cognitive scientists in which SR arises naturally, among them sensation and perception in general, detection of prey and predators in particular, and the functioning of neurons and groups of neurons, including synchronization of neural oscillations and other exotic phenomena of dynamical computational neuroscience. (Thus, if you need to be motivated to dig into the meat of stochastic resonance, skim those later chapters first, then read this chapter, then go back and read chapters 21 and 22 again, this time with enhanced understanding.)

Stochastic resonance was originally proposed as a mechanism whereby large fluctuations in the global climate of the earth (i.e., ice ages) could be explained by statistical resonance of the earth's temperature fluctuations with small regular fluctuations in the amount of solar energy reaching the earth's surface caused by perturbations of the earth's orbit around the

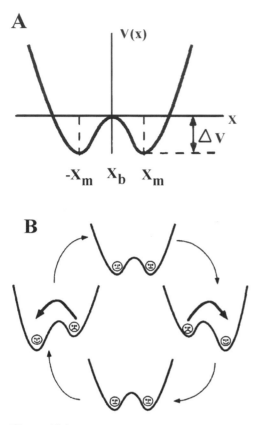

Figure 20.1
(*A*) Double-well potential; (*B*) effect of sine wave on probability of movement by a "kick" from well to well. (From Gammaitoni et al. 1998. © 1998 by The American Physical Society.)

sun. The mystery was how such small fluctuations in what is called "insolation" could cause large fluctuations such as the ice ages, during which earth's average temperature was many degrees below normal. To explain this effect, the earth's climate was modeled by a simple physical system called a "double-well potential" (figure 20.1A), in which noise-induced hopping between the two stable states, ice age and non–ice age, was synchronized with the weak periodic forcing caused by variations in the earth's orbit around the sun (Benzi, Sutera, and Vulpiani 1987). To explain the ice ages, the noise that induced the state changes was taken to be the yearly fluctuations in amount of solar radiation, which are not only random but also quite large and fast compared to the very small, slow, periodic fluctuations in solar radiation caused by the changes in the earth's orbit around the sun.

Stochastic resonance in the double-well potential system has been very well analyzed. Picture a tiny particle sitting in one of the two depressions (the stable states or "potential wells") in the diagram of figure 20.1A. If it were not acted on by any force, it would just sit there. However, suppose there is noise (random energy inputs to the system), and every once in a while the particle gets a "kick" (perhaps it is hit by a stray photon of light) that causes it to move toward the hump in the middle (the potential barrier). If the kick is large enough, the particle will jump over the hump, out of the well it is in, and into the other one. Clearly, the average time between such well-to-well jumps will depend on how often the particle is kicked by an amount equal to or greater than required to get over the hump. The average waiting time (T_w) is the inverse of the average rate (r_K) at which such jumps occur, called "Kramer's rate" after the physicist H. A. Kramers (1940), who derived it, and written

$$r_K = c \cdot e^{-\Delta V / \sigma}, \tag{20.1}$$

where c is a constant that depends on the particular characteristics of the physical system, ΔV is the height of the potential barrier (see fig. 20.1A), and e is the base of the natural logarithms ($e = 2.7183\ldots$). Thus the average waiting time can be written

$$T_w = \frac{1}{r_K} = \frac{1}{c \cdot e^{-\Delta V / \sigma}} = \frac{e^{\Delta V / \sigma}}{c}. \tag{20.2}$$

Clearly, for a particular double-well system characterized by a potential barrier ΔV, the average waiting time depends inversely on σ, the standard deviation of the statistical distribution of the noise (e.g., the standard deviation of a normal, bell-shaped, distribution): the larger the value of σ, the smaller the value of $\Delta V / \sigma$, thus the smaller the value of $e^{\Delta V / \sigma}$ and the smaller the average waiting time.

Now imagine we have a system in which the particle is "forced" by another, periodic energy input, say $a \sin(\omega t)$, where ω is some frequency and t is time and a is the (very small) amplitude of the sine wave. This input varies smoothly with time, rising and falling around a mean value. The effect of this varying energy input on the double-well system can be imagined pictorially as causing the double-well system to tilt back and forth, as in figure 20.1B, not by enough to cause the particle to jump into the other well, but just by a little bit. At each instant of time, then, the particle will have some energy $a \sin(\omega t)$ added to it plus another, random kick by the noise. If the total of the two energy inputs is enough to exceed the barrier, then the jump will happen. Effectively, the addition of the periodic forcing the $a \sin(\omega t)$ lowers the barrier slightly in one direction or the other, meaning that the kick required from the noise is slightly smaller in the lowered direction (and larger in the other). Now, if the frequency of the tilting is about the same as the rate at which the noise-induced transitions would ordinarily happen (Kramer's rate, r_K), then the two are said to be in "stochastic resonance." In other words, if the average waiting time between the noise-induced transitions between wells is roughly equal to one-half the period of the forcing, then the noise-induced hopping will be highly likely to happen at just the same time that the bias in one direction or the other is greatest. This hopping is *stochastic* resonance because a jump does not happen every time; it is only highly likely to happen at certain times, and less likely to happen at other times in between. In fact, the likelihood of a jump at any moment of time exactly mirrors the ups and downs of the sine wave. For this to happen, the noise amplitude, σ, must be just right—this is called "tuning the noise." This requirement for tuning the noise is critical to the demonstration of stochastic resonance; the system is resonant with the forcing only for a certain range of σ, below which the noise-induced transitions are too rare for the forcing to be visible, and above which the noise-induced transitions are too common and the periodic component is buried in the noise.

Stochastic resonance has been demonstrated in many bistable physical systems (those having two stable states), in excitable systems (which have only one stable state and a threshold to an unstable excited state), and in threshold detectors (which have no dynamics but rather fire a pulse each time an input exceeds a threshold). Gammaitoni et al. (1998) have provided an extensive and detailed review of the many manifestations of SR in these contexts. Because all examples of SR are characterized by maximum sensitivity to a weak perturbation at an optimal level of noise, the notion of stochastic resonance has been generalized to one of information transmission from the weak perturbation through a threshold-dominated system (e.g., Moss, Pierson, and O'Gorman 1994). Because this "informational" stochastic resonance is fundamentally a threshold phenomenon, its essential characteristics can be revealed by a study of threshold detectors, such as the one I now describe. (Experimental studies of stochastic resonance in excitable systems such as neurons and people are discussed in chapters 21 and 22.)

20.2   Stochastic Resonance in a Threshold Detector

Consider a detector that ignores any input below a threshold value, $a > 0$, and that responds with a "pulse" (say an output of 1) whenever the input is greater than the threshold. Let there be a weak signal $s(t)$ that is a function of time and that takes values less than a at all times. For simplicity, we will take $a = 1$ and $s(t) < 1$, that is, the signal is always below threshold so that, without noise, the detector would not respond to it at all. Let $t_i = i/n$, $i = 1 \ldots n$, be equally spaced time points in a 1 sec sampling interval, where n is the number of samples. Noise is represented by independent random variables ε_i with common continuous distribution function F. Remember from chapter 14 that a distribution function is the integral of a probability density function considered as a function of the upper limit of integration, x_u. Although F can be any distribution function we will assume that it is the distribution function of the Gaussian density function that has mean 0 and standard deviation σ. Thus

$$F(x_u) = \int_{-\infty}^{x_u} \frac{1}{\sigma\sqrt{2\pi}} \cdot e^{-x^2/2\sigma^2} \, dx. \tag{20.3}$$

At each time point the input to the detector is the noisy signal $s(t_i) + \varepsilon_i$. Whenever $s(t_i) + \varepsilon_i > a$ the detector fires. I will call these instances "exceedances," indicating that the noisy signal has exceeded the threshold, and they will be represented by the number "1." Thus the output of the detector, X_i, will be 1 if and only if there is an exceedance, and 0 otherwise. According to probability theory (see Greenwood, Ward, and Wefelmeyer 1999), the probability of an exceedance in this situation, $p(t_i)$, is

$$p(t_i) = 1 - F[a - s(t_i)]. \tag{20.4}$$

This situation is illustrated in figure 20.2, where the signal is a sine wave and $\sigma = 1$, and the y-axis represents the amplitude of the noisy signal at each time point. Notice the line at "1" on the y-axis: any dot above that line is an exceedance. The number of exceedances per unit time over short segments of time where the signal is roughly the same depends on the distance of the signal from the threshold over that time interval. Moreover, it should also be clear that noise with a smaller standard deviation will lead to less vertical spread of the noisy signal and to fewer exceedances everywhere, whereas noise with a larger standard deviation will have the opposite effect. Thus, for suitable σ, the signal is well represented by the time density of exceedances. Figure 20.3 shows the exceedances in

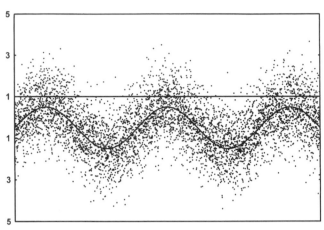

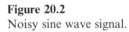

Figure 20.2
Noisy sine wave signal.

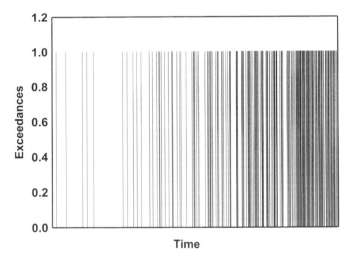

Figure 20.3
Exceedances from part of signal in figure 20.2.

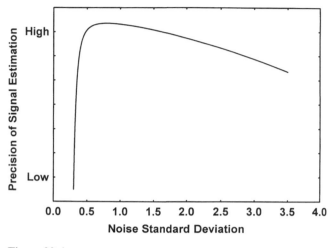

Figure 20.4
Typical stochastic resonance curve.

part of the signal from figure 20.2. It is clear that the time density of these varies regularly, although noisily, with the distance of the signal from the threshold of "1." It is easily possible to determine which part of the sine wave gave rise to this set of exceedences—it is the part from the trough of one cycle to the peak of the next.

To obtain an expression for an estimate of the signal at any given time point, $\hat{s}_h(t_i)$, we insert an estimate of $p(t_i)$ into equation 20.4 and solve for the estimate of $s(t_i)$, putting the little hats on $p(t_i)$ and $s(t_i)$ to indicate that these are estimates. The result is

$$\hat{s}_h(t_i) = a - F^{-1}[1 - \hat{p}_h(t_i)], \tag{20.5}$$

where the h subscript appears because of the way we estimate $p(t_i)$, averaging over a local region of size $2h$ around each time point (Müller 2000). Providing we know what the distribution function of the noise is, and that it has an inverse, we can estimate the signal at each time point by plugging the value of a and $F^{-1}[1 - \hat{p}_h(t_i)]$ into equation 20.5 and solving. The mean squared error of estimate for the entire signal, $MSE(h, t) = E(\hat{s}_h(t) - s(t))^2$, can be calculated approximately for large n for a known signal, or even for various ranges of signals (see Müller 2000). In fact, the "wiggliness" of the signal (its derivatives) and the standard deviation of the noise distribution both affect the mean squared error for a given sampling rate and threshold. If we assume that the noise is normally distributed, the threshold is 1, and the first and second derivatives of the signal are between -2 and 2, and then calculate the worst-case approximate mean squared error for a given σ, we obtain the values plotted in figure 20.4. As it turns out, this is a standard stochastic resonance curve, demonstrating the "tuning" of the noise. The y-axis of the graph is proportional to the amount of information recovered about the signal from the exceedances alone, rising steeply from near 0 at low values of σ to a peak at somewhat higher values and then gradually falling as σ increases further. The peak is at the value of σ at which the amount of noise is "just right" to reveal the subthreshold signal's fluctuations in the exceedances without swamping them.

Curves like that of figure 20.4 are diagnostic of the informational type of stochastic resonance and similar curves appear in physical stochastic resonance. They have been produced for many types of signals and many types of nonlinear systems, including signals that have no periodic components (random signals) and physical systems that have no strict thresholds (see Gammaitoni et al. 1998 for a review). The above-mentioned method of estimating the signal from the exceedances has been extended to the case of unknown signals with good results (Müller and Ward 2000). The technique is complicated, and works better for relatively smooth signals than for the more wiggly ones, but it gives good signal recovery for a wide range of subthreshold signals, and it is based on well-understood statistical procedures (see also Greenwood et al. 1999). Because we can now calculate the expected information recovery whenever a known subthreshold signal and its associated noise are to be estimated, we can know in advance whether a given signal can be efficiently recovered. These techniques should also be useful in modeling various systems that must contend with weak signals buried in noise, such as those discussed in chapter 21.

Chapter 21

Stochastic Resonance and Perception

Broadband stochastic resonance is manifest in the peripheral layers of neural processing in a simple sensory system, and ... it plays a role over a wide range of biologically relevant stimulus parameters.

—Jacob E. Levin and John P. Miller, "Broadband Neural Encoding in the Cricket Cercal Sensory System Enhanced by Stochastic Resonance"

21.1 Detection of Weak Signals by Animals

The watery world of a rippling brook is an inspiration to poets, but a very dangerous place for a crayfish. It must swim there to obtain its own food, but much larger and faster creatures prowl the same waters, hoping to make a tasty meal of the hapless crayfish. Although the rhythmical movements made by a swimming fish disturb the water ahead of a predatory fish, the fish often attacks so fast that the information about its imminent arrival is not detected by its prey until too late. In this situation, an early warning system has clear survival advantages. If the faint signals of a predator's attack could be detected early enough, the prey might have enough time to take appropriate action and avoid being eaten. In the case of our crayfish, there are sensory cells that are specialized to detect weak, coherent water motions such as those produced by a swimming predatory fish. The tiny hairs protruding from these cells bend in response to water motion, and this bending generates electrochemical signals, which are transmitted to the ganglia (interconnected groups of interneurons) that control escape movements. The hair cells react best to periodic bending of their hairs by water motion in just the frequency range produced by swimming predatory fish. The perennial problem for the crayfish is, can this sensory system detect the predatory fish in time for the crayfish to escape being eaten?

A rippling brook, or any other body of water, is a noisy place—it is constantly moving under the influence of so many factors that it is as if the creatures in it are immersed in a bath of white noise. This seems like the ideal place to exploit stochastic resonance. Perhaps the noisy water acts to amplify the weak signals of the crayfish's predators, allowing the crayfish to detect them earlier than it might otherwise with the apparatus at hand. In an attempt to simulate the actual watery environment of the crayfish, Douglass et al. (1993) generated weak, subthreshold, periodic (sine-wave) water motions like those of a swimming fish at a distance, and then added "white-water noise" (random water motions like those encountered on a white-water rafting trip) at various amplitudes to create noisy signals like those pictured in figure 20.2. In this noisy water, they immersed an excised piece of crayfish tail, which contained the required sensory hairs, as well as the nerve and ganglia connected to them. Recording the responses of single neurons in the nerve and the ganglia to various water motions, they compared the output of the crayfish neurons to the noisy weak periodic input signal by calculating the power spectrum (from a fast Fourier transform, or FFT; see chap. 14) of the time series of action potentials emitted by the neuron in response to the noisy signal.

Before taking up Douglass et al.'s results, let us briefly consider the common technique of power spectrum analysis in stochastic resonance situations. To begin with, if we calculated the power spectrum of the noisy input signal itself, the result would look something like figure 21.1, showing a "spike" of power at the frequency of the weak periodic signal (here a nominal 1 Hz; ignore the second, smaller spike at 2 Hz, the second harmonic of the signal), and a lower, flat, background representing the power spectrum of the noise. The ratio of the height of the spike to the

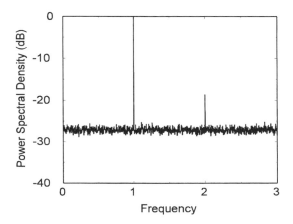

Figure 21.1
Power spectrum of a noisy periodic signal.

height of the noise is called the "signal-to-noise ratio" (SNR), and can be expressed as a difference in decibels (dB) between signal and noise. Because the y-axis in figure 21.1 is in decibels, the SNR of the spike at 1 Hz is just $0 - (-27)$ or about 27 dB. For the noisy input signal, the SNR would decrease as the noise increased because the background level in figure 21.1 would rise, but the signal level would stay the same (at 0). In the time series of action potentials from the sensory neurons exposed to the water motions, the SNR at the signal frequency indicates the extent to which the variation in the neuron's output of action potentials mirrors the ups and downs of the subthreshold periodic signal. A typical power spectrum of such a time series would also resemble figure 21.1, except that often the second, smaller spike would also be present. If stochastic resonance were present, a graph of SNR versus noise level for the sensory neurons should resemble figure 20.4, at first increasing and then gradually decreasing as the noise level increases. Notice that this is quite different from what happens with the SNR of the input signal itself, which steadily decreases with increasing noise. It is this paradox that makes stochastic resonance so intriguing.

Turning to Douglass et al.'s results (1993), let us look at the SNR for one sensory neuron in their experiment, shown by the solid squares in figure 21.2. Each square represents a measurement of the SNR for

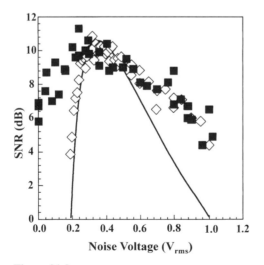

Figure 21.2
Stochastic resonance in the crayfish mechanoreceptor (From Wiesenfeld and Moss 1995. Reprinted with permission from *Nature*. © 1995, Macmillan Magazines, Limited.)

responses of the neuron to the noisy signal for a different amplitude of water noise. Stochastic resonance is clearly present, for the SNR of the neuron's response reaches a peak at an intermediate level of water noise. The open squares in the figure represent the SNR values for a computer simulation of a model neuron (see chap. 22; Moss et al. 1993) and the solid line a theoretical curve that characterizes many systems displaying stochastic resonance. The actual neuron responses are highly similar to those of the simulated neuron except at low noise levels. Douglass et al. speculated that this is because the actual neuron also has *internal* noise that may increase its ability to follow a subthreshold signal even in the absence of external water noise.

Other animals also seem to use stochastic resonance in a similar way to avoid predators or to capture prey. For example, it is thought that crickets avoid wasp predators at least partially through using stochastic resonance to detect very weak air currents generated by their attackers (Levin and Miller 1996). In this case, through similar experiments, Levin and Miller demonstrated that a combination of random air currents and the faint vibrations made by a predatory wasp's wings can be detected by the cricket's cercal hair cells well before they become detectable in the absence of the "air noise." Moreover, the noise-induced enhancement of coherence of the cricket's sensory response with the subthreshold signal occurred in just the frequency range of air movements generated by the wasp predator, and for just the same faint intensity of air motions where crickets really do escape from wasps. It thus seems plausible that the mechanism is actually in use by these noisy creatures.

Stochastic resonance appears in mammalian sensory systems as well. Collins, Imhoff, and Grigg (1996a) excised a piece of a rat's skin, along with its mechanoreceptors and the slowly adapting nerve fiber that comprised the axons of the receptor neurons, placed it in an appropriate physiological apparatus, and made recordings of individual receptors' action potentials emitted in response to precisely measured touches on the piece of skin. The touches varied in intensity corresponding to a near-threshold, slowly but randomly varying signal to which the receptors seldom responded. Random "touch noise" was also added to the skin stimulus. The correlation between the resulting noisy touch signal and the momentary firing frequency of the touch neurons was maximal for an intermediate level of touch noise, again displaying stochastic resonance, in this case, for an aperiodic signal.

Such experiments show that animals *can* use stochastic resonance in their sensory systems to avoid predators (or detect prey) but do they

actually do so? The first experiment to show that an animal does use stochastic resonance to its advantage was reported by Russell, Wilkens, and
Moss (1999), who put juvenile paddlefish into a stream of flowing, electrically noisy, water, and introduced daphnia, tiny plankton eaten by the
paddlefish, into the stream. In nature, a juvenile paddlefish uses an array
of electrosensors on its long snout (rostrum) to detect daphnia, which
it then pursues and eats. Russell, Wilkens, and Moss showed that the
paddlefish were able to capture more daphnia presented farther from the
rostrum in moderately electrically noisy water than in electrically quieter
or noisier water, indicating that stochastic resonance was enhancing
detectability of the faint electrical signals generated by the daphnia.
Greenwood et al. (2000) then showed that the relationship between the
probability of a paddlefish striking at a daphnia and the distance of the
daphnia from the rostrum, in the presence of the optimum amount of
noise, can be explained by a simple theory of how stochastic resonance
enhances information extraction from subthreshold signals.

An example more relevant to humans concerns the isolated sciatic nerve
of the toad *Xenopus laevis*, whose responses are used to predict those of
the human auditory nerve to vowel sounds coded by cochlear implants.
Surgically implanted in the cochleas (the inner ear structures that transform sound waves into electrical impulses) of profoundly deaf people,
cochlear implants electrically stimulate the auditory nerve in response to
external sounds. Morse and Evans (1996) found that, although standard
analog cochlear implants did not do well at stimulating a useful pattern of
nerve activity, adding noise to the speech stimulus enhanced the encoding
of distinguishing acoustic features of vowels in the pattern of toad sciatic
nerve neural activity. Subsequently, Zeng, Fu, and Morse (2000) showed
that adding noise to auditory stimuli did indeed improve the ability of
cochlear implant recipients to detect and discriminate the frequency of
pure tones. This and other results suggesting stochastic resonance led
Morse and Evans (1996), Moss, Chiou-Tan, and Klinke (1996), and
Zeng, Fu, and Morse (2000) to propose that noise be added deliberately
to the input of cochlear implants to enhance the ability of those receiving
them to distinguish speech and other natural sounds.

Cordo et al. (1996) demonstrated that stochastic resonance occurs in
human sensory systems too, using muscle spindle receptors, which detect
stretching of the muscle. They recorded the responses of a single afferent
fiber from the wrist and hand extensor muscles of each subject while the
wrist was being passively rotated (to stretch the muscles) back and forth
in a sinusoidal motion that covered about 2 degrees. They generated

"motion noise" by randomly vibrating the tendon attached to the extensor muscle, causing the muscle to stretch randomly. The very tiny rotary movement caused very few action potentials in the muscle spindle neuron in the absence of the motion noise and thus a very low SNR (near 0 dB) at the frequency of the weak periodic signal in the power spectrum of the time series of action potentials. When, however, they introduced the motion noise, the SNR increased, with the maximum SNR occurring for a moderate level of motion noise. For even higher levels of motion noise, the SNR gradually decreased, as the noise began to dominate the response of the neuron, indicating stochastic resonance was operating. Cordo et al. argued that internal noise generated by the intrafusal muscle fibers on which the stretch receptors lie provides the stretch receptors with the optimum amount of motor noise so that near-threshold movements can be detected and signaled by the stretch receptors, enhancing motor control.

21.2   Stochastic Resonance in Human Perception

Stochastic resonance also operates at the level of the whole organism in human perception. Perhaps the most dramatic example was provided by Simonotto et al. (1997). Although not used by them, figure 21.3 illustrates what they found. It contains three pictures of Big Ben, the famous London clock tower. To produce these, Simonotto et al. first digitized a standard photograph of Big Ben on a 256-level gray scale with a spatial resolution of 256 by 256 pixels. (A pixel is a picture element, usually a tiny square, which has the same color, or gray-scale value, everywhere, but can be different from its neighbors.) Then, to the gray scale value in every pixel,

Figure 21.3
Big Ben is seen best in optimal noise. (From Simonotto et al. 1997. © 1997 by The American Physical Society.)

initially $I < 30$, was added noise, which consisted of a random number, ξ, drawn from a normal distribution with zero mean and standard deviation σ. The resulting noisy gray scale values, $I + \xi$, were then replaced by white if $I + \xi < \Delta$ and by black if $I + \xi \geq \Delta$. In the black-and-white pictures shown in figure 21.3, $\sigma = 10$, 90, and 300, respectively, from left to right. As you can see, Big Ben is clearest when $\sigma = 90$, an intermediate level of gray-scale noise, displaying stochastic resonance in the picture-making process. In this case, the threshold was $\Delta = 30$, a level that was clearly too high to yield a recognizable picture when the noise level was low ($\sigma = 10$). At an intermediate noise level, however, the subthreshold picture is clearly apparent, whereas at a higher noise level it is beginning to be masked by the noise and it is not as clear.

In their experiment, Simonotto et al. (1997) created patterns of stripes by varying gray-levels sinusoidally across the face of a computer monitor, to which they added various amounts of noise that varied over time (dynamic visual noise; see Uttal 1969). They turned each gray-level pattern into a black-and-white pattern by applying a threshold, much as in figure 21.3. Each resulting dynamically noisy striped pattern was created in seven different degrees of contrast. The contrast of a pattern is the ratio of the luminance of its lightest part to that of its darkest part. Using gray-scale values and calling black "1," when the lightest part has a gray-scale value of 25 and the darkest part is black, the contrast is 25/1 or 25. The higher the gray-scale value of the white part, the greater the contrast. Lower contrast patterns are harder to see. Simonotto et al. asked their subjects to choose the lowest contrast noisy pattern for which they could just distinguish a particular fine detail (very thin stripe). This "contrast threshold," which represents the best resolving power of the visual system for these stimuli, varied with the intensity of the noise in the way predicted by stochastic resonance. That is, it was lowest (resolving power was highest) for an intermediate level of noise. Indeed, Simonotto et al. found that a simple model of threshold stochastic resonance fitted their data extremely well:

$$A_{th} = K\sigma \exp[\Delta^2 2\sigma^2] \tag{21.1}$$

According to this model, subjects detect the signal power, A_{th}, rather than the signal-to-noise ratio, where A_{th} corresponds to the contrast threshold mentioned above. Clearly A_{th} depends on σ, which represents the amount of noise and on K, which represents the extent to which different subjects were sensitive to fine details in a noisy pattern (ignore Δ, which has a technical meaning). Small K values mean low thresholds and high sensitivity. Of course, σ varied across patterns to give the stochastic resonance curve. That the model of stochastic resonance used was based on the power spectrum of a time series of identical pulses similar to the action potentials of neurons suggests that the visual system might perform similar computations when we look at noisy images.

Another example of perceptual stochastic resonance comes from a study of tactile sensation. As in their work with rat skin, Collins, Imhoff, and Grigg (1996b) touched their human subjects' skins with a probe. In this experiment, however, the skin remained attached to the subjects, who were only asked to say whether they had detected a subthreshold touch signal added to "touch noise" or only the noise itself. The touch signal was a constant touch applied for a quarter of a second at a force that was just subthreshold in the absence of noise. Collins, Imhoff, and Grigg (1996b) found that, as input noise level increased, performance rose from chance (at zero noise) to significantly above chance at moderate noise levels, and then declined to below chance again. Thus people seem to be able to exploit stochastic resonance in the touch perception system to improve their detection of faint touches.

In addition to their studies with cochlear implant recipients, Zeng, Fu, and Morse (2000) also showed that adding subthreshold noise to subthreshold tones allowed normal-hearing subjects to detect them. In my own laboratory, we are studying the use of stochastic resonance to improve normal-hearing subjects' detection of faint sinusoidal modulations of clearly audible sounds, reasoning that such abilities are most likely to have had evolutionary significance. In our experiments, human subjects are asked to tell which one of two roughly 70 Hz sounds is beating at 3 Hz. Various levels of noise are added to both sounds so that the only difference between them is the presence of the beats in one sound. Thus far, we have evidence that detection of the beats, measured with a bias-resistant measure, is best at nonzero levels of added noise, although the effect is small and very difficult to measure (Ward, Moss, Desai, and Rootman 2001). Similarly, when human subjects try to discriminate which of two patches on a computer monitor contains a square-wave grating (or a sinusoidal grating), they perform best at nonzero noise levels (Ward, Moss, Desai, and Tata 2001). Again, this effect is small and difficult to measure, but with sophisticated psychophysical techniques we have obtained the data shown in figure 21.4 (only square-wave grating detection shown). The mean contrast threshold data clearly show the prototypical stochastic resonance curve. Moreover, a model very similar to that of Simonotto et al. (1997) also fits these data very well (solid curve in figure 21.4). One

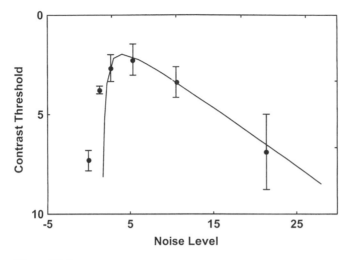

Figure 21.4
Stochastic resonance in the human visual system.(From Ward, Desai, Tata, and Moss 2001.)

implication of these demonstrations is that stochastic resonance could prove to be useful in ameliorating sensory deficits produced by aging or damaged receptor systems, in which sensory thresholds are raised, even in the absence of prostheses such as cochlear implants. It is conceivable that by adding the right amount of noise to sensory signals, they could be usefully amplified beyond the raised thresholds, enhancing perception of the previously subthreshold signals.

Stochastic resonance in human behavioral performance is somewhat controversial because the standard model used to measure performance in a bias-resistant way, signal detection theory (SDT; e.g., Green and Swets 1966; Macmillan and Creelman 1991), predicts that there should be no such thing as stochastic resonance (Ward 1999; Tougaard 2000). There is no threshold in SDT: the theory assumes that all signals will add an amount of energy to the background noise distribution such that the distribution of signal plus noise can always be discriminated from the distribution of noise alone given a sufficient number of samples from each. In the face of demonstrations of stochastic resonance in human perception, we need a way to understand the situation that both preserves the bias-resistant nature of SDT measures and also allows stochastic resonance. Moss, Neiman, and I (Ward 2000; Ward, Neiman, and Moss 2001) have argued that if any element of the signal processing system has a significant nonlinearity, such as a hard threshold (like that of the detector described in chap. 20), a soft threshold (a relatively steep but not discontinuous increase in the probability of detection as a function of input signal strength) or even a sufficiently nonlinear transfer function (an exponential will do), then stochastic resonance will result, even in a bias-resistant measure of performance such as that offered by signal detection theory. Demonstrations of this effect in two specific situations can be derived from the work of Bezrukov and Vodyanoy 1997 and in Stemmler 1996. Thus there are both demonstrations of stochastic resonance in human performance and the beginning of a theoretical understanding about how weak signals can be made detectable by adding optimum amounts of noise, creating an intriguing oxymoron: "useful noise."

Chapter 22

Stochastic Resonance in the Brain

As neurons in higher centers of the brain need to maintain a high signal-to-noise ratio as well as peripheral ones, it is plausible to presume that stochastic resonance is a general principle of biological information processing.

—H. E. Plesser and S. Tanaka, "Stochastic Resonance in a Model Neuron with Reset"

22.1 Stochastic Resonance in Neurons

Although, under the appropriate conditions, stochastic resonance may be exhibited by any level-crossing detector, it may play a particularly profound role in excitable systems such as cortical interneurons. A cortical interneuron produces an *action potential* (or *spike*) when the membrane electrical potential at the "trigger zone" of the neuron (where the axon extends from the soma) depolarizes to just above the resting potential of -70 mV, namely, at about -60 to -50 mV. The *membrane potential*, the voltage across the membrane, from the outside to the inside of the neuron, is negative when the neuron is "resting" (no inputs) because of a dynamic equilibrium of ion flows across the membrane and the presence of large, positively charged molecules inside the neuron. Each action potential triggered by a change in membrane potential at the trigger zone lasts about 1 to 2 msec, and the neuron's threshold for firing is higher than usual for an additional 1 to 2 msec after the end of the action potential. Thus, under optimal conditions, the neuron can fire at most only about every 2 msec, making the maximum firing rate about 500 Hz. Changes in membrane electrical potential relevant to action potentials are produced by excitatory (depolarizing—making membrane potential more positive) and inhibitory (hyperpolarizing—making it more negative) postsynaptic potentials (EPSPs and IPSPs, respectively) generated when excitatory or inhibitory transmitter substance is released across a dendritic synapse from the axonal endings of another neuron. EPSPs and IPSPs can directly affect the generation of an action potential in a resting neuron or can simply modulate a neuron's spontaneous rate of firing (see Eccles 1964 for details on postsynaptic potentials and neuron firing). Each release of transmitter substance causes a postsynaptic potential that quickly reaches a peak and then decays exponentially in time. Such membrane potential changes are largest near the receptor site and propagate to and across the soma and down the axon, decaying exponentially with distance from the source. EPSPs and IPSPs are usually thought to summate algebraically in their effect on the total membrane potential and across space and time. Thus inputs to the neuron that generate postsynaptic potentials while the effects of earlier ones are still present will add to those effects, possibly increasing or decreasing the likelihood of exceeding the neuron's threshold for an action potential. Koch (1997) has observed that even more complicated interactions can take place between postsynaptic potentials at different sites on the neuron, including multiplicative interactions.

Hodgkin and Huxley (1952) were the first to propose a mathematical model of the events surrounding the generation of, and recovery from, action potentials in neurons. Their model consists of four differential equations that faithfully reproduce the series of action potentials seen in real neurons, while also describing in some detail how inputs from other neurons and various membrane currents affect them. A simpler model of neural firing (involving only two differential equations) that preserves most of these features was suggested by Fitzhugh (1961) and by Nagumo, Arimoto, and Yoshizawa (1962). (This model is studied further in chapter 31 in the context of relaxation oscillators.) Finally, an even simpler model, called the "integrate-and-fire" model, describes only the ability of the neuron to integrate various subthreshold inputs over time and to fire a series of action potentials. A differential equation for this last, simplest model is

$$\frac{dv}{dt} = -av + a - \delta + S(t) + \xi(t), \tag{22.1}$$

where v is the voltage across the membrane (membrane potential), a and δ are constants, $S(t)$ is a subthreshold slowly varying but random signal representing the inputs of various other neurons to the neuron, and $\xi(t)$ is normally distributed noise that at each time is slightly correlated with the values at previous times (e.g., Collins et al. 1996; Plesser and Tanaka 1997). The voltage, v, is reset to its starting value (usually 0) every time it exceeds the threshold and an action potential is generated. Another way

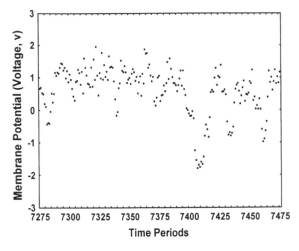

Figure 22.1
Membrane voltage fluctuations for an integrate-and-fire model neuron.

to write this model is as a time series,

$$v_{t+1} = v_t - av_t + a - \delta + S_t + \xi_t, \tag{22.2}$$

where the membrane potential at time $t + 1$, v_{t+1}, consists of the value at time t, v_t, plus the change over a small time interval given by equation 22.1, and typical values for the constants are $a = 0.5$ and $\delta = 0.01$. Figure 22.1 shows how the membrane voltage in this model fluctuates over time (200 time periods are shown from a much longer run), given these values of the constants and a particular series of values for S_t and ξ_t.

The threshold for firing an action potential in the integrate-and-fire model is set as a constant, for example $v = 1$. Considering this threshold for the series of voltages displayed in figure 22.1, you can see that a series of action potentials resulted whenever the voltage exceeded 1, separated by periods of time during which no action potentials occurred, much like the picture in figure 20.3. An interesting aspect of this integrate-and-fire model of a neuron is that the signal, $S(t)$, can be adjusted to be small enough that in the absence of the noise, $\xi(t)$, the voltage will never cross the threshold and the neuron will never fire. This is just the situation in stochastic resonance. Collins et al. (1996) showed that the mean firing rate of the integrate-and-fire model neuron (similar to the mean number of spikes in a short interval around the time of interest, for each time point in the series) tracked the variations in such a subthreshold signal best, and reasonably well at that, for an intermediate value of the noise intensity

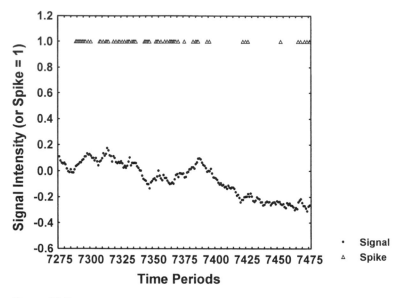

Figure 22.2
Signal and spikes for the same time periods as in figure 22.1.

(standard deviation of the distribution from which the noise was drawn). An example of such tracking, shown in figure 22.2, illustrates that when the (subthreshold) signal was relatively high, toward the left side of the graph, the frequency with which spikes were generated by the model neuron was much higher than when the signal was relatively low, toward the right side of the graph. A similar demonstration for a subthreshold periodic signal was accomplished by Plesser and Tanaka (1997). Thus the model integrate-and-fire neuron exhibits stochastic resonance; the same is true for the more complicated model neurons described earlier (e.g., Collins et al. 1996; Longtin 1993, 1997). Thus, too, real cortical interneurons may also exhibit stochastic resonance because these models are quite good descriptions of their dynamics. Indeed, researchers such as Plesser and Tanaka (1997) in the epigraph above have speculated that stochastic resonance is a general principle of biological information processing.

22.2 Neural Networks

Because each cortical interneuron receives inputs of transmitter substance from many other neurons (about 1,000 on average) via dendritic and somatic synapses with their axons, each is immersed in a complex environment of external signals. From the point of view of a single neuron sending a coherent signal to another neuron, that signal is in turn immersed in the noise generated by all of the other connecting neurons and other surrounding support cells and the intercellular medium, as well as by metabolic processes of the recipient neuron. Because all of the postsynaptic potentials summate (or even multiply) in their effect on action potential generation, and because a single action potential input from another neuron typically has a subthreshold effect on the total membrane potential (e.g., Thomson et al. 1996), the situation is exactly right for stochastic resonance to amplify a subthreshold signal above the action potential threshold. If all of the other inputs to a neuron are incoherent with each other, then they constitute noise. In such a context, a coherent input signal, even if subthreshold, could be amplified above the threshold by that noise and drive the output of the target neuron, in much the same way described for the integrate-and-fire model neuron.

This scenario was studied by Mato (1998) using such a model neuron, which received two input spike trains: one was periodic and subthreshold, and the other random with a given variability. Because the random input represented the unsynchronized inputs of other neurons, its variability represented the number of other, unsynchronized neurons actively stimulating the target neuron. The target neuron exhibited typical stochastic resonance behavior in that it tracked the periodic input signal best at an intermediate level of random input noise. Moreover, this finding demonstrated that the more usual scenario, in which many inputting neurons synchronize their inputs so as to deliver enough action potentials to the target neuron within a small enough time window to excite action potentials postsynaptically, is not the only way in which neurons can be driven by input signals. In the stochastic resonance scenario, one or a few neurons could drive the output of another neuron as long as they produced a synchronized input signal. The output of each neuron could also represent a blend of several different, subthreshold, input signals, each incoherent with the others, but all producing a complex, additive periodicity in the output of the target neuron. This process would happen best when just the right number of incoherent inputs (optimum noise) was being received.

As I mentioned earlier, a neuron integrates inputs over time as well as over space. The time constant, τ, over which such integration occurs varies from about 100 msec for inputs to sensory neurons, to 40–60 msec for inputs to the soma of pyramidal interneurons, to as short as 10 msec for inputs to the apical tufts of dendrites of pyramidal neurons in the prefrontal cortex (Seamans, Gorelova, and Yang 1997). Larger values of

τ make neurons act as integrators, whereas smaller values, such as those at the apical tufts, make them act as coincidence detectors (König, Engel, and Singer 1996). EPSPs and IPSPs, as well as action potentials, are produced by flows of ions across the cell membrane of the neuron. In many cases, a cascade of chemical reactions (second messenger system) is begun by reception of transmitter substance at the cell membrane. It is the time courses of such processes that set the value of the time constant τ. The electrochemical state of the neuron at any time is a complex balance of electrochemical forces influenced by synaptic and internal events that have occurred over a time window of width τ plus the constant diffusion of ions caused by electrical and concentration gradients and active pumps. The instantaneous rate of firing $(1,000/T$, where T is the interval between two successive action potentials in msec) of the neuron reflects all of these forces, and thus can be modeled as depending on inputs over a moving window of length τ.

Temporal integration in a neuron is represented in all of the model neurons I have mentioned, especially of course in the integrate-and-fire neuron. It has been shown that temporal integration in the form of kernel estimation (see chap. 20) allows even a simple threshold detector to produce outputs that closely follow a nonstationary subthreshold signal, at least at frequencies below the Nyquist cutoff, which is $2/\tau$ in this case (Müller and Ward 2000). Thus, for example, a particular neuron might produce spike trains that gradually increase in time density (number of

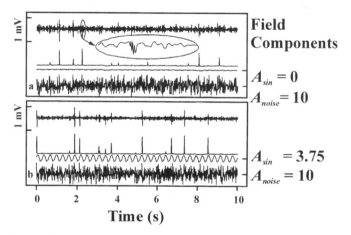

Figure 22.3
Stochastic resonance in the rat hippocampus. (From Gluckman et al. 1996. © 1996 by The American Physical Society.)

spikes per unit time) as the relatively small number of neurons synapsing with it, and responding in synchrony to an external stimulus, increases. Or its output could simply reflect an overall increase in the firing rate of the synchronized, driving neurons, which could in turn reflect the increasing intensity of the faint noises made by an approaching predator.

The growing body of theoretical work on model neurons has made it highly desirable to study stochastic resonance experimentally in neurons in the brain. To address the difficulty in delivering different levels of signal and noise to these neurons, Gluckman et al. (1996) used a technique adapted from their study of epileptic-like activity in slices of rat brain: they imposed an electrical field on an entire network of neurons in a slice from the rat hippocampus. They did this by placing the slice between two electrode plates, which produced an electrical field in the fluid bathing the neurons. The field induced ionic currents both inside and outside the neurons, and effectively shifted the spike threshold. The field was varied sinusoidally in a way that produced no action potentials, and then noise was added to this periodic variation in various amounts.

In contrast to previous studies, however, the behavior of individual neurons was not studied in this experiment. Instead, the synchronized bursting behavior of the entire network of neurons, which occurs spontaneously and is an emergent property of the network, was recorded as the electrical field varied. Burst firing occurs when neurons fire several spikes spaced closely in time (a "burst"), with relatively longer time periods between the bursts. Stochastic resonance has been demonstrated in models of such neurons, even without external forcing (e.g., Longtin 1997) but never before in real bursting neurons. As the top half of figure 22.3 shows for the case of the hippocampal slices, when the electrical field contained noise but no signal ($A_{sin} = 0$, $A_{noise} = 10$), synchronized bursts were also random. The bursts are indicated both by the field component graph at the top of each segment of the figure and by the graph just above the signal graph (the latter is just a straight line in the top half of the figure). But when there was a subthreshold signal, shown in the bottom half of the figure where $A_{sin} = 3.75 < A_{threshold} = 7$ and $A_{noise} = 10$, the bursts tended to occur at the peaks of the signal (i.e., phase-locked to the signal). This tendency was most pronounced for intermediate levels of the electrical noise: stochastic resonance again. Thus it seems that groups of neurons act like individual neurons in displaying stochastic resonance. It seems possible that stochastic resonance is a general property of brain activity, although just how extensive a role it plays is not yet known.

Chapter 23

Chaos

For my part, at least, I am convinced that He doesn't throw dice.

—Albert Einstein

And then we see unexpected things ... our imagination is stretched to the utmost, not, as in fiction, to imagine things which are not really there, but just to comprehend those things which *are* there.

—Richard Phillips Feynman, *Character of Physical Law*

23.1   Chaos Is Not What You Think It Is

At one time, chaos theory seemed like the answer to Einstein's quest for a theory that would at the same time be deterministic and yet give the appearance of randomness (in order to satisfy the requirements of quantum physics). In the late 1980s, it captured the imagination of the media, and of many scientists; as a result, many excellent popularizations have been written about it (e.g., Gleick 1987; Stewart 1989). There are also deep texts if you have the stomach for them (e.g., Devaney 1989; Thompson and Stewart 1986). In this chapter I will merely skim the surface, introducing some of the ideas critical to understanding what occurs in the following few chapters, which are by way of a progress report. Far from being dead, chaos theory is alive and well and being applied fruitfully in many areas, including dynamical cognitive science. As we might have guessed, however, it has proved not to be a panacea, and many matters that were before mysterious remain so, despite the best efforts of many brilliant minds.

My desk dictionary (Merriam-Webster 1971, 81) defines chaos as "the confused unorganized state existing before the creation of distinct forms" or as "complete disorder." And that is indeed part of what chaos theory is about: the surface appearance of disorder, even randomness. But chaos theory is really about nonlinear dynamical systems and their maps, which are the mathematical functions that determine the behavior of the system. One of the most important goals of the theory of dynamical systems is "to understand the eventual or asymptotic behavior of an iterative process" (Devaney 1989, 17). The dynamical system could be specified by a system of nonlinear differential equations in time, in which case understanding the system involves solving the equations, a very difficult, often impossible undertaking. (For cases where solution is possible, and for techniques to use when solution is too difficult, see, for example, Devaney 1989; Morrison 1991; see also chaps. 8–10 and 31.) Alternatively, and what we are most concerned with in this chapter, the system could be specified as the iteration of a discrete function, where we want to know what happens to the value of the function as we continue to iterate it. Because iteration is not something we are used to doing with functions, I will tell you a bit more about it before we go on into chaos.

To iterate a function $f(x)$ means to calculate the value of the function for some starting value, x, and then to put that value, called $f^1(x)$, back into the function in place of the initial x value, so we have $f^2(x) = f(f^1(x))$, $f^3(x) = f(f^2(x)) = f(f(f^1(x)))$, and so forth. Notice that the superscripts do not have their usual meaning of multiplication here, but rather refer to the number of times a function has been applied to the starting value of the independent variable. Let us look at, for example, what happens to the *map* $f(x) = x^2$ if we start with $x = 2$. ("Map" is just another word for function because functions map a set of numbers into another set in the sense of connecting pairs of numbers.) Clearly, the value of the function increases without limit. ($2^2 = 4$, $4^2 = 16$, $16^2 = 256$, etc.) Indeed, it will do so for any starting value greater than 1 or, after the initial iteration, for any starting value less than -1, in what is called an "exploding process." Nonetheless, this outcome is extremely sensitive to the starting value. If we start with $x = 0.1$, the process dives toward an asymptote of 0 ($0.1^2 = 0.01$, $0.01^2 = 0.0001$, $0.0001^2 = 0.00000001$, etc.), in what is called a "collapsing process." The same outcome will occur for any number between -1 and 1 except for 0. If $x = 0$, since $0^2 = 0$, the system will stay at 0. Similarly, if $x = 1$, then the system stays right at 1, since $1^2 = 1$. Any such points, for which $f(x) = x$, are called "fixed points" of $f(x)$. Finally, for $x = -1$, the first iteration of $f(x) = x^2$ will produce $(-1)^2 = 1$ and any subsequent iterations will then stay at 1. In this case, the behavior of the function as it is repeatedly iterated is clear and easy to see. If we knew that our dynamical system was described by this function, we would simply have to know the starting value to be able to predict how it would behave, as summarized in table 23.1. Notice that

Table 23.1
Behavior of Iterated Function $f(x)$

Starting x	< -1	-1	$-1 < x < 0$	0	$0 < x < 1$	1	> 1
Behavior	Explodes	1	Collapses	0	Collapses	1	Explodes

the graph of $f(x) = x^2$, although useful in many contexts, is not particularly useful here. What we are interested in is the behavior of the function under iteration, that is, as it takes on new values at discrete time points in the future or in the past.

As interesting as the function $f(x) = x^2$ is, it does not display the really interesting and useful behavior of periodicity or of chaos. A slight modification will take care of periodicity. Consider the function $f(x) = x^2 - 1$. This map has fixed points at $(1 \pm \sqrt{5})/2$; for example, $((1 + \sqrt{5})/2)^2 - 1 = (1 + \sqrt{5})/2)$, although that is not obvious (go ahead, do the calculations for yourself). More interestingly, the points 0 and -1 are *periodic points* of the function, and they form a *periodic orbit*, which means that the value of the function cycles between these points forever if it ever gets to one or the other from some other point. To see this, start with $x = 0$. Then, $x^2 - 1 = 0^2 - 1 = -1$. For $x = -1$, $x^2 - 1 = (-1)^2 - 1 = 1 - 1 = 0$. We are back at 0. And so it goes, the function simply flips back and forth between 0 and -1 forever, a periodic orbit of period 2 (meaning it takes two iterations to come back to the starting point).

23.2 What Chaos Really Is

But what about chaos? How do we get chaos? Surprisingly (for those who have never experienced it, at least), a further simple modification seems to do the trick. Consider the function $f(x) = 4x - 4x^2$. According to my twelve-digit-precision calculator, for a starting value of $x = 0.3$, the first thirteen iterations are as follows: 0.84, 0.5376, 0.99434496, 0.02249224209, 0.0879453645, 0.32084391, 0.871612381, 0.4476169529, 0.989024066, 0.004342185149, 0.166145577, 0.554164898, 0.9882646555. The numbers just keep jumping around like that, seemingly at random, never repeating (although there is a larger pattern, which we will discuss shortly), in what seems more like the "complete disorder" of the dictionary definition of *chaos*. But it is not. Because any finite precision calculation of the values of any function must eventually repeat a number, chaos can never be displayed in a list of numbers written with finite precision: only a finite number of different numbers can be represented, and from that point on it is periodic—the same as the last time that particular number occurred. To see this informally, consider making the above calculations with only two-digit precision, that is, we simply round off any digits higher than the two to the right of the decimal point (because all numbers will be between 0 and 1 inclusive). Thus, starting with $x = 0.30$ again, we get 0.84, 0.54, 0.99, 0.04, 0.15, 0.51, 1.00, 0.00, 0.00, 0.00, 0.00, 0.00, 0.00, forever. What? A fixed point! If we add a few more digits of precision we can get periodic behavior, a cycling between, say, 9, 10, or even 13 periodic points. But no matter how many digits of precision we add, rounding always occurs and we end up in periodic behavior, although it can look quite random indeed, even with only twelve-digit precision. How, then, do we know we have chaos? And what is chaos anyway, if we can never see it?

As you might have expected, chaos is an abstract mathematical concept that can only be approximated in our real, quantized world. Here is one respectable mathematical definition, slightly modified from Devaney (1989). Let V be a set. A function f that maps V into itself is said to be "chaotic" on V if (1) f has sensitive dependence on initial conditions, (2) f is topologically transitive, and (3) periodic points are dense in V. To take the easy one first, "dense periodic points" means that there is a very large number of periodic points everywhere in V, that is, that in any small neighborhood near a particular point in V, there must be a very large number of periodic points (the word *infinite* springs to mind, but is not precisely what is meant here). This condition holds so that the function can return to that neighborhood again and again without ever repeating exactly—otherwise, it would be strictly "periodic," although perhaps with a very long period. If you think that a "nonperiodic function with a very large number of periodic points" sounds like an oxymoron, you are right. It is. To have so many periodic points that they can never all be reached, and none repeated, is the ultimate in periodicity—the function is so intensely periodic that it is not periodic any more: it has become chaotic. In a sense, chaos is the asymptote of periodicity as the number of periodic points increases without limit. "Topologically transitive" means that a map will eventually move under iteration from one arbitrarily small neighborhood of phase space to any other, so that the system cannot be decomposed into disjoint sets that are invariant under the map, that is, it cannot become trapped in some small neighborhood, similar to a fixed point, forever. Finally, and probably most importantly, "sensitive dependence" means that there exist points in phase space arbitrarily close to every point x that eventually diverge from x by at least some amount δ

under iteration of f. All points need not diverge, but at least one in every neighborhood must do so. This means that the map defies numerical computation—the smallest roundoff error becomes magnified by iteration and the calculated orbit bears no resemblance to the real one. Moreover, this means that precise prediction of the future behavior of such an equation is impossible if that prediction depends on numerical calculation. Thus the behavior appears to be "random" or "stochastic" (see chap. 24 on the relationships between chaos and randomness).

Sensitive dependence is also probably the easiest and most "empirical" attribute of chaos because we can see it happen even in calculations of limited precision. For example, consider what happens in our iteration of $f(x) = 4x - 4x^2$. Let us start at the same place, with $x = 0.30$, but on the second iteration make a small change. Instead of using 0.5376, let us use 0.5377, a difference of only 0.0001. The sequence continues: 0.5377, 0.99431484, 0.02261135582, 0.0884003296, 0.311342845, 0.857633911, 0.48839194147, 0.999461012, 0.00215479033, 0.00860058883, 0.00341064748, 0.1317728928, 0.045763519. Now compare the two sequences. They do stay close together for a while, about the first eight iterations. But then they diverge drastically—where the original sequence had 0.166145577, 0.554164898, 0.9882646555, the new one has 0.00860058883, 0.00341064748, 0.1317728928. The orbits are now far from each other: the difference on the thirteenth iteration (0.9882646555 − 0.1317728928 = 0.856491627) is nearly 10,000 times as large as the original difference, although this difference is arbitrary and will fluctuate up and down as the sequences are iterated further. The point is that the two sequences are now apparently unrelated, although they began very close together, and unless they happen to both converge on the same number on some future iteration, they will continue to fluctuate independently of each other.

What kinds of functions have this behavior, and why are they interesting? Certain nonlinear differential and difference equations and certain iterated nonlinear functions (which are similar to difference equations) are just such kinds, which are interesting because they describe dynamical systems. Unfortunately, however, because precise prediction is impossible, we must think of new uses for such descriptions. They can be used to predict the general form of the system's behavior (its attractors; see sec. 23.3), but not its precise state (see Kellert 1993). They are also interesting because, and this can defy imagination, they are completely deterministic. That is, there is a precisely statable algorithm for calculating the next value of any iteration on such a function, although the calculation must

A

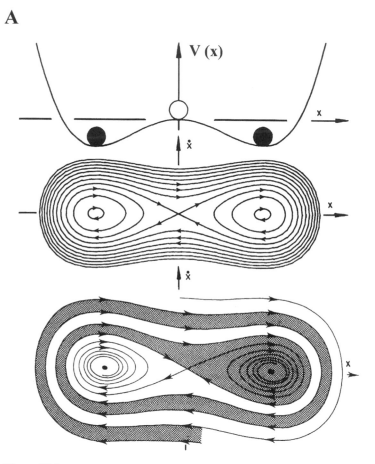

Figure 23.1
Phase space drawings of the behavior of (A) a nonlinear oscillator, and (B) a model of a neural network. (From Thompson and Stewart 1986. © 1986 by John Wiley & Sons, Ltd. Reprinted by permission.)

be made from less than full precision. We are not sampling from a probability distribution here; we are calculating a function value. And yet the function behaves so strangely, even with limited precision calculations (say anything beyond ten digits), that precise prediction is impossible, and the result looks random. Some have argued that this means that we can explain the unpredictability and apparent randomness of some behavior of the universe (and of humans), and yet salvage Einstein's belief that God does not play at dice, by modeling that behavior with such equations. Because they are deterministic, they are not truly random, and yet

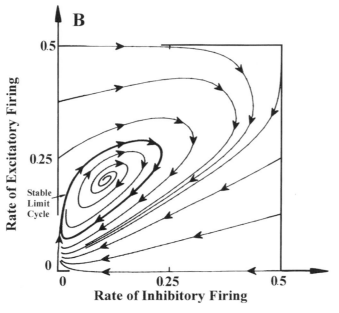

Figure 23.1 (continued)

they defy our puny human attempts at prediction, forcing us into elaborate subterfuges like quantum physics to deal with the apparent randomness. I discuss this idea in chapter 29 for human behavior; the physics community is still wondering about the possibility of quantum chaos.

23.3   Phase Space Drawings and Strange Attractors

Although the iterated behavior of the function $f(x) = 4x - 4x^2$ appears to be random, there is a way to describe its behavior that displays an underlying order. This way is also useful for functions that display periodic behavior, such as the oscillators discussed in chapter 31, which can be quite complex (we will use some for examples here). Moreover, many iterated functions display different transient behavior, sometimes chaos, before settling down onto a fixed point or a periodic orbit. For example, a damped oscillator such as a grandfather clock pendulum (friction provides the damping force) will oscillate in a series of ever-smaller swings until it stops at the fixed point of 0. Other, forced oscillators perform several oscillations in one fashion before settling down into a different stable periodic orbit (or one of several possible ones). Still others oscillate in one fashion for a while before settling into a "stable" chaotic behavior.

In all of these cases, the final, stable behavior is called an "attractor" of the function because it can be reached by iteration (or the flow of time) from many different starting points. The metaphor evokes the behavior of iron filings in the vicinity of a magnet. The attractor of a chaotic function is called a "strange attractor" because the "stable" behavior is so strange: the function jumps around a limited region of *phase space* (a space in which the axes are the variables that describe the system's states) without ever landing on exactly the same point. When there are several attractors in the phase space, which one determines the ultimate behavior of the system depends on where the system starts, or on outside inputs to the system that might perturb it out of one attractor and into another.

One way, perhaps the easiest, to understand such behavior is to draw pictures of it. These pictures can be quite complex, and an exotic vocabulary describing them has arisen (see Thompson and Stewart 1986). Figures 23.1A and 23.1B are drawings of the behavior of two interesting and useful functions. Figure 23.1A shows a damped (and an undamped) nonlinear oscillator in the form of the double-well potential of chapter 20, starting with the ball high up one wall. This oscillator has two, competing attractors. The undamped attractors (middle) are stable periodic orbits that depend on the starting point, whereas the damped attractors (bottom) are fixed points (the bottoms of the wells). Figure 23.1B is a picture of the behavior of a model of excitatory and inhibitory firing in a discrete neural network. This network is a general one, constructed from a set of excitatory model neurons and a set of inhibitory model neurons that are interconnected to each other in a random way. Each model neuron has some excitatory inputs and some inhibitory inputs, and the variables of interest are the *firing rates* of the neurons—the proportions of each type of neuron firing per unit time. To arrive at the final set of differential equations for the entire system, various assumptions were made about firing thresholds, refractory periods, response functions, and values of coefficients representing proportions of excitatory and inhibitory connections and external excitation (cf. secs. 18.4 and 22.2). Under certain assumptions, this system exhibits both a damped oscillatory response to a short-duration external excitation and a stable limit cycle (or periodic orbit) similar to the electroencephalogram rhythms, such as the alpha rhythm, that have been studied for years (see also chap. 27). In chapter 31, we will consider such oscillators in greater detail as a foundation for modeling in dynamical cognitive science. For now, it is enough to get a rough idea of how such strange mathematical objects behave.

Chapter 24

Chaos and Randomness

It was none other than Henri Poincaré who recognised ... that initial-value sensitivity is a fundamental source of randomness.

—Kung-Sik Chan and Howell Tong, *Chaos from a Statistical Perspective*

24.1 A Random Walk through the Logistic

Chapter 23 discussed the behavior of a function, $f(x) = 4x - 4x^2$, that, when iterated, gave rise to a series of random-appearing numbers. This function is one example of a large class of functions that are called collectively the "logistic difference equation" or more simply, the "logistic." Equations 24.1a and 24.1b are the most general expressions of this equation, written in a standard form that emphasizes its iterative nature:

$$x_{n+1} = a \cdot x_n - a \cdot x_n^2, \tag{24.1a}$$

or in the equivalent form seen in most books on the topic:

$$x_{n+1} = a \cdot x_n \cdot (1 - x_n). \tag{24.1b}$$

Equations 24.1a and 24.1b say that each new value of x, x_{n+1}, is calculated by inserting the previous value of x, x_n, into the equation and solving. The starting value, $0 < x_0 < 1$, determines the initial behavior of the iterated function but its influence soon fades away. The constant a is the parameter of the equation, and determines its behavior (after the first few iterations) in a profound way. When a is smaller than 3.0, the iterating equation moves toward a final, steady state point attractor, whose value depends on a. For a between 3.0 and about 3.58, the equation behaves as a simple periodic function, with the number and values of the periodic points depending on the value of a. Finally, for $a > 3.58$, the number of periodic points varies from one to very, very many. When the number of periodic points becomes so large that they could be called "dense," for example, when $a = 4.0$, the behavior of the iterated function is said to be "chaotic," that is, it meets the three criteria mentioned in chapter 23: dense periodic points, topological transitivity, and sensitive dependence. The values of the function jump around in a random-seeming way, although they are constrained to a strange attractor: a particular region of phase space in which the function stays without repeating itself exactly. I have drawn the strange attractor, or actually an approximation of the strange attractor, of the logistic difference equation in figure 24.1A. To get the approximation, I iterated equation 24.1 with $a = 4.0$ for 1,000 iterations, which I discarded, and then further for 4,096 iterations, which I plotted in the following way. I took each pair of values x_n, x_{n+1} as the coordinates of a point in a kind of "reconstructed" phase space. I then plotted all such pair coordinates on a graph of x_n versus x_{n+1}. This is called the "method of delay coordinates" and under certain conditions, which are satisfied here, it provides a picture of the attractor of a dynamical system even though its dimensions are not those of the actual phase space (see also Chan and Tong 2001). Interestingly, the graph of the approximate strange attractor for the logistic difference equation for this value of $a = 4.0$ is exactly the same as the graph of the uniterated map itself, $f(x) = 4x - 4x^2$—they are identical parabolas. The picture of the approximate strange attractor demonstrates that although the iterations of the logistic equation appear to be random, they actually stay within a small region of phase space, and the approximate behavior of the iterated function can indeed be described, although never predicted with any accuracy for more than a few iterations (because of sensitive dependence).

Compare Figure 24.1A with Figure 24.1B, the latter constructed using samples from a uniform (0, 1) probability distribution (see chap. 14). Notice that the plotted points in figure 24.1B tend to fill the x_n versus x_{n+1} space uniformly. Figures 24.1A and 24.1B dramatize the difference between the strange attractor of a deterministic process and the same plot for a stochastic process. This difference is exploited in some methods for distinguishing between randomness and deterministic chaos. From the perspective of the method of delay coordinates, deterministic chaos is certainly not the same as randomness, even though it entails a similar inability to predict the future.

Nonetheless, chaos does look like randomness from other perspectives. For example, consider the power spectrum of a chaotic process. Figures 24.2A and 24.2B display plots of both the time series for 600 of the iterations, or iterates, and the power spectrum of the entire series I generated to produce the strange attractor. Compare them with figures 14.2A and 14.2B. They are highly similar, except that the time series of the chaotic

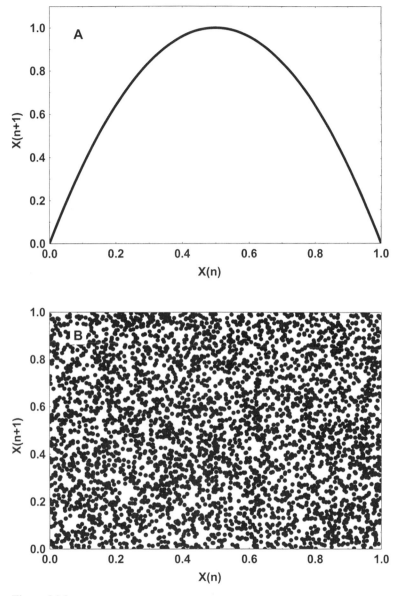

Figure 24.1
(*A*) Graph and strange attractor of the logistic difference equation (eq. 24.1b), $a = 4.0$; (*B*) "attractor" of time series of random samples from a uniform distribution.

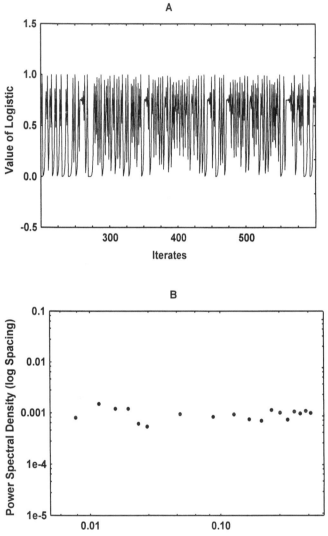

Figure 24.2
(*A*) Time series from the logistic difference equation; (*B*) power spectrum of time
series from the logistic difference equation.

process more regularly approaches its numerical limits (0 and 1 in this case). Both power spectra are flat. The time series and power spectrum generated by the uniform (0, 1) distribution look similar to those in figures 14.2A and 14.2B except that the time series values are constrained to be between 0 and 1, as they are in figures 24.2A and 24.2B. Of course the power spectrum of the logistic looks like this only for "chaotic" values of the parameter a. For other values of a, the spectrum either reflects the periodicity of the process, with peaks at the appropriate frequencies, or does not exist (for the values of a that give fixed points). Interestingly, at $a = 3.97$, at what Kauffman (1992) called the "edge of chaos," the power spectrum at low frequencies approaches $1/f$ (Clayton and Frey 1997; see also chap. 15), which means that a single, deterministic equation can behave in several very different ways, from fixed point attractors and periodicity of various kinds to the very edge of chaos and on into chaos itself. Moreover, many usual ways of characterizing stochastic processes, such as displaying their probability distributions and power spectra, can give insight into the behavior of deterministic dynamical systems (see Chan and Tong 2001 and chaps. 25–27).

24.2 Dimensionality of an Attractor

One of the most popular ways in which to display the difference between randomness and chaos is to show that the attractor of many chaotic systems can be described in a geometrical space of much lower dimensionality than that of a typical stochastic system. Indeed, the attractors of chaotic systems often display *fractal* dimensionality, that is, the number of dimensions they occupy is expressed as a fraction rather than as an integer (see Mandelbrot 1982). The easiest way to think about the dimensionality of an attractor is to think about the extent to which it fills space. Clearly, the "random attractor" in figure 24.1B fills space uniformly and requires all of the two-dimensional space available within the limits of its possible values. In fact, if we were to plot triples of uniform distribution time series points, the plot would fill three dimensions; for quadruples, it would fill four; and so forth. The more coordinates, the more dimensions would be required, and space would be filled up uniformly in each plot. If, however, we were to take triples, quadruples, and so forth of points from the logistic time series, we would find that, no matter how many coordinates we plotted, the attractor would fit easily within a two-dimensional subspace; indeed, it would look exactly like figure 24.1A in that subspace. Because it takes more than one dimension but less than two to hold the attractor of the logistic difference equation (fig. 24.1A), we say that the attractor has "fractal dimensionality."

Box-counting dimensionality nicely captures this idea of space filling. To determine box-counting dimensionality, we take a set of "boxes" (actually the mathematicians use "balls" because they can be described by a single parameter, their radius, ε), of a certain, relatively large, size and count how many of them we need to just cover all of the points in the attractor. Of course there will be some empty space in the covering set of balls because the shape of the attractor will not necessarily be such that balls would just cover all of the occupied points leaving no unoccupied points. Hence we reduce the size of the balls. With smaller balls, we will need more of them, but they will leave less unoccupied space, thus we will get a better approximation of the attractor. We continue to do this, making smaller and smaller balls, until we have enough observations of ball size, ε, and numbers of balls, $N(\varepsilon)$, to deduce their relationship. We will find that $N(\varepsilon) \approx k/\varepsilon^{D}$, where D represents the required box-counting dimensionality. Using this procedure, $D \approx 1.15$ for the chaotic attractor in figure 24.1A, and $D \approx 2$ for the random attractor in figure 24.1B, as expected.

Most of the chaotic systems that have been studied have turned out to have attractors with relatively low fractal dimensionality, often lower than 2 (e.g., the Hénon map, the tent map, the logistic and other quadratic maps) but sometimes higher. For example, the Lorenz attractor for a system of three differential equations formulated to describe the evolution of weather systems has a dimensionality of about 2.5 (depending on which formal definition of *dimensionality* is used, and there are several in addition to box-counting, for example, Hausdorff, information, correlation, Renyi, and Lyapunov; see Chan and Tong 2001). This property led many researchers to calculate the dimensionality of the approximate, reconstructed attractor of a long time series by using one of the available algorithms. If, as the number of coordinates plotted increased, the calculated dimensionality at first increased and then leveled off at a relatively small value (< 7), the researcher was tempted to conclude that the attractor was that of a chaotic dynamical system (see, for example, Mayer-Kress 1986 for some of these early studies). However, Osborne and Provencale 1989 burst that bubble by showing numerically that even time series from random processes could be expected to yield relatively low dimensionality when treated in this way. And then Cutler (1997), in addition to refining the mathematical notion of the dimensionality of a stochastic process, showed formally that random processes could be expected eventually to give rise to a time series that would be locally low dimensional to any extent desired. Hence this procedure is no longer viable except as a trigger for further analyses. Even then, it should be done on several relatively short time series from the suspected chaotic process, and these compared statistically with several time series of the same length from null-hypothesized stochastic processes. In later chapters, we will briefly review a few other other methods of distinguishing deterministic chaos from randomness, or more precisely, chaotic randomness from stochastic randomness. For now, let us turn to another aspect of the relationship between chaos and randomness, that of the behavior of a deterministic dynamical system subject to random noise.

24.3 Chaos and Noise

When we consider real dynamical systems, we have to cope with noise. One of the most important distinctions about noise made in chapter 14 was that between external and internal noise. External noise was not of the system under study and could in principle be turned off or bypassed. Internal noise arose from the quantization of the system processes and could not be turned off. The same distinction applies here, only perhaps more clearly stated as one between measurement noise (external) and dynamical noise (internal). Measurement noise is added when we try to measure the state of a dynamical system; it is added separately to each observation we make and is not carried over into the next measurement or into the time evolution of the dynamical system itself. Figure 24.3 shows an example of uniform (between -0.5 and 0.5) measurement noise added to the computer-generated logistic attractor with $a = 4.0$. Compare it to figure 24.1A, the (approximate) noiseless attractor of the iterated logistic equation. Measurement or observational noise renders the attractor "fuzzy," making it more difficult to discern its true form. Of course the fuzziness grows worse the more noise there is, and has worse effects for a given noise level the more complicated the attractor being sought. Because we can easily mistake noise-created forms for attractor features (witness the Rorschach inkblot test), we must take care in interpreting diagrams such as figure 24.3.

Dynamical noise, in contrast to measurement noise, is a part of the system's observable behavior even when no measurement error is present, although it can be considered to be separate from the deterministic dynamical system itself. It forms part of the observable dynamical system behavior because it is incorporated into the system's state at any instant and thus influences the system's next state. Perhaps the easiest way to see

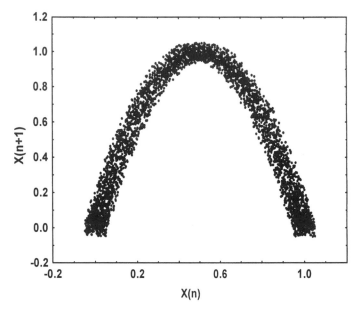

Figure 24.3
Logistic attractor with measurement noise added to each point.

this is to consider a kind of Langevin equation for the logistic difference equation:

$$x_{n+1} = a \cdot x_n \cdot (1 - x_n) + \gamma_n, \qquad (24.2)$$

where γ_n is a random variable representing independent, identically distributed (i.i.d.) noise. Clearly the noise is incorporated additively into the iterative evolution of this equation. Another way in which this could happen is multiplicatively, as in

$$x_{n+1} = a \cdot x_n \cdot (1 - x_n) \cdot \gamma_n \qquad (24.3)$$

Both of these noisy or stochastic dynamical systems will behave somewhat differently from the deterministic skeleton (the logistic). Because of sensitive dependence, they will amplify the noise, and if the noise gets very large, the system can jump from one attractor to another, collapse, or explode (see Chan and Tong 2001). For a simple system such as the logistic difference equation, this means that even very small amounts of dynamical noise can have drastic effects. For example, I computed iterations of the logistic equation with various amounts of noise added to each iteration, as in equation 24.2. I added computer-generated i.i.d. samples from the uniform (0, 1) distribution that had been linearly transformed by subtracting 0.5 (making the mean zero instead of 0.5) and multiplied by a number less than 1 to shrink the variance. When iterated without noise, the logistic stays between zero and one. With noise, it can go outside these boundaries, and when it does, it usually explodes toward negative infinity within about ten iterations. The larger the noise, the sooner the boundaries are breached and the sooner the process explodes. For more complicated dynamical systems, with multiple strange attractors, the noise could propel the system from one attractor to the other. In such a system, it is useful to think of the attractors themselves as "macrostates" that represent different types of system behavior. The predictability of these macrostates might actually approach that of the microstates of a conventional linear system. In a noisy dynamical system, however, noise can play the important role of determining the trajectory of macrostates over time and limiting predictability to that achievable for any other stochastic system.

Chapter 25
Nonlinear Time Series
Analysis

From the viewpoint of practical applications, the most fundamental task is to start with the data ... and explore the impact of various notions relating to chaos on their analysis.

—Kung-Sik Chan and Howell Tong, *Chaos from a Statistical Perspective*

Given that deterministic equations in a small number of variables can generate complicated behaviour, the question arises: how much of the complicated behaviour observed in nature can be described by deterministic equations with a small number of variables?

—Martin Casdagli, "Chaos and Deterministic versus Stochastic Non-linear Modelling"

25.1 State Space Reconstruction

The fundamental data of dynamical cognitive science, and of any study of dynamical systems, is a time series of univariate, real data values. To the naked eye, a time series generated by a nonlinear deterministic process looks just like a time series generated by some linear stochastic process, they are both simply lists of numbers and only the most obvious trends or cycles can be discerned without statistical help. The simplest way to aid the naked eye is to plot the data on a graph. Previous chapters have shown examples of several such plots, including plots of the data values against time, plots of power spectra, and plots of current values against immediately previous values. In addition, chapter 11 mentions linear time series analysis plots (and techniques), although these do not tend to be very helpful when undertaking nonlinear time series analysis. (For descriptions of many useful plots and techniques, and for more sophisticated statistical generalizations of the techniques discussed in this book, see Chan and Tong 2001.) I will describe only one of the most fundamental and intriguing techniques; later chapters will introduce a few others.

As I mentioned in chapter 23, drawings of the approximate attractor of a dynamical system, often called "delay maps," can be constructed by plotting adjacent pairs of time series data values, x_n and x_{n+1}, against each other (see figures 23.1, 24.1, and 24.3). Such maps were introduced by Packard et al. (1980), and their usefulness firmly established by Takens (1981). Because mathematically estimating the dimensionality of a strange attractor (see chap. 24) was, for many systems of differential equations, extremely difficult and often impossible, delay maps were employed to attack the problem. If a particular time series behaved like a dynamical system with a small number of dimensions, then it could possibly be usefully modeled with a small number of simpler differential equations, yielding insight not available for the larger, more complicated system. The basic idea is that, provided a sufficient number of sufficiently long time series of observations of the dynamical system of interest is obtained, the dimensionality of the actual strange attractor of the system can be approximated by the dimensionality of the approximate strange attractor displayed by the delay map.

In keeping with their use in plotting delay maps, or "phase portraits," as some call them, the sets of data values used as coordinates are called "delay vectors." These delay vectors can be of any length m, called the "embedding dimensionality," and *delay time* τ, the time between the observations in the delay vector, consistent with the nature of the time series. For example, consider the following time series with observations taken 1 sec apart: 3, 5, 7, 1, 8, 5, 7, 1, 4, 3, 9, 3, 6, 5, 8, 1, 7, 2, 5, 6, 3, 4, 8, ... The respective observations are typically labeled x_1, x_2, x_3, ..., x_i. The delay vectors of length $m = 2$ for $\tau = 1$ sec, then, are $\{x_2, x_1\}$, $\{x_3, x_2\}$, $\{x_4, x_3\}$, ... or $\{5, 3\}$, $\{7, 5\}$, $\{1, 7\}$, ..., and the delay vectors of length $m = 3$ and $\tau = 2$ sec are $\{x_5, x_3, x_1\}$, $\{x_6, x_4, x_2\}$, $\{x_7, x_5, x_3\}$, ... or $\{8, 7, 3\}$, $\{5, 1, 5\}$, $\{7, 8, 7\}$, ..., and so forth. For this particular time series we could have no delay times shorter than 1 sec or longer than the number of elements in the series, and no noninteger numbers of seconds. Because, in plotting these delay vectors in a delay map, we use each element of the delay vector as a coordinate on a separate dimension, it is of course difficult to graphically portray delay vectors longer than $m = 3$. Usually, delay vectors of length $m = 2$ are plotted on delay maps, with different values for τ in order to explore the temporal structure of the time series. The most interesting thing about delay vectors, however, is that as long as the embedding dimensionality is greater than D, the dimensionality of the process generating the delay vectors, then the delay vectors almost always fill out a reconstructed attractor that has the same geometric properties as the original attractor (Casdagli 1991). Figures 25.1A and 25.1B show two such reconstructed attractors for some physical data: the amount of light given off by a flame. Figure 25.1A is from a place in the flame where the attractor displays periodicity, whereas figure 25.1B is from a place in the flame where the attractor displays low-dimensional chaos.

25.2   Out-of-Sample Forecasting

Another very important use for delay vectors is in what is called "out-of-sample forecasting," which attempts to predict the future behavior of a time series from its past behavior. The relative success in this endeavor can help determine whether a time series was generated by a nonlinear dynamical process, by a purely stochastic process, or by a nonlinear stochastic process (Farmer and Sidorowich 1987). Casdagli (1991) created an algorithm for out-of-sample forecasting using the simplest possible approach, which is probably not much worse than the most sophisticated approach and much easier to use. In Casdagli's approach, a piecewise linear approximation of the attractor of the time series is constructed, in various embedding dimensionalities, m, and used to test whether the attractor belongs to a low-dimensional deterministic system (see Chan and Tong 2001 for a more sophisticated version of the algorithm.)

   In Casdagli's algorithm, the time series is divided into two parts: a *fitting set* and a *test set*. The idea is to estimate the local straight-line approximations from the delay vectors in the fitting set that most resemble each delay vector in the test set because such vectors will be nearby in the phase space, and then to see how the goodness of predictions based on these approximations changes as we increase the size of the region of the phase space we are using for the estimates. Because of sensitive dependence, in a chaotic sequence nearby trajectories eventually diverge, which should be reflected in increasingly poor predictions of the trajectory as the region of phase space on which the predictions are based becomes larger. As an example of the application of the algorithm, consider the time series segment from section. 25.1 Let the first seventeen values, 3, 5, 7, 1, 8, 5, 7, 1, 4, 3, 9, 3, 6, 5, 8, 1, 7, be the fitting set, and the next six values, 2, 5, 6, 3, 4, 8, be the test set. (Usually we use much longer time series, say 1,000 observations, with 800 observations in the fitting set and 200 in the test set). Now let us consider each of the delay vectors of length $m = 2$ in the test set. We will use $\tau = 1$ throughout, and we will choose a prediction time of $T = 1$ sec, which means we will try to predict the next observation

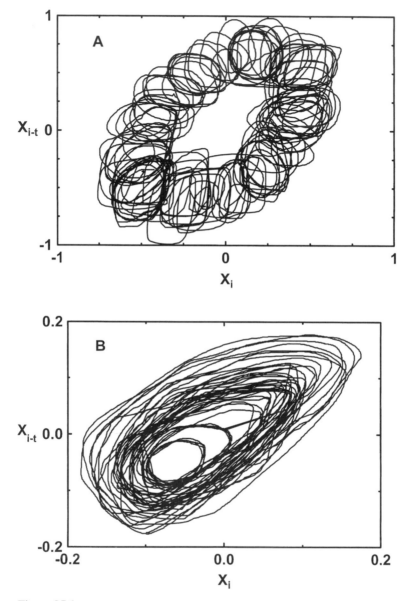

Figure 25.1
(*A*) Reconstructed attractor of a flame exhibiting periodicity; (*B*) reconstructed attractor of a flame exhibiting low-dimensional chaos. (After Casdagli 1991.)

in the time series for each delay vector. In this case, there are four testable delay vectors of length $m = 2$ in the test set: $\{5, 2\}$, $\{6, 5\}$, $\{3, 6\}$, and $\{4, 3\}$. There are only four because we need both the delay vector and the value after it, which is the one to be predicted, for each test. Now we calculate the "distance" between each of the four test vectors and all delay vectors of length m in the fitting set, for example, $\{5, 3\}$, $\{7, 5\}$, and so on. The distance can be Euclidean or some other measure, it usually does not matter much. In my implementation of the algorithm, I used Euclidean distance,

$$d_{ij} = \sum_{ijn} (x_{in} - x_{jn})^2,$$

where $n = 1$ to m, that is, the sum is over the embedding dimensionality. For each test set delay vector, we find the k nearest neighbors in the fitting set, that is, the k delay vectors with the smallest distance to the test vector in (Euclidean) space. Here k is the parameter that represents the size of the region of phase space we are using to make predictions, and it will be varied from a number as small as 2 up to a number that represents an appreciable fraction of all the vectors in the fitting set. Now we create a separate linear prediction function for each delay vector in the test set by estimating its parameters from the delay vectors of its k nearest neighbors in the fitting set and their respective next values. This function is of course likely to be different for each delay vector in the test set. Here we are trying to find out where each test set delay vector is in the reconstructed attractor represented by the delay vectors of the fitting set. We are predicting the next value of the test set to be the same as the next value predicted from the linear function based on that particular region of the reconstructed attractor. To see this, look at figure 25.1B. Pick a place on the attractor and see where the nearby lines are going. Now imagine you have arrived at a place near that place and you want to see where you will be at some (relatively short) time in the future. Clearly, it is reasonable to expect it will be close to where the nearby lines are going.

Once we have our set of linear functions, one for each test vector, we use them to predict the next observation for each delay vector in the test set (the values 6, 3, 4, and 8 for the four vectors, respectively, in our example). The difference between the actual next values and the predicted next values is used to calculate the error of prediction, which is squared, summed across the test set, and divided by the number of values in the test set. The square root of this average squared error divided by the standard deviation of the entire time series forms the root mean squared

(RMS) error. Once we have the RMS error for given values of m and k, we do the same thing for other values of m and k, choosing several different values of m and many different values of k (from a few to most of the delay vectors in the fitting set). These are displayed in a plot of the RMS error for each of our prediction attempts versus k, usually plotting the series of values for different values of m on the same graph. Figures 25.2A and 25.2B show two examples. Because these plots can be used to differentiate between the two types of processes, Chan and Tong (2001) called them "deterministic versus stochastic plots" or simply, "DVS plots." They and the algorithm that generates them must, of course, be implemented on a computer. (A commercial program from Physics Academic Software called "Chaos Data Analyzer: The Professional Version," programmed by Sprott and Rowlands, accomplishes similar kinds of analyses, among many others. Also, I have written a fairly efficient, albeit somewhat limited, program just for DVS analysis in ANSI-standard C for PCs that should be portable to other computers; I will supply the source code to anyone who asks.)

Casdagli (1991) showed that for chaotic systems, the RMS error is very near zero for the appropriate value of m and small k, and rises sharply to near 1.0 as the number k of nearest neighbors on which prediction is based increases. This is exactly the behavior of the DVS plot displayed in figure 25.2A (attend to the line labeled "$ns = 0$," where "ns" stands for "noise") for a time series generated by the Hénon map (a chaotic map similar to the logistic). Because a chaotic process is very sensitive to slight differences in initial conditions, processes beginning at very slightly different values at a given time (near neighbors in the strange attractor) quickly become very different from each other. The larger the number of nearest neighbors used (the larger k is), the more different they can be and still be "nearest," thus the more different are the starting places of the process compared, and the more different they can be expected to be in their predictions of the next value in the process. In contrast, the algorithm gives rise to dramatically different plots of RMS error versus k for linear and nonlinear stochastic processes. For a linear stochastic process or even a high-dimensional chaotic process, which is about the same thing, the plot begins at a value of RMS error near 1 and decreases gradually with k, never becoming very small (near zero). This behavior arises because in any noise-dominated process, increasingly large samples allow sample statistics, such as the mean, to become increasingly better estimates of population statistics, such as the expectation. Moreover, even large sampling variations can be swamped by very large sample sizes. At

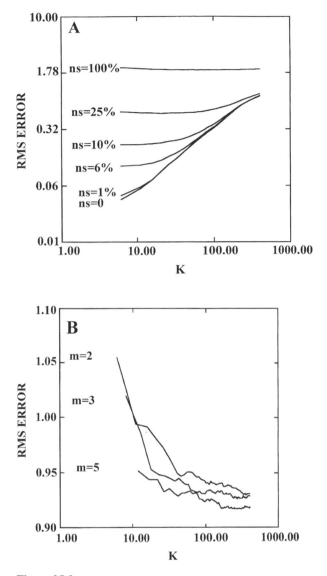

Figure 25.2
(*A*) Deterministic versus stochastic (DVS) plots for logistic map with various amounts of observational noise; (*B*) DVS plots for Gaussian noise. (From Ward 1996.)

RMS error $= 1$, the error of prediction is equal to the sample standard deviation, which is what happens when the algorithm predicts the mean for every point. Figure 25.2B (note the different range of values on the RMS error axis) shows an example of a DVS plot for a linear stochastic process, a series of 1,000 random samples from a Gaussian distribution. Notice that the excursion of the curves is very small, from about 1.05 down to only about 0.94 for the one with the largest excursion, quite different from the curve for the Hénon map, which spans several orders of magnitude from very near zero to near 1. For a nonlinear stochastic process, the plot begins at a value of RMS error somewhere between zero and 1, decreases to a minimum at an intermediate value of k, and then increases with increasing k to level off near 1. These plots of RMS error versus k can therefore, under certain conditions, be used to identify from which of these different types of dynamic process a given time series could have arisen. The presence of observational or measurement noise (noise that does not participate in the dynamic process, but only obscures it) makes it harder to identify low-dimensional deterministic structure using DVS plots. This difficulty can be seen in figure 25.2A, where different amounts of observational noise have been added to the Hénon time series. The plots with successively more noise (larger SDs of the Gaussian distribution from which the noise was sampled) begin at successively higher RMS error levels, and increasingly resemble the plots of nonlinear (lower noise levels) or linear (higher noise levels) stochastic processes. Using this technique, Casdagli (1991) confirmed the presence of low-dimensional chaos in some physical systems, for example, the flame whose phase plots are displayed in figure 25.1, and also demonstrated its absence in some time series previously thought to be characterized by chaos, such as that of EEG data. I will demonstrate how to use DVS plots to do the same thing with human behavioral data in chapter 26, although the high levels of noise in such data make conclusions less clear.

25.3 Surrogate Data

DVS plots are useful because they make an explicit comparison between the behavior of deterministic and stochastic dynamic systems. Although, in practice, the DVS plot may yield only an ambiguous conclusion as to the nature of a particular time series, the idea of comparing the behavior of a particular time series with the behavior of various representative "null hypothesis" time series, especially those generated by stochastic processes, is an important one. In the early days of searching for chaos in nature, investigators were often incautious in the application of algorithms to determine dimensionality, Lyapunov exponents, and other signatures of chaos. It turns out that stochastic processes can often mimic low-dimensional deterministic processes (see, for example, Cutler 1997; Osborne and Provencale 1989), and data that are dominated by noise can sometimes appear to be chaotic. Thus it is not acceptable simply to show that some time series has an attractor of low dimensionality, or a positive Lyanpunov exponent. Appropriate comparisons with the same analyses of null-hypothesized time series must be made.

Probably the most widely used procedure for making such comparisons, the "method of surrogate data" promoted by Theiler et al. (1992) involves three steps: (1) specify some linear process as a null hypothesis; (2) generate several sets of surrogate data under this hypothesis, normalizing them to have the same mean and variance as the original data; and (3) calculate and compare the relevant property (e.g., dimensionality) for the surrogate data sets and for the original data sets. Usually the set of values for the surrogate sets can be used to estimate the properties of a probability distribution, most commonly the Gaussian, and the statistic from the original data set can be tested for a significant difference using an appropriate statistic, for example, the z-statistic. Say the average dimensionality of 100 computer-simulated time series composed of 1,000 i.i.d. successive samples from a (computer-simulated) Gaussian distribution is 10.6, with a standard deviation of 3.0, and an original data set has a calculated box-counting dimensionality of 3.1 (see chap. 24). The z-score for obtaining a box-counting dimensionality of 3.1 by random sampling from the distribution exemplified by the surrogate data is $z = (3.1 - 10.6)/3.0 = -2.5$. Because the probability of a z-score as extreme as, or more extreme than, ± 2.33 is 0.01, we can conclude that the original data set probably was not a series of i.i.d. samples from a Gaussian. This conclusion gives us some confidence that the low dimensionality we observed is actually that of a deterministic dynamical system, rather than a red herring thrown our way by mischievous Mother Nature. A similar approach is to randomly shuffle the original data set several times, recording the relevant statistics for each shuffle. Again, the mean and variability of the original data set can be compared with those for the reshuffled sets, giving confidence that the shuffling has destroyed whatever structure was being indicated by the nonlinear analysis, and making it at least plausible the structure was nonlinear, possibly chaotic.

Chapter 26

Chaos in Human Behavior?

The current interest in chaos theory is matched only by the number of pronouncements on consciousness and cognition.
—Karl H. Pribram, "Chaos Edge"

After a while, though, I got pretty bored with chaos.
—Doyne Farmer, quoted in M. Mitchell Waldrop, *Complexity*

26.1 Could Unexplained Variance Be Chaos?

Linear techniques for time series modeling do not account for considerable response variance. For example, in my study of psychophysical judgment (Ward 1987), I found that a linear regression equation that predicted current response from a linear combination of present stimulus with immediately previous stimulus and response accounted for about 80% of the total response variance in magnitude estimations and category judgments and for about 60% in cross-modality matches (see also chap. 11). Adding similar additional terms to the equation accounted for less than another 1% of variance. Similarly, the ARIMA models used to analyze time estimation data in chapter 11 leave much variance unaccounted for. This pesky residual variance could arise from random uncorrelated noise, which is how it has been treated for many years. Alternatively, it could arise from correlated noise operating at more than one timescale, such as $1/f$ noise. Certainly this is true for time estimations and reaction times in several cognitive tasks (see chap. 16), and would have similar implications for how the judgments were generated by a brain that operates at many, equally weighted, timescales. Finally, and this need not exclude other causes, it could also arise from chaos (see Gregson 1988; Killeen 1989; and Townsend 1992). Because chaos is a form of randomness (see chap. 24), such an eventuality would explain why the residual variance remains unaccounted for in a linear regression. However, the implications of a chaotic source for the residual variance, especially a low-dimensional chaotic source, are different from those of a random or multiscale-correlated noise source. Indeed, a simple deterministic equation might be found to model a low-dimensional chaotic source, although of course the values of the relevant state variable could not be predicted from this equation for more than a few time steps because of sensitive dependence. Nonetheless, such a discovery would increase our understanding, especially if the parameters of such a chaotic equation could be tied to empirical variables such as stimulus modality, stimulus intensity, or arousal state. If in this were so, we might be able to predict and understand the general form of the variance, that is, whether it would reside inside one attractor or another, depending on the parameter values operative in the particular empirical situation. Given this possibility, it seems reasonable to explore residual variance for evidence of nonlinear structure. This chapter will summarize three examples of such an exploration.

26.2 Nonlinear Analysis of Time Estimation

There is more to nonlinear time series analysis than discussed in chapter 25. One technique not mentioned there resembles the hypothesis-testing approach most psychologists take for granted. Let me briefly describe one such analysis on time estimations (Ward 1996), before I tell you what I found. This technique was developed by economists based on work done by physicists using the *correlation integral*, $C_m(\varepsilon, T)$, where T is the length of a time series and ε represents the size of a neighborhood in phase space (Grassberger and Procaccia 1983a). The correlation integral measures the extent to which the different delay vectors of length m (see chap. 25) of a time series clump together (relative to the neighborhood size ε) in phase space. As usual, each delay vector is taken as a set of Cartesian coordinates in phase space. Delay vectors from random time series fill up phase spaces of any dimensionality uniformly, as illustrated in chapter 24, so that for a random process $C_m = (C_1)^m$. In contrast, delay vectors from time series generated by chaotic processes tend to clump together in a subspace in the strange attractor; thus C_m does not change with m when m is larger than the dimensionality of the attractor. William Brock and his associates (Brock, Dechert, and Scheinkman 1986; Brock, Hsieh, and LeBaron 1991) developed a family of statistics based on the difference between the correlation integrals in these two situations: $D_m = C_m - (C_1)^m$. This difference measures the extent to which the delay vectors of length m

from a particular time series diverge from those characterizing a series derived from independent, identically distributed (i.i.d.) noise. One statistic based on D_m is calculated as follows:

$$\frac{\text{BDS}}{\text{SD}} = \frac{(T - m + 1)^{1/2} \cdot D_m}{\text{SD}}, \tag{26.1}$$

where SD is the standard deviation of the statistic (from another formula; see Brock et al. 1991). BDS/SD is distributed as $N(0,1)$ under the null hypothesis of a time series from i.i.d. noise. This statistic can therefore be treated as a standard z-test. A sufficiently large z-score indicates rejection of the null hypothesis of i.i.d. noise for a particular time series with the probability of "type I" error equal to α. Unfortunately, departures from linearity other than those indicative of nonlinear deterministic structure can be detected by the BDS/SD statistic (Hseih 1991). One type of misleading departure from linearity that is a particular problem with this technique is conditional heteroscedasticity, in which the variance of the time series in a local region depends on the values the measured variable takes in that region. Also, nonstationary linear processes and even stationary nonlinear processes such as nonlinear stochastic processes, can generate sufficiently large values of the statistic to reach statistical significance. A large value of BDS/SD is therefore not sufficient evidence that the underlying process is a low-dimensional chaotic one. However, the statistic can be applied to short time series, such as the present ones, to obtain statistically convincing evidence for nonlinear structure (Casdagli 1991).

I calculated BDS/SD statistics for the normalized residuals from the ARIMA analysis of the time estimation data described in chapter 11. Remember that in that experiment, human subjects generated time series of 1,000 time intervals by pressing a key under four different instruction sets: (1) to generate 1 sec intervals; (2) to generate 3 sec intervals; (3) to generate intervals at their "natural" pace; or (4) to generate "random" intervals. Because the differenced time series were stationary, and the ARIMA residuals had had all detectable linear structure removed, it is unlikely that any linear process would give rise to large values of the statistic. This is the recommended procedure for using the BDS/SD statistic. Table 26.1 summarizes the results of this analysis (see Ward 1996 for details). I also calculated BDS/SD for 10 different random shuffles of each series in the 1 sec experiment (see sec. 25.3 for the rationale for this procedure, a type of surrogate data technique). These random shuffles all gave mean BDS/SD near zero, as they should for random time series, so I

Table 26.1
BDS/SD Values for Autoregressive Integration and Moving Average (ARIMA)
Residuals of Time Estimations

Subject	1-Second	3-Second	Random	Natural
1	6.65	16.54	3.44	15.94
2	10.05	17.24	5.18	22.03
3	8.43	11.08	6.08	33.56
4	14.06	15.69	4.01	14.46
5	15.00	14.70	9.63	8.15
6	5.97	6.77	8.24	7.59
Mean	10.02	13.67	6.10	19.96

Source: Ward 1996.

have not listed them in table 26.1. Thus the large values of BDS/SD
shown in the table for the unshuffled ARIMA residuals are not artifacts
of the particular numbers produced by the removal of linear structure
through ARIMA analysis. Table 26.1 shows that there is considerable
evidence for nonlinear structure in these data. All BDS/SD statistics are
significant at the $\alpha = 0.01$ level ($z = 2.33$). Thus, we can reject the hypothesis that the residuals of the ARIMA analysis are i.i.d. for all subjects
in all of the experiments. It seems that the evidence for nonlinear structure
is greatest in the natural intervals series, since the values of BDS/SD are
greatest there.

I also applied the Casdagli forecasting algorithm described in chapter
25 to the time estimation data to create deterministic versus stochastic
(DVS) plots. For this analysis the raw time series were first differenced
to render them stationary because the algorithm fails for nonstationary
series. A range of m values was explored to find the minimum error curves
for each series. Typical results for one subject who participated in all four
experiments are shown in Figure 26.1. Again, the strongest evidence for
low-dimensional nonlinear deterministic structure comes from the natural
interval series (lower right-hand panel). The curves for five out of six
subjects were very similar to the one shown in the figure. Minimum error
was clearly reached at a low value of k (6, 8, 11, 13, 33, and 48 for the six
subjects). Unfortunately, degradation of predictability at high k, which
would be expected if the time series were chaotic, was not very great. For
the natural interval experiment, it ranged from 13% to 24%. Even extra-
polating the curves to $k = 800$ only adds about 5%, yielding 18% to 29%.
These results are therefore ambiguous: the data represent either a very

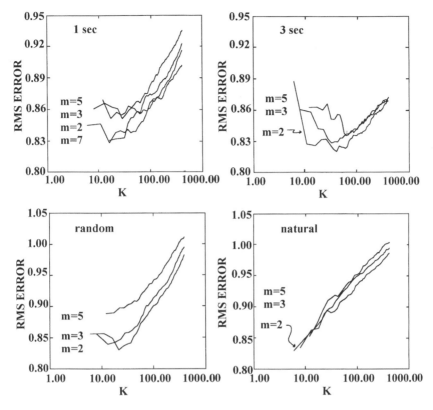

Figure 26.1
Deterministic versus stochastic (DVS) plots for time estimation data of one subject. (From Ward 1996.)

noisy but nonlinear deterministic process or a nonlinear stochastic process. On the other hand, because not a single one of the twenty-four curves (four conditions by six subjects) resemble those of figure 23.2B, there is no evidence whatsoever in these data for a linear stochastic or a random model. Remembering that these data also display a $1/f$-like power spectrum (see chap. 16), the nonlinear stochastic model seems to be a good bet for further work.

26.3 Nonlinear Analysis of Mental Illness

One of the best places to find techniques for discovering the presence of nonlinear structure in cognitive science time series data is in Scheier and Tschacher 1996, whose approach, though similar to my own, has been

Table 26.2
Test Profile for Analyzing Short, Noisy Time Series

Type of Process/ Statistic	Sugihara-May: Forecasting Degeneracy with Time	Determinism vs. Chaos: Forecasting Degeneracy with Number of Neighbors	Surrogate Data: Standardized Difference of Correlations for i.i.d. Correlated		Noise vs. Chaos: Standardized Difference of Prediction Errors
Nonlinear deterministic	$\gg 0$	$\gg 0$	>2	>2	<-3.72
Linear stochastic:					
AR	≈ 0	$\ll 0$	>2	<2	>-3.72
MA	$\gg 0$	$\ll 0$	>2	<2	>-3.72
White noise	≈ 0	≈ 0	<2		$\gg -3.72$

Source: Scheier and Tschacher 1996.

developed in a more systematic way. In particular, the authors provide a table of time series statistics, a version of which is shown in table 26.2 above, in which they compare the outcomes of various tests for several prototypical types of time series, including chaotic ones. These tests include the method of surrogate data (described in chap. 25) and DVS plots from nonlinear forecasting, as well as two other techniques not covered here: a type of nonlinear forecasting analysis created by Sugihara and May (1990), and a different approach to surrogate data analysis called "noise versus chaos" invented by Kennel and Isabelle (1993). When all of these types of analysis are applied to a set of short, noisy time series such as the ones we commonly find in dynamical cognitive science, the profile of statistics nicely differentiates chaotic time series from linear stochastic time series (ARIMA) and from time series generated by a white noise process (see table 26.1).

Scheier and Tschacher 1996 also shows the results of an application of the technique to a set of "real" behavioral time series. The time series consisted of 200 to 800 daily ratings of a patient's "psychoticity" on a seven-point scale by staff at a small residential clinic. The clinic treats people experiencing a first psychotic manifestation using what is called "milieu therapy" and "affect logic" (how these techniques work and how effective they might be are not relevant to the analysis). Of the fourteen time series analyzed, five had a profile like that of a time series generated by a nonlinear deterministic process, three more looked somewhat similar to that profile, five had a profile like that of an autoregressive linear stochastic process, namely, ARIMA(n, 0, 0), and two had a profile like that of a white noise time series. According to Scheier and Tschacher 1996, a white noise time series occurs when the patient's behavior is under control of fluctuating external stimuli, whereas nonlinear deterministic dynamics imply the existence of an internally controlled process unfolding without much influence of external stimuli. Clearly these two different sources for psychotic symptoms imply different treatment regimens and prognoses. Thus, like Markovian analyses in the marriage clinic (Gottman 1999), nonlinear time series analysis may turn out to have important practical as well as research uses.

26.4 Memory and the Logistic Difference Equation

In their nonlinear analysis of memory and choice data, Clayton and Frey (1996) reported the results of analyzing four different types of response latency time series. In all cases, the correlation dimension was estimated for both the scrambled and unscrambled time series (see chaps. 24 and 25); in all cases, the scrambled time series had the same behavior as the unscrambled ones, indicating that the time series was probably not created by a nonlinear deterministic process of low dimensionality. You might remember the experiments (described in chap. 16) by Gilden and by Ward and Richard showing that response latency time series contained $1/f$ noise. For several reasons, dimensionality analysis does not seem to work well for behavioral data.

Undeterred by the disappointing results of their analysis of correlation dimension, Clayton and Frey (1996) presented a nonlinear deterministic model of the dynamics within each trial of a prototypical memory task. I will describe it here, even though it was not supported by their data, because it is an interesting example of an early attempt to produce a nonlinear deterministic model that might be relevant to human cognitive processes. Clayton and Frey adapted their model from models of animal populations competing in the same niche, models that use equations similar to the logistic difference equation. Clayton and Frey's model is specified by the following two equations:

$$x_{t+\Delta t} = x_t + \left(1 - \frac{x_t + y_t}{K}\right) \cdot r_x \cdot x_t - c \cdot x_t \cdot y_t \tag{26.2a}$$

$$y_{t+\Delta t} = y_t + \left(1 - \frac{x_t + y_t}{K}\right) \cdot r_y \cdot y_t - c \cdot x_t \cdot y_t. \tag{26.2b}$$

The first part of each equation is analogous to the logistic difference equation; the last, subtractive term has been added to introduce competition between the two processes. In this model, the main variables, x (whose dynamics are described by eq. 26.2a) and y (whose dynamics are described by eq. 26.2b), represent the dispositions to respond correctly and incorrectly, respectively, in some memory task. For example, they could be the disposition to say that a particular word either had or had not been seen previously in a study list, when the word actually had been present in the study list. Clearly, these are competitive dispositions. In equations 26.2a and 26.2b, $x_{t+\Delta t}$ and $y_{t+\Delta t}$ represent the values of the variables x and y at time $t + \Delta t$, where Δt is an interval after time t. The two variables increase over the interval Δt proportionally to their own values at time t and to their growth rates, r_x and r_y ($1 < r_x, r_y < 3$). K is a constant that limits the growth of each disposition to the capacity of working memory, and the constant c ($0 < c < 1$) directly represents the competition between x and y so that each process is diminished in proportion to the strength of the other. The model shows interesting dynamics: temporary dominance by one process before the other, having a higher growth rate, takes over (and presumably determines the ultimate response), and chaotic behavior by the winning process after it dominates. Such models represent first steps in the attempt to provide nonlinear deterministic models of memory and choice that compete with the traditional, probabilistic models. Although which type of model will ultimately prove to be more useful is moot at this time, a nonlinear model does have some attractive metatheoretical features. For many, the most important of these is that it can mimic the unpredictability of behavioral time series while at the same time providing a deterministic basis for that unpredictability.

Chapter 27

Chaos in the Brain?

Our studies have led us as well to the discovery in the brain of chaos [which] is not harmful in the brain. In fact, we propose it is the very property that makes perception possible. We also speculate that chaos underlies the ability of the brain to respond flexibly to the outside world and to generate novel activity patterns, including those that are experienced as fresh ideas.

—Walter J. Freeman, "The Physiology of Perception"

27.1 The Smell of Chaos

That the brain is a nonlinear dynamical system seems beyond dispute. The question is whether saying so enhances our understanding. Can linear statical theories of brain function capture all of the important properties? Do the nonlinear dynamics create chaotic or edge-of-chaos functioning? Is the chaos high dimensional, in which case it could be modeled as noise (perhaps $1/f$ noise; see chap. 19), or low dimensional, in which case it makes sense to try to model the dynamics deterministically. Whatever the case, does understanding the brain and its relationship to behavior and the mind *require* understanding its dynamics? This book, of course, tries to make a case for the necessity, but not the sufficiency, of understanding the brain's dynamics. Even though many authors, such as Freeman (1991; see epigraph above) and Lashley (1951; see chap. 2) agree, the position has yet to penetrate mainstream neuroscience.

Freeman (1991; Skarda and Freeman 1987) has provided an eloquently argued vision of the role that chaotic dynamics might play in brain and behavior. Freeman and his associates trained rabbits and other animals to recognize several different smells and to behave in specific ways when they did, for example, to lick or chew. Using an electroencephalogram (EEG), during and after training his team recorded the large-scale ionic currents of the olfactory bulb and the olfactory cortex generated in response to the presentation of smell stimuli. The olfactory bulb is the

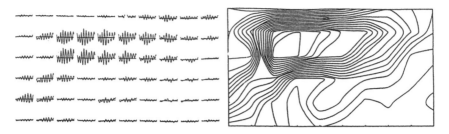

Figure 27.1
Electroencephelaogram (EEG) carrier wave patterns (*left*) and contour maps (*right*) of olfactory cortex activity in response to a recognized smell stimulus. (From Freeman 1991.)

brain area nearest the olfactory sensory surface to which the smell receptors project, and it projects in turn to the olfactory cortex. The EEG recordings, which reflected the activity of many neurons, showed a burst of neural activity while the animal was inhaling. The burst was composed of synchronous waves of neural firing whose frequency was the same at each recording site, but whose amplitude varied in a particular way across the olfactory bulb or olfactory cortex for each different type of smell stimulus. Freeman called these waves "carrier waves" by analogy to the radio waves that carry music or talk signals because, through their amplitude modulations across the different parts of the olfactory bulb or olfactory cortex, the synchronous waves carried the information about which substance was being smelled. Importantly, the recognized smell stimulus was represented by the entire pattern of carrier wave activity across the cortex, not by the activity of any one small group of neurons. Figure 27.1 shows an example of the carrier wave pattern of the olfactory cortex for a particular smell stimulus and the associated contour map of carrier wave amplitude. The carrier wave varied in frequency from exposure to exposure, usually in the range 20 Hz to 70 Hz (often called "40 Hz oscillation"), but the contour map of amplitudes was always the same for the same smell stimulus until the situation changed. If another stimulus was introduced to the learning situation, the contour maps of all of the stimuli currently recognized changed to accommodate it, and the new patterns were now stable until further changes occurred. Figure 27.2 shows the change in the contour map for the recognized smell of sawdust after a rabbit had learned to recognize the new smell (in that situation) of banana (amyl acetate). The sawdust pattern on the left is the original map for the smell of sawdust, before the banana smell was introduced. After

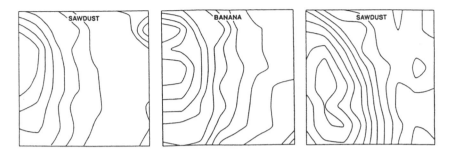

Figure 27.2
Change in contour maps of olfactory bulb activity with the introduction of a new
smell stimulus. (From Freeman 1991.)

the animal learned to respond to the banana smell, generating the pattern
shown in the middle panel for it, the sawdust map changed to the pattern
shown in the right-hand panel.

To understand how the rabbits' olfactory systems responded to recognized smells, Freeman and his colleagues constructed a model of the
olfactory system based both on structural (anatomical) information about
these parts of the brain (see chap. 9) and on some assumptions about how
the neurons in these regions functioned. The model's activity is based on
neural circuits constructed through experience according to the Hebbian
learning rule: when synchronous firing of neurons is accompanied by a
reward, connections between these neurons become stronger (structural
part of model). These neural circuits fire in response to a recognized smell,
and that firing ignites the synchronized burst of firing in all of the other
neurons of the bulb, which is then transmitted to the olfactory cortex and
ignites a similar burst there. This model accounts for both the bursts of
neural activity and also the properties of the contour maps of this activity
discussed earlier.

Rapid state changes in response to weak inputs are a signature of
chaos, indicating sensitive dependence (see chap. 23). Freeman and colleagues speculated that the bursts of neural activity in the rabbits' olfactory systems in response to smells were an indication that the olfactory
system could be usefully thought of as a chaotic dynamical system.
Although there were other indications as well, the most convincing one
arose when they ran their model for longer than the usual few seconds
of neural activity. These long runs produced phase portraits of neural
activity that very much resembled the strange attractors discussed in
chapter 23. These attractors not only did not fill phase space in the way

a random process would (e.g., uniformly, for a uniformly distributed random variable), but also had the "loose coils of wire" shape characteristic of strange attractors of more complex chaotic systems (see Gleick 1987 for more examples). Because behavior similar to that modeled for the olfactory system has been found in other sensory systems, such as vision, Freeman speculated that all of perception involves repeated transitions between the myriad strange attractors of the chaotic dynamical system of the brain, with each strange attractor representing a particular meaningful stimulus. The important departure of Freeman's approach from more conventional models is that in this model perceptual representations involve all of the neurons in entire cortical and subcortical regions, not just small groups of neurons, and that these representations are dynamic—they change in response to the changing stimulus and reinforcement situation. This picture is strikingly similar to the vision of Lashley (1951) described in chapter 2.

27.2 Dimensionality of the Electroencephalogram

How should we search for chaos in the brain? In chapter 24, I mentioned that the earliest applications of chaos theory in dynamical cognitive science included modeling the conventional EEG as a chaotic time series. This took the form of using the correlation integral to estimate the correlation dimensionality of the phase portrait of a time series (Grassberger and Procaccia 1983b; see Pritchard and Duke 1992 for a detailed discussion). Under ideal conditions, the correlation dimensionality of a chaotic process is the slope of the straight line relating the log of the correlation integral to the log of the size of the neighborhood at which it was measured over a large range of neighborhood sizes. In practice, the correlation dimensionality is estimated from the slope of a linear region of the graph of the log correlation integral plotted against the log neighborhood size for several different embedding dimensionalities (length of the delay vectors involved), and a saturation point is sought. The saturation point is a place on the graph of the estimated dimensionality plotted against the embedding dimensionality where the dimensionality estimate begins leveling off even though the embedding dimensionality is still increasing. If a time series reflects a chaotic process, then the correlation dimensionality should be the same, regardless of the embedding dimensionality, as long as the latter is greater than the true dimensionality of the process. Thus, for a chaotic process the estimated correlation dimensionality should increase with embedding dimensionality until the true dimensionality is reached and then should increase no further, creating a saturation point; the saturation point represents the estimated correlation dimensionality of the chaotic process. Pritchard and Duke (1992) cautioned that this saturation point should be taken only as an estimate of what they called "dimensional complexity," or correlation dimensionality used in a relative rather than in an absolute sense, because the limitations of the estimation procedure guarantee that the estimate of the correlation dimensionality is biased, usually downward.

The earliest studies using this technique measured the dimensional complexity of time series of EEG recordings taken from human subjects under various conditions and then compared the estimates. The expectation was that, at least under some conditions, the dimensional complexity should be low, or at least lower for one condition than for another. Pritchard and Duke (1992) identified two broad patterns of results in such studies: (1) dimensional complexity of EEG time series is lower when people have their eyes closed than when they have them open, at least partly because the alpha wave that dominates the EEG for many people with eyes closed has relatively low dimensional complexity, and (2) dimensional complexity of EEG time series is higher when people are doing a mental task than when they are not. Other findings mentioned by Pritchard and Duke were lower dimensional complexity of the EEG during some stages of sleep than during wakefulness, and lower than normal dimensional complexity of the EEG in the presence of some diseases such as epilepsy. This kind of research continues, with more recent findings of lower than normal dimensional complexity in EEGs of depressed people (Pezard and Nandrino 1996) and an increase in dimensional complexity of EEG time series caused by stimulation of the trapezius muscle or of the earlobe (Heffernan 1996).

Probably the most dramatic illustration of the dangers of analysis of EEG time series for dimensional complexity comes from Theiler and Rapp 1996, who reanalyzed EEG data previously analyzed for correlation dimensionality by Rapp et al. 1989, in which human subjects alternately rested or performed mental arithmetic, all with eyes closed. A sophisticated implementation of the correlation integral procedure was used in the original analysis, and a significant difference was found between the estimated correlation dimensionality during rest (mean = 4.0) and that during a difficult mental task (mean = 4.7). However, when the dimensionality estimation procedure was changed in several reasonable ways, for example, by demanding a larger region of linearity of log correlation integral with log neighborhood size than that used by Rapp et al.

(1989), no evidence for low-dimensional behavior was found in the outcomes of the new analyses. Moreover, when the correlation dimensionality estimated from the EEG data was compared with that estimated from surrogate data using the same procedure (see chap. 25), once again, no evidence for low-dimensional dynamical behavior was found. The model that seemed to fit these EEG time series best was one of linearly filtered white noise, which echoes the finding of Casdagli (1991), who applied nonlinear forecasting to similar EEG data and found no evidence for low-dimensional nonlinear deterministic behavior.

In addition to the somewhat discouraging results described above, there are further arguments that the search for low-dimensional dynamical behavior in the brain will be very difficult, if not fruitless (e.g., Rapp 1993). Nonetheless, if the brain is a nonlinear dynamical system, then it should be possible to find evidence of this in observations of brain activity. Theoretical work suggests that at least at some times, low dimensionality should characterize brain activity. For example, Freeman's work (1991) implies that, during the synchronous bursts of activity that encode stimuli in a sensory system, the system is in a low-dimensional attractor region of phase space. There may be other such states that imply low dimensionality, and improved methods for estimating fractal dimensionality might eventually reveal it in the (in comparison to physics) relatively uncontrolled experimental settings of dynamical cognitive science (see sec. 27.3). Moreover, dimensional complexity, although conceptually convenient, might not be the most meaningful aspect of dynamical behavior to model. One possibility is that the brain is usually characterized by high-dimensional, $1/f$ noise at the edge of chaos, but from time to time is pushed into a low-dimensional strange attractor by appropriate stimulation either from without or from within. To find evidence of the low-dimensional chaos, then, we must search for it in the appropriate time series as well as with the appropriate tools. We must be careful in this search, however, because even $1/f$ noise can lead to spuriously low dimensionality estimates (Osborne and Provencale 1989; Theiler 1991).

27.3 Chaotic Event-Related Potentials?

If we wish to stick with the EEG, a promising place to look would be in event-related potentials, or ERPs, which are EEG recordings taken in the second or so after an eliciting external event, such as a sound, or a smell (see chaps. 17 and 33 for more on ERPs). Indeed, ERPs might be recording the manifestations of the neural bursts discovered by Freeman

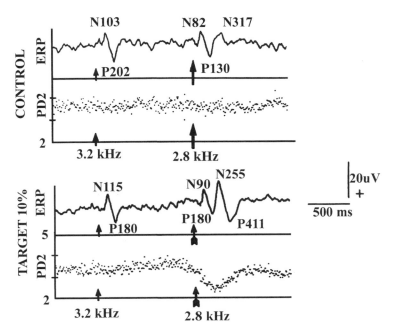

Figure 27.3
Event-related potentials (ERPs) and point D2 (PD2) values for control and target
stimuli (From Molnar and Skinner 1992. © 1992 by Overseas Publishers Association, N.V. Reprinted with permission from Gordon and Breach Publishers.)

(1991). This approach was taken by Molnar and Skinner (1992), who also
invented a new way to use correlation dimensionality to characterize the
complexity of the underlying brain processes producing an ERP, a way
that could accommodate the epoch of the ERP after a sensory stimulus
not being at all stationary because of the dramatic changes caused by the
various components of the ERP (see fig. 17.4). Indeed, stationarity is
always violated for ERPs; hence the conventional estimates of correlation
dimensionality (hereafter, "D2") obtained for ERPs in previous work
were suspect, even though the conclusions based on those estimates were
consistent with those of Freeman: lower dimensionality in the epoch following an ERP-eliciting stimulus than in other epochs (Rapp et al. 1989).
To get around the stationarity problem, Molnar and Skinner (1992)
developed the "point D2," or "PD2," the D2 based only on delay vectors
meeting two strict criteria: (1) linearity of the log of correlation integral
with the log of the neighborhood size, from which correlation dimensionality is estimated for each value of the embedding dimensionality,

and (2) saturation of the plot of D2 against embedding dimensionality. Although application of these criteria to individual delay vectors is difficult (see Molnar and Skinner 1992), the result is easy to understand: the PD2 is not sensitive to the violations of stationarity that characterize ERPs or often other biological or cognitive time series. Again, it is prudent to use the PD2 only as an indication of dimensional complexity rather than a measure of D2 because there is no rigorous proof that it converges to D2 in the limit.

Using the PD2, Molnar and Skinner (1992) examined both conventional chaotic and nonchaotic time series and time series of EEGs during ERP epochs. They showed that the PD2 is not sensitive to aspects of the time series that are of no interest and that do not relate to correlation dimensionality, such as frequency and amplitude of periodic components. Moreover, PD2 does a very good job of estimating D2 of processes for which D2 is known, for example the Lorenz attractor (D2 = 2.06, PD2 = 2.14), the Hénon map (D2 = 1.26, PD2 = 1.22), and a nonchaotic sine wave (D2 = 1.00, PD2 = 1.03). Molnar and Skinner (1992) also showed that PD2 decreases significantly when a human subject detects a low-probability target sound that usually also elicits a large and diagnostic component of the ERP, often called the "P300" (it begins approximately 300 msec after the stimulus onset in young normal humans) or just the "P3" because it is usually the third positive-going component of the ERP. Figure 27.3 shows the average ERPs (solid tracing at top of graphs) and PD2s (fuzzy series of dots at bottoms) from eleven human subjects for sounds that did not elicit a P3 component (control panel and first ERP in target panel) and for a sound that did (labeled "P411" in target panel). The reduction of the PD2 associated with the ERP to the low-probability target (2.8 kHz tone when it occurred only 10% of the time) is clear. Because the PD2 reduction occurs prior to the onset of the P3 component, it is likely that the reduction reflects a change in brain dynamics caused by the initiation of the process that also generates the P3. Because the P3 is seen in response to a low-probability stimulus event, and presumably marks the initiation of brain processes that update a representation of expected environmental events, apparently part of the brain momentarily enters a state of low dimensionality while engaged in this updating task. Such results are promising evidence that we may yet be able to study in intact humans the low-dimensional chaos created by the response of a cognitive system to a meaningful stimulus.

Chapter 28

Perception of Sequence

It is remarkable that a science which began with the consideration of games of chance should have become the most important object of human knowledge.

—Laplace, quoted in Warren Weaver, *Lady Luck*

The next three chapters attempt to answer the question, can humans behave chaotically if they want to? Because, however, chaos and randomness are so closely related (see chap. 24) I want to frame the question in the larger context of perception and behavior with respect to *randomness* before proceeding to an answer in chapter 30. Thus I will discuss the perception of random and not-so-random sequences in the present chapter, before considering attempts to get people to behave randomly (chap. 29) and chaotically (chap. 30).

28.1 The Gambler's Fallacy

Imagine yourself in Caesar's Palace in Las Vegas. Hundreds of people are gambling at slot machines, rolling dice at craps tables, and playing blackjack, and many more are crowded around roulette tables. You are among those playing roulette and you are doing something that the casino very much disapproves of: keeping careful track of all of the numbers the little steel ball lands on. You have noticed that in the past hour, the ball simply has not landed on the number "21" at all. Chance has simply passed by that number. You know that the casino is very careful to make sure that the roulette wheels have no long-run biases, so that people like yourself cannot break the bank by recording the plays, figuring out the bias, and then betting heavily on the most likely numbers or colors. But you have another scheme: you reason that because the rolls of the steel ball land randomly on the various numbers, the overall probability of it landing on each number is the same in the long run, as the casino intends it to be. But, you think, the short run is different. If the ball did not land on a particular number for a long while, that would violate the rule of randomness, or equal probability. Thus, you reason, the probability of the ball landing on a given number can be the same as it is for the other numbers in the long run, given an extended time period during which the ball never lands on that number, only if the ball is *more* likely to land on that number for a while after the run of nonlandings in order to compensate for the period of nonlandings. That is, you think you have discovered a loophole in the laws of chance and that you will become rich by exploiting it.

In this particular case, you act on your discovery that the number "21" has not been landed on in an hour at this roulette table by betting 20% of your money on that number in each of the next five rolls of the wheel. You reason that the ball simply "must" land there soon, perhaps several times, in order to make the long-run probability of that number the same as the others. Unfortunately, in the next five rolls of the wheel, the ball lands in the numbers 38, 20, 17, 3, and 3 again. You walk away from the wheel and out of the casino, broke and disillusioned. You have become the latest victim of the "gambler's fallacy." You are not alone. Most people, when asked, answer that the law of large numbers, the idea that long-run proportions approach exact probabilities, works by compensation. Which is to say, although runs of certain events might occur that distort the proportions of the various types of events away from the exact probabilities in the short run, the exact probabilities are approached closely in the long run because there are compensating runs of other events in the later portions of the series. Moreover, even if you are not one of those who consciously think this way, chances are that if you were asked to decide which of several series of zeros and ones looked the most "random," you would choose the one that seemed to alternate the most. For example, which of the following sequences do you think is most random-looking:

010101001011010101110

or

10110100011001110100001?

Most people find the upper sequence more random-looking; when asked why, they answer that the lower sequence has too many runs to be random. This conclusion is also a manifestation of the gambler's fallacy: either sequence could have been produced by a random process. If produced by a stochastic process in which $p(0) = p(1) = 0.5$ at all times, however, sequences that have many alternations (e.g., 0101) like the upper one actually occur somewhat less often than sequences like the lower one.

The law of large numbers in fact does *not* work by compensation; it works by *swamping* (see Feller 1968 or Weaver 1963). In any random process where the events occur independently according to some probability distribution, the proportions of types of events do indeed approach the exact probabilities ever more closely as the length of the sequence increases. But this is because low-probability subsequences, such a run of 100 ones in a sequence of ones and zeros like the one illustrated above, simply do not have much impact on a ratio like $5 \times 10^{100000000}/1 \times 10^{100000001}$. The large numbers of the "long run" simply swamp the short-run anomalies. The long-run proportion of ones can approach the nominal probability of 0.5 ever more closely the longer the sequence even though a compensating run of 100 zeros did not occur.

If belief in compensation, leading to the gambler's fallacy, can have such painful consequences, why is it still so prevalent? One reason might be because the correct understanding of random sequences requires some subtlety of thought. But a better answer might be that, except at the gaming tables, probabilities in the real world really do not remain the same over really long periods of time. If we see a run of some event, for example, the same animal showing up at a water hole three days in a row after failing to visit there for the previous week, perhaps something really has changed. We might indeed be rewarded for staking out the same water hole the next day (the opposite of the gambler's fallacy because this is not a random sequence). Sensitivity to short-run probabilities has become a habit of humans because the contingency structure of our environment requires it (see Skinner 1974). Before we consider that further, however, let us look at how we do when we have to perform such short-run probability estimation.

28.2   Estimation of Short-Run Probabilities

Studies of probability estimation became suddenly popular in cognitive psychology during the 1960s and 1970s, in the wake of a number of studies showing that both humans' and other animals' behavior is sensitive to short-run or "local" contingencies. A dramatic example in lower animals is the "matching law," discovered and named by Herrnstein (1961) in his classic study of choice behavior in pigeons. The pigeons pecked at one or the other of two keys, labeled "A" and "B," in proportion to how fast and often food was provided as a result of pecking each key. This result was expressed as the matching law:

$$\frac{R_A}{R_A + R_B} = \frac{r_A}{r_A + r_B}, \tag{28.1}$$

where R_A is the rate of pecking at key A and r_A is the rate of reinforcement obtained by pecking at that key. Because the times in each rate cancel in the fractions, these numbers also represent proportions of responses and reinforcements, or estimates of probabilities of response and reinforcement, respectively. This result can therefore be interpreted as "probability matching"; pigeons can be thought to peck the key at which the momentary probability of a reinforcement was the highest. In the types of reinforcement schedules used by Herrnstein (1961) and others since then, in which reinforcement occurs on the first peck after a variable interval of time, the probability of obtaining a reinforcement at a particular key increases with the time interval since that key was last pecked. By keeping track of these short-term changes in probability of reinforcement, a pigeon could distribute its pecking over the two keys so as to obtain the maximum number of reinforcements. Another explanation for the matching law is that the pigeon balances the local *rates* of reinforcement per time or per unit of effort over a slightly longer timescale so they are the same for all alternatives, with the goal of maximizing the overall rate of return for effort. In either case, the animal has to be sensitive to probabilistic contingencies that change over relatively short timescales (seconds to minutes).

Probability-matching behavior is common to many species of animals and humans, and occurs in humans even when the reward is quite abstract, for example "being correct" (Lee 1971). Indeed, humans are quite good at probability matching, and consistently probability match when asked to predict outcomes in a stochastic series, even when they know such a strategy will cost them money (see Lee 1971 for review). They have many rationalizations for this behavior, most of which display a concern with local probabilistic contingencies, that is, with the effects of immediately previous stimuli or choices on what is happening now. The sensitivity to local probabilistic contingencies seems to be a nearly universal characteristic of animals.

One arena in which sensitivity to short-run contingencies has been thoroughly studied, and in which it also biases performance (sometimes for the better), is in a task called "numerical signal detection," used to test the fundamental assumptions of *signal detection theory* (SDT; see Green

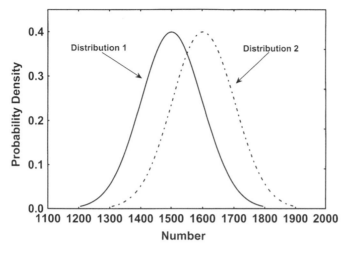

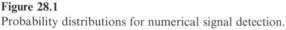

Figure 28.1
Probability distributions for numerical signal detection.

and Swets 1966; Macmillan and Creelman 1991 for discussions), an application of statistical decision theory to the detection of weak signals, either by a radio receiver or a human observer, and probably the most used and useful quantitative theory in psychology. In their study of numerical signal detection, Kubovy, Rapoport, and Tversky (1970) asked human subjects to decide from which of two Gaussian probability distributions a particular number was sampled; they repeated the procedure for many trials with many different samples from the two distributions. Distribution 1 had a mean of 1,500, distribution 2 had a mean of 1,600, and both had a standard deviation of 100. As plotted in figure 28.1, this decision situation resembles that of SDT except that in SDT the Gaussian distributions are assumed to underlie subjects' decisions about the presence, absence, or identity of sensory or other stimuli, and their relative locations are inferred from a number of those decisions. When numbers are sampled from distribution 1 or 2 according to a second probability distribution, for example $p(1) = p(2) = 0.5$, the optimal decision procedure is to choose a particular number as a criterion and respond "1" if the sample on a particular trial is below that number and "2" if it is above it. Which number to select as criterion depends on the probability of sampling from each number distribution and on the reward for each decision outcome (see Green and Swets 1966 for a discussion). For example, if the values of the responses are equal and the probability of sampling from each distribution is equal to 0.5, then the criterion should be fixed at

1,550. Theoretically, a series of such decisions should become mechanical: simply ascertain whether the sampled number is greater than or less than 1,550 and make the indicated decision, over and over again.

Somewhat surprisingly, especially because money was at stake, subjects in Kubovy, Rapoport, and Tversky's experiment did not always do what was optimal. Instead, on about 5% of trials, they made the opposite decision from that dictated by the optimal decision rule. This decision cost them money, just as betting according to the gambler's fallacy at Las Vegas could cost someone money. The three researchers had no explanation—the irrational behavior of their subjects mystified them. Later on, Tversky and his colleague Kahneman (see Tversky and Kahneman 1981) discovered behaviors, called "heuristics," that people use when they are in difficult, probabilistic decision situations, behaviors that help explain, in a general way, some aspects of such seemingly irrational behavior. When I read Kubovy, Rapoport, and Tversky 1970, however, having studied sequential dependencies between psychophysical judgments (see chap. 11), it occurred to me that the numerical detection situation was ripe for similar dependencies. Indeed, I had read in Friedman and Carterette 1964 and Sandusky 1971 that when stimuli in SDT experiments were presented in Markov chains, there were contingencies between the trials (see chap. 2). I had also conjectured (Ward and Lockhead 1971) that at least some sequential dependencies in psychophysical judgments arose from subjects' knowing that small differences between successive numbers in a random sequence are more common than large ones because there are more ways in which such small differences could occur. For example, in a random sequence of the numbers 1–10, there are eighteen ways a one-unit difference could happen (1–2, 2–1, 2–3, 3–2, and so forth) but only two ways for a nine-unit difference to occur (1–10 and 10–1). Our subjects seemed to be resolving their uncertainty about which response to select by choosing the smallest difference between preceding and current stimuli that was consistent with the sensory evidence.

It seemed to me that if subjects were scrutinizing the previous sequence of stimuli and responses in such a way as to produce sequential dependencies in their psychophysical judgments, then they might be sensitive to real sequential dependencies between the stimuli. To test this hypothesis, I produced Markov chains of samples from the two numerical detection distributions displayed in figure 28.1 to use as stimuli for numerical signal detection (Ward 1973). In some chains of samples, the probability of an alternation (a sample from distribution 1 followed by a sample from distribution 2 or vice versa) was 0.9 (*alternation* condition); in others, the probability of an alternation was 0.1 (*run* condition); and in still others, it was exactly 0.5 (an independent, identically distributed, or i.i.d., sequence—*random* condition). A short segment of the alternation condition might look like this: 121212122121121222121121212121212211212, whereas a segment of the run condition might look like this: 1111112222221111222122221111111122222. If subjects were sensitive to these dependencies between trials in distribution sampled from, they could do better than the ideal observer of SDT, who could obtain a d' of 1.0, where d' is the distance between the two distributions in standard deviation units; in this case, $d' = (1,600 - 1,500)/100 = 1.0$. And they did. Performance was significantly better than $d' = 1.0$ in both the alternation and run conditions, although not quite optimal. However, in the random condition, subjects performed significantly worse than the ideal SDT observer, just as they had in Kubovy, Rapoport, and Tversky 1970. Moreover, subjects violated the ideal decision rule in the random condition on even more trials than subjects had in that study. In Ward, Livingston, and Li 1988, we replicated Ward 1973 and extended SDT by assuming that subjects make short-run estimates of the transition probabilities in the Markov chain of stimuli and use these to tell them where to put their decision criterion on each trial. This behavior causes their performance to be worse than ideal in the random condition because their short-run estimates of the transition probabilities are unstable and often quite different from the true probabilities. The model, however, asserts that they continue to use these unstable estimates even when it makes their performance worse because when there *are* real sequential dependencies in the sequence of samples, when the probability of an alternation is different from 0.5, doing so improves their performance dramatically. A similar theory developed by Treisman and Williams (1984) has the decision criteria influenced by two competing tendencies: *tracking*, which monitors short-run changes in relevant probabilities, and *stabilization*, which makes sure that the unstable short-run estimates do not overly influence the decision criteria. In both theories, short-run estimation of probabilities is both as accurate as the situation permits and adaptive in the sense that it improves performance when contingencies actually are present.

28.3 Evolution of Contingency Perception

Sensitivity to contingencies at several timescales is adaptive because of the temporal structure of the world: contingencies between survival-relevant events exist at several timescales. Often, perhaps even usually, these contingencies are probabilistic and the probabilities can change on all timescales, although change on shorter timescales is more common. Consider a predator: the better it is at finding and killing its prey, the greater the number of its viable offspring (all things being equal) and the more likely its genes will dominate in future generations. Optimal foraging, the most efficient strategy for intake of food, by predator and nonpredator alike, can require several decisions to be made based on probabilistic data. For example, the redshank, a type of shore bird that inhabits the English mudflats, eats two different kinds of prey: a more desirable crustacean and a less desirable worm. Although it would be best to take only the more desirable prey, the redshank cannot always find and catch it and sometimes must settle for the more common but less desirable prey. When the redshank happens on a worm, it must "decide" whether to take it or to wait and possibly get a crustacean (but possibly go hungry). Calculations from optimal foraging theory, like those done by economists on optimal business strategies (see Stephens, and Krebs 1986), predict that the redshank will take the less desirable prey in inverse proportion to the probability of encountering the more-desirable prey. And indeed it does. It (seems to) estimate the short-run probability (which changes daily or even hourly depending on many factors, such as tides and weather) of encountering the more-desirable crustacean, taking fewer worms if that probability is high and more if it is low (Goss-Custard 1977). In other cases, an animal that has access to several "patches," areas where food is available, must estimate the relative density of feeding opportunities in each patch and then select the "best" one for exploitation. Animals usually do this in accordance with optimal foraging theory, spending the optimum amount of time sampling the patches to discover their relative goodness (e.g., Krebs, Kacelnik and Taylor 1978). Thus sensitivity to local contingencies plays an important role in the determining the fitness of animals.

Both long-term stabilization and short-term tracking are adaptive behaviors (see Treisman and Williams 1984 for a compelling argument). I propose that the memory mechanisms that evolved under the selection pressures of optimal foraging (and also of reproduction, avoidance of predators, etc.) help to explain the vicissitudes of probability estimation and sequence perception in humans. Long-term memory is relatively unlimited but imprecise (e.g., Norman 1982), whereas short-term memory is relatively precise but quite limited (e.g., Miller 1956; Simon 1974). Long-term probability estimation (stabilization) could be based on what

Neisser (1981) called "repisodic" memories: repeated episodes of similar events over long time periods, from a few days to many years, result in knowledge of stable long-run probabilities that can be quite accurate and approach the optimal (Bayesian) estimates (see Feller 1968). A good example is the feeling physicians have for the conditional probabilities of various diseases when given the symptoms of a patient (e.g., Kleinmuntz 1968). Short-run estimates (tracking) could be based on memories of specific events in the recent past, from a few seconds to perhaps a few hours (if the events are dramatic enough). But the short-term memory mechanism is limited: for example, in Ward, Livingston, and Li 1988, we found that transition probability estimates were based on about 7–15 trials back in the sequence of numerical signal detection trials, allowing subjects to discriminate large probability differences but not small ones and making it appear to the subjects that even long-term stable probabilities are fluctuating dramatically in the short run. This limited view should lead to the gambler's fallacy and other suboptimal performances when the sequence is truly random. To see this more clearly, consider the following (random) sequence of ones and zeros: 1100000001101100110001101011101010111. The probability of a one occurring in the first seven events, estimated from the proportion of ones in that subsequence, is 2/7, while in the last seven events it is 5/7. Similarly, the estimated probabilities of an alternation in those two subsequences are, respectively, 1/6 and 4/6. These are not only quite far from the "true" probabilities (1/2 in all cases), but also fluctuate greatly from segment to segment of the sequence, giving the impression of a somewhat unstable world at the shorter timescale. I propose that these short-run and long-run mechanisms operate automatically, giving rise to "intuitions" about what is about to occur that result both in suboptimal performances like the gambler's fallacy or poor numerical signal detection when the sequence is random, and in near-optimal foraging or clinical diagnosis when there are real contingencies to be perceived in a sequence of events.

Chapter 29
Can People Behave Randomly?

Human[s] are incapable of generating a random series of selections from a finite number of alternatives. . . .
—G. S. Tune, "A Brief Survey of Variables That Influence Random Generation"

Producing a random series of responses is a difficult, if not impossible, task to human[s], even when they are explicitly instructed to approximate randomness as closely as possible.
—Willem A. Wagenaar, "Generation of Random Sequences by Human Subjects"

29.1 No!

From the epigraphs above, it would seem that people are just as poor at generating random behavior as they are at perceiving it—even though such behavior would be adaptive in many situations, for example, when avoiding a predator or when competing for a mate or for food. My own research experience confirms this inability to behave randomly. In Ward and Lockhead 1971, we asked subjects to predict the output of an electromechanical random number generator that generated random sequences of the digits 0–9. The sequences generated by the subjects were not at all random, although they performed their guessing task no better than chance: they were correct on only 10% of their predictions, exactly as would be expected from random guessing. Indeed, as shown by the graph in figure 29.1, they displayed one of the same sequential dependencies we had found in sequences of psychophysical judgments: successive responses were close together or exact repeats more often than they would be in a random sequence and far apart less often than in a random sequence. The subjects' pattern of guessing is an exaggeration of the tendency mentioned in chapter 28 for small differences between random digits to be relatively more frequent and large ones less frequent (probability-matching curve in

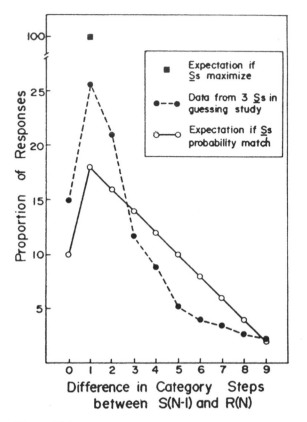

Figure 29.1
Relative frequency distribution of subjects' guessing responses compared to theoretical predictions. (From Ward and Lockhead 1971.)

fig. 29.1), and in the opposite direction from what the gambler's fallacy
would predict. Before exploring these results more fully, however, let us
look at some of the other evidence for nonrandom behavior.

According to Budescu (1987), Reichenbach (1949) was the first to
comment in print about whether people could behave randomly: in his
book on probability theory, Reichenbach speculated that people would
not be able to generate a random sequence because the behavior of stochastic processes was too subtle for an untrained person to emulate. He
predicted people would fall prey to the gambler's fallacy and generate too
many alternations, just as they perceive sequences with too many alternations to be more random than truly random sequences. And, indeed,
that has been found nearly always to be the case. (For a good review of

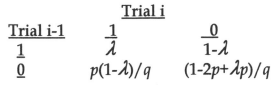

Figure 29.2
Budescu's Markov chain model of "random guessing." (After Budescu 1987.)

the early literature, see Wagenaar 1972; for reviews of the more recent literature, see Neuringer 1986 and Kareev 1992.)

In replicating the results of many previous experiments to establish the ubiquity of the gambler's fallacy in behavior, Budescu (1987) asked his subjects to generate series of hypothetical coin tosses by repeatedly pressing one or the other of two keys on a computer keyboard. Although informed about several of the properties of random sequences and given accurate information about the probabilities of the "heads" and "tails" they were to produce, they were given only very general feedback on how they were doing. The very first series for each subject was to be a series of tosses of a "fair" coin with $P(\text{heads}) = P(\text{tails}) = 0.5$. Twelve of eighteen subjects generated too many alternations, three generated too few, and three had no consistent bias. On later runs with a higher probability of "heads," some of the run-biased or inconsistent subjects also showed an alternation bias. Budescu described these data using a simple Markov chain model, with a parameter, $\lambda = P(x_i = \text{heads} \mid x_{i-1} = \text{heads})$, to account for the sequential dependencies in the generated series. According to this model, with $p = P(\text{heads})$ and $q = P(\text{tails}) = 1 - p$, the Markov transition matrix (see chap. 2) describing the chain of responses looks like figure 29.2. Because p and q are set by the experimenters and known to the subjects, only λ must be estimated from the data. If $\lambda < p$, then the sequence has too many alternations (gambler's fallacy), whereas if $\lambda > p$, then the generated series has too many runs. If $\lambda = p$, then the successive guesses are independent, a random series. The parameter λ is easily estimated from the generated series by $\hat{\lambda} = \#$ "heads heads" $/$ ($\#$ "heads heads" $+ \#$ "heads tails"), where $\#$ "heads heads" means number of pairs with a "heads" followed by a "heads." This model captures both the departures from randomness in subjects' generated series for a wide range of values of p, and also the tendency of subjects to use the response alternatives equally over short segments of the series ("local representativeness," one of the heuristics described by Tversky and Kahneman 1981). On the other hand, the model tells us neither why subjects would choose a particular value of λ nor why, when they know they are supposed to make $\lambda = p$, they usually do not do so.

29.2 Sometimes

In chapter 11, we encountered time estimation data from three subjects who had produced series of 1,000 "random" intervals in which the autocorrelation function was null, an indication that these subjects were capable of producing random behavior (although the data were not subjected to more stringent tests of randomness). Three other subjects were unable to produce random time series: their series were well described by ARIMA (0, 1, 2) or ARIMA (1, 1, 1) models. In Budescu 1987, three of eighteen subjects generated at least a few series of coin tosses that had no consistent bias, an instance of the randomness demonstrated by a few subjects in most experiments. Are these subjects different? Do they have a talent the other ones lack? Or does this random behavior simply occur at random?

Not trusting our subjects' answers (for good reasons), psychologists do not usually them to report either on their understanding of the task before them or on the strategy they propose to use to deal with it. We attempt to infer these from their performance or, better, to manipulate them explicitly. In an attempt to test the idea that subjects' nonrandom performance reflected imperfect understanding of the concept of randomness (a problem that sometimes affects even mathematicians), Neuringer (1986) conducted a sophisticated computer-based experiment. He asked subjects to press the "1" and "2" keys on a computer keyboard as randomly as possible and at their own speed. As a baseline, he collected 6,000 responses, in 60 blocks of 100 trials, from each of seven subjects. After subjects had generated these series, he began to give them feedback as to how well their series matched one generated by a random number generator implemented on the same computer. In one experiment, he gave feedback on five different series descriptors: uncertainty of successive responses (or information—see Garner 1962), uncertainty of responses two trials apart (RNG2), number of runs (ALTS), uncertainty of responses at the same position across 100-trial blocks, and uncertainty of responses at positions two trials apart across 100-trial blocks (XC2). In another, he gave feedback on a group of ten descriptors, the first five and five additional ones that implemented an even more demanding criterion of randomness. He compared each subject's series, both before and after feedback was initiated, to the outputs of the computer random number generator using the

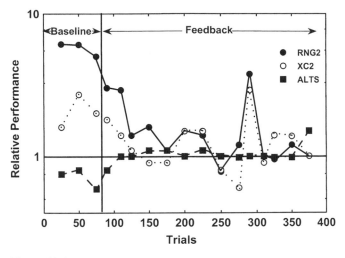

Figure 29.3
One subject's data. (Data from Neuringer 1986.)

Kolmogorov-Smirnov test (a nonparametric test of proportions; see Siegel 1956).

During the baseline period, all subjects' series differed significantly from the random number generator on most of the descriptors. For example, in the first experiment, all subjects differed from the random number generator on both of the first two descriptors, and four of the seven differed significantly on each of the other three. Interestingly, all of Neuringer's subjects (1986) displayed $\lambda > p$ behavior, to use Budescu's schema (1987), generating too few alternations, the opposite of the usual finding. Neuringer speculated that this may have occurred because of the ease of quickly generating strings of the same response on the computer keyboard. Figure 29.3 displays the baseline data for three of the descriptors for one typical subject in the form of the ratio of the subject's score on a descriptor divided by the random number generator's score on that same descriptor: random performance would be indicated by a ratio of 1.0. Each point in the figure is an average over twenty 100-digit blocks, (called "trials" by Neuringer). Figure 29.3 is also representative of the general finding of both experiments: after feedback was initiated, eventually all subjects were able to generate series that passed all of the tests for randomness for at least two successive sets of 60 "trials." For most subjects, this took a long time (remember a "trial" refers here to a 100-digit series). The subject shown in figure 29.3 required about 300 such "trials" to reach consistent randomness; other subjects required over 500 (or

50,000 responses). In the second experiment, with ten descriptors, three subjects required nearly 1,000 such "trials"; one even required some 1,700 "trials" (170,000 responses) after feedback was initiated. Thus, when humans are told exactly what to do, and given feedback on how they are doing, they can even behave randomly, if given enough time to learn how to adjust their behavior to the requirements.

Although people must be extensively trained to achieve the most stringent standards of randomness, there is evidence that they do have a reasonable idea of what random behavior is, at least in the sense of relative frequency. As we have noted, small differences are more common than large ones in a random sequence of more than two alternatives. There are similar "proportions" in the various subsequences of longer random sequences. Consider a long sequence of "fair" coin tosses and subsequences of ten tosses in the longer sequence. There are $2^{10} = 1,024$ possible such subsequences, and of these, 252 have five heads and five tails, and 210 have either 4 heads and 6 tails or vice versa. Clearly, a 10-toss subsequence with about equal numbers of heads and tails is by far the most common type: 67.2% of the possible subsequences are of this type. Kareev (1992) argued that people know that such roughly equally balanced subsequences are most common in a longer sequence, although of course he did not ask them directly. Instead, he reasoned that young children would be less likely to know this fact than college-age adults. Kareev argued that, when asked to produce a random sequence, people try to produce subsequences resembling the most common one in longer sequences; and that they are limited by short-term memory capacity to producing a subsequence of a length consistent with that capacity (between five and seven items for most people). Tune (1964) had proposed a similar explanation for violations of randomness based on short-term memory limitations. Kareev (1992) hypothesized that, because children also have less short-term memory capacity than adults, they would be limited to even shorter subsequences, thus would depart from randomness more often than would adults. He confirmed this hypothesis for short sequences of ten hypothetical coin tosses; analyzing the alternation rate in sequences of hypothetical coin tosses of various lengths for various probabilities of heads in the sequence, he showed that the most commonly reported alternation rate of about 0.6 is the expected one for a short-term memory capacity of between five and six items. Finally, he showed that the alternation rate observed in his data decreased with increasing age of subject, and was smaller for a task that put more emphasis on each individual trial than on the entire sequence. For the adults doing the trial-by-trial task, it was 0.53, just about the expected 0.5 for a truly random sequence, but still slightly biased in the usual way.

The theoretical approach taken in chapter 28 for perception of sequences would seem appropriate for production of sequences, as well. Although it is hardly a well-worked-out theory, associating the contingency estimation processes described in chapter 28 based on long-term and short-term memory, respectively, with the stabilization and tracking processes of Treisman and Williams (1984), goes some way toward making the approach more sophisticated. Treisman and Faulkner (1987) showed that by assuming subjects possess an internal generator of randomly varying activation (internal noise?) that can be categorized like that produced by an external stimulus under the influence of the effects of stabilization and tracking on criterion settings, one can account for all of the previous data and their own new data on random sequence generation. And their theory is very well worked out indeed. An alternative is the theory my colleagues and I proposed in Ward et al. 1988, a different generalization of SDT with an explicit memory parameter that, when applied to the generation of sequences, produces results roughly similar to those of Treisman and Faulkner (1987).

29.3 Sequential Dependencies and Extrasensory Perception

Many people associate Duke University with the work of J. B. Rhine on parapsychology, although he left there in the early 1960s to start an independent foundation located in Durham, North Carolina, for research into unexplained phenomena, mostly parapsychology. As a graduate student in experimental psychology at Duke, supervised by G. R. Lockhead, I became very aware of the mixed feelings that Rhine's work had generated. Thus, when I ran the experiment I mentioned in section 29.1, where human subjects were told to try to guess the next number a mechanical random number generator would generate, I realized that it could also be seen as an experiment in extrasensory perception (ESP). If subjects could do better than chance at this task, which was quite out of any human's control (the machine was driven by the electrical noise from a Zener diode), perhaps there was some way in which humans could have access to the subatomic world. At any rate, the disappointing, but expected, result that all subjects performed at chance accuracy dashed any secret hopes at taming parapsychology, but revealed an even more interesting behavior, another manifestation of the sequential dependencies I have been studying off and on for over thirty years.

Just before I left Duke, Rhine's foundation entertained a prominent Caribbean psychic named Lance Harribance. Many of my fellow graduate students were excited by this visit, and several went to be "read" by Harribance. The tales of this man's wondrous psychic abilities of course got back to the Psychology Department, and though I scoffed at their gullibility, I was impressed by Harribance's ability to fool these very bright students. My mentor, Greg Lockhead, was also impressed and determined to put Harribance's abilities to an objective test. He invited Harribance to our laboratory to participate in the same experiment I described above: trying to predict which numeral (1–5) would be the next one chosen by our mechanical random number generator. I had to leave before Harribance took the test, but I read all about it in Lockhead's paper (1974), unfortunately still unpublished.

Supplied with food and drink, and made comfortable in our laboratory, Harribance felt confident that his abilities were equal to the task. He made a series of 1,000 guesses and, after each guess, he rated the confidence he felt in the correctness of that particular guess. On each trial, he received as feedback the numeral actually chosen by the machine before making his next guess. After the test, he was even more confident, and felt he had done very well and had exceeded chance performance. Nevertheless (as you may have guessed), he performed very close to chance: 21.1% correct predictions, less than one standard deviation from the predicted 20%. The sequential dependencies in his guesses, however, were of exactly the same form as the ones we had described in Ward and Lockhead 1971, but the greatest in magnitude either of us had ever seen. Indeed, it was possible to predict which number Harribance would guess next with far higher accuracy than he could predict the machine's next number, using a model based on his tendency to repeat the previous machine-generated number, or choose a number at most one removed from it. When he did make such a guess, which was frequently, his confidence was high; on the infrequent occasions when he guessed a number farther away from his last guess his confidence was low. Harribance's feeling that he had done well came from the fact that he was within one number of the correct one on many occasions, because, as noted, small differences occur most frequently in random series. By guessing a number close to the previous feedback, he ensured that even if he was incorrect, he would be close on many occasions. Unfortunately, close counts only in horseshoes and in psychic readings. In this test, rather than psychic ability, Harribance displayed only the more mundane ability to exploit a property of random sequences (cf. Goodfellow 1938; Hansel 1966).

Chapter 30

Can People Behave Chaotically?

The presence of chaotic-like human behavior is consistent with a complete determinism.... Yet the slightest uncertainty in knowledge makes prediction of chaotic behaviors highly unreliable.

—Allen Neuringer and Cheryl Voss, "Approximating Chaotic Behavior"

30.1 Yes!

Human behavior is vexingly unpredictable, and yet it is (usually) not random either (see chap. 29). Whether a "reformed" killer will kill again or a relationship with a person to whom we are attracted will last are questions that plague us. We need to be able to predict some aspects of human behavior and yet are notoriously bad at it. For example, it has been argued that forensic psychiatrists and psychologists are completely unable to speak with any authority about whether a particular criminal will relapse into criminal behavior if released into society, and that the testimony of such experts should not be admissible in hearings concerning such questions (Faust and Ziskin 1988). And the divorce rate is testimony that, on average, we are not good at choosing marriage partners. Where does this unpredictability come from if not from randomness? Many would answer "free will." If we accept this answer, we must admit that the prospects for understanding human behavior are dim because, at a whim, a person can produce some unexpected behavior whose causal antecedents are in principle unavailable. We could possibly still discover general (nomothetic) laws having a statistical basis. For example, we could discover that, on average, 25% of rapists commit rape again within one year of release into society. However, when the question is about the behavior of a single individual rapist, does this general law say anything useful? It does only if we wish to set a criterion of 0 or 1 for the probability of a repeat offense. Then we can either release (if our criterion is 1) or retain (if it is 0) all rapists on the basis of the "general law." Otherwise, our finding provides no basis for saying whether any particular individual will commit the same offense again. On the other hand, some researchers argue that the eventual discovery of the basis in brain activity for behavior, even covert behavior such as cognition, will allow us to predict with near certainty what an individual will do. Even better, if the individual is likely to do something we do not like, we can adjust the brain so as to prevent that behavior from emerging, a future envisaged with horror (albeit with cruder technology) by Anthony Burgess in *A Clockwork Orange*. Moral debates aside, the likelihood of this occurring is uncertain at present: we simply do not know enough about how the brain generates behavior and cognition.

On the other hand, as the chapter epigraph indicates, chaos holds out the possibility that absolute determinism and relative unpredictability may coexist. Indeed, chaos may explain why human behavior is at the same time unpredictable and yet completely determined by discoverable laws. Although this may not help us predict future criminal behavior, where we may have to continue to rely on the dictum "The past is the best predictor of the future," it might bring us philosophical solace, letting us dispense with the notion that human behavior has essentially hidden causes, or perhaps no causes at all. Chapter 26 reviewed some evidence that sequences of human behaviors might contain some nonlinear structure indicative of low-dimensional deterministic generators. Here I am going to discuss a different approach to the problem of establishing a role for chaos theory in human behavior, that of trying to teach humans to emulate a chaotic system.

In a provocative article published in *Psychological Science*, Allen Neuringer and Cheryl Voss (Neuringer and Voss 1993) claimed they had taught humans to approximate chaotic sequences generated by the logistic difference equation (eq. 24.1b):

$$x_{n+1} = a \cdot x_n \cdot (1 - x_n),$$

with $a = 4.0$ (for a display of the strange attractor of eq. 24.1b, see fig. 24.1B; for a brief discussion of the behavior of the logistic difference equation, see sec. 24.1). Neuringer and Voss used a technique similar to the one Lockhead (1974) used to investigate the sequential behavior of a psychic (see chap. 29): they asked subjects to predict what number would occur next in a series (a one-step forecast) and then gave them feedback as to what number had actually occurred. The series in question was generated by a computer implementing equation 24.1b with seven-digit pre-

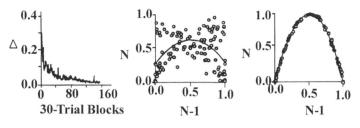

Figure 30.1
One subject's data. (From Neuringer and Voss 1993. Copyright © 1993 by
Blackwell Publishers.)

cision but displaying it with three-digit precision. They also had subjects
perform an analog version of this task, predicting the next location on a
line that ran the width of the computer monitor. Both with lines and with
digits the results were the same: subjects learned to generate forecasts
that were not far from the actual numbers in the sequence based on the
last number that actually occurred (the "seed"). In figure 30.1, the left-
hand graph shows the deviation of one subject's forecasts from the computer-generated numbers over about 4,500 trials, and the middle and
right-hand graphs represent that subject's forecasts on each trial as a
function of the computer-generated number on the previous trial for the
first and last 120 trials of this subject's data, respectively. If the subjects
are behaving according to the logistic equation, then such plots should
resemble figure 24.1B; indeed, the plot for the final 120 trials does. Neuringer and Voss also subjected these data to other tests for nonlinear
determinism, such as comparing the entropy (uncertainty, information) of
the subjects' sequences with those of the logistic-generated sequences and
with that of a random-number generator, and also fitted their phase plots
with quadratic equations. Finally, they ran an experiment in which they
ceased giving the feedback at a certain point and then observed the divergence of the subjects' sequences from the computer-generated sequence,
an indication of sensitive dependence (see chap. 23). On the basis of these
data, they concluded that their subjects were approximating chaotic
behavior, with the implications mentioned earlier.

30.2 Not Really

As I was reading Neuringer and Voss's paper (1993), I could not help
thinking of several *non*chaotic ways in which subjects could be generating
sequences that "approximated" chaotic ones. People could be simply

learning the rough shape of the logistic map, a parabola in which numbers near either 0 or 1 on the x-axis are paired with numbers near 0 on the y-axis, whereas numbers near 0.5 on the x-axis are paired with numbers near 1 on the y-axis, and so on. Enlisting the nearest family member, my daughter, I confirmed that, after only a few trials, she could easily emulate Neuringer and Voss's subjects' behavior using only a simple heuristic that had nothing to do with chaos. Metzger (1994) had a similar thought and proposed a model in which subjects memorized several seed-feedback pairs of numbers and noticed that they fell along a parabola. Linear interpolation between these memorized pairs could then provide predictions for any other seeds. Without feedback, the subject could simply use each previous prediction as the seed for the next one.

In Ward and West 1994, Robert West and I took a slightly different tack in print. We argued that from Neuringer and Voss's results it is difficult to tell whether subjects were iterating a chaotic equation, and thus producing a chaotic sequence and a strange attractor, or simply following a nonchaotic heuristic such as memorizing pairs of numbers and interpolating between them, when the map and the attractor are identical as they are in equation 24.1b with $a = 4.0$. We pointed out that when a is changed from 4.0 to 3.66, although the quadratic form of the map stays the same (it is still a parabola, albeit with a slightly different pairing of numbers), the attractor of the map changes drastically, as shown in figure 30.2A: most of the left leg and large parts of the right leg of the map are now missing. We reasoned that if we taught subjects this map and then asked them to iterate it without feedback, they would produce the map (noisily) if they were using a heuristic such as Metzger's but the attractor if they were indeed iterating the equation they had learned, even if only approximately. As you can see from the example in figure 30.2B, our subjects did not produce the attractor, but only a noisy version of the map.

With Metzger (1994), West and I also pointed out some subtle technical problems involving precision of computer representation of numbers for any such experiments. The crux of the matter is this: to get a good approximation of chaos from a computer, it is necessary to represent the numbers involved with at least seven-digit precision, preferably, with fourteen- or fifteen-digit precision. Neuringer and Voss (1993), however, presented their subjects with numbers (or line lengths) having only three-digit precision, although they used seven-digit precision in the computer. With only three-digit precision, the logistic equation generates sequences that settle into limit cycles of from one to only a few points, depending on

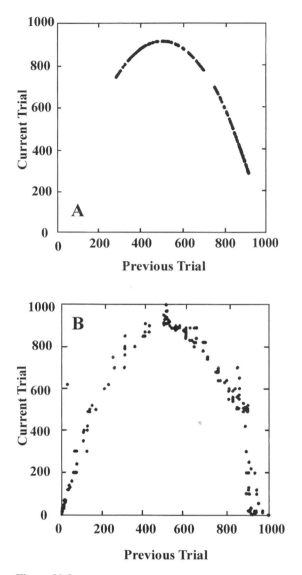

Figure 30.2
(*A*) Strange attractor of the logistic difference equation (eq. 24.1b), *a* = 3.66; (*B*) one subject's data. (From Ward and West 1994. Copyright © 1994 by Blackwell Publishers.)

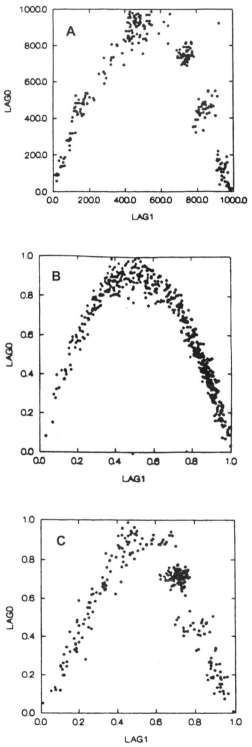

the value of a, the starting number, and the rounding or truncating procedure used. Moreover, the actual seed-feedback pairings that occur in a sequence generated at seven-digit precision but rounded to three-digit precision do not properly represent even the seven-digit-precision sequence, let alone the "real" sequence of the logistic equation (which requires infinite precision). On the other hand, three-digit precision is probably all that humans can comfortably deal with. In Ward and West 1994, our subjects had trouble even with that level of precision. Thus it seems that the need to use numbers of limited precision in experiments with humans calls into question the interpretation of even clear and provocative results.

30.3   Heuristics and Chaos

Despite the problems mentioned in section 30.2, it is worth investigating further how human subjects behave in the face of learning to approximate the logistic equation. Even if they are using a heuristic, it is not clear that it is the one we (Ward and West 1994) and Metzger (1994) promoted. Finding out what they are doing and how they are doing it would be of value both in understanding how people might produce unpredictable behavior, and in how they might cope with unpredictability of the form produced by chaos.

To do this, West and I (Ward and West 1998) ran some additional subjects in our version of the logistic learning task. Setting the constant a in equation 24.1b to 3.66, we compared the data generated by two models to those generated by our additional subjects. One model was a computer simulation of the memory pairs model suggested by Metzger (1994); the other, a version of the logistic iteration equation model proposed by Neuringer and Voss (1993). The novel feature of our study was the analysis of both subject-generated and model-generated data using Casdagli's nonlinear forecasting technique (1991). Figure 30.3A shows a phase plot of data from a typical one of our additional subjects. It is clear that, as in Ward and West 1994, subjects failed to reproduce the strange attractor of the chaotic map they learned (fig. 30.2A). Rather they produced a phase plot that approximated the logistic map itself, in this case with added

Figure 30.3 (facing page)
(*A*) Phase plot for human subject; (*B*) phase plot for noisy logistic; (*C*) phase plot for fuzzy memory model of subject in figure 30.3A. (From Ward and West 1998.)

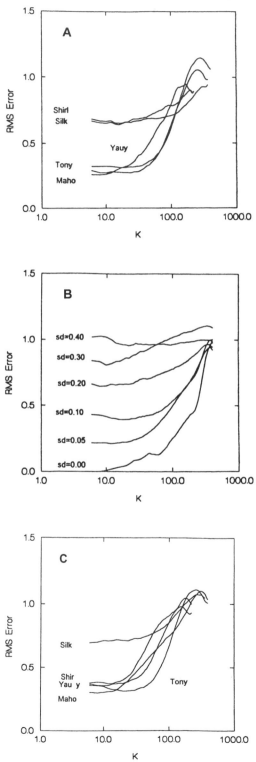

structure in the form of clumping of points in certain areas. As far as we knew, there were no such attractors in the logistic family, but we nevertheless entertained, as a model of this behavior, Equation 30.1, which is just equation 24.1b with an added term representing a sample of Gaussian (observational) noise, ε_n:

$$x_{n+1} = a \cdot x_n \cdot (1 - x_n) + \varepsilon_n \qquad (30.1)$$

When, however, we simulated this model with different amounts (standard deviations) of added noise, the resulting phase plots (e.g., fig. 30.3B) did not contain clumping like that in the subjects' data (e.g., fig. 30.3A). Interestingly, neither did our first version of Metzger's memory pairs model (1994), in which we chose a few specific memory pairs for each subject based on their phase plot and then used simple linear interpolation between these pairs for other points. Although adding noise helped, in the end, we had to resort to using two types of interpolation, "fine" (the usual) and "gross," which consisted of choosing the midpoint between the guesses indicated by the nearest memorized pairs. We also assumed that people used fuzzy or noisy, rather than precise, representation of the memory pairs. This approach was successful at reproducing most of the features of each subject's phase plot, in particular, the clumps. Figure 30.3C is an example for the subject data shown in figure 30.3A. Clearly, what we called the "fuzzy memory pairs model" fitted the phase plots the best.

The above discussion seems to imply that subjects were not iterating the logistic equation to produce chaotic sequences of numbers, a somewhat disappointing conclusion. Nonetheless, we wanted to see whether there was any nonlinear structure in the sequences produced by both subjects and models. Perhaps the heuristic used by subjects to comply with the experimenters' instructions produced a different kind of chaotic sequence. Thus we subjected both subject-generated and model-generated sequences to the nonlinear forecasting analysis described in chapter 25. Figures 30.4A–30.4C show deterministic versus stochastic (DVS) plots of the subjects' data and the computer-generated data from each of the two models. The DVS plots of subjects' data (fig. 30.4A) show evidence of nonlinear deterministic structure: they are similar to the plots of the logistic equation with some observational noise added (fig. 30.4B). Three of the subjects' DVS plots seem well approximated by the noisy logistic

Figure 30.4 (facing page)
(*A*) Deterministic versus stochastic (DVS) plots for human subjects; (*B*) DVS plots for noisy logistic; (*C*) DVS plots for fuzzy memory model. (From Ward and West 1998.)

DVS plots for noise of between SD = 0.05 and SD = 0.10, whereas the other two required noisy logistic sequences with SD = 0.20. Thus the noisy logistic model could fit subjects' DVS plots with the choice of a single parameter, the standard deviation of the noise distribution. Second, the DVS plots of data from the fuzzy memory pairs model for the best-fitting sequences (fig. 30.4C) are nearly identical to the corresponding plots for the subjects' data with one exception (subject Shir's model curve indicates less noise than the data curve). Thus the memory pairs model, which reproduces both the subjects' phase plots and their DVS plots, is a good model, but not a chaotic one. Or is it? After all, its output does show the same evidence of nonlinear structure as the subjects' plots, and could also be fitted by the noisy logistic model (compare figs. 30.4B and 30.4C). We are left in a quandry, then, regarding such models, although we do know that the fuzzy memory model heuristic is effective at approximating chaotic behavior. Perhaps similar heuristics could be used to produce unpredictable behavior in other situations, or even to cope with chaos itself.

Chapter 31

Relaxation Oscillators: A Foundation for Dynamical Modeling

Now that the general equation for *relaxation oscillations* is known, it is an easy matter to devise further electrical systems of the same type.

—Balthasar van der Pol, "On 'Relaxation-Oscillations'"

Van der Pol's equation for a relaxation oscillator is generalized.... The resulting ... model serves as a simple representative of a class of excitable-oscillatory systems including the Hodgkin-Huxley (HH) model of the squid giant axon.

—Richard A. FitzHugh, "Impulses and Physiological States in Theoretical Models of Nerve Membrane"

It is time, book time that is, for a change. Chapters 16 through 30 have dealt with specific problem areas in dynamical science: $1/f$ noise, stochastic resonance, and chaos theory. In the final chapters, I am going to broaden the scope of the discussion to deal with more speculative topics. I hope these last five chapters will be fun and their ideas worth thinking about, but I cannot guarantee that they will be even as solidly based as the admittedly incomplete work on the topics already discussed. Let us begin with a general perspective on building dynamical models.

31.1 A Brief Taxonomy of Oscillators

Time, in one way or another, is central to every chapter in this book. A dynamical system is characterized by change over time, and change over time is most compactly represented by differential equations, although not all differential equations are equally useful when it comes to modeling dynamical cognitive systems. One especially promising class of differential equations defines *oscillators*, systems that change in some more or less regular way, and that are therefore ideal both for measuring time and for describing processes that evolve in time. A good example of an oscillator is the pendulum of a grandfather clock, which keeps reasonably good time because it has a roughly constant period. As we noted in chapter 4, pendulums were the first precise measurement devices for time, and they have been thoroughly studied and described in all of their incarnations. Another useful example is what is called a "simple, damped, unforced linear oscillator," such as the small gold ore cart with mass m (gold ore plus cart) and frictionless wheels attached to a gold mine wall via a spring with stiffness s, pictured in figure 31.1. Notice that, attached in parallel to the spring, is something called a "dashpot damper," a container filled with oil and a piston that tends to act against the force exerted by the spring on the cart. Imagine we have attached a mule to the cart and we make the mule pull the cart away from the wall to which the spring is attached. When the mule begins to complain that the load is getting heavy, we release the cart. It rushes back toward the mine wall until the spring is compressed somewhat, at which point it is pushed away again, and so on, oscillating back and forth until it finally slows to rest, its oscillations "damped out" by the dashpot damper, which provides a force opposing both inward and outward movements. Although hardly a good way to go about getting gold ore out of a gold mine, this system does have some useful properties, which physicists and engineers have exploited. A particular variant of it, called a "relaxation oscillator," has the potential to form the foundation for modeling a wide class of dynamical cognitive systems, including the brain itself.

The typical differential equation that describes the motion of an oscillator such as that shown in figure 31.1 is

$$m\frac{d^2x}{dt^2} + r\frac{dx}{dt} + sx = 0, \tag{31.1}$$

where x is position, t is time, m and s are mass and spring stiffness, as mentioned, and r represents the amount of damping provided by the dashpot. Here d^2x/dt^2 is simply a compact way of writing $d(dx/dt)/dt$, the rate of change of the rate of change of position, or acceleration (formally called the "second derivative of position with respect to time"), which we first encountered in section 4.1. Typically, equation 31.1 is divided by the mass, m, to put it in standard form:

$$\frac{d^2x}{dt^2} + b\frac{dx}{dt} + cx = 0, \tag{31.2}$$

where $b = r/m$ and $c = s/m$. This equation describes a spiral path in phase space (left side of figure 31.1) as the amplitude of the sinusoidal,

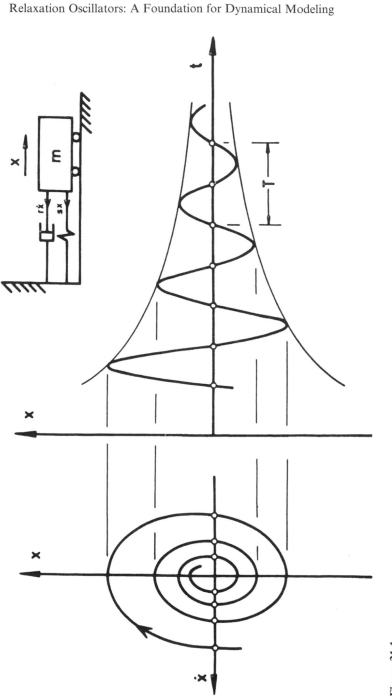

Figure 31.1
Simple damped, unforced, linear oscillator. (From Thompson and Stewart 1986. © 1986 by John Wiley & Sons, Ltd. Reprinted by permission.)

back-and-forth motion of the ore cart gradually decreases until the cart finally comes to rest (right side of figure 31.1).

Oscillators in general can be categorized with respect to the three attributes just mentioned: linearity, damping, and forcing. Differential equations, for their part, can be divided into two large groups: linear and nonlinear. *Linear* differential equations have all terms of either degree one or degree zero (degree refers to the exponents of the derivatives). Equations 31.1 and 31.2 are linear because the derivatives in their terms all have degree one (including the first term, which, as we noted represents the *second* derivative, not the square of the first derivative). Squaring dx/dt, among other possibilities, would make them *nonlinear*. Linear differential equations exhibit some very special properties (symmetries) that often allow them to be solved exactly, whereas nonlinear equations lack such symmetries and are very difficult to work with. The real world is always nonlinear but often can be approximated usefully by linear equations. *Damping* refers to a force opposing the "natural" oscillation of the system. Without the dashpot damper, the system portrayed in figure 31.1 would continue its sinusoidal oscillations forever at the same amplitude. The damping in equation 31.2 is linear because the damping term, $b(dx/dt)$, is proportional to the velocity of the cart, (dx/dt). If it were proportional to the square of the velocity the damping would be nonlinear. Oscillators in the real world are always damped; that is, they are not perfectly efficient—they lose or dissipate energy. Sometimes the damping can be negligible over the given time period, but usually it is not. Finally, *forcing* refers to energy inputs from outside the given system. If our mule pulled at and pushed at the cart repeatedly even as it oscillated under the influence of the spring (which stores and then releases the energy of the initial displacement), the oscillation would be forced. In the real world, oscillations are always forced because no system can be completely isolated from the rest of the universe. The forcing can, however, sometimes be so small that it can be neglected. The oscillators with the most interesting behavior are both damped and forced. The interaction of damping and forcing with the basic structure of a system can generate complex dynamics—often chaotic—and a complicated phase space picture, showing qualitatively different behaviors for different parameter regimes. Thompson and Stewart (1986) describe in some detail the various types of oscillators that can be generated from various combinations of linearity, damping and forcing. Although a number of these oscillators could be applied in dynamical cognitive science, either to model the temporal unfolding of cognitive phenomena or to measure systemic time, section 31.2 concentrates on one particular type of nonlinear oscillator that I believe could become a foundation stone of dynamical cognitive science.

31.2   The van der Pol Relaxation Oscillator

Let us first consider the van der Pol equation, which describes an unforced, damped, nonlinear oscillator:

$$\frac{d^2v}{dt^2} + \alpha(v^2 - 1)\frac{dv}{dt} + \omega^2 v = 0, \tag{31.3}$$

where the variable v could stand for the voltage across a resistance in an electrical circuit. In his initial studies of the equation, van der Pol (1926, 992) suggested several such circuits, of which the simplest was a neon lamp in parallel with a capacitor, this pair in series with a resistance and a battery, and "perhaps also heart-beats." Notice that the damping term (the second term) is what makes the equation nonlinear: because the function $\alpha(v^2 - 1)$ multiplies the first derivative (dv/dt), this term is of third degree. The relationship between α and ω is crucial to the behavior of the oscillator. When $\alpha \ll \omega$, the oscillator behaves like a linear oscillator with a very small amount of damping, generating a very slowly decaying sine wave, as portrayed in figure 31.2 (top panel). When $\alpha \approx \omega$,

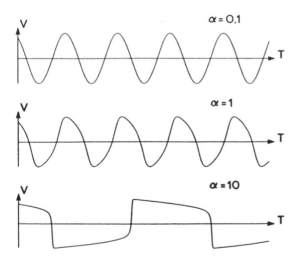

Figure 31.2
Behaviors of the van der Pol equation (eq. 31.3) for $\omega = 1$. (From Thompson and Stewart 1986. © 1986 by John Wiley & Sons, Ltd. Reprinted by permission.)

the oscillatory behavior becomes less sinusoidal but is still fairly regular (middle panel). When, however, $\alpha \gg \omega$, the oscillation approaches a square wave (bottom panel). Notice in the bottom tracing of figure 31.2 that each sudden transition (nearly vertical trace) is preceded by a considerable time period during which the voltage changes only slowly. Van der Pol (1926) called this phenomenon a "relaxation oscillation" because each slow change followed by a quick jump resembles the buildup and release of charge in a capacitor with capacitance C and "relaxation time" $\tau = RC$ (where R is the resistence of the circuit), the time it takes for the capacitor to charge. In this system relaxation, or the time taken for the "memory" of the previous state to decay, is the important feature, not the restoring force ($\omega^2 v$). A relaxation oscillator is highly prone to phase locking with an external driving frequency (forcing), even one that does not correspond to the natural frequency of the unforced oscillations, all the while maintaining a relatively constant oscillation amplitude. These properties make such oscillators ideal systems for controlling a system that should produce a response of fixed amplitude but variable frequency, for example, the heart or a neuron. Recognizing this, van der Pol and van der Mark (1928) made an analog model of the electrical activity of the heart consisting of three coupled relaxation oscillators: one to generate sine wave forcing of the auricles, a second to represent the auricles, and a third to represent the ventricles (contraction of the auricles drives that of the ventricles). This model explained (qualitatively) both the normal heartbeat, including the "all-or-nothing law" and various irregularities, and some disorders of the heartbeat such as heart block, in which decoupling the auricle from the ventricle leads to heart failure.

Relaxation oscillators can even give rise to chaos. In another famous paper, van der Pol and van der Mark (1927) reported that the neon tube oscillator they were to use later as a model of the heart had a remarkable property. If a forcing oscillator was added to the circuit in series with the neon tube, the nonlinearity of the relaxation oscillator made the whole circuit produce oscillations at frequencies that were equal to the forcing frequency divided by various whole numbers (2, 3, 4, 5, 6), the whole number increasing as the parallel capacitance was increased. This phenomenon, illustrated in figure 31.3, turned out to be very useful for electronic engineering. But the two researchers also noted an anomaly in this circuit: at certain values of the capacitance, "often an irregular noise is heard in the telephone receivers before the frequency jumps to the next lower value" (p. 364), a phenomenon represented by the hatched areas in figure 31.3, mostly at higher capacitances but at lower ones as well. This

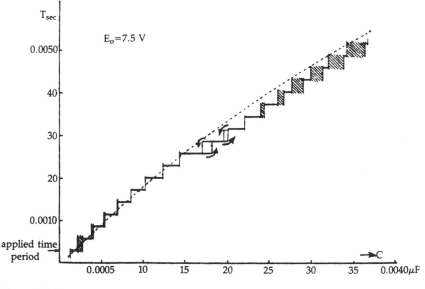

Figure 31.3
Chaos in a relaxation oscillator. (From van der Pol and van der Mark 1927. ©
1927, Macmillan Magazines, Limited. Reprinted with permission from *Nature*.)

noise was chaos (Kellert 1993 also noted this). Note that the equation
describing this circuit is equation 31.3 with a simple sinusoidal forcing
term added ($E_0 \sin \omega t$), thus completely deterministic. Moreover, although
there was certainly random circuit noise present, it was so small that
it does not show in the graph at the middle values of capacitance. The
"irregular noise" only showed up just as the system was switching to a
different oscillatory mode (attractor). Finally, note also the hysteresis
diagrammed in figure 31.3 at a capacitance of about 20 μF. Hysteresis is
also an important signature of nonlinearity, in this case indicating the
importance of knowing the path by which a system has reached a certain
state, yet it was not even mentioned by van der Pol and van der Mark in
their 1927 paper.

Relaxation times in physical systems correspond to "memory" in cognitive systems. That is, a "relaxation" is a time period during which the
influence of previous events on current behavior gradually declines. In a
time series, this is measured by correlations between current behavior and
behavior at various lags. Human behavior is characterized by time series
that generate rhythms, orders, sequences, and so forth, even chaos. The
relaxation oscillation is a formal construct, represented by the behavior of

equations such as equation 31.3, that could be used to model the ubiquitous temporal correlations found in human cognitive and other behavior. Because such relaxations can happen at several scales in human behavior, coupled systems of relaxation equations would be required, making the task of analysis very difficult (even the analysis of equation 31.3 is very difficult). Several such systems have been described in chapters 16, 18 and 19 in the context of $1/f$ noise, as well as in the chapters on chaos theory. Section 31.3, describes how the van der Pol equation can be applied to the oscillations of neurons in the brain.

31.3   Noisy Oscillators in the Brain

Neurons display relaxation time behavior par excellence: they fire an action potential (spike) when the voltage across the cell membrane in the trigger zone of the soma (around the base of the axon that leaves the soma) exceeds a threshold, and then "gradually" build back up again, usually under the influence of input from other neurons, until the threshold is crossed again and then they fire another spike, and so forth. Hodgkin and Huxley (1952) developed an influential mathematical model of this process based on studies of action potentials in the squid giant axon. The model consists of four first-order differential equations that describe the flow of ions through the cell membrane arising from several physiological mechanisms (e.g., the sodium pump, passive diffusion). The equations are not easy to solve or analyze, and they have been the subject of much study, even though they do not produce all of the phenomena shown by vertebrate neurons (for example, they do not show adaptation to a constant stimulus; Yamada, Koch, and Adams 1998). Richard Fitz-Hugh (1960) was one of those who worked on the analysis of the Hodgkin-Huxley equations. He first tried describing their behavior using phase space methods, such as those discussed earlier in this book, combined with reducing the system of equations to a more manageable size by holding one or more of the variables of state constant, that is, by assuming that their derivatives were equal to zero. Finding that approach inadequate to describe how trains of impulses occur, he noticed that neural action potentials are actually relaxation oscillations similar to those described by van der Pol and van der Mark (1928) for the heartbeat. In an influential paper, FitzHugh (1961) described a model of a neuron based on a special case of equation 31.3 ($\omega = 1$) plus some additional terms, including a forcing input, and showed how it mimicked the behavior of the Hodgkin-Huxley equations. The resulting equations were studied further by Na-

gumo, Arimoto, and Yoshizawa (1962); they have come to be called the
"FitzHugh-Nagumo model" (although FitzHugh modestly called it the
"Bonhoeffer-van der Pol model").

The FitzHugh-Nagumo equations, in one popular form, look like this:

$$\frac{dv}{dt} = \alpha(w + v - v^3/3 + z) \tag{31.4}$$

$$\frac{dw}{dt} = -(v - a + bw)/\alpha, \tag{31.5}$$

where v is a voltage across the neuronal membrane that represents a fast,
excitation process, w is a voltage that represents a slower, recovery process, z is the input stimulus intensity (the forcing term representing input
from other neurons), α is the damping constant (greater than $\omega = 1$, so
that the system shows relaxation oscillations), and a and b are constants
that affect the recovery rate. FitzHugh (1961), in showing that this system
mimicked the Hodgkin-Huxley equations, also showed that the neural
action potential is a form of relaxation oscillation.

Since 1961, the FitzHugh-Nagumo model of the neuron has been used
in many biophysics applications, especially in the study of stochastic
resonance in excitable systems (see chap. 22), where stochastic (noise)
forcing is added to the "fast" equation 31.4 and deterministic forcing is
added to the "slow" equation 31.5 (Longtin 1993). Such additions are
consistent with the usual case that the noise is at a much faster timescale
(comparable to spike duration) than is the signal (comparable to recovery
duration). Longtin's equations (1993) look like this:

$$\varepsilon\frac{dv}{dt} = v(v - a)(1 - v) - w + \xi(t) \tag{31.6}$$

$$\frac{dw}{dt} = v - cw - b - r\sin(\beta t) \tag{31.7}$$

where $\xi(t)$ is the noise forcing (an Ornstein-Uhlenbeck process; see chaps.
14–15) and $r\sin(\beta t)$ is the deterministic forcing (replacing the z in
eq. 31.4). (There are also a few other changes in equations 31.6 and 31.7
from equations 31.4 and 31.5, but they do not change the essence of the
process.) Longtin (1993) showed that these equations behave much like
neurons (see fig. 31.4) and also demonstrate stochastic resonance (see
chap. 22). In further papers, he has shown how the equations' behavior
can be synchronized to periodic forcing (Longtin 1995a) and that it demonstrates stochastic phase locking (Longtin 1995b).

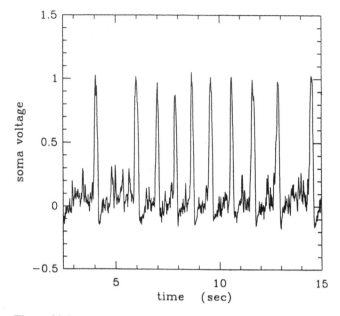

Figure 31.4
Sequence of spikes from Longtin's Fitzhugh-Nagumo model of a neuron. (From Longtin 1993.)

Many more examples of the relevance of relaxation oscillators to dynamical cognitive science can be adduced, including the double potential well Haken, Kelso, and Bunz (HKB, 1985) model discussed in chapter 3. This model can be generalized to as many wells as necessary (even infinite), to model ever more complex brain systems. I am suggesting that systems of coupled relaxation oscillators (neurons) at many scales are sufficient to produce rhythm, timing, serial order, and many of the other phenomena of the unfolding of human behavior in time, including the recurrence of thoughts analyzed by Crovitz (1970) and the stream of consciousness described by James (1890). Indeed, modeling such phenomena with relaxation oscillators allows us to understand the sense in which such dynamical systems create their own time—the system itself is oscillating, and oscillations are the only means we have of measuring time. In a deep sense, oscillations *are* time. Models based on relaxation oscillators would explain why the behavior emerges "when" it does, and why there are correlations between behaviors at many scales, including possibly chaotic behavior. Stochastically driven and deterministically driven relaxation oscillators comprise stochastic processes such as those described in chapters 12 and 13, and some of the modern tools of mathematics and physics can be brought to bear on their analysis. Such models should be particularly well suited to describe the synchronization of neurons and the temporal coding of information thought to underlie much neural activity (e.g., Singer 1993, 1994) and possibly also to form the basis of human consciousness (e.g., Tononi and Edelman 1998; see chap. 35). Already the influence of relaxation oscillators in neural modeling is pervasive (see, for example, Koch and Segev 1998). The promise is that modeling human cognitive phenomena with relaxation oscillators will allow current and future neural models to be coupled to behavioral models, bringing dynamical modeling to a new level of complexity and usefulness.

Chapter 32
Evolution and Ecology of Cognition

The half-art, half-instinct of language still bears the stamp of its gradual evolution.
—Charles Darwin, *The Descent of Man*

Animal cognition is a biological feature that has been molded by natural selection. Hence, to understand cognition, one must study its ecological consequences and evolution.
—Reuven Dukas, *Cognitive Ecology*

32.1   Evolution of Cognition

Thus far, we have considered dynamical cognitive systems at many time-scales, from milliseconds to seconds, minutes, hours, even days. Although "historical" timescales, such as years, decades, centuries, and millenia, are highly relevant to understanding and predicting human behavior and there is every reason to believe dynamical models will illuminate human behavior on such timescales, that is the work of disciplines other than dynamical cognitive science. The very longest timescales, however, those on which the processes of evolution work, are directly relevant to the topic of this book. Evolutionary theory can often provide the answers to ultimate "why" questions, both about morphology (what an animal is like physically) and about behavior. For example, evolutionary theory sheds light on the mysteries of the male peacock's tail and doves' court-ship rituals, among dozens of other profound questions (see Lea 1984 for an excellent introduction to this function of evolutionary theory in un-derstanding behavior). It has the promise to do the same for questions about cognition, such as why nonhuman animals exhibit selective atten-tion and short-term memory but not explicit, episodic memory, or why bacteria do not have (or need) short-term memory. Evolutionary theory also provides a framework within which to appraise current systems.

There is even a new field of psychology, called "evolutionary psychology," that takes this approach to the study of human behavior (see Buss 1999 for a survey). Of course biology has been studying animal behavior in this way for many years, and Nobel prizes have been awarded to Karl von Frisch, Niko Tinbergen, and Konrad Lorenz for the development of the methods and early results of comparative ethology. However, both evolutionary psychology, which emphasizes the study of human mating strategies, and comparative ethology, which emphasizes the study of aggression and reproduction in nonhuman animals, have neglected what Dukas (1998a) calls "cognitive ecology," the study of the evolution of cognitive capacities and their influence on animal-environment interactions, even though such a study was clearly mandated by Darwin (see first epigraph above). This chapter discusses a few of the possibilities for dynamical cognitive science engaging with evolutionary timescales.

Darwin's great theory of evolution by natural selection was based on two simple observations and a conclusion that followed "naturally" from them. First, within each species there is quite dramatic variation of structure, even though all members of the species share certain characteristics. For example, although each human has a head with two eyes, a nose, a mouth, hair, and so on, human heads come in all sorts of shapes and colors, and so do their parts. A similar statement can be made for every characteristic of every animal, although the amount of variation can be more or less than that of human heads. Moreover, Darwin observed that this variation tends to be inherited. Short parents tend to have short children, muscular parents tend to have muscular children, and so forth. Second, every species produces many more offspring than could possibly survive. Darwin calculated for many species how long it would take for an unsustainable number of its members to be born, at species-typical reproductive rates and assuming survival of all offspring. It was a surprisingly short time, even for the slowest reproducers. For example, a female cod lays millions of eggs each time she reproduces, which can happen several times a year. If each egg grew into an adult, and survived and reproduced in turn, the oceans would literally be overflowing with cod after only a few months. From these two observations, he concluded that if living creatures vary and not all survive, the survivors must possess the inheritable characteristics that are best adapted to the local environment in which the creature must live. This *principle of natural selection* was called the "survival of the fittest" because it was originally thought to amount to a struggle between individuals to see who would, literally, live on from day to day. But gradually, it has come to be interpreted in a more useful way, as a struggle for successful reproduction. Of course an organism that does not survive to reproductive age cannot reproduce, and its genes are lost to the species. Thus the struggle to live long enough to reproduce is part of natural selection. But there are also more subtle factors at work, such as which stag can attract and hold the largest harem of does against competing stags, or which male peacock can attract the locally most fecund female with his magnificent plumage. Today, *fitness* is defined simply as the ability to produce viable offspring, and it is the universal yardstick of evolution; the genes that persist in a species are the ones that maximize the fitness of their possessors. It is simply a numbers game—Darwinian roulette.

Because evolution by natural selection (with modern revisions and with additions such as population genetics; see especially Luria, Gould, and Singer 1981) is one of the two theoretical cornerstones of biology (the other is the "central dogma" of molecular biology on the pivotal role of DNA), I cannot possibly survey it here. I can, however, point out a few aspects relevant to dynamical cognitive science. One of these has to do with the origin of traits. Although Darwin concentrated on explaining the origin of species (albeit with only modest success), the general approach of evolutionary theory can also usefully be applied on a smaller scale to the understanding of the origin of traits. For example, senescence has been usefully analyzed, and its role in the overall functioning of a species in its niche elucidated, from this point of view. Similarly, many behavior traits have been successfully analyzed in this way, especially mating rituals among nonhuman animals. A similar analysis should reveal how information processing abilities evolved among animals, from the simplest one-celled animals such as bacteria, whose cell membrane responds directly to chemical gradients, to the most complex human accomplishments such as performing a piece of music or creating a scientific theory. Methods of comparative ethology could be adapted to deduce evolutionary trends in, for example, memory use, or communication techniques. Although some have begun to study cognition in this way, there is still much to be learned about how and why the ability to write a book such as this came to be among those abilities possessed by humans.

Of course the resulting picture is not likely to be simple. One complication is that collections of traits could have coevolved. For example, it has been suggested that, because speech motor patterns seem to be the substrate for speech perception (e.g., Liberman and Mattingly 1985), the mechanisms for the perception of and for the production of human speech must have coevolved. Another possibility is a mutation of a "regulator gene." Ordinary genes code for only a single trait, and sometimes only for a part of a trait. Regulator genes, on the other hand, do just what the name suggests—they regulate the expression of many genes, in turn influencing many traits. One or more such mutations could have been the change that led to the emergence of humans (see Stanley 1981 for a development of this theory). Similarly, mutation in a regulator gene that governs expression of the genes that code for brain structure could have simultaneously affected several information-processing mechanisms together, producing an animal that had both enhanced visual pattern recognition abilities and the ability to focus them on particular patterns in the visual field.

Another complication is that the modern view of evolution has replaced Darwinian gradualism (many small changes over many years) with a more interesting dynamical process, called "punctuated equilibrium," in which things are relatively stable for millions of years and then something dramatic happens, either an explosion of new species or an extinction of huge numbers of existing species (see again Stanley 1981). This represents a kind of oscillation of species production within a time series lasting billions of years. Looking at evolution this way focuses on macroevolutionary trends, for example, the way that the appearance of new species changes the distribution of traits in the world. Evolution is essentially historical, and cannot create traits out of whole cloth: it works with what is available. Macroevolution, on the other hand, works with the species available, and can be responsible for dramatic changes that have nothing to do with individual fitness but only with the corresponding concept defined at the species level, which involves both how long a given species persists and how fecund it is with respect to giving rise to offspring species. An example of how this could work is displayed in figure 32.1. Here a hypothetical evolutionary change in shape portrayed in the top graph takes place simply because species tend to last longer (middle graph), and to give rise to more new species (bottom graph), the farther they are to the right on the "shape" axis. Thus either micro- or macroevolution or both could be involved in producing changes in information-processing abilities of animals. Moreover, the long-term oscillations of macroevolution can also be treated with the same tools that we have developed for dealing with shorter-term changes. Figure 32.2 shows how the logistic equation (eq. 8.6) can be fitted both to the growth of a bacterial colony over a period of several hours and to the growth in the numbers of marine orders (collections of species) over hundreds of millions of years.

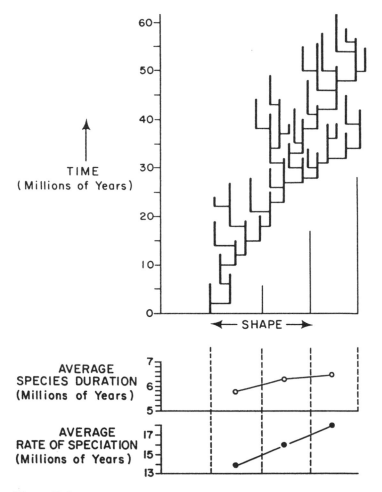

Figure 32.1
Macroevolutionary trend. (From Stanley 1981. © 1981 by Steven M. Stanley.
Reprinted by permission of Basic Books, a member of Perseus Books, L.L.C.)

Although the Darwinian approach to evolution has been modified in
many ways, one of its sacred cows is the idea that evolution is "blind,"
that it does not proceed by design but rather by chance, that it does not
always lead to "progress." This idea is eloquently defended by Dawkins
(1986) in his book *The Blind Watchmaker*. Moreover, as explained by
Dawkins (1976) in his earlier book, *The Selfish Gene*, much if not most
evolution is at the level of the individual organism, where the genes have
only self-interest. Evolution is not supposed to be for the good of the
organism's own species, much less than for the good of other species. On

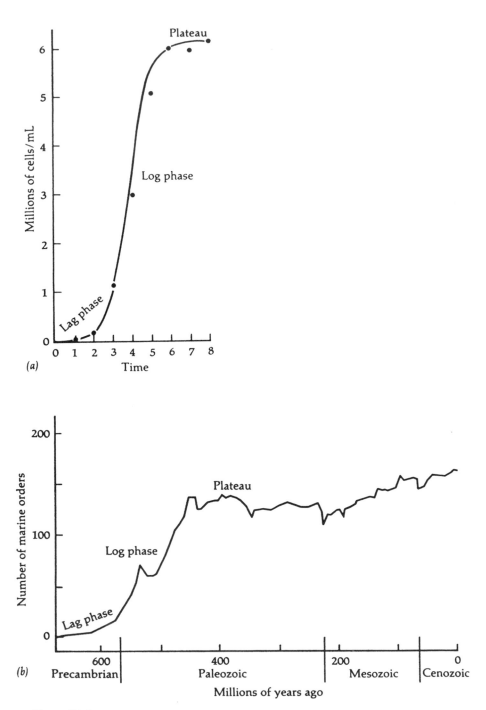

Figure 32.2
Time series at two time scales conform to the logistic equation. (From Luria, Gould, and Singer 1981. © 1981 by The Benjamin/Cummings Publishing Company, Inc. Reprinted by permission of Addison Wesley Longman, Inc.)

the other hand, this and other evolutionary sacred cows have also been challenged, nowhere more forcefully than by Stuart Kauffman (1993) in his profound but difficult work *The Origins of Order*. Kauffman argued that complex systems poised at the "edge of chaos" are the most able to adapt and change through the processes of mutation and natural selection. The edge of chaos is a place in the phase space of a complex dynamical system where the orbit is highly complex but not quite chaotic. Typically, only a small change in one or more parameters is necessary to push the system into chaos. For example, the logistic difference equation (eq. 24.1a) iterating with a value of the parameter $a = 3.57$ would be at the edge of chaos; if $a \geq 3.58$, the attractor can be chaotic. Kauffman also argued that coevolving complex systems could be pushed by selection to form ecosystems where all species mutually attain the edge of chaos, and thus symbiotically maintain the maximum possible fitness for all. If Kauffman's arguments are correct, then our own information processing mechanisms could have evolved mutually with those of the other animals around us, to the mutual benefit of all. If so, we cannot understand our own mechanisms without also understanding those of our coevolvers.

32.2   Ecology of Cognition

How an animal obtains and processes information about its environment clearly constrains that animal's interactions with that environment, its "cognitive ecology," which in turn determine an animal's fitness: the survival of its genes into future generations. And that fitness, in turn, determines which of those information-processing capabilities will be present in those future generations. The same selection pressures that brought about the male peacock's gorgeous (but heavy) tail plumage are responsible for such things as selective attention, implicit and explicit memory, classical and operant conditioning, language, and so forth. (For useful discussions of the evolutionary perspective and the study of particular cognitive constraints on animal behavior within a particular ecological niche, see Dukas (1998c.)

Dukas's introduction and chapter (1998a,b) contain much of the material most relevant to dynamical cognitive science. In his chapter (Dukas 1998b) on the effects of information-processing constraints on animal behavior, Dukas sees selective attention as an adaptation to the requirement of some niches for highly demanding computations to accomplish predator and prey recognition. The focus of attention provides a restricted range over which such computations can be performed efficiently with a limited neural apparatus, albeit with associated costs to detection of predators or prey in parts of the environment outside the attentional focus. One cost of attentive focus is that it requires effort, effort that, when directed at focusing continuously on a difficult task, results in an increasing decrement in performance the longer the task lasts. Since its discovery among radar monitors during World War II, this vigilance decrement has been studied extensively in humans. Attentive focus is required by animals during foraging, a ubiquitous and vitally important activity of all animals, or by humans during the typical work-day (which has replaced foraging for many of us). Satisfactory performance during foraging or working in an office, factory, or store demands occasional rest periods for recovery from vigilance decrement (among other decrements). This observation suggests that an animal should alternate (oscillate) between foraging and rest periods during its foraging activity rather than simply foraging until it is satisfied.

Dukas and Clark (1995) proposed a dynamical model of foraging that has just this character. First, they assumed that a foraging animal's vigilance level declines linearly during active foraging according to equation 32.1:

$$\frac{dv}{dt} = -\alpha v, \tag{32.1}$$

where α is the rate of vigilance decrement, which is associated both with task difficulty (larger, the more difficult the task) and with the individual animal. Dukas and Clark also assumed that the forager's vigilance level recovers during a rest period according to

$$\frac{dv}{dt} = \beta(1 - v), \tag{32.2}$$

where β is the rate of recovery, associated both with the quality of rest the animal is able to attain and with the individual animal. These two linear differential equations can be combined into one equation by assuming that the foraging animal devotes some fraction, $0 < \theta < 1$, of its time to foraging, and the remaining amount of time, $1 - \theta$, to resting. In this model, θ reflects the proportion of its time the animal puts into foraging, thus its foraging effort. Forming a linear combination of equations 32.1 and 32.2 with weights θ and $1 - \theta$, respectively, for foraging and resting, results in

$$\frac{dv}{dt} = -\theta\alpha v + (1 - \theta)\beta(1 - v). \tag{32.3}$$

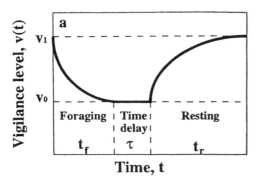

Figure 32.3
Optimal length of a foraging bout. (From Dukas 1998, p. 109. © 1998 by The University of Chicago.)

One (not so natural) way to use this equation is to assume that a forager alternates rapidly between periods of foraging and periods of rest and thus maintains an equilibrium level of vigilance, $\bar{v}(\theta)$. This equilibrium level of vigilance can be found by setting dv/dt equal to zero and solving for v. The result is

$$\bar{v}(\theta) = \frac{(1-\theta)\beta}{\theta\alpha + (1-\theta)\beta}. \tag{32.4}$$

Several things can be discovered by contemplating (or even better, graphing) this equation for various values of α, β, θ, and that for average food intake, expressed by

$$\bar{f}(\theta) = \lambda\theta\bar{v}(\theta). \tag{32.5}$$

One thing we discover is that equilibrium vigilance level is lower, the greater the ratio α/β. Thus difficult tasks such as foraging for cryptic (well-camouflaged) prey, which produce greater rates of vigilance decrement (higher α), also produce lower equilibrium levels of vigilance. Moreover, although increases in foraging effort (increases in θ) result at first in increases in food intake when θ is small (eq. 32.5), when θ is large, such increases actually decrease food intake because of the simultaneous decrease in the equilibrium vigilance level. Thus, for any ratio α/β, there is an optimum proportion of time to spend foraging, and that proportion increases the easier the foraging task is. This somewhat counterintuitive conclusion is typical of the results one can obtain from such dynamical models even when treated statically (at equilibrium).

A more dynamical way to view this model, in which it was assumed that a forager would initiate foraging activity when it was well rested, was also discussed by Dukas and Clark (1995). The animal's vigilance level would start at v_1 and then decrease with time (exponentially, because this is a solution of the simple linear differential eq. 32.1) to some level v_0, at which time it would be fatigued and would begin to rest. They also assumed that there would be a time delay, τ, after foraging before the animal could actually begin to rest (a cost of the switch in activities— perhaps the time it takes the animal to find a predator-free refuge). Then, once resting, vigilance would build back up again, logarithmically, to the rested level, v_1. Figure 32.3 shows one foraging cycle. Clearly, if the rate of decrement of vigilance, α, is large, then the optimal foraging bout will be short, and if the cost of switching activities, τ, is large, then foraging bouts also should be short. In this linear model, an animal's days consist of a sequence of alternating periods of foraging and resting, foraging and resting, with perhaps an occasional bout of running from a predator, until death.

Of course in this model the foraging and rest periods are of fixed length, and thus would not model any animal's actual life. If, however, we introduce some nonlinearities, or some noise, or both, then the alternations become more irregular, and thus more lifelike. Notice that if we extend the single cycle of figure 32.3 to an indefinite sequence of such cycles, including the irregularities, they very much resemble the cycles of a relaxation oscillator. In fact, a very similar picture could be produced using a van der Pol relaxation oscillator. In such a nonlinear, dynamical model, however, the transitions between foraging and resting would be more sudden, and the curves of decreasing vigilance and increasing capacity would have different shapes (see fig. 32.2). Again, introducing noise into this picture would create the irregularity observed in nature and also perhaps create the rare departures from a regular pattern. In such a model, the parameters would be the amount of damping (equivalent to the rate of vigilance decrement) and the restoring force (equivalent to the rate of regaining attentional capacity). A similar model could be proposed for humans to describe both performance in vigilance situations and the rhythm of work and rest during a typical day. Whether the original linear model proposed by Dukas and Clark (1995) would be sufficient to account for the many different aspects of vigilance behavior, especially when applied to human activities, or the nonlinear model just sketched out would be required, is left for future researchers to ascertain. What is clear, however, is that looking at the dynamics of cognition in the context of the demands of survival in a biological niche during evolutionary times promises many insights not attainable from a statical view of cognitive capacities.

Chapter 33
Dynamical Cognitive Neuroscience

In studying the relationship of mind and brain ... neuroimaging techniques are of paramount importance, for only these techniques can provide pictures of the active, living human brain.
—Michael I. Posner and Marcus E. Raichle, *Images of Mind*

Neocortical dynamic behavior at multiple spatial scales, ranging from molecules to neurons to overlapping local and regional cell groups of different sizes to global fields of synaptic action density. Interaction across these hierarchical levels (or spatial scales) may be essential to the dynamics (and by implication to behavior and cognition)....
—Paul L. Nunez, "Toward a Quantitative Description of Large-Scale Neocortical Dynamic Function and EEG"

To study the dynamics of the brain, we must measure brain activity. For many years such measurement was impossible. In the mid-1800s, eminent scientists like Gustav Teodor Fechner, the founder of psychophysics, believed that we would never be able to study "inner psychophysics," the relationship between brain activity and the mind. This belief stimulated him to develop "outer psychophysics," the study of the relationship between the world of physical stimuli and the mind, or at least conscious sensations. Nonetheless, beginning in the late 1800s, scientific and technical developments combined to produce a plethora of techniques now used to study brain activity (see Posner and Raichle 1994 for a nontechnical introduction and Kandel, Schwartz, and Jessell 2000 for a technical survey of the state of our current knowledge of the brain). Many of these, such as inserting electrodes directly into the brain, are quite invasive and, as such, can only be performed on nonhuman animals or used on human patients when the information they provide will help with diagnosis or therapy. In recent years, however, several less invasive techniques have emerged and are beginning to provide very useful information about brain function in intact, normal humans. Some of these techniques have been mentioned already: magnetoencephalography and electroencephalography are particularly suited to providing time series of brain activity with millisecond accuracy for time periods of up to many minutes. Other techniques, depending on the fact that more neural activity requires more blood flow to replenish oxygen and energy used in generating action potentials and other neural activities, can provide more precise spatial localization of neural activity associated with particular cognitive functions. Together these techniques promise to illuminate the relationship between brain and mind to an extent undreamed of when Fechner lived. This chapter briefly describes some of the techniques and their potential role in dynamical cognitive science, conveying the flavor of current dynamical brain models, which involve various nonlinear oscillators such as those described in chapter 31.

33.1   Brain Imaging

We have known since Galvani made a frog's leg twitch that electrical currents run in our bodies. Nowhere is this more true than in our brains, where the basic mode of communication between neurons involves the exchange of chemicals, the neurotransmitters, that affect the permeability of the neurons' cell membranes to ions, which are particles that carry electrical charge. The flow of electrical charge creates electrical currents, and when enough neurons, aligned in parallel, are active, the resulting electrical currents can become quite large—large enough to reach the surface of the scalp and be detected there by special electrodes. Recording electrical fluctuations at the scalp, or in special cases from the dura of the brain (the sheath of the brain beneath the skull), called "electroencephalography," was invented by Hans Berger in the early 1930s. The electroencephalogram (EEG) can provide long (up to several hours), precise (millisecond accuracy) time series of the global (arising from many neurons) electrical activity of the brain. A standard EEG simply records the activity from several sites on the scalp while an animal or a person does various activities. A set of such tracings from a rat brain is shown in figure 33.1. Notice how the oscillatory trace varies with the rat's activities and experiences. In particular, notice that there are several scales of oscillations in these tracings, and that the more global ones are more closely associated with moment-to-moment changes in behavior, such as moving while sleeping, jumping, turning the head, chattering the teeth, whereas the more local ones seem to differ more when the animal is in

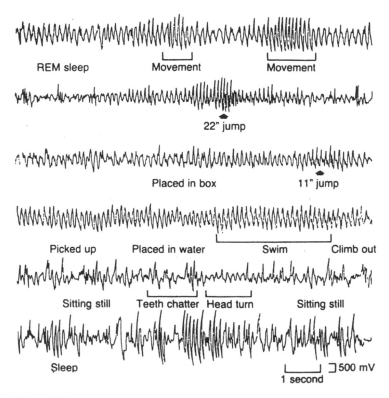

REM sleep   Movement   Movement

22" jump

Placed in box   11" jump

Picked up   Placed in water   Swim   Climb out

Sitting still   Teeth chatter Head turn   Sitting still

Sleep   500 mV
                              1 second

Figure 33.1
Electroencephalogram (EEG) time series of rat brain electrical activity. (From Whishaw and Vanderwolf 1973.)

different general behavioral states, such as sitting, sleeping, or swimming. Various frequencies of EEG waves are associated with particular states or activities. For example, the "alpha" frequency of about 10 Hz indicates a state of relaxation, whereas the "gamma" frequency of about 40 Hz is associated with strenuous mental activity. EEGs can be used to define various behavioral states, such as the stages of sleep or relaxation versus stimulation. Because the time series of electrical activity is affected noticeably by the abnormal brain tissue, comparisons of the EEG tracings of normal people with those suspected of a disease (such as a brain tumor) can often provide valuable diagnostic information. Chapter 27 describes how the standard EEG can be used as an index of chaos in the brain.

Another way to use the EEG is to record the less regular fluctuations in brain electrical activity associated with the perception of external stimulus events (see Picton, Lins, and Scherg 1995). Such *event-related potentials*

(ERPs) provide time series over the range of a few milliseconds to perhaps a second or two. Because ERPs are very small in relation to the overall activity of the brain, usually many of them are averaged to provide a clean record. When this averaging is done, specific features in the time series can be linked to specific cognitive operations, such as processing a visual stimulus in the occipital cortex, where differences, say as a function of whether the visual stimulus was attended to or not, can be detected as differences between ERPs under the two conditions. These differences provide converging evidence to model cognitive processes (see Hillyard and Picton 1987 or Näätänen 1992 for more). Because their vulnerability to noise makes study of individual, unaveraged ERPs difficult, it would seem to be impossible to investigate ERPs at longer timescales, but there are ways around this problem. Chapter 22 describes the search for $1/f$ noise in time series of individual ERPs; chapter 27 describes an attempt to find chaos in ERPs; and there are now techniques available to filter the noise from individual ERPs so that time series of "cleaned-up" ERPs can be generated (e.g., Jaśkowski and Verleger 1999, 2000). This should allow ERP and behavioral time series to be coordinated.

Electrical currents generate magnetic fields; those generated by the electrical currents flowing in the brain can be detected and recorded with a technique more recent than electroencephalography—magnetoence-phalography. Using an expensive and cranky device called a "supercooled quantum interference device" (SQUID), the magnetoencephalogram (MEG) provides time series of magnetic field measurements across the brain that are possibly even more useful than the EEG. Because the SQUID has better spatial resolution with the same temporal resolution, we can observe not only what the brain is doing from moment to moment but also more exactly which part of the brain is doing it. Chapter 17 reviews some early work on $1/f$ noise in MEG time series.

Neural activity in the brain is also accompanied by changes in the flow of blood to the neurons and to their surrounding supporting glial cells, a phenomenon first noticed by Mosso in the late 1800s and turned into a general hypothesis by Roy and Sherrington in 1890 (see Posner and Raichle 1994). Not until the 1970s, however, did these early observations bear fruit, in the form of several imaging techniques that are now quite commonly used to provide precise information on exactly where in the brain neural activity occurs in response to various cognitive tasks. One of these, called "positron-emission tomography" (PET), involves introduc-ing a weak radioactive tracer into the brain and then detecting the pho-tons produced by collisions of the positrons emitted by the tracer in the blood with the electrons that are part of every brain tissue molecule. More of the tracer builds up in regions of high blood flow, where the brain tissue is more active; the greater number of collisions between positrons and electrons produces more photons to be detected. In another technique, called "functional magnetic resonance imaging" (fMRI), active regions of the brain are imaged by surrounding the brain with an intense, fluctuating magnetic field with which deoxygenated hemoglobin molecules in the brain resonate, producing a resultant inhomogeneity of the magnetic field that can be detected. Regions of greater neural activity cause local vasodilation, bringing in increased amounts of oxygenated hemoglobin and relatively decreasing the amounts of deoxygenated hemoglobin. On the other hand, because they depend on blood flow, and blood flow is slower to respond to neural activity than are electrical or magnetic fields, PET and fMRI have somewhat poorer temporal resolution than the EEG and the MEG. Some newer imaging techniques, which detect the scattered remnants of weak laser beams injected directly into the brain (Gratton and Fabiani 1998) also show promise of combining high spatial and temporal resolution while not harming the brain.

All these imaging techniques have the potential to produce a unique type of time series—the temporal unfolding of a three-dimensional map of neural activity in the brain. Ideally, the spatial scales would range from the microscopic to entire functional areas; the temporal scales, from milliseconds to minutes or even hours. Although techniques to analyze this enormous, complex mass of data are still in their infancy, such time series, obtained noninvasively while the brain engages in various cognitive tasks, indeed while similar time series of behavioral data are being collected, would allow the many links between behavior, cognition, and brain activity to be explored in detail. Some aspects of this relationship are already beginning to be studied, as discussed in section 33.2.

33.2   Brain Dynamics

Brains evolve (see chap. 32), and individual brains are born, develop into maturity, age, and finally die. Although the basic structure of the brain seems to be fixed for each species, individual brains do not attain this structure invariably. Deprivation of experience at critical periods leads to structural abnormalities that persist, whereas exposure to experience leads a brain to develop more closely to its potential. Even the adult brain is plastic. For example, if the tactile cortex of an adult monkey is deprived of innervation from an arm, the part of the tactile cortex that previously encoded touch and pain information from that arm is invaded by inner-vation from neighboring regions of skin and subsequently encodes touch and pain information from those regions instead (Pons et al. 1991). In humans, extensive musical training over many years results in permanent changes in the brain, both in enhanced tactile representations of the fingers used in playing the violin (Elbert et al. 1995), and in enhanced auditory responses to piano tones (Pantev et al. 1998). Such plasticity occurs in the short term as well. For example, after listening for three hours to music from which a small band of frequencies around 1,000 Hz had been removed, people appeared to have fewer auditory cortical neurons devoted to coding sound in that frequency region. This tendency reversed between listening sessions, suggesting that the frequency tuning of neurons in the auditory cortex depends dynamically on the current soundscape (Pantev et al. 1999). Even short-term training on frequency discriminations in a particular frequency region can enhance the brain's responses to the relevant frequencies (Menning, Roberts, and Pantev 2000). These studies show more than simply changes in the brain as a consequence of learning. They demonstrate that the very structure and organization of the brain are dynamical (see also Ward 2001).

The dynamics of the brain are nowhere more apparent than at the scale of the individual neurons and their connections to other neurons. At one time, these relationships were thought to be adequately modeled by the influence of one neuron on another neuron's rate of generating action potentials ("firing rate"). This influence is relevant to "rate coding" by neurons, that is, expressing the presence of a trigger feature by an increase or decrease in firing rate. Recently, however, a different kind of influence has been gaining prominence (see Singer 1993). In this view, the *timing* of a neuron's action potentials is influenced by the timing of its inputs from other neurons. *Synchronization* of neural activity is thus considered to be important to the way the brain's state evolves in time and for the way in which it generates cognitive and behavioral states. Indeed, it amounts to a second possibility for neural coding, one especially useful for solving what is described as the "binding problem"—the coding of necessary relations between neural activity in anatomically separated but functionally related brain areas (see Singer 1999). Because relaxation oscillators are easily entrained by forcing inputs (see chap. 31), we might suspect that such oscillators would play a role in contemporary theories of synchronization mechanisms. They do.

A striking example is the theory of Nunez (1995, 2000), according to which, neurons do act very much like relaxation oscillators, producing standing and traveling waves of neocortical activity that influence global

and local oscillations and cognitive and behavioral states, even consciousness (see chap. 35; Wright and Liley 1996). The theory begins with
the observation that *synaptic action density* (the number of active synapses in a particular volume of neocortex), averaged over millions of
neurons, is measured crudely by scalp EEG. The approach emphasizes
coherences (squared correlation coefficients—closely related to synchronization) between paired locations of EEG recordings as estimates of the
interactions of the neural networks found in these brain regions. The
general principles of the theory are (1) brain state is described by physio-
logically based control parameters that depend on neuromodulatory
action and that determine prominent EEG frequencies; (2) neural networks operate in a background of standing waves of synaptic action—
oscillatory changes in the number of active synapses; (3) excitatory and
inhibitory synaptic action density and action potential density are treated
as macroscopic field variables; (4) cognitive and overt behavior depend
on, among other things, the levels of these variables in various brain
regions. The goal is to describe the brain system's input-output relationship in a general theory stated thus:

$$\hat{\mathbf{D}}[f(x, t)] = g(x, t), \tag{33.1}$$

where $f(x, t)$ is the input, $g(x, t)$ is the output, and $\hat{\mathbf{D}}$ is a mathematical
operator that represents the dynamical properties of the system. This
operator is quite complicated (as might be expected) and also certainly
nonlinear, which means that there is no easy way to decompose it into
subterms that can be dealt with easily. Nunez (2000) points out, however,
that it may be possible to use local linear approximations (see chap. 25)
for certain brain states, or over certain parameter values, and thus begin
to work with the theory. He does this in the context of EEG data in
Nunez 1995 and 2000. Although there is not the space here to describe
this complicated theory and its empirical plausibility in detail, it dovetails
impressively with the ideas I have been trying to express in this book. The
multiple scales of dynamics mentioned in the chapter epigraph from
Nunez 2000 are collapsed for pragmatic reasons to two prominent scales
of oscillations in synaptic action density and their interactions. *Local
oscillations* arise from interactions between neurons in relatively small,
functionally segregated areas of the brain, connected in neural networks
through both excitatory and inhibitory connections. *Global oscillations*
arise from interactions between such segregated areas, with longer communication delays caused by the longer axonal pathways, and possibly by
the many intervening synapses, involved. Under some conditions, described in more detail by Nunez (1995, 2000), it is possible to derive simple

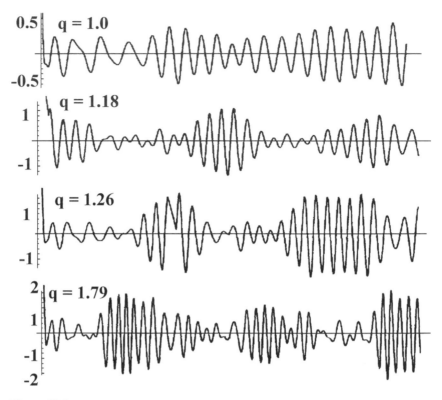

Figure 33.2
Local and global oscillations. (From Nunez 2000. Reprinted by permission of
Cambridge University Press.)

expressions for local and global oscillations and their interactions. In one
such case, where the nonlinearity of the dynamics is small and the various
global-local resonances do not interact, a set of five second-order differential equations can be obtained, each one like the following equation:

$$\frac{d^2Z}{dt^2} - \varepsilon(1 - Z^2)\frac{dZ}{dt} + [k_n^2 - (1 + \varepsilon)Z^2]Z = 0, \tag{33.2}$$

which closely resembles equation 31.3, the van der Pol relaxation oscillator: Z stands for the synaptic action density (like voltage in the van der
Pol equation), ε is the damping parameter, and $[k_n^2 - (1 + \varepsilon)Z^2]Z$ is the
restoring force term. If the nonlinearity is stronger, and the resonances are
coupled, more complicated versions of equation 33.2 apply (right side not
equal to zero). Numerical solutions to one set of such equations are
shown in figure 33.2 for various local oscillation frequencies (q). Both

local (faster) and global (slower) oscillations are apparent in figure 33.2. It has been suggested that gamma and theta frequencies of the EEG interact in this way to limit working memory (Lisman and Idiart 1995). In this theory, one "rehearsal" of all working memory "slots" takes place during every (global) theta cycle of about 6 Hz, rehearsal of each item taking place at the (local) gamma frequency of about 40 Hz, or one item every 25 msec, the maximum rate at which short-term memory can be "scanned" (Sternberg, 1966). Thus some 7 ± 2 items can be retained in working, or short-term, memory (Miller 1956). In the service of confirming their model, Lisman and Idiart (1995) published plots of embedded oscillations recorded from both human auditory cortex and from rat hippocampus that look remarkably like those of figure 33.2.

33.3   Hybrid Models

The brain has a definite structure, both anatomical and functional and in part modular (Swindale 1990, 1998); this structure is plastic at many scales of space and time. Although the prospect of describing the brain in a way that integrates anatomical and functional structure with dynamics is daunting, it is nonetheless beginning to be attempted. An excellent first pass is Arbib, Érdi, and Szentágothai 1997 (see also Arbib and Érdi 2000). Primitive, but illuminating, models can be suggested for cognitive tasks such as memory scanning, attentional orienting, or navigating space, in terms of which brain areas "light up" in a particular temporal sequence. One particularly influential such model has been the "disengage-shift-engage" model of visual attention reorienting. In this model, disengaging of visual attention from a current location in visual space is mediated by activity in the posterior parietal cortex, shifting to a new location in visual space is mediated by activity in the superior colliculus, and reengaging attention at the new location is mediated by activity in the pulvinar nucleus of the thalamus (e.g., Posner and Raichle 1994). Because attentional orientation changes intermittently over time (oscillates?—see Large and Jones 1999), its time evolution would consist of a series of episodes of shifting (the above sequence); these episodes of shifting would alternate with dwell times of various durations depending partly on the nature of the cognitive task being done (e.g., reading) and partly on the person's "span of attention." Ultimately, it should be possible to coordinate more sophisticated models of brain activity with equally sophisticated models of cognitive operations to produce models that integrate brain and cognitive or behavioral dynamics in the way envisioned by Arbib and colleagues (Arbib, Érdi, and Szentágothai 1997; Arbib and Érdi 2000).

Chapter 34

Dynamical Computation

No artifact devised by man is so convenient for this kind of functional description as the digital computer.

—Herbert A. Simon, *The Sciences of the Artificial*

If the bits of computers are someday scaled down to the size of individual atoms, quantum mechanical effects may profoundly change the nature of computation itself.

—D. P. DiVincenzo, "Quantum Computation"

34.1 Numerical Methods

The digital computer is probably the most important weapon in the armamentarium of the dynamical cognitive scientist. Because dynamical equations are so difficult to understand and solve analytically, the computer is the tool of choice for analyzing dynamical systems. I have already alluded to numerical methods implemented on a digital computer for doing Fourier analysis, for simulating chaos and stochastic processes, for solving ordinary differential equations, and for understanding nonlinear differential and difference equations (usually involving iteration of a function; see chap. 23). Computers are modeling tools par excellence. Indeed, it is hard to see how anyone could comprehend complex systems of differential or difference equations without computer analysis. With computer analysis, we can often see how a complex model behaves under various parameter regimes and thus come to understand it. We can also use computer methods to obtain new predictions, often counterintuitive consequences of "innocent" assumptions.

Of all of the techniques mentioned or suggested in this book, perhaps the most mundane and yet useful one for dynamical approaches is that of numerical integration of a differential equation. Because numerical integration can be used to solve *any* differential equation approximately for certain ranges of variable and parameter values, and because differential equations form the foundation of dynamical modeling, it is definitely worth knowing about. Integrating a differential equation produces a solution to it that expresses the relationship between a set of variables over some range of their values. Although a given differential equation may express how the changes in the state variables of a system depend on some other variables, especially on time in the dynamical case, the actual evolution of the system in time is expressed by the solution to the equation, thus the need to integrate. Remember, in this case integration is not done to obtain a measure of a set (for example the area under a probability density function), but rather to find a function relating the system's variables to time. Although there are many sources of computer algorithms for numerical integration, the one I have found most useful is Press et al. 1992, which contains descriptions of algorithms for this and many other numerical techniques of use to dynamical modeling (including random number and probability distribution generators), and which comes with an impressive array of software to implement these algorithms and with a website for news and problem reports.

To get a taste of numerical integration without going into its complexities, let us begin with an ordinary differential equation (ODE) of any order. This equation can be reduced to a set of first-order ODEs by choosing new variables, as FitzHugh did when deriving his neuron model from the van der Pol relaxation oscillator (see chap. 31). We can apply numerical integration to each equation in this set, one at a time. Consider what is called an "initial-value problem" for a single ODE: given x_s at a starting time t_s, we want to know what value x_f has at some final time, t_f, or what value x_i has at some discrete list of time points t_i between t_s and t_f, perhaps to plot the function between t_s and t_f. The basic idea of numerical integration is to construct the trajectory of the function $x(t)$ piece by piece by adding a series of small increments to the initial value, x_s, each one consisting of a step-size multiplied by a derivative. The simplest way to do this is called the "Euler method." Often used for modeling neurons, this method is also valuable for insight into what is happening in the numerical integration process: it approximates the solution function by a series of straight lines (local linear approximation; see chap. 25), with each new point calculated according to

$$x_{n+1} = x_n + \Delta t \cdot f(t_n, x_n), \tag{34.1}$$

where Δt is the small increment in time, and $f(t_n, x_n)$ is the right-hand side of the differential equation we are integrating. As a simple example, consider the first-order ODE

$$\frac{dx}{dt} = at,$$

which you might remember as equation 8.1, whose solution,

$$x = a\frac{t^2}{2},$$

was equation 8.2. Let us say we want to plot the function that yields equation 8.1, but we do not know the solution, equation 8.2 (we pretend it is too difficult to solve analytically). First we rewrite the differentials, dx and dt, in equation 8.1 as differences, Δx and Δt, and multiply both sides by Δt, producing

$$\Delta x = \Delta t \cdot at. \tag{34.2}$$

Now we can calculate the value of x at a point Δt in the future from the starting point, t_0, by adding the increment, Δx, specified by equation 34.2 to the starting value of x, x_0:

$$x_1 = x_0 + \Delta x = x_0 + \Delta t \cdot at. \tag{34.3}$$

Clearly, equation 34.3 can be applied recursively, generating a series of values, x_i, that can be plotted against the successive values of t, yielding a graph of the function (the integral solution of the differential equation). Thus, in the absence of an analytical solution of a differential equation, we can use this and similar numerical techniques to obtain numbers that are close to those taken by the solution: we can plot orbits of such equations in phase space, even if we cannot solve them analytically.

Figure 34.1 shows an example of a series of points generated in this way from equation 34.3 with $a = 0.5$ and $x = 0$ at $t = 0$. It also shows the analytical solution, equation 8.2, plotted in the same graph for comparison. The Euler method generates a reasonable approximation, although there is some error—in this case, all of the solution points are over-estimated by a small amount. For equations that are less well behaved, the error can be large at some points, for example, at points of inflection. This error can be reduced by using a more sophisticated method such as the fourth-order Runge-Kutta, which creates several Euler steps, one at beginning of each time interval, twice at the midpoint and once at a trial endpoint and the final function estimate is calculated based on these four derivatives, hence "fourth-order Runge-Kutta" (see Press et al. 1992).

Another approach to dealing with intractable dynamical system descriptions is to begin with a potentially interesting difference equation

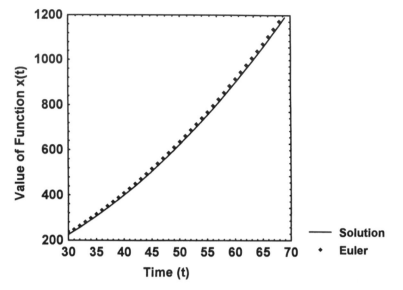

Figure 34.1
Euler approximation and solution to Equation 34.2.

and study its behavior by computer. Gregson (1988) studied a complex cubic difference equation in this way as part of a model of psychophysical judgment. His difference equation can be written as

$$Y_{j+1} = -a(Y_j - 1)(Y_j + ie)(Y_j - ie), \tag{34.4}$$

where the variable Y is complex, that is, each value of Y is a vector composed of a real value and an imaginary value, often written as $y = x + iz$, where the multiplier $i = \sqrt{-1}$ creates the imaginary part. Through his computer analysis of this function, Gregson was able to find parameter values for which chaos appeared in the imaginary component and affected the time evolution of the real component. This is an excellent example of how computer exploration of a complicated, in this case nonlinear, difference equation can inform dynamical theory.

34.2 Neural Network Models

The computational power of the digital computer is critical to the implementation of *neural network models*, also called "parallel distributed processing models" and "connectionist architectures," which have augmented traditional symbolic artificial intelligence in computer science (e.g., Hudson and Cohen 2000; Lewis, Jagannathan, and Yeşildirek

1999), and which have also proved capable of explaining many perceptual and cognitive behaviors in humans and other animals (e.g., Rumelhart and McClelland 1986; Parks, Levine, and Long 1998). Neural network models are inherently dynamical—they must "learn" to model a particular behavior or to accomplish a particular task. Such learning is accomplished by implementing a graphlike structure of processing elements whose interconnections change over time until the structure is correctly accomplishing the task before it. Thus neural network models are potentially capable of realizing the program described in chapter 9 of building dynamical models on a plausible structural base.

Any neural network model must have a minimum set of elements, each of which can be more or less complicated (e.g., Golden 1996; Rumelhart, Hinton, and McClelland 1986). Figure 34.2A shows these aspects in a schematic form. First, the network is composed of a set of *processing units*, u_i, $i = 1$ to N. In the simplest neural network in use today, there are three types of units: *input*, *output*, and *hidden*, as shown in figure 34.2B. Input units receive input from an environment and connect to either hidden units or to output units, whereas output units provide output signals to that environment and receive connections from either input or hidden units. Hidden units are called that because they do not interact directly with the environment: they receive inputs from either input or other hidden units and output to either output units or other hidden units. Networks without hidden units are called "perceptrons," which lack the computational power to model the complexities of human cognition (Minsky and Papert 1967). Each processing unit has a *state of activation*, a_i, and an *output function*, $o_i(t) = f_i(a_i)$, that transforms the unit's state of activation into an output signal. Processing units are connected to one another by weighted connections (similar to a directed, weighted, graph; see chap. 9) that together represent what the network "knows" and thus how it responds to any input. The *connection weights*, $w_{i,j}$, are positive if the output from u_i excites u_j, and negative if u_i inhibits u_j. The size of $w_{i,j}$ represents the magnitude of the effect of u_i on u_j. It is possible for a single unit to have many inputs, and these are referred to collectively as "net_j." The *rule of propagation* specifies for each type of connection what the resulting net input is into each unit; it is often simply the weighted sum of the inputs of a given type. The *activation rule* specifies how the various net inputs to a unit are combined with its current state of activation through a function, F, to produce its new state of activation for the next time period. The activation rule can be quite simple, such as the sum of net inputs and the current activation level, or it can be more complicated, such as a logistic or other threshold function or a Gaussian. The activation function

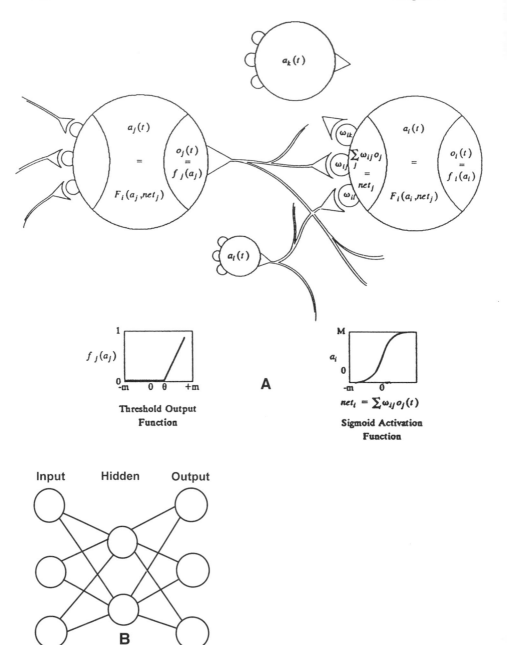

Figure 34.2
(*A*) Elements of neural network models (From Rumelhart, Hinton, and McClelland 1986. Reprinted by permission of The MIT Press.); (*B*) three-layer neural network.

might be some complicated processing that involves many computations, and that might even implement a semiautonomous agent. Initially, processing units are connected randomly or uniformly, with meaningless connection weights. The connection weights, or *strengths*, change over time as a result of implementation of a *learning rule*, as the network learns to do its task. Most learning rules are variants of the famous Hebbian learning rule (Hebb 1949), in which the connection between two units is strengthened if both units are highly active at the same time, and weakened if they are active at different times. Quite often the rule is modified so that weights are changed in proportion to the difference (delta) between the achieved activation and a target activation for the receiving unit; this is called the "delta rule." In the *backpropagation* process, an error signal calculated at the output units is propagated backward into the network, so that the weights on each layer are changed successively based on the "error" calculated for that layer. Finally, in most neural network models, the environment is represented as some probability distribution over the set of possible input patterns, perhaps varying over time as well.

Although neural network models are inherently dynamical, and are a foundation stone of modern artificial intelligence research, they have proven difficult to accept as models of human cognition (e.g., Green 1998). Ironically, their strength is also their weakness in this regard: their "knowledge" of the problem domain is represented in the connection weights between the processing units. The pattern of activation of the hidden units, in particular, appears on the surface to be fairly random with respect to the critical aspects of the patterns presented to the input units. The problem is that the processing units are all the same, and often bear no direct relationship to the concepts of the phenomenon being modeled. This problem is common to all distributed representations (see Lashley 1950), in contrast to more traditional models, in which the model units themselves represent processing modules or conceptual units more directly related to the concepts of the problem domain. For example, a neural network model of visual pattern recognition may correctly classify patterns, even partial and novel patterns, but it is difficult to see exactly how it is doing that task. In contrast, when a more traditional model performs, say, recognition by feature detection, it is clear what is going on because the concepts of the model are the same as those of the problem —in this case, features of visual patterns. Connectionist models must be analyzed to find representations of cognitive concepts and to discover how the representations arose through the learning process, not an easy task because usually the more useful the model, the more complex it is. Progress is being made, however, on developing methods by which to analyze neural network models for representations of cognitive concepts. For example, Berkeley and Dawson (1995) reported finding clear representations of rules for making various logical deductions in the patterns of activations of the hidden units in their neural network. Others have used such multivariate techniques as factor analysis and discriminant function analysis to accomplish similar analyses.

Consider a neural network made up of relaxation oscillators (see chap. 31). Here the processing done by individual units (activation rule) would be fairly complex, although the propagation rule could be simpler. Inputs from various units would represent stochastic and deterministic forcing, and different activation rules could endow different units with agentlike capabilities. Networks of similar processing units have been explored to some extent by Grossberg (1988), who introduced the concept of *adaptive resonance* in classifying patterns. In adaptive resonance, top-down signals from higher-level units interact with bottom-up signals from lower-level units to stabilize the network and create resonance when the input is sufficiently close to a stored category prototype. During learning, both the top-down and bottom-up connection weights are changed adaptively, so that the category prototypes change to reflect experience. More purely mathematical work on systems of coupled oscillators can be found in Kopell 1988 and Rand, Cohen, and Holmes 1988.

Another way to modify traditional neural networks is to introduce temporal coding, that is, to make the timing of signals between processing units important to their activation by those signals. This was done by Berger and Liaw (2000) in a simple neural network (11 neurons and 30 links) designed to do recognition of isolated spoken words presented in "babble" noise (essentially nonsense talking), a very difficult task for humans. In this network, the learning rule allowed the temporal properties as well as the magnitudes of the connection weights to change as learning progressed. The network recognizes human speech in babble noise much better than any previous models can, including neural networks with thousands of neurons and connections, and also better than humans can, even when the noise is hundreds of times as intense as the speech signal. Thus there are two important timescales in neural networks: the scale of the learning and the scale of the signals between the units, which is tuned by the learning process.

34.3   Exotic Computers

Digital computers are composed of logic circuits implementing elementary (Boolean) logic: OR, NOT, AND, XOR, NAND, NOR, and so forth, and memory registers consisting of functionally organized groups of flip-flops. A digital computer is a logic machine that simply repeats the same logic operations over and over again in different sequences. These sequences of operations, though specific to the task being accomplished, are implemented in the same way regardless of whether the task is numerical computation or human speech processing. Essentially, the various patterns of bits and the operations and groups of operations performed on them represent different symbols during different tasks. These symbols must be interpreted by a user. In a sense, the typographical level of operation, the level of simple logical operations performed on bits of information, is insulated from the semantic level of the user interpretation (Hofstadter 1979). Recently, large groups of interlinked digital computers have been formed to allow massively parallel processing. Some neural networks, such as that of Berger and Liaw (2000), are actually implemented as groups of simple computers, rather than being simulated by a single computer.

Any digital computer, including a massively parallel one, can be emulated (the same calculations performed in the same way) by a universal Turing machine (Turing 1936) consisting of only an unbounded storage tape, a movable tape read/write head, and a set of elementary operations on the bits encoded on the tape. Such a machine has been said to be able to perform all physically possible computations (the Church-Turing thesis), although this is difficult to prove. Indeed, there have been proposals of systems that could compute things that the Turing machine cannot. One such is the analog shift map of Siegelmann (1995), created from a chaotic dynamical system similar to the logistic difference equation discussed in chapter 24. An "analog shift" replaces one dotted substring (consisting of symbols and one dot, for example, 0.1) with another equally long one according to a function G; then the string is shifted an integer number of places to the left or to the right (relative to the dot) according to another function, F. For example, starting with the sequence 1010.101, if the function G operates on the subsequence 0.1 by replacing "0.1" with "1.1", then $G(1010.101) = 1011.101$. If F then specifies that the dot is to be moved one place to the left, then $F(1011.101) = 101.1101$. This process continues until the functions G and F specify no further changes; the result of the computation is the final sequence, and the input-output map is the transformation from the initial dotted sequence to the subsequence to the right of the dot in the final sequence. Siegelmann (1995) proved that this process can compute a class of functions that contains the class of functions computed by the universal Turing machine as a subset, thus it represents a more powerful computer. Moreover, the analog shift map computes in a way similar to that of neural networks and analog computers, and could possibly describe real physical systems. Realizations of this hypothetical computer could come in the form of physical systems that behave chaotically, making it possible to exploit chaos as a computational device, and also making it possible to simulate very complicated neural networks directly.

Among the other exotic, hypothetical computers that have been suggested in recent years (including ones based on DNA), at least one has properties that might become useful for dynamical cognitive science. This is the quantum computer (e.g., Feynman 1985; DiVincenzo 1995). The most important difference between classical digital computers and quantum computers is in the state of the elements that encode the user's symbols. A digital computer's flip-flops always have a definite state at any moment of time, for example, an 8-bit register might read 10101111. In a quantum computer, however, the bits of information are sometimes described by a wave function (see chap. 13). When this is the case, as during a computation, the different possible states of a group of bits are superimposed in the wave function

$$\Psi = a|10101111\rangle + b|11111111\rangle + c|00000000\rangle + \cdots, \qquad (34.5)$$

where $a, b, c, \ldots$ are complex numbers whose phases (the parts multiplied by i) can be such that the different possible states interfere either constructively or destructively. When the state of the computer is measured, this wave function collapses and the bits assume one of the possible states with probabilities $|a|^2, |b|^2, |c|^2, \ldots$ The trick is to make the incorrect answers to a computation interfere destructively so that their probabilities are vanishingly small, whereas that of the state corresponding to the correct answer is near one. If this can be done, because complex calculations are accomplished in parallel across huge numbers of bits, they can be accomplished in much less time than in a conventional digital computer. With this much computing power, it should prove possible to emulate the human brain's activity over time at any necessary level of detail (cf. Tipler 1994). Moreover, it has even been suggested that the human brain implements a quantum computer that is responsible in some way for the noncomputable aspects of human consciousness (Hameroff 1998; Penrose 1994; but see also Tegmark 2000). Thus understanding quantum computers could provide insights into the temporal unfolding of human cognition more directly than attained by simulations of complicated dynamical models.

Chapter 35
Dynamical Consciousness

O, what a world of unseen visions and heard silences, this insubstantial country of the mind!... And the privacy of it all!... This consciousness that is myself of selves, that is everything, and yet nothing at all—what is it? And where did it come from? And why?

—Julian Jaynes, *The Origin of Consciousness in the Breakdown of the Bicameral Mind*

Consciousness, then, does not appear to itself chopped up in bits.... It is nothing jointed; it flows.... In talking of it hereafter, let us call it the stream of thought....

—William James, *The Principles of Psychology*

We propose that a large cluster of neuronal groups that together constitute, on a time scale of hundreds of milliseconds, a unified neural process of high complexity be termed the "dynamic core," in order to emphasize both its integration and its constantly changing patterns.

—Giulio Tononi and Gerald M. Edelman, "Consciousness and Complexity"

Human consciousness is itself a huge complex of memes (or more exactly meme-effects in brains) that can best be understood as the operation of a "von Neumanesque" virtual machine implemented in the parallel architecture of a brain that was not designed for any such activities.

—Daniel C. Dennett, *Consciousness Explained*

35.1 Consciousness

Arguably the greatest challenge of dynamical cognitive science in the future will be to provide a basis for understanding the unique and fascinating phenomena of human consciousness. The project is of gigantic proportions, and although breakthroughs may come in the next few years, indeed, may have already been initiated, it is unlikely that a detailed understanding of the mechanisms of human (and other animal) consciousness will be attained in less than many years (the title of Dennett

1991 to the contrary notwithstanding). Although consciousness has been neglected for years in psychology, the group studying it has become both vast and interdisciplinary, with physicists and neuroscientists joining the psychologists and philosophers in telling their stories around the campfire. Here I will touch on a few of the most promising (in my opinion) and dynamically relevant ideas that swirl around this topic.

The consciousness so aptly and poetically alluded to in the first two chapter epigraphs clearly includes wakefulness, our awareness of or attention to environmental events, our ability to report on our mental states, our ability to remember episodes in our past life at will, our ability to contemplate our own mental states and our own behavior, and, above all, our *experience* of mental life, what the philosophers call "what it is like to be me (or you, or a bat)." Chalmers (1996) argued that explaining the first several items on this list (and some others) is "easy" relative to explaining the last one, that of experience, which he called the "hard problem." Indeed, we could not hope to use the ordinary methods of cognitive science (including dynamical cognitive science) to achieve a satisfactory account of the problem of experience because nothing in any functional or mechanistic explanation of any aspect of consciousness could possibly *entail* that the function or mechanism in question would be accompanied by experience. Chalmers (1996) speculated that the only way to deal with experience is to grant it fundamental status, in the same way that we grant electrons, photons, and quarks fundamental status. We could do this by asserting that at least some information (the difference that makes a difference; Bateson 1972) has two distinct aspects or properties, one physical and the other phenomenal. This is consistent with suggestions that information, rather than matter, is the most fundamental physical concept (e.g., Wheeler 1990), and that information can take different aspects depending on the point of view of the observer (Pribram 1986). We can study the phenomenal aspect, as we study the physical one, but there is no use asking *why* there is a phenomenal aspect to information, any more than it makes sense to ask why there is a physical aspect. This view denies that conscious experience is an eternal mystery (traditional dualism) but also denies that it will be possible to explain it in a reductionist functional or mechanistic way (scientific materialism, a form of monism).

Dennett (1991) has argued compellingly that we should abandon the traditional view of the mind/brain as having a place, the Cartesian theater, where "it all comes together," where consciousness lives. Instead, he has proposed, the mind/brain contains many parallel channels of information processing (he called them "multiple drafts") and that different parts of this stream of parallel processing form the dominant narrative, a virtual von Neuman serial computer, at different times. There is no Cartesian theater—the theater of consciousness is the entire brain. Indeed, from the evidence gathered thus far, it seems clear that some kind of massive parallelism must be the case, and that it must form a foundation stone of any explanation of how the brain generates experience and the other attributes of consciousness.

Why are we conscious? Many (e.g., Shallice 1972) have sought to discover something that consciousness does, that can be accomplished by no other mechanism. One prominent recent suggestion (e.g., Delacour 1995; Donald 1995) is that the usefulness of the huge computational power of the massively parallel organization of the human brain (and mammalian brains in general) is somewhat compromised by a lack of integration; at any moment each parallel process could be doing its own thing, and the whole organism could be paralyzed or could oscillate wildly between inconsistent perceptions and actions. Consciousness, by allowing competing processes to interact in the same "global workspace" (e.g., Baars 1988), could achieve a level of integration that would counteract these negative qualities of parallel computing. This "virtual serial von Neumanesque" aspect of the mind/brain would be responsible for intentionality and models of the self in the world—or, at least, these would be the metaphors used by modern humans to describe this integrative activity (cf. Jaynes 1976).

What form could the brain activity associated with consciousness take? The modern search for the *neural correlates of consciousness* was greatly stimulated by Crick and Koch 1990. One neural correlate of consciousness they suggested, might be found in the roughly 40 Hz oscillations discovered by Gray and Singer (1989) in the cat visual cortex (see also Singer 1999), where neural activity was synchronized via locking to a common firing frequency. Not only could such synchronization bind together the disparately coded features (color, shape, motion, etc.) of visual stimuli; perhaps it could also be the sine qua non of consciousness (or at least visual awareness) itself. Whereas Crick and Koch continued to search for some property of individual neurons that would confer consciousness, several others focused on the temporal synchrony itself as the critical feature. One of the most impressive demonstrations of the importance of such synchronization builds on an ingenious technique for studying consciousness first exploited by Logothetis and Schall (1989): presenting visual stimuli that engage in *binocular rivalry* (cf. Levelt 1968) and simultaneously directly recording neural activity from neurons in visual cortex that are responding to these stimuli. In binocular rivalry, conflicting stimuli, such as a square-wave grating with stripes oriented vertically and another with stripes oriented horizontally, are presented at the same time, one to each eye (see fig. 35.1). The viewer is generally only aware of (conscious of) one of the two stimuli, and the "seen" grating alternates randomly. What happens in the visual cortex when the "seen" grating switches from one to the other, that is, when awareness changes? According to one hypothesis, the firing rates of various neurons undergo modulation as the view changes, with the neurons responding to the newly "seen" grating increasing their firing rate just as the view changed, and those responding to the newly "unseen" grating decreasing their firing rate at the same time. Although such modulation does not consistently occur in the cortical areas that do the early processing of visual stimuli (areas V1, V2, and V3), it does appear to occur in inferotemporal cortex, where the later stages of visual processing take place (Sheinberg and Logothetis 1997)

According to a second hypothesis, in addition to, or instead of, modulation of firing rate, awareness changes are accompanied by a change in the *synchrony* of the firing of the various neurons that encode the stimuli. This hypothesis was confirmed for neurons in areas V1 and V2 in a clever study of binocular rivalry in cats by Fries et al. (1997). Figure 35.1 shows their experimental setup and results. The cat was watching mirrors that presented one drifting (slowly moving in the direction of the arrow) grating to each eye (panel A). Under rivalry conditions, with two gratings present, which one the cat was aware of was inferred from which one was causing optokinetic nystagmus (slow tracking eye movements interrupted by abrupt "return" eye movements that indicate that the cat was tracking the grating). Because the eyes move together, the directions of the slow and abrupt eye movements indicated which grating was being "seen" at any moment. When only one grating was presented to only one eye as a control (panels B and D), the neurons responding to that grating were quite synchronized (large amplitude and oscillatory nature of correlation functions below the gratings in the figure) and there was no difference in the synchrony between the two gratings. When both stimuli were presented together, however, the neurons responding to the "seen" grating (panel C) were much more highly synchronized than were those responding to the "unseen" grating (panel D).

These are dramatic results, but do they apply to human consciousness? Much recent work using electroencephalography and magnetoencephalography (EEG and MEG; e.g., Sauve 1999, see chap. 33) suggests that

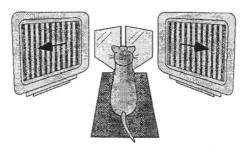

A

B   selected suppressed   C   selected suppressed

D   selected suppressed   E   selected suppressed

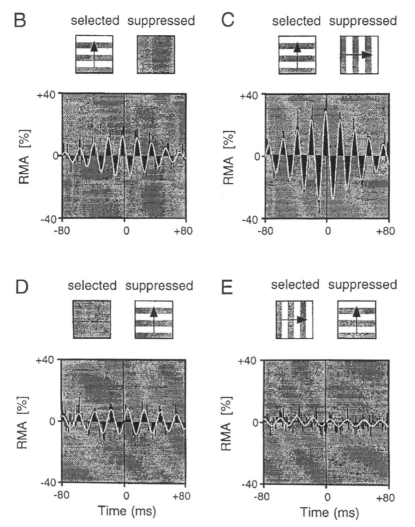

Figure 35.1
Neural synchronization under binocular rivalry. (From Engel et al. 1999.)

they do. One result using MEG, in particular, is especially suggestive. Tononi et al. (1998) reported that, when humans are conscious of a particular stimulus among rivaling visual grating stimuli, there is widespread coherence between MEG measurements at various brain sites and the MEG measurements of the activity of the neurons in visual cortex responding to the seen grating, whereas such coherence is lacking for the unseen grating (*coherence* relates to the square of the correlation coefficient between two time series). Tononi et al.'s experimental setup was similar to that of Fries et al. (1997), except that the rivaling gratings were flickered at different temporal frequencies. Because visual cortical neurons phase lock their firing to the flicker frequency of stimuli to which they are responding, the power in the appropriate frequency band of a Fourier spectrum of the MEG time series could be compared across brain sites when a given stimulus was "seen" and when it was suppressed. These comparisons indicated that widespread, coherent neural firing was associated with consciousness of a particular grating. Not all neural synchrony is associated with consciousness, however. The rigid, hypersynchronous firing characteristic of petit mal seizures is associated with an unconscious state. Apparently, before synchrony becomes associated with consciousness, there must be a large number of possible patterns of neural synchrony, of which the occurring pattern is only one (differentiation). Tononi and Edelman (1998) suggested that both *differentiation* and *integration* are fundamental aspects of consciousness, and that both are achieved by the emergence of a *dynamic core*, namely, "a large cluster of neuronal groups that together constitute, on a time scale of hundreds of milliseconds, a unified neural process of high complexity" (p. 1849). The dynamic core is similar to Kinsbourne's "dominant focus" (1988) and to Dennett's von Neumanesque computer (1991), in both of which massively parallel computing in the brain is integrated in consciousness. Various aspects of the current sensory and cognitive activity constitute the dynamic core and are thus "in consciousness," whereas other aspects, being outside the dominant focus, are outside of consciousness. Neural synchrony across widespread areas of the brain is the "force" that binds various neural activity into the dynamic core, with unsynchronized activity continuing outside of awareness (with often significant consequences, as ideas "pop" into our minds, problem solutions "just appear," and our bodies react in unpredicted ways to unperceived stimuli). An interesting implication of this view, consistent with Dennett's multiple drafts model (1991), is that time and space are "smeared" at the scale of the dynamic core process: several hundreds of milliseconds across the spatial extent of the brain. Because consciousness itself is a temporally smeared process it makes no sense to ask exactly when some aspect of the brain's information processing becomes conscious relative to when a stimulus is presented in eotemporal time (see Dennett and Kinsbourne 1992 for a deep discussion of this implication). The dynamic core generates its own biotemporal or nootemporal scales (see chap. 4), according to which conscious events (measured in clock time) are temporally indeterminate.

The plausibility of this view has been demonstrated by a large-scale simulation of thalamocortical circuits in the brain (65,000 neurons and 5 million connections; Lumer, Edelman, and Tononi 1997). In this simulation, individual neurons were modeled as integrate-and-fire neurons (see chaps. 22 and 31) described by

$$\tau_m \frac{dV_i(t)}{dt} = -V_i + E_0 - \sum_j g_j(t)(V_i - E_j), \tag{35.1}$$

where $V_i(t)$ is the voltage across the cell membrane at time t, E_0 is the resting potential, $g_j(t)$ is the synaptic potential generated by a spike at synapse j at time t (realistically modeled as several different types of synapses), E_j is the reversal potential for synapse j, and τ_m is a passive membrane time constant set at 16 msec for excitatory and 8 msec for inhibitory neurons. Whenever the membrane potential reached a threshold (about -51 mV) it was reset to -90 mV and a spike was recorded. As illustrated in figure 35.2, neurons were grouped into various layers, with various pathways and reentrant loops. Based on other evidence, the reentrant loops are particularly important to visual consciousness (Lamme and Roelfsema 2000), probably because they facilitate across-area synchrony. An attempt was made to realistically represent the various pathways in the visual system, even to the inclusion of primary (subscript p in fig. 35.2) and secondary (subscript s) areas in each region of the brain, and also several cortical layers. Visual inputs consisted of two superimposed square-wave gratings, with added noise, moving in perpendicular directions. When this neural network was simulated with continuous input, multilevel synchronous oscillations at roughly 50 Hz emerged, as shown in figure 35.3 by the population-averaged membrane potentials from cells in various layers of the model (based on from several hundred to several thousand simulated neurons in each layer). These oscillations were not programmed into the simulation in any way; they simply occurred as a consequence of the interactions between the neural activity in the various simulated brain areas in response to the stimulus input. Variation of parameters such as synaptic strengths, inhibitory time

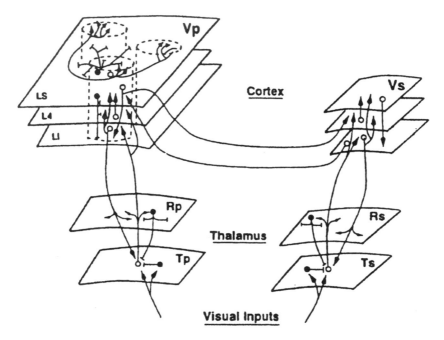

Figure 35.2
Organization of neural systems that generates spontaneous oscillations. (From Lumer, Edelman, and Tononi 1997. Reprinted by permission of Oxford University Press.)

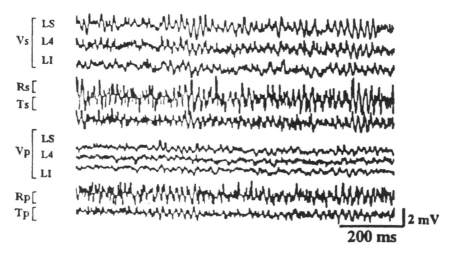

Figure 35.3
Spontaneous oscillations from a simulated thalamocortical system. (From Lumer, Edelman, and Tononi 1997. Reprinted by permission of Oxford University Press.)

constants, transmission delays, and lesions of various parts of the network affected the frequencies, but not the presence, of oscillations.

How does the peculiarly human feel to consciousness arise? We humans have a sense of self that often dominates our conscious awareness. We are aware of being aware and we talk about being aware, even to ourselves. The awareness of self seems to be restricted to humans, apes (chimpanzees, gorillas, and orangutans), and whales (e.g., dolphins and killer whales). Such awareness can be ascertained by testing whether an animal learns to recognize itself in a mirror (Gallup 1977), and to reverse roles in a social situation (Povinelli 1993). There is clearly a basis for the construction of a nonverbal self-concept in the basic facts of perception and social interaction; for example certain objects (our hands, our feet) cannot get smaller than a certain apparent size, no matter how we move about, whereas others (our car, a tree) can be made indefinitely small simply by moving in a particular direction (see Bermudez 1998 for a detailed discussion). Without language, animals can only have such a nonverbal self-concept based on perceptual-motor schemata, similar to a preverbal child, whereas with language, things change dramatically. Children learn to have a verbal self-concept, so that they can consistently use the word "I" to refer to behaviors, desires, and states of a particular entity (to which they have privileged access), and "you," "he," "she," and "they" to refer to the actions, desires, and (inferred) states of everyone else. They appear to do this via a massive infusion of memes (Dennett 1991), simple idea units introduced by Dawkins (1976) to describe how cultural information seems to undergo selective evolution similar to that experienced by genetic information. (Cavelli-Sforza 1981 expands on this theme with a quantitative model of cultural transmission based on standard evolutionary theory.) Dennett (1991) probably was wrong, however, to assert that these memes created from scratch the von Neumanesque serial processor running in the parallel architecture of the brain. Apparently, the complexly interlinked relaxation oscillators that make up the brain spontaneously self-organize into the dynamic core. Without language and the memes it makes possible, however, even a human would be left with a simple, nonverbal, perceptual-motor concept of self, and could not achieve elaborate simulations of self in the metaphorical world to which verbal humans are prone (see Jaynes 1976; Kahneman and Tversky 1982).

All of this has not yet answered the "hard problem." Why is the synchronized neural processing of the dynamic core accompanied by "experience?" What is it about spatially distributed, temporally synchronized neural processing that generates experience? It is possible that exotic mechanisms are responsible. Hameroff (1998) and Penrose (1994) have suggested that the brain acts as a quantum computer (see chap. 34) and that this action is responsible for consciousness: physically, conscious awareness is a quantum field effect, similar to an electromagnetic field. Hameroff (1998) suggested that anesthetics interrupt the necessary physical conditions necessary for the large-scale quantum coherence that generates consciousness, perhaps by binding electrons in the microtubule skeletons of the neurons so that they cannot participate in the quantum field (called a "Bose-Einstein condensate"). Although it has been argued that the timescale for such a field in the brain is much too short to approximate the time scale of consciousness (Tegmark 2000), the dynamic core of neural processing may indeed generate some kind of field effect, possibly electromagnetic, that results in "subjectivity." Certainly electromagnetic fields are what is measured by MEG and EEG, and these are more closely associated with cognitive states than are the detailed activities of individual neurons (e.g., Nunez 2000). These assertions must remain speculations, but they refer to provocative questions that will stimulate dynamical cognitive science for many years, even though we may never answer them (see Kurthen, Grunwald, and Elger 1998).

35.2 Unity of Science

It is appropriate to close this book with a discussion of consciousness, the study of which is inherently dynamical and interdisciplinary, with a strong need for complementary explanations. As we pass into an era when machines may think, when intelligence may evolve beyond that of humans (see Fogel 2000; Pfeifer and Scheier 1999) and quantum computation may allow us to emulate the human brain at the level of quarks (Tipler 1994), dynamical cognitive science, informed by complementary approaches from all of the sciences, will play a central role in our continuing effort to understand ourselves and our place in the cosmos.

References

Alvarez de Lorenzana, J. M. (2000). Closure, open systems and the modeling imperative. In J. R. Chandler and G. Van der Vijver, eds., *Closure, Emergent Organizations and Their Dynamics*, 91–99. New York: New York Academy of Sciences.

Alvarez de Lorenzana, J. M., and Ward, L. M. (1987). On evolutionary systems. *Behavioral Science*, 32, 19–33.

Anderson, J. R. (1976). *Language, Memory, and Thought*. Hillsdale, NJ: Erlbaum.

Anderson, J. R., Matessa, M., and Leabiere, C. (1997). Act-R: A theory of higher level cognition and its relation to visual attention. *Human-Computer Interaction*, 12, 439–462.

Arbib, M., and Érdi, P. (2000). Précis of *Neural Organization: Structure, Function and Dynamics. Behavioral and Brain Sciences*, 23, 513–571.

Arbib, M., Érdi, P., and Szantágothai, J. (1997). *Neural Organization: Structure, Function, and Dynamics*. Cambridge, MA: MIT Press.

Ashby, W. R. (1958). Requisite variety and its applications for the control of complex systems. *Cybernetics*, 1, 83–99.

Baars, B. J. (1988). *A Cognitive Theory of Consciousness*. Cambridge: Cambridge University Press.

Baggott, J. E. (1992). *The Meaning of Quantum Theory*. New York: Oxford University Press.

Baird, J. C. (1997). *Sensation and Judgment: Complementarity Theory of Psychophysics*. Mahwah, NJ: Erlbaum.

Bak, P. (1990). Self-organized criticality. *Physica A*, 163, 403–409.

Bak, P., Tang, C., and Weisenfeld, K. (1987). Self-organized criticality: An explanation of $1/f$ noise. *Physical Review Letters*, 59, 381–384.

Bateson, G. (1972). *Steps to an Ecology of Mind*. New York: Ballentine.

Beckers, R., Deneubourg, J. L., Goss, S., and Pasteels, J. M. (1990). Collective decision making through food recruitment. *Insectes Sociaux*, 37, 258–267.

Beer, S. (1974). *Designing Freedom*. Toronto: Canadian Broadcasting Company Publishing Corporation.

Beer, R. D. (2000). Dynamical approaches to cognitive science. *Trends in Cognitive Sciences*, 4, 91–99.

Bell, D. A. (1960). *Electrical Noise*. London: Van Nostrand.

Benzi, R., Sutera, S., and Vulpiani, A. (1987). The mechanism of stochastic resonance. *Journal of Physics*, A14, L453–L457.

Berge, G. (1985). *Graphs*. Amsterdam: North-Holland.

Berger, T. W., and Liaw, J. S. (2000). Machine demonstrates superhuman speech recognition abilities. USC News Service [On-line]. Available: ⟨http://www.usc.edu/ext-relations/news_service/releases/stories/3013html⟩.

Berkeley, I. S. N., and Dawson, M. R. W. (1995). Density plots of hidden value unit activations reveal interpretable bands. *Connection Science*, 7, 167–187.

Bermudez, J. L. (1988). *The Paradox of Self-Consciousness*. Cambridge, MA: MIT Press.

Bezrukov, S. M., and Vodyanoy, I. (1997). Stochastic resonance in non-dynamical systems without response thresholds. *Nature*, 385, 319–321.

Boon, J. P., and Decroly, O. (1995). Dynamical systems theory for musical dynamics. *Chaos*, 5, 501–508.

Born, M. (1962). *Einstein's Theory of Relativity*. New York: Dover.

Bouisson, M. (1960). *Magic: Its Rites and History*. London: Rider.

Box, G. E. P., and Jenkins, G. M. (1976). *Time Series Analysis: Forecasting and Control*. Rev. ed. San Francisco: Holden-Day.

Braida, L. D., and Durlach, N. I. (1988). Peripheral and central factors in intensity perception. In G. M. Edelman, W. Gall, and W. M. Cowan, eds., *Auditory Function*, 559–583. New York: Wiley.

Bremermann, H. J. (1962). Optimization through evolution and recombination. In M. C. Yovits et al., eds., *Self-Organizing Systems*, 93–106. Washington, DC: Spartan.

Bringhurst, R. (1995). *The Calling: Selected Poems, 1970–1985*. Toronto: McClelland and Stewart.

Brock, W. A., Dechert, W. D., and Scheinkman, J. (1986). A test for independence based on the correlation dimension. Department of Economics, University of Wisconsin, Madison, University of Houston, and University of Chicago.

Brock, W. A., Hsieh, D., and LeBaron, B. (1991). *Nonlinear Dynamics, Chaos, and Instability: Statistical Theory and Economic Evidence*. Cambridge, MA: MIT Press.

Brockwell, P. J., and Davis, R. A. (1996). *An Introduction to Time Series and Forecasting*. New York: Springer.

Bryden, M. P. (1967). A model for the sequential organization of behaviour. *Canadian Journal of Psychology*, 21, 37–56.

Budescu, D. V. (1987). A Markov model for generation of random binary sequences. *Journal of Experimental Psychology: Human Perception and Performance*, 13, 25–39.

Burgess, A. (1962). *A Clockwork Orange*. London: Heinemann.

Bush, R. R., and Mosteller, F. (1955). *Stochastic Models for Learning*. New York: Wiley.

Buss, D. M. (1999). *Evolutionary Psychology: The New Science of the Mind*. Boston: Allyn and Bacon.

Casdagli, M. (1991). Chaos and deterministic versus stochastic non-linear modelling. *Journal of the Royal Statistical Society B*, 54, 303–328.

Cavalli-Sforza, L. L., and Feldman, M. W. (1981). *Cultural Transmission and Evolution: A Quantitive Approach*. Princeton, NJ: Princeton University Press.

Chalmers, D. J. (1996). *The Conscious Mind: In Search of a Fundamental Theory*. New York: Oxford University Press.

Chan, K. S., and Tong, H. (2001). *Chaos from a Statistical Perspective*. New York: Springer.

Clancy, W. J. (1997). *Situated Cognition: On Human Knowledge and Computer Representations*. New York: Cambridge University Press.

Clancy, W. J. (1999). *Conceptual Coordination: How the Mind Orders Experience in Time*. Mahwah, NJ: Lawrence Erlbaum Associates.

Clayton, K., and Frey, B. (1997). Studies of mental "noise." *Nonlinear Dynamics, Psychology, and Life Sciences*, 1, 173–180.

Collins, J. J., Chow, C. C., Capela, A. C., and Imhoff, T. T. (1996). Aperiodic stochastic resonance. *Physical Review E*, 54, 5575–5584.

Collins, J. J., Imhoff, T. T., and Grigg, P. (1996a). Noise-enhanced information transmission in rat SA1 cutaneous mechanoreceptors via aperiodic stochastic resonance. *Journal of Neurophysiology*, 76, 642–645.

Collins, J. J., Imhoff, T. T., and Grigg, P. (1996b). Noise-enhanced tactile sensation. *Nature*, 383, 770.

Cordo, P., Inglis, J. T., Verschueron, S., Collins, J. J., Merfeld, D. M., Rosenblum, S., and Moss, F. (1996). Noise in human muscle spindles. *Nature*, 383, 769–770.

Coren, S., Ward L. M., and Enns, J. T. (1999). *Sensation and Perception*. 5th ed. Fort Worth: Harcourt Brace.

Corsini, G., and Saletti, R. (1987). Design of a digital $1/f^v$ noise simulator. In C. M. Van Vliet, ed., *Ninth International Conference on Noise in Physical Systems*, 82–86. Singapore: World Scientific.

Cowell, R. G., Philip, D. A., Lauritzen, A. L., and Spiegelhalter, D. J. (1999). *Probabilistic Networks and Expert Systems*. New York: Springer.

Crick, F. H. C., and Koch, C. (1990). Towards a neurobiological theory of consciousness. *Seminars in the Neurosciences*, 2, 263–275.

Crovitz, F. (1970). *Galton's Walk : Methods for the Analysis of Thinking, Intelligence and Creativity*. New York: Harper and Row.

Cutler, C. D. (1997). A general approach to predictive and fractal scaling dimensions in discrete-index time series. *Fields Institute Communications*, 11, 29–48.

Darwin, C. (1871). *The Descent of Man, and Selection in Relation to Sex.* London: Murray

Dawkins, R. (1976). *The Selfish Gene.* New York: Oxford University Press.

Dawkins, R. (1986). *The Blind Watchmaker.* New York: Norton.

De Bono, E. (1970). *Lateral Thinking: Creativity Step by Step.* New York: Harper and Row.

Delacour, J. (1995). An introduction to the biology of consciousness. *Neuropsychologia*, 33, 1061–1074.

Dement, W. C. (1974). *Some Must Watch While Some Must Sleep.* San Francisco: Freeman.

Dennett, D. C. (1991). *Consciousness Explained.* Toronto: Little, Brown.

Dennett, D. C., and Kinsbourne, M. (1992). Time and the observer: The where and when of consciousness in the brain. *Behavioral and Brian Sciences*, 15, 183–247.

Devaney, R. L. (1989). *An Introduction to Chaotic Dynamical Systems*, Second Edition. New York: Addison-Wesley.

DeCarlo, L. T., and Cross, D. V. (1990). Sequential effects in magnitude scaling: Models and theory. *Journal of Experimental Psychology: General*, 119, 375–396.

Dirac, P. A. M. (1958). *The Principles of Quantum Mechanics.* 4th ed. Oxford: Clarendon Press.

DiVincenzo, D. P. (1995). Quantum computation. *Science*, 270, 255–261.

Donald, M. (1995). The neurobiology of human consciousness: An evolutionary approach. *Neuropsychologia*, 33, 1087–1102.

Douglass, J. K., Wilkens, L., Pantazelou, E., and Moss, F. (1993). Noise enhancement of the information transfer in crayfish mechanoreceptors by stochastic resonance. *Nature*, 365, 337–340.

Dukas, R. (1998a). Introduction. In Dukas, ed., *Cognitive Ecology: The Evolutionary Ecology of Information Processing and Decision Making*, 1–19. Chicago: University of Chicago Press.

Dukas, R. (1998b). Constraints on information processsing and their effects on behavior. In Dukas, ed., *Cognitive Ecology: The Evolutionary Ecology of Information Processing and Decision Making*, 89–127. Chicago: University of Chicago Press.

Dukas, R., ed. (1998c). *Cognitive Ecology: The Evolutionary Ecology of Information Processing and Decision Making.* Chicago: University of Chicago Press.

Dukas, R., and Clark, C. W. (1995). Sustained vigilance and animal performance. *Animal Behaviour*, 49, 1259–1267.

Dunne, J. W. (1934). *The Serial Universe.* London: Faber and Faber.

Eccles, J. C. (1964). *The Physiology of Synapses.* Berlin: Springer.

Einstein, A., H. Born, and M. Born (1969). Brief zum Max Born, 4 December 1926 in *Einstein und Born Briefwechsel: 1916–1955*. Kommentiert von Max Born. München.

Einstein, A. (1906). Zur Theorie der brownschen Bewegung. *Annalen der Physik*, 19, 371–381.

Einstein, A. (1961). *Relativity. The Special and General Theory. A Popular Exposition.* New York: Crown Publishers.

Elbert, T., Pantev, C., Weinbruch, C., Rockstroh, B., and Taub, E. (1995). Increased cortical representation of the left hand in string players. *Science*, 270, 305–307.

Engel, A. K., Fries, P., König, P., Brecht, M., and Singer, W. (1999). Temporal binding, binocular rivalry, and consciousness. *Consciousness and Cognition*, 8, 128–151.

Enns, J. T., and Di Lollo, V. (2000). What's new in visual masking? *Trends in Cognitive Sciences*, 4, 345–352.

Ericsson, K. A., and Simon, H. A. (1993). *Protocol Analysis: Verbal Reports as Data.* Cambridge, MA: MIT Press.

Falmagne, J.-C. (1985). *Elements of Psychophysical Theory.* New York: Oxford University Press.

Farmer, J. D., and Sidorowich, J. J. (1987). Predicting chaotic time series. *Physical Review Letters*, 59, 845–848.

Faust, D., and Ziskin, J. (1988). The expert witness in psychological and psychiatry. *Science*, 241, 31–35.

Fechner, G. T. (1860). *Elemente der Psychophysik.* Leipzig: Breitkopf and Härtel.

Feller, W. (1968). *An Introduction to Probability Theory and Its Applications.* Vol. 1. 3d ed. New York: Wiley.

Feller, W. (1971). *An Introduction to Probability Theory and Its Applications.* Vol. 2. 2d ed. New York: Wiley.

Feynman, R. P. (1965). *Character of Physical Law.* Cambridge, MA: MIT Press.

Feynman, R. P. (1985). *QED: The Strange Theory of Light and Matter.* Princeton, NJ: Princeton University Press.

Feynman, R. P., Leighton, R. B., and Sands, M. (1963). *The Feynman Lectures on Physics.* Reading, MA: Addison-Wesley.

FitzHugh, R. A. (1960). Thresholds and plateaus in the Hodgkin-Huxley nerve equations. *Journal of General Physiology*, 43, 867–896.

FitzHugh, R. A. (1961). Impulses and physiological states in theoretical models of nerve membrane. *Biophysical Journal*, 1, 445–466.

Fogel, D. B. (2000). *Evolutionary Computation: Toward a New Philosophy of Machine Intelligence.* New York: Institute of Electrical and Electronics Engineers.

Fraser, J. T. (1982). *The Genesis and Evolution of Time: A Critique on Interpretation in Physics.* Amherst: University of Massachusetts Press.

Freeman, W. J. (1991). The physiology of perception. *Scientific American*, 264(2), 78–85.

Friedman, M. P., and Carterette, E. C. (1964). Detection of Markovian sequences of signals. *Journal of the Acoustical Society of America*, 36, 2334–2339.

Fries, P., Roelfsema, P. R., Engel, A. K., König, P., and Singer, W. (1997). Synchronization of oscillatory responses in visual cortex correlates with perception in interocular rivalry. *Proceedings of the National Academy of Sciences USA*, 94, 12699–12704.

Gall, J. (1977). *Systemantics*. New York: *New York Times*.

Gallup, G. G., Jr. (1977). Self-recognition in primates: A comparative approach to the bi-directional properties of consciousness. *American Psychologist*, 32, 329–338.

Gammaitoni, L., Hänggi, P., Jung, P., and Marchesoni, F. (1998). Stochastic resonance. *Reviews of Modern Physics*, 70, 223–287.

Garner, W. R. (1962). *Uncertainty and Structure as Psychological Concepts*. New York: Wiley.

Geschieder, G. A. (1997). *Psychophysics: The Fundamentals*. 3d ed. Mahwah, NJ: Erlbaum.

Gilden, D. L. (1997). Fluctuations in the time required for elementary decisions. *Psychological Science*, 8, 296–301.

Gilden, D. L., Thornton, T., and Mallon, M. W. (1995). $1/f$ noise in human cognition. *Science*, 267, 1837–1839.

Gleick, J. (1987). *Chaos: Making a New Science*. New York: Viking.

Gluckman, B. J., Netoff, T. I., Neel E. J., Ditto, W. L., Spano, M. L., and Schiff, S. J. (1996). Stochastic resonance in a neuronal network from mammalian brain. *Physical Review Letters*, 77, 4098–4101.

Gödel, K. (1931). Über formal unentscheidbare Sätze der *Principia Mathematica* und Verwandter Systeme I. *Monatskefte für Mathematik und Physik*, 38, 173–198.

Gold, T. (1965) The arrow of time. In S. T. Butler and H. Messel, eds., *Time: Selected Lectures*, 143–165. Oxford: Pergamon Press.

Goldberg, S. (1986). *Introduction to Difference Equations*. New York: Dover.

Golden, R. M. (1996). *Mathematical Methods for Neural Network Analysis and Design*. Cambridge, MA: MIT Press.

Goodfellow, L. D. (1938). A psychological interpretation of the results of the Zenith Radio Experiments in telepathy. *Journal of Experimental Psychology*, 23, 601–632.

Goss-Custard, J. D. (1977). The energetics of prey selection by redshank, *Tringa totanus* (L.), in relation to prey density. *Journal of Animal Ecology*, 46, 1–19.

Gottman, J. M. (1999). *The Marriage Clinic: A Scientifically Based Marital Therapy*. New York: Norton.

Gottman, J. M., and Roy, A. K. (1990). *Sequential Analysis: A Guide for Behavioral Researchers*. New York: Cambridge University Press.

Graf, P. (1994). Explicit and implicit memory: A decade of research. In C. Umiltà and M. Moscovitch, eds., *Attention and Performance 15: Conscious and Nonconscious Information Processing*, 682–692. Cambridge, MA: MIT Press.

Granger, C. W. J. (1980). Long memory relationships and the aggregation of dynamic models. *Journal of Econometrics*, 14, 227–238.

Granger, C. W. J., and Ding, Z. (1996). Varieties of long memory models. *Journal of Econometrics*, 73, 61–77.

Grassberger, P., and Procaccia, I. (1983a). Measuring the strangeness of strange attractors. *Physica D*, 9, 189–208.

Grassberger, P., and Procaccia, I. (1983b). Characterization of strange attractors. *Physical Review Letters*, 50, 346.

Gratton, G., and Fabiani, M. (1998). Dynamic brain imaging: Event-related optical signal (EROS) measures of the time course and localization of cognitive-related activity. *Psychonomic Bulletin and Review*, 5, 535–563.

Gray, C. M., and W. Singer. (1989). Stimulus-specific neuronal oscillations in orientation columns of cat visual cortex. *Proceedings of the National Academy of Sciences USA*, 91, 6339–6343.

Green, C. D. (1998). Are connectionist models theories of cognition? *Psycholoquy*, 9(4).

Green, D. M., and Swets, J. A. (1966). *Signal Detection Theory and Psychophysics*. Reprint, New York: Krieger, 1974.

Greenwood, P. E. (1997). Lecture notes for Mathematics 608. Vancouver, Canada: University of British Columbia.

Greenwood, P. E., and Ward, L. M. (2001). $1/f$ noise and autoregressive processes. Unpublished manuscript, University of British Columbia.

Greenwood, P. E., Ward, L. M., Russell, D. F., Neiman, A., and Moss, F. (2000). Stochastic resonance enhances the electrosensory information available to paddlefish for prey capture. *Physical Review Letters*, 84, 4773–4776.

Greenwood, P. E., Ward, L. M., and Wefelmeyer, W. (1999). Statistical analysis of stochastic resonance in a simple setting. *Physical Review E*, 60, 4687–4695.

Gregg, L. W., and Simon, H. A. (1967). An information-processing explanation of one-trial and incremental learning. *Journal of Verbal Learning and Verbal Behavior*, 6, 780–787.

Gregson, R. A. M. (1983). *Time Series in Psychology*. Hillsdale, NJ: Erlbaum.

Gregson, R. A. M. (1988). *Nonlinear Psychophysical Dynamics*. Hillsdale, NJ: Erlbaum.

Gregson, R. A. M. (1992). *N-Dimensional Nonlinear Psychophysics: Theory and Case Studies*. Hillsdale, NJ: Erlbaum.

Grimmett, G., and Stirzaker, D. (1992). *Probability and Random Processes*. 2d ed. New York: Oxford University Press.

Grossberg, S. (1988). Nonlinear neural networks: Principles, mechanisms, and architectures. *Neural Networks*, 1, 17–61.

Haken, H. (1983). *Synergetics*. New York: Springer.

Haken, H., Kelso, J. A. S., and Bunz, H. (1985). A theoretical model of phase transitions in human hand movements. *Biological Cybernetics*, 51, 347–356.

Hall, E. T. (1983). *The Dance of Life*. Garden City, NY: Doubleday.

Hameroff, S. R. (1998). "Funda-mentality": Is the conscious mind subtly linked to a basic level of the universe? *Trends in Cognitive Sciences*, 2, 119–124.

Hansel, C. E. M. (1966). *ESP: A Scientific Evaluation*. New York: Scribner.

Hausdorff, J. M., and Peng, C. K. (1996). Multiscaled randomness: A possible source of $1/f$ noise in biology. *Physical Review E*, 54, 2154–2157.

Hebb, D. O. (1949). *The Organization of Behavior*. New York: Wiley.

Hecht, S., Schlaer, S., and Pirenne, M. H. (1942). Energy, quanta, and vision. *Journal of General Physiology*, 25, 819–840.

Heffernan, M. (1996). Comparative effects of microcurrent stimulation on EEG. *Integrative Physiological and Behavioral Science*, 31, 202–209.

Heisenberg, W. (1927). The physical content of quantum kinematics and mechanics. *Zeitschrift für Physik*, 43, 172.

Herrnstein, R. J. (1961). Relative and absolute strength of response as a function of frequency of reinforcement. *Journal of the Experimental Analysis of Behavior*, 4, 267–272.

Hillyard, S. A., and Picton, T. W. (1987). Electrophysiology of cognition. In F. Plum, ed., *Handbook of Physiology: The Nervous System*. Vol. 5, *Higher Functions of the Nervous System*, 519–584. Bethesda, MD: American Physiological Society.

Hodgkin, A. L., and Huxley, A. F. (1952). A quantitative description of membrane current and its application to conduction and excitation in nerve. *Journal of Physiology*, 117, 500–544.

Hofstadter, D. R. (1979). *Gödel, Escher, Bach: An Eternal Golden Braid*. New York: Basic Books.

Honerkamp, J. (1998). *Statistical Physics: An Advanced Approach with Applications*. New York: Springer.

Houghton, G., and Tipper, S. P. (1994). A model of inhibitory mechanisms in selective attention. In D. Dagenbach and T. H. Carr, eds., *Inhibitory Processes in Attention, Memory, and Language*, 53–112. San Diego, CA: Academic Press.

Houston, C. E. (1999). Thought suppression of episodic memories and susceptibility to erroneous suggestion regarding sequence. *Dissertation Abstracts International: Section B: The Sciences and Engineering*, 60(1-B), 0411.

Hsieh, D. (1991). Chaos and nonlinear dynamics: Application to financial markets. *Journal of Finance*, 46, 1839–1877.

Hudson, D. L., and Cohen, M. E. (2000). *Neural Networks and Artificial Intelligence for Biomedical Engineering*. New York: Institute of Electrical and Electronics Engineers.

Iberall, A. S. (1972). *Toward a General Science of Viable Systems*. New York : McGraw-Hill.

Jaffe, J., and Feldstein, S. (1970). *Rhythms of Dialogue*. New York: Academic Press.

James, W. (1890). *The Principles of Psychology in Two Volumes.* Vol. 1. New York: Holt.

Jaśkowski, P., and Verleger, R. (1999). Amplitudes and latencies of single-trial ERPs estimated by a maximum likelihood method. *IEEE Transactions on Biomedical Engineering,* 46, 987–993.

Jaśkowski, P., and Verleger, R. (2000). An evaluation of methods for single-trial estimation of P3 latency. *Psychophysiology,* 37, 153–162.

Jaynes, J. (1976). *The Origin of Consciousness in the Breakdown of the Bicameral Mind.* Boston: Houghton Mifflin.

Jesteadt, W., Luce, R. D., and Green, D. M. (1977). Sequential effects in judgments of loudness. *Journal of Experimental Psychology: Human Perception and Performance,* 3, 92–104.

John, E. R. (1977). Neurometrics. *Science,* 196, 1393–1410.

Jourdain, R. (1997). *Music, the Brain, and Ecstasy.* New York: Avon.

Just, M. A., and Carpenter, P. A. (1976). Eye fixations and cognitive processes. *Cognitive Psychology,* 8, 441–480.

Just, M. A., and Carpenter, P. A. (1987). *The Psychology of Reading and Language Comprehension.* Boston: Allyn and Bacon.

Kac, M. (1983). What is random? *American Scientist,* 71, 405–406.

Kac, M. (1984). More on randomness. *American Scientist,* 72, 282–283.

Kahneman, D. (1968). Method, findings, and theory in studies of visual masking. *Psychological Bulletin,* 70, 404–425.

Kahneman, D., and Tversky, A. (1982). The simulation heuristic. In Kahneman, P. Slovic, and Tversky, eds., *Judgement under Uncertainty: Heuristics and Biases,* 201–208. Cambridge: Cambridge University Press.

Kalmus, M., and Bachmann, T. (1980). Perceptual microgenesis of complex visual pattern: Comparison of methods and possible implications for future studies. *Acta et Commentationes Universitatis Tartuensis,* 529, 134–159.

Kandel, E. R., Schwartz, J. H., and Jessell, T. M., eds. (2000). *Principles of Neural Science.* 4th ed. New York: McGraw-Hill.

Kareev, Y. (1992). Not that bad after all: Generation of random sequences. *Journal of Experimental Psychology: Human Perception and Performance,* 18, 1189–1194.

Kauffman, H., and Noyes, H. P. (1996). Discrete physics and the derivation of electromagnetism from the formalism of quantum mechanics. *Proceedings of the Royal Society of London A,* 452, 81–95.

Kauffman, S. A. (1992). Applied molecular evolution. *Journal of Theoretical Biology,* 157, 1.

Kauffman, S. A. (1993). *The Origins of Order.* New York: Oxford University Press.

Kaulakys, B. (1999). Autoregressive model of $1/f$ noise. *Physics Letters A,* 257, 37–42.

Kaulakys, B., and Mešauskas, T. (1998). Modeling $1/f$ noise. *Physical Review E*, 58, 7013–7019.

Kellert, S. H. (1993). *In the Wake of Chaos*. Chicago: University of Chicago Press.

Kelso, J. A. S. (1995). *Dynamic Patterns: The Self-Organization of Brain and Behaviour*. Cambridge, MA: MIT Press.

Kennel, M. B., and Isabelle, S. (1992). Method to distinguish possible chaos from colored noise and to determine embedding parameters. *Physical Review A*, 46, 3111–3118.

Killeen, P. R. (1989). Behavior as a trajectory through a field of attractors. In J. R. Brink and C. R. Haden, eds., *The Computer and the Brian: Perspectives on Human and Artificial Intelligence*, 53–82. New York: Elsevier Science Publishers.

Kilmister, C. W. (1992). Space, time, discreteness. *Philosophica*, 50, 55–71.

Kinsbourne, M. (1988). Integrated field theory of consciousness. In A. J. Marcel and E. Bisiach, eds., *Consciousness in Contemporary Science*, 239–256. New York: Oxford University Press.

Klein, R. M. (2000). Inhibition of return. *Trends in Cognitive Sciences*, 4, 138–147.

Kleinmuntz, B. (1968). The processing of clinical information by man and machine. In B. Kleinmuntz, ed., *Formal Representation of Human Judgment*. New York: Wiley.

Klir, G. J. (1972a). *Trends in General Systems Theory*. New York: Wiley.

Klir, G. J. (1972b). *Introduction to the Methodology of Switching Circuits*. New York: Van Nostrand.

Koch, C. (1997). Computation and the single neuron. *Nature*, 385, 207–210.

Koch, C., and Segev, I. (1998). *Methods in Neuronal Modeling: From Ions to Networks*. 2d ed. Cambridge, MA: MIT Press.

König, P., Engel, A. K., and Singer, W. (1996). Integrator or coincidence detector? The role of the cortical neuron revisited. *Trends in Neuroscience*, 19, 130–137.

Kopell, N. (1988). Toward a theory of modelling central pattern generators. In A. H. Cohen, S. Rossignol, and S. Grillner, eds., *Neural Control of Rhythmic Movements in Vertebrates*, 369–413. New York: John Wiley & Sons.

Kosslyn, S. M., and Koenig, O. (1992). *Wet Mind: The New Cognitive Neuroscience*. New York: Free Press.

Kramers, H. A. (1940). Brownian motion in a field of force and the force and the diffusion model of chemical reactions. *Physica*, 7, 284–304.

Krebs, J. R., Kacelnik, A., and Taylor, P. (1978). Optimal sampling by birds: An experiment with great tits (*Parus major*). *Nature*, 275, 27–31.

Kubvoy, M., Rapoport, A., and Tversky, A. (1970). Deterministic vs. Probabilistic strategies in detection. *Perception and Psychophysics*, 9, 427–429.

Kurthen, M., Grunwald, T., and Elger, C. E. (1998). Will there be a neuroscientific theory of consciousness? *Trends in Cognitive Sciences*, 2, 229–234.

Lamme, V. A. F., and Roelfsema, P. R. (2000). The distinct modes of vision offered by feedforward and recurrent processing. *Trends in Neurosciences*, 23, 571–579.

Large, E. W., and Jones, M. R. (1999). The dynamics of attending: How people track time varying events. *Psychological Review*, 106, 119–159.

Lashley, K. S. (1950). In search of the engram. *Symposia of the Society for Experimental Biology*, 4, 454–482.

Lashley, K. S. (1951). The problem of serial order in behavior. In L. A. Jeffress, ed., *Cerebral Mechanisms in Behavior*, 112–136. New York: Wiley.

Lauk, M., Chow, C. C., Pavlik, A. E., and Collins, J. J. (1998). Human balance out of equilibrium: Nonequilibrium statistical mechanics in posture control. *Physical Review Letters*, 80, 413–416.

Lauritzen, S. L. (1996). *Graphical Models.* Oxford Statistical Science Series, vol. 17. New York: Oxford University Press.

Lea, S. E. G. (1984). *Instinct, Environment and Behaviour.* London: Methuen.

Lee, W. (1971). *Decision Theory and Human Behavior.* New York: Wiley.

Leibniz, G. F. (1714/1956). *Monadologie.* Paris: Delagrave.

Leipus, R., and Viano, M. C. (2000). Modeling long-memory time series with finite or infinite variance: A general approach. *Journal of Time Series Analysis*, 21, 61–74.

Levelt W. J. M. (1968). *On Binocular Rivalry.* Hague: Mouton.

Levin, J. E., and Miller, J. P. (1996). Broadband neural encoding in the cricket cercal sensory system enhanced by stochastic resonance. *Nature*, 380, 165–168.

Lewis, F. L., Jagannathan, S., and Yeşildirek, A. (1999). *Neural Network Control of Robot Manipulators and Nonlinear Systems.* London: Taylor and Francis.

Liberman, A. M., and Mattingly, I. G. (1985). The motor theory of speech perception revised. *Cognition*, 21, 1–36.

Link, S. W. (1992). *The Wave Theory of Difference and Similarity.* Hillsdale, NJ: Erlbaum.

Link, S. W. (1994). Rediscovering the past: Gustav Fechner and signal detection theory. *Psychological Science*, 5, 335–340.

Lisman, J. E., and Idiart, M. A. P. (1995). Storage of 7 ± 2 short-term memories in oscillatory subcycles. *Science*, 267, 1512–1515.

Lockhead, G. R. (1974). Sequential behavior and parapsychology. Unpublished manuscript, Duke University.

Logothetis, N. K., and Schall, J. D. (1989). Neuronal correlates of subjective visual perception. *Science*, 245, 761–763.

Longtin, A. (1993). Stochastic resonance in neuron models. *Journal of Statistical Physics*, 70, 309–327.

Longtin, A. (1995a). Synchronization of the stochastic FitzHugh-Nagumo Equations to periodic forcing. *Il Nuovo Cimento*, 17D, 835–846.

Longtin, A. (1995b). Mechanisms of stochastic phase locking. *Chaos*, 5(1), 209–215.

Longtin, A. (1997). Autonomous stochastic resonance in bursting neurons. *Physical Review E*, 55, 1–9.

Luce, R. D. (1986). *Response Times: Their Role in Inferring Elementary Mental Organization*. Oxford Psychology Series, vol. 8. New York: Oxford University Press.

Lumer, E. D., Edelman, G. M., and Tononi, G. (1997). Neural dynamics in a model of the thalamocortical system: 1 Layers, loops and the emergence of fast synchronous rhythms. *Cerebral Cortex*, 7, 207–227.

Lundström, I., and McQueen, D. (1974). A proposed $1/f$ noise mechanism in nerve cell membranes. *Journal of Theoretical Biology*, 45, 405–409.

Luria, S. E., Gould, S. J., and Singer, S. (1981) *A View of Life*. Menlo Park, CA: Benjamin-Cummings.

Machlup, S. (1981). Earthquakes, thunderstorms, and other $1/f$ noises. In P. H. E. Meijer, R. D. Mountain, and R. J. Soulen, Jr., eds., *Sixth International Conference on Noise in Physical Systems*, 157–160. Washington, DC: National Bureau of Standards.

Macmillan, N. A., and Creelman, C. D. (1991). *Detection Theory: A User's Guide*. New York: Cambridge University Press.

Mandelbrot, B. B. (1982). *The Fractal Geometry of Nature*. New York: Freeman.

Mandelbrot, B. B. (1998). *Multifractals and $1/f$ Noise: Wild Self-Affinity in Physics*. New York: Springer.

Mandler, G. (1980). Recognizing: The judgment of previous occurrences. *Psychological Review*, 87, 252–271.

Marcel, A. J. (1983). Conscious and unconscious perception: Experiments on visual masking and word recognition. *Cognitive Psychology*, 15, 197–237.

Marks, L. E. (1974). *Sensory Processes: The New Psychophysics*. New York: Academic Press.

Maslov, S., Tang, C., and Zhang, Y. C. (1999). $1/f$ noise in Bak-Tang-Wiesenfeld models on narrow stripes. *Physical Review Letters*, 83, 2449–2452.

Mato, G. (1998). Stochastic Resonance in neural systems: Effect of temporal correlation of spike trains. *Physical Review E*, 58, 876–880.

Mayer-Kress, G., ed. (1986). *Dimensions and Entropies in Chaotic Systems*. New York: Springer.

McCleary, R., and Hay, R. A., Jr. (1980). *Applied Time Series Analysis for the Social Sciences*. Beverly Hills, CA: Sage.

McDonald, J. J., and Ward, L. M. (1998). Nonlinear dynamics of event-related human brain activity. Unpublished manuscript, University of British Columbia.

Meadows, D. H., Meadows, D. L., Randers, J., and Behrens, W. W., III. (1972). *The Limits to Growth*. Washington, DC: Potomac.

Menning, H., Roberts, L. E., and Pantev, C. (2000). Plastic changes in the auditory cortex induced by intensive frequency discrimination training. *Neuroreport*, 11, 817–822.

Merriam-Webster. (1971). *The New Merriam-Webster Dictionary*. New York: Pocket Books.

Metcalfe, J. (1986). Premonitions of insight predict impending error. *Journal of Experimental Psychology: Learning Memory and Cognition*, 12, 623–634.

Metcalfe, J., and Wiebe, D. (1987). Intuition in insight and noninsight problem solving. *Memory and Cognition*, 15, 238–246.

Metzger, M. A. (1994). Have subjects been shown to generate chaotic numbers? Commentary on Neuringer and Voss. *Psychological Science*, 5, 111–114.

Miller, G. A. (1952). Finite Markov processes in psychology. *Psychometriks*, 17, 149–167.

Miller, G. A. (1956). The magical number seven, plus or minus two: Some limits on our capacity for processing information. *Psychological Review*, 63, 81–97.

Milotti, E. (1995). Linear processes that produce $1/f$ or flicker noise. *Physical Review E*, 51, 3087–3103.

Minelli, A. (1971). Memory, morphogenesis and behavior. *Scientia*, 106, 798–806.

Minsky, M. L., and Papert, S. A. (1967). *Perceptrons*. Cambridge, MA: MIT Press.

Molnar, M., and Skinner, J. E. (1992). Low-dimensional chaos in event-related brain potentials. *International Journal of Neuroscience*, 66, 263–276.

Morrison, F. (1991). *The Art of Modeling Dynamic Systems: Forecasting for Chaos, Randomness, and Determinism*. New York: Wiley-Interscience.

Morse, R. P., and Evans, E. F. (1996). Enhancement of vowel coding for cochlear implants by addition of noise. *Nature Medicine*, 2, 928–932.

Moss, F., Pierson, D., and O'Gorman, D. (1994). Stochastic resonance: Tutorial and update. *International Journal of Bifurcation and Chaos*, 4, 1383–1397.

Moss, F., Chiou-Tan, F., and Klinke, R. (1996). Will there be noise in their ears? *Nature Medicine*, 2, 860–862.

Moss, F., Douglass, J. K., Wilkens, L., Pierson, D., and Pantazelou, E. (1993). Stochastic resonance in an electronic FitzHugh-Nagumo model. In J. R. Buchler and H. E. Kandrup, eds., *Stochastic Processes in Astrophysics, Annals of the New York Academy of Sciences*, 706, 26–41.

Müller, U. U. (2000). Nonparametric regression for threshold data. *Canadian Journal of Statistics*, 28, 301–310.

Müller, U. U., and Ward, L. M. (2000). Stochastic resonance in a statistical model of a time-integrating detector. *Physical Review E*, 61, 4286–4294.

Musha, T. (1981). $1/f$ fluctuations in biological systems. In P. H. E. Meijer, R. D. Mountain, and R. J. Soulen, Jr., eds., *Sixth International Conference on Noise in Physical Systems*, 143–146. Washington, DC: U.S. Department of Commerce and National Bureau of Standards.

Näätänen, R. (1992). *Attention and Brain Function.* Hillsdale, NJ: Erlbaum.

Nagumo, J., Arimoto, S., and Yoshizawa, S. (1962). An active pulse transmission line simulating nerve axon. *Proceedings of the Institute of Radio Engineers,* 50, 2061–2070.

Nakao, H. (1998). Asymptotic power law of moments in a random multiplicative process with weak additive noise. *Physical Review E,* 58, 1591–1600.

Nass, G. (1970). *The Molecules of Life.* New York: McGraw-Hill.

Neisser, U. (1981). John Dean's memory: A case study. *Cognition,* 9, 1–22.

Neuringer, A. (1986). Can people behave "randomly"? The role of feedback. *Journal of Experimental Psychology: General,* 115, 62–75.

Neuringer, A., and Voss, C. (1993). Approximating chaotic behavior. *Psychological Science,* 4, 113–119.

Newell, A. (1990). *Unified Theories of Cognition.* Cambridge MA: Harvard University Press.

Newell, A. (1992). Précis of Unified Theories of Cognition. *Behavioural and Brain Sciences,* 15, 425–492.

Nordsieck, A., Lamb, W. E., and Uhlenbeck, G. E. (1940). On the theory of cosmic-ray showers: 1. The Furry model and the fluctuation problem. *Physica,* 7, 344–360.

Norman, D. A. (1982). *Learning and Memory.* San Francisco: Freeman.

Norwich, K. H. (1993). *Information, Sensation, and Perception.* Toronto: Academic Press.

Novikov, E., Novikov, A., Shannahoff-Khalsa, D., Schwartz, B., and Wright, J. (1997). Scale-similar activity in the brain. *Physical Review E,* 56, R2387–R2389.

Nunez, P. L. (1995). *Neocortical Dynamics and Human EEG Rhythms.* New York: Oxford University Press.

Nunez, P. L. (2000). Toward a quantitative description of large-scale neocortical dynamic function and EEG. *Behavioral and Brain Sciences,* 23, 371–437.

Osborne, A. R., and Provenzale, A. (1989). Finite correlation dimension for stochastic systems with power law spectra. *Physica D,* 35, 357–381.

Packard, N. H, Crutchfield, J. P., Farmer, J. D., and Shaw, R. S. (1980). Geometry from a time series. *Physics Review Letters,* 45, 712–716.

Pacut, A. (1978). Stochastic model of the latency of the conditioned escape response. *Progress in Cybernetics and System Research,* 3, 633–642.

Pantev, C., Oostenveld, R., Engelien, A., Ross, B., Roberts, L. E., and Hoke, M. (1998). Increased auditory coritcal represenation in musicians. *Nature,* 392, 811–814.

Pantev, C., Wollbrink, A., Roberts, L. E., Engelein, A., and Lutkenhöner, B. (1999). Short-term plasticity of the human auditory cortex. *Brain Research,* 842, 192–199.

Parks, R. W., Levine, D. S., and Long, D. L. (1998). *Fundamentals of Neural Network Modeling: Neuropsychology and Cognitive Neuroscience.* Cambridge, MA: MIT Press.

Penrose, R. (1990). *The Emperor's New Mind.* Oxford: Oxford University Press.

Penrose, R. (1994). *Shadows of the Mind: A Search for the Missing Science of Consciousness.* Oxford: Oxford University Press.

Pezard, L., and Nandrino, J.-L. (1996). Depression as a dynamical disease. *Biological Psychiatry*, 39, 991–999.

Pfeifer, R., and Sheier, C. (1999). *Understanding Intelligence.* Cambridge, MA: MIT Press.

Piaget, J. (1954). *The Construction of Reality in the Child.* Cambridge, MA: MIT Press.

Picton, T. W., Lins, O. G., and Scherg, M. (1995). The recording and analysis of event-related potentials. *Handbook of Neuropsychology*, 10, 3–73.

Platt, J. (1964). Strong inference. *Science*, 146, 347–353.

Plesser, H. E., and Tanaka, S. (1997). Stochastic resonance in a model neuron with reset. *Physics Letters A*, 225, 228–234.

Plischke, M., and Bergersen, B. (1994). *Equilibrium Statistical Physics.* 2d ed. Singapore: World Scientific.

Pons, T. P., Garraghty, P. E., Ommaya, A. K., Kaas, J. H., Taub, E., and Mishkin, M. (1991). Massive cortical reorganization after sensory deafferentation in adult macaques. *Science*, 252, 1857–1860.

Port, R. F., and van Gelder, T. (1995). *Mind as Motion: Explorations in the Dynamics of Cognition.* Cambridge, MA: MIT Press.

Posner, M. I., and Raichle, M. E. (1994). *Images of Mind.* New York: Scientific American Library.

Povel, D. J. (1981). Internal representation of simple temporal patterns. *Journal of Experimental Psychology: Human Perception and Performance*, 7, 3–18.

Povinelli, D. J. (1993). Reconstructing the evolution of the mind. *American Psychologist*, 48, 493–509.

Press, W. H., Teykolsky, S. A., Vetterling, W. T., and Flannnery, B. P. (1992). *Numerical Recipes in C: The Art of Scientific Computing.* 2d ed. New York: Cambridge University Press.

Pribram, K. H. (1986). The cognitive revolution and mind/brain issues. *American Psychologist*, 41, 507–520.

Pribram, K. H. (1996). Chaos edge. In W. Sulis and A. Combs, eds., *Nonlinear Dynamics in Human Behavior*, v–x. Singapore: World Scientific.

Prigogene, I., and Stengers, I. (1984). *Order Out of Chaos.* Toronto: Bantam.

Pritchard, W. S., and Duke, D. W. (1992). Measuring chaos in the brain: A tutorial review of nonlinear dynamical EEG analysis. *International Journal of Neuroscience*, 67, 31–80.

Ramirez, R. W. (1985). *The FFT: Fundamentals and Concepts.* Englewood Cliffs, NJ: Prentice-Hall.

Rand, R. H., Cohen A. H., and Holmes, P. J. (1988). Systems of coupled oscillators as models for central pattern generators. In Cohen, A. H., Rossignol, S., and Grillner, S., eds., *Neural Control of Rhythmic Movements in Vertebrates* 333–368. New York: John Wiley & Sons.

Rapoport, A. (1972). The uses of mathematical isomorphism in general systems theory. In G. J. Klir ed., *Trends in General System Theory*, 42–77. New York: Wiley-Interscience.

Rapp, P. E. (1993). Chaos in the neurosciences: Cautionary tales from the frontier. *Biologist*, 40, 89–94.

Rapp, P. E., Bashore, T. R., Martinerie, J. M., Albano, A. M., and Meos, A. I. (1989). Dynamics of brain electrical activity. *Brain Topography*, 2, 99–118.

Reichenbach, H. (1949). *The Theory of Probability.* (E. Hutton and M. Reichenbach, Trans.) Berkeley: University of California Press. (Originally published as *Wahrscheinlichkeitslehre* in 1934).

Rinkus, G. J. (1996). A combinatorial neural network exhibiting episodic and semantic memory properties for spatio-temporal patterns. *Dissertation Abstracts International: Section B: The Sciences and Engineering*, 57(5-B), 3428.

Roediger, H. L., III. (1996). Memory illusions. *Journal of Memory and Language*, 35, 76–100.

Rumelhart, D. E., Hinton, G. E., and McClelland, J. L. (1986). A general framework for parallel distributed processing. In Rumelhart, D. E. and McClelland, J. L., eds., *Parallel Distributed Processing: Explorations in the Microstructure of Cognition.* Vol. 1, *Foundations*, 45–77. Cambridge: MIT Press.

Rumelhart, D. E., and McClelland, J. L., eds. (1986). *Parallel Distributed Processing: Explorations in the Microstructure of Cognition.* Vol. 1, *Foundations.* Cambridge, MA: MIT Press.

Russell, B. (1945). *A History of Western Philosophy.* New York: Simon and Schuster.

Russell, D. F., Wilkens, L. A., and Moss, F. (1999). Use of behavioral stochastic resonance by paddlefish for feeding. *Nature*, 402, 291–294.

Sandusky, A. (1971). Signal recognition models compared for random and Markov presentation sequences. *Perception and Psychophysics*, 10, 339–347.

Sattath, S., and Tversky, A. (1977). Additive similarity trees. *Psychometrika*, 42, 319–345.

Sauvé, K. (1999). Gamma-band synchronous oscillations: Recent evidence regarding their functional significance. *Consciousness and Cognition*, 8, 213–224.

Scheier, C., and Tschacher, W. (1996). Appropriate algorithms for nonlinear time series anaylsis in psychology. In W. Sulis, A. Combs, eds., *Nonlinear Dynamics in Human Behavior*, 27–43. Singapore: World Scientific.

Scholem, G. G. (1965). *On the Kabbalah and its Symbolism.* New York: Schocken.

Schottky, W. (1918). Über spontane Stromschwankungen in verschiedenen Elektrizitätsleitern. *Annalen der Physik*, 57, 541–567.

Schrödinger, E. (1944). *What is Life? and Mind and Matter*. Reprint, Cambridge: Cambridge University Press, 1967.

Schroeder, M. (1991). *Fractals, Chaos, Power Laws: Minutes from an Infinite Paradise*. New York: Freeman.

Seamans, J. K., Gorelova, N., and Yang, C. R. (1997). Contributions of voltage-gated Ca^{2+} channels in the proximal versus distal dendrites to synaptic integration in prefrontal cortical neurons. *Journal of Neuroscience*, 17, 5936–5948.

Shallice, T. (1972). Dual functions of consciousness. *Psychological Review*, 79, 383–393.

Shannon, C. E., and Weaver, W. (1949). *The Mathematical Theory of Communication*. Urbana: University of Illinois Press.

Sheinberg, D. L., and Logothetis, N. K. (1997). The role of temporal cortical areas in perceptual organization. *Proceedings of the National Academy of Sciences USA*, 94, 3408–3413.

Sherrington, C. S. (1940). *Man and His Nature*. Cambridge: Cambridge University Press.

Siegel, S. (1956). *Nonparametric Methods for Behavioral Sciences*. New York: McGraw-Hill.

Siegelmann, H. T. (1995). Computation beyond the Turing limit. *Science*, 268, 545–548.

Simon, H. A. (1969). *The Sciences of the Artificial*. Cambridge, MA: MIT Press.

Simon, H. A. (1974). How big is a chunk? *Science*, 183, 482–488.

Simon, H. A., and Newell, A. (1971). *Human Problem Solving*. Englewood Cliffs, NJ: Prentice Hall.

Simonotto, E., Riani, M., Seife, C., Roberts, M., Twitty, J., and Moss, F. (1997). Visual perception of stochastic resonance. *Physical Review Letters*, 78, 1186–1189.

Singer, W. (1993). Synchronization of cortical activity and its putative role in information processing and learning. *Annual Review of Physiology*, 55, 349–374.

Singer, W. (1994). The organization of sensory motor representations in the neocortex: A hypothesis based on temporal coding. In C. Umiltà, and M. Moscovitch, eds., *Attention and Performance 15: Conscious and Nonconscious Information Processing*, 77–107. Cambridge, MA: MIT Press.

Singer, W. (1999). Neuronal synchrony: A versatile code for the definition of relations? *Neuron*, 24, 49–65.

Skarda, C. A., and Freeman, W. J. (1987). How brains make chaos in order to make sense of the world. *Behavioral and Brain Sciences*, 10, 161–195.

Skinner, B. F. (1974). *About Behaviorism*. New York: Knopf.

Sokolov, E. N. (1975). The neuronal mechanisms of the orienting reflex. In Sokolov and O. S. Vinogradova, eds., *Neuronal Mechanisms of the Orienting Reflex*, 217–238. New York: Wiley.

Squire, L. R. (1987). *Memory and Brain.* New York: Oxford University Press.

Stanley, S. M. (1981). *The New Evolutionary Timetable: Fossils, Genes, and the Origin of Species.* New York: Basic Books.

Stemmler, M. (1996). A single spike suffices: The simplest form of stochastic resonance in model neurons. *Network: Computation in Neural Systems,* 7, 687–716.

Stephens, D. W., and Krebs, J. R. (1986). *Foraging Theory.* Princeton: Princeton University Press.

Sternberg, R. J. (1986). A triangular theory of love. *Psychological Review,* 93, 119–135.

Sternberg, S. (1966). High-speed scanning in human memory. *Science,* 153, 652–654.

Stevens, S. S. (1975). *Psychophysics: Introduction to its Perceptual, Neural, and Social Prospects.* New York: Wiley-Interscience.

Stewart, I. (1989). *Does God Play Dice? The Mathematics of Chaos.* Cambridge, MA: Basil Blackwell.

Sugihara, G., and May, R. M. (1990). Nonlinear forecasting as a way of distinguishing chaos from measurement error in time series. *Nature,* 344, 734–741.

Swindale, N. V. (1990). Is the cerebral cortex modular? *Trends in Neuroscience,* 13, 487–492.

Swindale, N. V. (1998). Cortical organization: Modules, polymaps and mosaics. *Current Biology,* 8, R270–R273.

Takakura, K., Sano, K., Kosugi, Y., and Ikebe, J. (1979). Pain control by electrical nerve stimulating using irregular pulse of $1/f$ fluctuation. *Applied Neurophysiology,* 42, 314–315.

Takens, F. (1981). Detecting strange attractors in fluid turbulence. In D. A. Rand and L.-S. Young, eds., *Dynamic Systems and Turbulence,* 366–381. New York: Springer.

Tegmark, M. (2000). Importance of quantum decoherence in brain processes. *Physical Review E,* 61, 4194–4206.

Theiler, J. (1991). Some comments on the correlation dimension of $1/f^{\alpha}$ noise. *Physics Letters A,* 155, 480–493.

Theiler, J., and Rapp, P. E. (1996). Re-examination of the evidence for low-dimensional, nonlinear structure in the human electroencephalogram. *Electroencephalography and Clinical Neurophysiology,* 98, 213–222.

Theiler, J., Eubank, S., Longtin, A., Galdrikian, B., and Farmer, J. D. (1992). Testing for nonlinearity in time series: The method of surrogate data. *Physica D,* 58, 77–94.

Thelen, E., Schöner, G., Schier, C., and Smith, L. B. (2001). The dynamics of embodiment: A field theory of infant perseverative reaching. *Behavioral and Brian Sciences,* 24.

Thompson, J. M. T., and Stewart, H. B. (1986). *Nonlinear Dynamics and Chaos: Geometrical Methods for Engineers and Scientists.* Chichester, U.K.: Wiley.

Thomson, A. M., West, D. C., Hahn, J., and Deuchars, J. (1996). Single axon IPSPs elicited in pyramidal cells by three classes of interneurons in slices of rat neocortex. *Journal of Physiology (London)*, 496, 81–102.

t'Hooft, G. (1989). On the quantization of space and time. In S. Deser, ed., *Themes in Contemporary Physics II: Essays in Honor of Julian Schwinger's Seventieth Birthday*, 77–89. Singapore: World Scientific.

Thorne, K. (1994). *Black Holes and Time Warps: Einstein's Outrageous Legacy*. New York: Norton.

Thurner, S., Feurstein, M. C., and Teich, M. C. (1997). Conservation laws in coupled multiplicative random arrays lead to $1/f$ noise. Unpublished manuscript.

Thurstone, L. L. (1927). A law of comparative judgment. *Psychological Review*, 34, 273–286.

Tipler, F. J. (1994). *The Physics of Immortality*. New York: Doubleday.

Tononi, G., and Edelman, G. M. (1998). Consciousness and complexity. *Science*, 282, 1846–1851.

Tononi, G., Srinivasan, R., Russell, D. P., and Edelman, G. M. (1998). Investigating neural correlates of conscious perception by frequency-tagged neuromagnetic responses. *Proceedings of the National Academy of Sciences USA*, 95, 3198–3203.

Tougaard, J. (2000). Stochastic resonance and signal detection in an energy detector-implications for biological receptor systems. *Biological Cybernetics*, 83, 471–480.

Townsend, J. T. (1992). Chaos theory: A brief tutorial. In A. F. Healy, S. M. Kosslyn, and R. M. Shiffrin, eds., *Essays in Honor of William K. Estes, Vol. 2: From Learning Processes to Cognitive Processes*, 65–96. Hillsdale, NJ: Lawrence Erlbaum Associates.

Townsend, J. T., and Ashby, F. G. (1983). *Stochastic Modeling of Elementary Psychological Processes*. New York: Cambridge University Press.

Trabasso, T., and Bower, G. (1968). *Attention in Learning*. New York: Wiley.

Treisman, M., and Faulkner, A. (1987). Generation of random sequences by human subjects: Cognitive operations or psychophysical process? *Journal of Experimental Psychology: General*, 116, 337–355.

Triesman, M., and Williams, T. C. (1984). A theory of criterion setting with an application to sequential dependencies. *Psychological Review*, 91, 68–111.

Tulving, E. (1983). *Elements of Episodic Memory*. London: Clarendon Press.

Tune, G. S. (1964). A brief survey of variables that influence random generation. *Perceptual and Motor Skills*, 18, 705–710.

Turing, A. M. (1936). On computable numbers with an application to the *Entscheidungs problem. Proceedings of the London Math Society*, 42, 230–265 and 43, 544–546.

Tversky, A., and Kahneman, D. (1981). The framing of decisions and the psychology of choice. *Science*, 211, 453–458.

Usher, M., Stemmler, M., and Olami, Z. (1995). Dynamic pattern formation leads to $1/f$ noise in neural populations. *Physical Review Letters*, 74, 326–329.

Uttal, W. R. (1969). Masking of alphabetic character recognition by dynamic visual noise (DVN). *Perception and Psychophysics*, 6, 121–127.

Van Bendegem, J. P., ed. (1992). *Modern Perspectives on the Philosophy of Space and Time. Philosophica*, 50(2). Special issue.

van der Pol, B. (1926). On "relaxation-oscillations." *Philosophical Magazine and Journal of Science*, 2, 978–992.

van der Pol, B., and van der Mark, J. (1927). Frequency demultiplication. *Nature*, 120, 363–364.

van der Pol, B., and van der Mark, J. (1928). The heartbeat considered as a relaxation oscillation, and an electrical model of the heart. *Philosophical Magazine and Journal of Science*, 2, 763–775.

Van Essen, D. C., and Deyoe, E. A. (1995). Concurrent processing in the primate visual cortex. In M. S. Gazzaniga, ed., *The Cognitive Neurosciences*, 383–400. Cambridge, MA: MIT Press.

van Gelder, T. (1998). The dynamical hypothesis in cognitive science. *Behavioral and Brain Sciences*, 21, 615–628.

van Gelder, T., and Port, R. F. (1995). It's about time: An overview of the dynamical approach to cognition. In Port and van Gelder, eds., *Mind as Motion: Explorations in the Dynamics of Cognition*, 1–43. Cambridge, MA: MIT Press.

van Kampen, N. G. (1976). The expansion of the master equation. *Advances in Chemical Physics*, 34, 245–309.

van Kampen, N. G. (1985). *Stochastic Processes in Physics and Chemistry*. Amsterdam: North-Holland.

van Kampen, N. G. (1987). Some theoretical aspects of noise. In C. M. Van Vliet, ed., *Ninth International Conference on Noise in Physical Systems*, 3–10. Singapore: World Scientific.

Van Vliet, K. M. (1981). Classification of noise phenomena. In P. H. E. Meijer, R. D. Mountain, and R. J. Soulen, Jr., eds., *Sixth International Conference on Noise in Physical Systems*, 3–11. Washington, DC: U.S. Department of Commerce and National Bureau of Standards.

von Bertelanffy, L. (1968). *General Systems Theory*. New York: George Braziller.

von Bertelanffy, L. (1972). The history and status of general systems theory. In G. J. Klir, ed., *Trends in General Systems Theory*, 21–41. New York: Wiley-Interscience.

Voss, R. F., and Clarke, J. (1975). "$1/f$ noise" in music and speech. *Nature*, 258, 317–318

Wagenaar, W. A. (1971). Serial nonrandomness as a function of duration and monotony of a randomization task. *Acta Psychologica*, 35, 70–87.

Wagenaar, W. A. (1972). Generation of random sequences by human subjects: A critical survey of literature. *Psychological Bulletin*, 77, 65–72.

Waldrop, M. M. (1992). *Complexity: The Emerging Science at the Edge of Order and Chaos*. New York: Simon and Schuster.

Ward, L. M. (1973). Use of Markov-encoded sequential information in numerical signal detection. *Perception and Psychophysics*, 14, 337–342.

Ward, L. M. (1979). Stimulus information and sequential dependencies in magnitude estimation and cross-modality matching. *Journal of Experimental Psychology: Human Perception and Performance*, 5, 444–459.

Ward, L. M. (1987). Remembrance of sounds past: Memory and psychophysical scaling. *Journal of Experimental Psychology: Human Perception and Performance*, 13, 216–227.

Ward, L. M. (1990). Critical bands and mixed-frequency scaling: Sequential dependencies, equal-loudness contours, and power function exponents. *Perception and Psychophysics*, 47, 551–562.

Ward, L. M. (1991). Informational and neural adaptation curves are asynchronous. *Perception and Psychophysics*, 50, 117–128.

Ward, L. M. (1992). Mind in psychophysics. In D. Algom, ed., *Psychophysical Approaches to Cognition*, 187–249. Amsterdam: North-Holland.

Ward, L. M. (1996). Hypothesis testing, nonlinear forecasting, and the search for chaos in psychophysics. In W. Sulis and A. Combs, eds., *Nonlinear Dynamics in Human Behavior*, 77–89. Singapore: World Scientific.

Ward, L. M. (1999). The psychophysics of stochastic resonance. In P. Killeen, ed., *Fechner Day '99*, 389–394. Tempe, AZ: International Society for Psychophysics.

Ward, L. M. (2000). Signal detection theory and stochastic resonance. In C. Bonnett, ed., *Fechner Day 2000*, 357–362. Strasbourg: International Society for Psychophysics.

Ward, L. M. (2001). Human neural plasticity. *Trends in Cognitive Sciences*, 5, 325–327.

Ward, L. M., Livingston, J. W., and Li, J. (1988). On probabilistic categorization: The Markovian observer. *Perception and Psychophysics*, 43, 125–136.

Ward, L. M., and Lockhead, G. R. (1971). Response system processes in absolute judgement. *Perception and Psychophysics*, 9, 73–78.

Ward, L. M., Moss, F., Desai, S., and Rootman, D. (2001). Stochastic resonance in detection of auditory beats by humans. Unpublished manuscript, Univ. of British Columbia.

Ward, L. M., Moss, F., Desai, S., and Tata, M. (2001). Stochastic resonance in detection of visual grating by humans. Unpublished manuscript, Univ. of British Columbia.

Ward, L. M., Neiman, A., and Moss, F. (2001). Stochastic resonance in psychophysics and in animal behavior. Unpublished manuscript, Univ. of British Columbia.

Ward, L. M., and Richard, C. M. (2001). $1/f^{\infty}$ noise and decision complexity. Unpublished manuscript, Univ. of British Columbia.

Ward, L. M., and West, R. L. (1994). On chaotic behavior. *Psychological Science*, 5, 232–236.

Ward, L. M., and West, R. L. (1998). Modeling human chaotic behavior: Nonlinear forecasting analysis of logistic iteration. *Nonlinear Dynamics, Psychology and Life Sciences*, 3, 261–282.

Weaver, W. (1963). *Lady Luck: The Theory of Probability*. Garden City, NY: Doubleday.

Wegner, D. M., Quillian, F., and Houston, C. E. (1996). Memories out of order: Thought suppression and the disturbance of sequence memory. *Journal of Personality and Social Psychology*, 71, 680–691.

Weinberg, G. M. (1975). *An Introduction to General Systems Thinking*. New York: Wiley.

Weissman, M. B. (1981). Survey of recent $1/f$ theories. In P. H. E. Meijer, R. D. Mountain, and R. J. Soulen, Jr., eds., *Sixth International Conference on Noise in Physical Systems*, 3–11. Washington, DC: U.S. Department of Commerce and National Bureau of Standards.

Wheeler, J. A. (1990). Information, physics, quantum: The search for links. In W. Zurek, ed., *Complexity, Entropy, and the Physics of Information*. Redwood City, CA: Addison-Wesley.

Whishaw, I. Q., and Vanderwolf, C. H. (1973). Hippocampal EEG and behavior: Changes in amplitude and frequency of RSA (theta rhythm) associated with spontaneous and learned movement patterns in rats and cats. *Behavioral Biology*, 8, 461–484.

White, J. A. Rubenstein, J. T., and Kay, A. R. (2000). Channel noise in neurons. *Trends in Neuroscience*, 23, 131–137.

Wiesenfeld, K., and Moss, F. (1995). Stochastic resonance and the benefits of noise: from ice ages to crayfish and SQUIDs. *Nature*, 373, 33–36.

Wise, M. N. (1979). The mutual embrace of electricity and magnetism. *Science*, 203, 1310–1318.

Wittgenstein, L. (1961). *Tractatus Logico-Philosophicus*. Trans. D. F. Pears and B. F. McGuiness. London: Routledge and Kegan Paul.

Woltz, D. J., Bell, B. G., Kyllonen, P. C., and Gardner, M. K. (1996). Memory for order of operations in the acquisition and transfer of sequential cognitive skills. *Journal of Experimental Psychology: Learning, Memory, and Cognition*, 22, 438–457.

Woodworth, R. S. (1938). *Experimental Psychology*. New York: Holt, Rinehart and Winston.

Wright, R. D., and Liley, D. T. J. (1996). Dynamics of the brain at global and microscopic scales: Neural networks and the EEG. *Behavioral and Brain Sciences*, 19, 285–320.

Wright, R. D., and Ward, L. M. (1998). Control of visual attention. In Wright, ed., *Visual Attention*, 132–186. New York: Oxford University Press.

Yamada, W., Koch, C., and Adams, P. R. (1998). Multiple channels and calcium dynamics. In Koch and I. Segev, eds., *Methods in Neuronal Modeling: From Ions to Networks*. 2d ed., 137–170. Cambridge, MA: MIT Press.

Yarbus, A. L. (1967). *Eye Movements and Vision*. New York: Plenum Press.

Zeki, S. (1993). *A Vision of the Brain*. London: Blackwell.

Zeng, F. -G., Fu, Q. -J., and Morse, R. (2000). Human hearing enhanced by noise. *Brain Research*, 869, 251–255.

Index

Action potential, 145–147, 150, 184–186, 188, 190, 193–195, 197–199, 280–281, 296, 300–301
Adaptation, 37–38, 280, 291
Aliasing, 32
ARIMA, 89–92, 94, 96– 98, 102, 141, 169, 229, 231–232, 234–235, 258
Artificial intelligence, 308, 311
Attention, 5, 32, 41, 46, 62, 67, 74, 84, 135, 163, 291, 303, 316
Attractor, 205, 207–210, 213–217, 220–221, 223, 227, 230, 239, 242, 244, 266, 271, 279, 291
Autocorrelation, 91–94, 258
Autoregression, 90–92, 94, 96–97, 102–104, 106, 140, 169–171. *See also* ARIMA

Baggott, J. E., 55, 112, 114, 116
Bak, P., 157–159
Bell, D. A., 122, 130, 147, 155, 165, 167–170
Binocular rivalry, 317–318
Biology, 4, 6, 55, 68, 75, 286–287
Bohr, N., 114
Bremermann limit, 46
Bringhurst, R., 3
Brock, W., 230–231
Brownian motion, 91, 100, 117–118, 125–126, 130
Budescu, D. V., 256–259
Bunz, H., 21, 282

Calculus, 26, 33, 51, 65, 99
Casdagli, M., 219, 221, 224, 226, 231–232, 242, 269
Chalmers, D. J., 316
Chance, 13, 29, 167, 190, 245–246, 255, 261–262, 289
Chaos, 29, 59, 83, 87, 96, 103–105, 112, 125–126, 138–139, 173, 201–205, 207–210, 213–215, 219, 221, 224, 226–227, 229–232, 234, 236–237, 239–242, 244–245, 263–266, 269, 271–273, 276, 278–280, 282, 291, 297–298, 305, 308, 313–314
dynamics, 237
edge of, 138, 155, 213, 237, 242, 291
Chaos theory, 112, 139, 173, 201, 229, 240, 264, 273, 280
dense periodic points, 210
map, 75, 83, 168, 202–205, 210, 214, 224, 226, 238–239, 244, 266, 269, 299, 313
sensitive dependence, 59, 189, 202, 204–205, 210, 216, 221, 224, 230, 239, 244, 247–248, 250–251, 265
strange attractor, 208, 210, 217, 220, 224, 230, 239, 240, 242, 264, 266, 269
topological transitivity, 204, 210
Chemistry, 4, 55
Clancey, W. J., 12–13, 42
Clark, C. W., 292, 294
Clarke, J., 135–136
Clayton, K., 138–139, 141, 144, 213, 235
Clock, 18, 26–27, 29, 30, 35, 137–138, 188, 207, 273, 321
Cognitive neuroscience, 74, 146
Colored noise. *See* Noise, colored
Complementarity, 8, 59–60, 62, 69, 87, 113–114, 324
Complexity, 20, 45–48, 82, 173, 229, 241, 243, 283, 315, 320
Computation, 46, 163, 205, 305, 313–314, 324
Computer, 29, 42, 46, 58, 66–67, 72–73, 81, 83, 94, 110, 124, 126, 143, 157, 159, 186, 189, 190, 215–216, 224, 227, 257– 259, 264–266, 269, 271, 305–306, 308, 313–314, 317, 320
digital, 46, 305, 308, 312–314
quantum, 314, 324
Computer simulation, 67, 83, 110, 143, 159, 186, 269
Consciousness, 10–11, 28, 30, 43, 50, 63, 75, 132, 229, 282–283, 295, 301, 314–318, 320–321, 323–324